Encyclopedia of entrepreneurship

edited by

Calvin A. Kent

Herman W. Lay Professor of Private Enterprise
Director, Center for Private Enterprise and Entrepreneurship
Baylor University

Donald L. Sexton

Caruth Professor of Entrepreneurship
Director of Entrepreneurial Programs
Center for Private Enterprise and Entrepreneurship
Baylor University

Karl H. Vesper

Joseph F. Schoen Visiting Professor of Private Enterprise
and Entrepreneurship, Baylor University
Professor of Business Administration
University of Washington

encyclopedia of entrepreneurship

PRENTICE-HALL, INC.
Englewood Cliffs, New Jersey 07632

Library of Congress Cataloging in Publication Data

Main entry under title:

Encyclopedia of entrepreneurship.

Includes bibliographies and index.
1. Entrepreneur. 2. Technological innovations.
3. Small business. I. Kent, Calvin A. II. Sexton, Donald L. III. Vesper, Karl H.
HB615.E59 338'.04 81-10602
ISBN 0-13-275826-1 AACR2

Printed in the United States of America

10 9 8 7 6 5 4 3 2 1

Editorial/production supervision by Joan L. Lee
Manufacturing buyer: Ed O'Dougherty

PRENTICE-HALL INTERNATIONAL, INC., *London*
PRENTICE-HALL OF AUSTRALIA PTY. LIMITED, *Sydney*
PRENTICE-HALL OF CANADA, LTD., *Toronto*
PRENTICE-HALL OF INDIA PRIVATE LIMITED, *New Delhi*
PRENTICE-HALL OF JAPAN, INC., *Tokyo*
PRENTICE-HALL OF SOUTHEAST ASIA PTE. LTD., *Singapore*
WHITEHALL BOOKS LIMITED, *Wellington, New Zealand*

Contents

Section Three
Entrepreneurship and Progress, 231

Section Four
Entrepreneurship and Academia, 317

Biographical sketches of contributors

Robert H. Brockhaus, Sr., is an Associate Professor of Management at St. Louis University and is also President of Progressive Management Enterprises, Ltd., a management consulting firm which he founded. He is the Director of the Small Business Institute at St. Louis University; Vice President of the national Small Business Institute Directors Association; and Vice President of the International Council for Small Business. He also serves on the Editorial Advisory Board of the *Journal for Small Business Management.*

In addition to teaching graduate and undergraduate courses on entrepreneurship, Dr. Brockhaus conducts research on the entrepreneurial decision from psychological, sociological, and environmental perspectives. This research has appeared in the *Academy of Management Journal*, *Academy of Management Review*, the *Journal for Small Business Management*, the *Proceedings of the International Symposium on Entrepreneurship and Enterprise Development*, and the *Proceedings of the 1980 White House Conference on Small Business.*

Wayne G. Broehl, Jr., the Benjamin Ames Kimball Professor of the Science of Administration at the Amos Tuck School of Business Administration, Dartmouth College, is author or coauthor of eight books in the fields of business history, management theory, and economic development. The corporation's role in society has been of central interest to Dr. Broehl over the past two decades. His research has centered on corporate governance and the role of the board of directors. He has conducted extensive research on entrepreneurship in developing countries.

More recently, Dr. Broehl has completed a Ford Foundation research project in India on entrepreneurial patterns in agro-industry companies. The project also involved an "action" phase, where Dr. Broehl conducted a series of innovation seminars to encourage the development of change agents among rural entrepreneurs. He has taught business administration in Ireland, Argentina, and India and has consulted with various multinational companies.

David J. Brophy is an Associate Professor of Finance and Director of the Graduate School of Bank Management at the University of Michigan. He received his Ph.D. from Ohio State University. He is the founder and director of Michigan Savings and Loan Association, and a co-founder and director of Vector Research, Inc. In addition, he is a consultant to the National Bank of Detroit and the National Venture Capital Association. Dr. Brophy has authored two textbooks and twelve papers in the area of venture finance. His articles have been published in the *Financial Review, Michigan Business Review*, and the *Journal of the Midwest Financial Association.*

Wayne S. Brown is a Professor of Mechanical Engineering and Director of the Utah Innovation Center at the University of Utah. He has been instrumental in forming several companies, including Kenway Engineering, Inc., now a $100 million division of Eaton Corporation and Terra Tek. He currently serves as Chairman of the Board of Terra Tek and Native Plants. As director of the Utah Innovation Center, he is concerned with the development of high-technology business enterprise.

Albert V. Bruno is a Professor of Marketing, Chairman of the Marketing Department, and Director of the Center for Entrepreneurial Research, Innovation, and Management at the University of Santa Clara. His degrees include B.S., M.S., Purdue University, and Ph.D., Krannert School, Purdue. He has published over 30 articles, chapters, and research notes in a diverse set of publications including *Journal of Marketing Research, Journal of Consumer Research, Journal of Advertising Research, Research Management, Sloan Management Review, Journal of Business Research*, and *Educational and Psychological Measurement.* His most recent publications on entrepreneurship are: "Success Among High-Technology Firms" (with A. C. Cooper) in *Business Horizons* and "An Empirical Examination of Venture Capital Association Decisions and Their Performance" (with Tyzoon T. Tyebjee) in *National Science Foundation.*

Robert E. Coffey is a Professor of Management and former Director of the Entrepreneur and Venture Management Program at the University of

Southern California. He received his M.B.A. from Northwestern and his Ph.D. from the University of Illinois. Bob is active in professional organizations and served as secretary of the Academy of Management from 1972–75. He has published a number of books and articles. He is also active in the consulting and in Management Development Programs at the University of Southern California. He is listed in *American Men and Women of Science.*

James A. Constantin is David Ross Boyd Professor of Business Administration at the University of Oklahoma. He received his Ph.D. from the University of Texas in 1950. Prior to joining the faculty at the University of Oklahoma in 1953, he had taught at Texas, Alabama, and Washington. He is author or coauthor of four books, several dozen articles in scholarly and business publications, and several monographs. He has owned and operated several successful businesses. He introduced the entrepreneurship course at Oklahoma in 1967, and also teaches courses in corporate planning, logistics, and marketing.

Arnold C. Cooper is a Professor at the Krannert Graduate School of Management, Purdue University. He holds a B.S. and M.S. from Purdue and a D.B.A. from Harvard. He has previously served on the faculties of Harvard, Stanford, Manchester Business School (England), and IMEDE Management Development Institute (Switzerland). He teaches courses in new enterprises and strategic management. He is author, coauthor, or coeditor of five books on entrepreneurship and small business. In addition to his many publications, Dr. Cooper is an active consultant and serves on the editorial boards of the *Academy of Management Journal* and the *Strategic Management Journal.*

Yvon Gasse is an Associate Professor of Organization Theory and Behavior at Laval University in Québec, Canada. He holds a B.S. and M.S. from Laval University and a M.A. and Ph.D. from Northwestern. Prior to joining Laval, he held teaching positions at the University of Moncton and the University of Sherbrooke. He has published 17 articles dealing primarily with the psychological aspects of entrepreneurs and small businessmen.

Edwin Harwood is currently Professor of Sociology and Chairman of the Department of Sociology at Mercer University in Macon, Georgia. He has taught previously at Rice University, Harvard University, Kenyon College, and New College. He obtained his B.A. from Stanford and his Ph.D. in sociology from the University of Chicago. His research includes youth unemployment, the sociology of work, black labor force adjustment, and the sociology of entrepreneurship. He has published in *The Public Interest*, the *Wall Street Journal*, and *Society Magazine*, among other publications. At New College in Sarasota, where he last taught, he created a program in entrepreneurial studies for liberal arts undergraduates; the objective of the program was to prepare students for new venture start-ups and management. He is currently interested in special situation investing.

John A. Hornaday is currently Chairman of the Division of Management and Organizational Behavior and Director of the program in Entrepreneurial Studies at Babson College. His education was in the field of applied psychology at Duke University, where he received the A.B., M.A., and Ph.D. degrees. Prior to joining the Babson faculty, he was employed at Houghton-Mifflin, and since 1958 he has been on the editorial staff of two professional journals, *Personnel Psychology* and *Educational and Psychological Measurement*. In addition to his present teaching and editorial activities, Dr. Hornaday is on the board of directors of several corporations, and is an external consultant with many organizations. Dr. Hornaday specializes in the application of the behavioral sciences to problems of management, especially in the area of organizational development. His research is concerned with developing and evaluating psychological tests and with assessment and development of entrepreneurial characteristics in individuals.

Deszö Horváth is Associate Professor of Business Policy and Chairman of the Department of Policy at the Faculty of Administrative Studies, York University, Toronto. Prior to joining the faculty at York he taught at Umea University, Sweden, and at the Management Centre, Stockholm School of Economics, Sweden. He received his M.B.A. and Ph.D. degrees at the University of Umea, Sweden.

Dr. Horvath has worked with a number of business organizations and governmental agencies in the areas of strategic management, organizational design and control, and international business. He is author of *Criteria and Principles for Organizational Design* and *Contingency Organizations: Theory and Practice* and has contributed many articles to academic and professional journals in business policy, general management, and international business.

Dr. Horvath's current research includes strategy and structure in large enterprises, strategic decision processes, organization design and control, management of international operations, and strategic management of smaller firms.

Calvin A. Kent is the Herman W. Lay Professor of Private Enterprise at Baylor University, and Director of the Center for Private Enterprise and Entrepreneurship. Dr. Kent was formerly Professor of Economics at the University of South Dakota and chief economist to the South Dakota Legislature. He has served as a consultant to many major corporations and government entities, including the Internal Revenue Service and the United States Senate Finance Committee. He received his B.A. from Baylor University and his M.A. and Ph.D. in economics from the University of Missouri. His postdoctoral work has been completed at the universities of Virginia and Chicago. He is listed in most major directories, including *Who's Who in America*. Currently he is serving as President of the National Association of Economic Educators, and is on the executive committee of the Association for Private Enterprise Education and the Business

Taxation Committee of the National Tax Association. He has written five books and 50 articles on various economic subjects.

Herbert E. Kierulff is a Professor of Finance and Entrepreneurship at Seattle-Pacific University. Prior to beginning a full-time teaching career, he spent seven years in industry in line and staff positions. In 1972, Dr. Kierulff co-founded the entrepreneur program at U.S.C.'s Graduate School of Business Administration. He now teaches and consults to government and business in the areas of new venture formation, acquisitions, and turnaround management. He is the author of *The Economics of Decision* and numerous articles appearing in such journals as the *Harvard Business Review*, *California Management Review*, *Business Horizons*, and the *Journal of Small Business Management*.

Israel M. Kirzner is a Professor of Economics at New York University. A noted publisher and speaker, Dr. Kirzner has published six textbooks and approximately 30 articles and has presented roughly 100 papers. His most recent text, *Perception, Opportunities and Profit: Studies in the Theory of Entrepreneurship*, was published in 1979. Recent articles include "Entrepreneurship, Entitlement and Economic Justice," in the *Eastern Economic Journal*, and "Entrepreneurship, Choice and Freedom," in *ORDO*.

Dr. Kirzner received his B.A. from Brooklyn College and his M.B.A. and Ph.D. from New York University. In addition to his work at New York University, he has been actively involved in the Price Institute of Entrepreneurial Studies.

Russell Knight is an Associate Professor at the University of Western Ontario. He holds a B.S.E.E. from McGill, a Master's in industrial management from MIT, and a Ph.D. in business administration from Harvard. His research interests lie in the areas of venture capital, entrepreneurship, and business failures. He currently has a text in progress entitled "Small Business Management in Canada."

O. J. Krasner is a Professor of Management and Chairman of MBA–International Programs at Pepperdine University. He holds a B.S., an M.A., an M.S., and a Ph.D. from the University of Southern California. Prior to teaching, he had over 25 years of experience with firms such as Rockwell International and General Electric. He is currently the President of Rensark Associates, a management consulting firm specializing in strategic planning. His previous teaching experience was at the California Institute of Technology; UCLA; U.S. International University; Loyola-Marymount; and the University of Southern California. He is a member of several professional societies, and is listed in *Who's Who in the West* and *American Men and Women in Science*. He has had numerous publications.

Harold C. Livesay received his Ph.D. in American economic and business history from Johns Hopkins University after a number of years of business experience. He previously taught at the University of Michigan and is currently Professor of History at the State University of New York at Binghamton. His publications include *Merchants and Manufacturers, Studies in the Changing Structure of Nineteenth-Century Marketing, Andrew Carnegie and the Rise of Big Business, Samuel Gompers and Organized Labor in America, American Made (Men Who Shaped the American Economy),* and a number of articles, two of which have won the Newcomen Society Award in Business History.

Justin G. Longenecker is the Harry and Hazel Chavanne Professor of Christian Ethics in the Hankamer School of Business at Baylor University, having joined that faculty in 1955. He is the author (with H. M. Broom) of *Small Business Management* and a number of journal articles on small business and entrepreneurship. He is a member of the International Council for Small Business and serves as Chairman of its publications committee. He holds an M.B.A. from Ohio State University and a Ph.D. from the University of Washington.

Kenneth E. Loucks received his M.B.A. and Ph.D. from the University of Western Ontario. He is currently Professor in the School of Commerce and Administration at Laurentian University, teaching entrepreneurship, small business management, and business policy. He is responsible for the Small Business Counseling Program (equivalent to the U.S. Small Business Institute Program). He is also President of Trillium Institute of Management, Inc., which conducts small business consulting activities. His most recent research was a survey of entrepreneurship and small business management educational activities in Canada, which is currently being published by the Small Business Secretariat of the federal government. Prior research investigated methods of dealing effectively with owners of small business on management development programs. The results were reported at the Fourth International Symposium on Small Business in Seoul, Korea. He also served as Visiting Professor of Small Business Management at the University of New England, Armidale, New South Wales, Australia.

Joseph Mancuso is the founder of the Center for Entrepreneurial Management. He is a respected educator and author and a compulsive entrepreneur. He started his first business while an undergraduate at Worcester Polytechnic Institute. In all, he has launched seven businesses and serves as a board member and advisor for a score of entrepreneurial ventures. He holds a B.S.E.E. from Worcester Polytechnic Institute, an M.B.A. from Harvard Business School, and a Doctorate in Education from Boston University. He has written and edited six books, including *Fun and Guts: The Entrepreneur's Philosophy, Entrepreneurship and Venture Management,* and *How to Start, Finance and Manage Your Own Small Business,* his current best-seller. Articles by Dr. Mancuso have been published in *The Harvard Business Review, The Journal of Marketing, The Journal of Small Business, Business Horizons,* and many other national magazines.

Albro Martin is a Lecturer in Business History at Harvard University and is Editor of the *Business History Review.* As both an economist and a historian, he teaches courses in political, social, and economic history as well as business history. His research interests are the role of enterprise in economic life and the relationship between economic and political leadership in American and European history. He is currently working on a definitive history of the Cabot Corporation, a high-technology firm in the fields of carbon black, oil and gas exploration and production, natural gas distribution, and high-performance alloys.

Jacquetta J. McClung began work on her Ph.D. in Business Administration in 1976 at the University of Oklahoma. Her dissertation field is marketing, and her supporting fields are accounting and entrepreneurship. She holds a B.S. degree from Southwestern Oklahoma State University (1962) and a Master of Accountancy degree from the University of Oklahoma (1976). She worked as an accountant from 1962 to 1972 and as a part-time Instructor in Accounting at Cameron University from 1973 to 1976. Since 1974 she has been a Graduate Assistant in both accounting and marketing. She has completed a bibliography on entrepreneurship with over 1100 entries in 21 major categories and is currently completing her dissertation proposal in the entrepreneurship area.

William L. Paulin is sales manager of Vandling Corporation and former Assistant Professor of Management at the University of Southern California where he taught in the Entrepreneur Program. He received his Ph.D. in business policy from the University of Washington, an M.B.A. in finance from the University of Washington and his B.S. in mechanical engineering from the University of California at Berkeley. His work experience was gained in firms such as the Boeing Company, Western Electric, and Rocket Research Corporation (now Rockor). He has taught operations management, business policy, small business management, entrepreneurship, and small business consulting at the University of Washington and the University of Southern California. Dr. Paulin's major professional interests are in the areas of small business management and entrepreneurship. One article has been published to date, two are slated for the next six months, and several research projects are currently underway.

Johannes M. Pennings is a Professor in the Graduate School of Business at Columbia University. Prior to joining Columbia he was an Associate Professor of Industrial Management at Carnegie-Mellon University. He received his B.A. and M.A. at the University of Michigan and has published over 20 articles, several texts, and many chapters in other texts. He has also completed several funded research projects. He is currently a member of the editorial boards of *Organization and Administrative Sciences* and the *Administrative Science Quarterly*.

M. Ray Perryman is Herman Brown Professor of Economics and Director of the Center for the Advancement of Economic Analysis, Baylor University. Dr. Perryman holds a B.S. in mathematics from Baylor University and a Ph.D. in economics from Rice University. He has published or presented more than one hundred academic articles in the fields of economics, mathematics, statistics, history, and management. He is best known for his research on monetary and fiscal policy, economic modeling, and econometric and economic theory. He is currently serving as Director of the State of Texas Econometric Model Project, the largest regional modeling program currently in existence. He has won numerous awards for his research efforts, including the Distinguished Professor Award from the Hankamer School of Business, the SHAZAM Award for outstanding contributions to economic research by a Rice alumni, and the outstanding young economist and social scientist in the United States award from a major national research organization.

Rein Peterson is on leave from his position as Professor and Director of Entrepreneurial Studies at York University and the Director of the York Enterprise Development Centre. The Centre has provided consulting help to over 2500 small firms and has been instrumental in the start-ups of more than 50 new companies. Prior to coming to York, Dr. Peterson was associated with Columbia University, the University of Western Ontario, and Harper College. His current research includes entrepreneurial education; technological innovation; and the encouragement, development, and financing of small business.

Dr. Peterson is an active consultant and advisor to corporations, banks, and government groups at both the provincial and federal level. His consulting work has taken him abroad, most recently to Indonesia where he served for 4 months as a consultant, on economic development through the small business sector, to the International Bank for Reconstruction and Development (The World Bank).

Hans Schollhammer is an Associate Professor in the Graduate School of Management, University of California, Los Angeles. He received his D.B.A. from Indiana University and has taught at Columbia University, the Cranfield Institute of Technology, and the Institute for International Studies and Training. He has held management positions in industry and in recent years has been involved in consulting with new and small business ventures through the Small Business Institute of the Small Business Administration. Dr. Schollhammer has published books, monographs, and articles treating international and comparative management issues. One of his recent publications (coauthored with Arthur Kuriloff) is *Entrepreneurship and Small Business Management.*

Richard C. Scott is Dean of the Hankamer School of Business at Baylor University. Before assuming these duties he had a distinguished career as an entrepreneur and businessman, having started his own contracting, real estate, and insurance firms. In addition to his academic responsibilities he continues as an active entrepreneur and has started several successful businesses in the past few years. His services are in constant demand as a consultant to various business and governmental agencies in the fields of management strategy, acquisition, sale of business, and management training.

Dean Scott's undergraduate and M.B.A. degrees are from Baylor and he holds a DBA from Indiana. Among his many achievements as dean has been the completion of the Bessie Blume Conference Center. The Professional Development Program was established and has branches in Houston, Dallas, and Waco. The Center for Private Enterprise and Entrepreneurship which he initiated is nationally recognized as a leader in economics education and entrepreneurial programs.

Donald L. Sexton is the Caruth Professor of Entrepreneurship and Director of Entrepreneurial Programs in the Center for Private Enterprise and Entrepreneurship at Baylor University. He received his M.B.A. and Ph.D. from Ohio State University. Prior to joining Baylor he served on the faculty at Sangamon State University where he established a Small Business Unit within the Center for Policy Studies. He has an extensive background in industry, primarily as a "turnaround" manager of failing firms. He has published several articles in the area of small business and entrepreneurship, the most recent in *Internationales Gewerbearchiv.* One of his books, *Experiences in Entrepreneurship and Small Business* (coauthored with Phil Van Auken), will be published in January 1982.

Albert Shapero is the William H. Davis Professor of American Free Enterprise System at Ohio State University. Prior to joining Ohio State he was a Professor of Management at the University of Texas. He is a former national vice-president of the Society for General Systems Research and is president of the Society of Entrepreneurship Research and Application. He is listed in *Who's Who in the South* and in *American Men of Science.* His publications include numerous articles, papers, and major addresses.

Edward Shils is the George W. Taylor Professor in Entrepreneurial Studies at the Wharton School of Finance and Commerce at the University of Pennsylvania. He also holds an Honorary Doctor of Laws degree from the Philadelphia College of Textiles and Science. He received his B.S., M.A., and Ph.D. at the University of Pennsylvania. He has been actively involved as a consultant to industry and serves on the board of directors of a number of firms. He has published over 50 papers and books. A recent article, "The Development of a Model of Internal Entrepreneurship which Replicates the Environment and Design of the Autonomous Entrepreneurial Companies," has appeared in *Social Science.*

Lisa Sokol is an Assistant Professor of Management Sciences at the Ohio State University. She holds a Ph.D. in Operations Research from the University of Massachusetts. Since joining Ohio State she has become involved in entrepreneurship and small business and particularly the problems of financing new ventures. She has several research projects in process and is working with Albert Shapero on a number of other projects.

Jeffry A. Timmons is Professor of Human Resources and Area Coordinator for the entrepreneurship major at Northeastern University. His primary teaching and research interests are in organizational behavior, entrepreneurship, and new venture development. He has published over 60 articles, papers, and teaching cases, which have appeared in *Harvard Business Review, Business Horizons, Executive*, and elsewhere. He is senior author of *New Venture Creation* and recently edited *A Region's Struggling Savior: Small Business in New England.*

Professor Timmons has had extensive experience in the design and delivery of management and entrepreneurship programs for U.S. and foreign business and government organizations. As a founding principal of and consultant to Venture Founders Corporation and the Institute for New Enterprise Development, he has developed a program to find, evaluate, and invest in growth-oriented new companies seeking venture capital. He has worked with over 800 founders and presidents since 1972. This six-year effort has resulted in a 32-company portfolio with combined 1979 sales of nearly $90 million.

Professor Timmons received his Bachelor's degree from Colgate University, and his M.B.A. and Doctorate from Harvard Business School.

Tyzoon T. Tyebjee is Assistant Professor of Marketing at the University of Santa Clara. He was formerly an Assistant Professor at the Wharton School, University of Pennsylvania. His degrees include a B.S. in chemical engineering from the Indian Institute of Technology, an M.S. in chemical engineering from the Illinois Institute of Technology, an M.B.A. and a Ph.D. from the University of California at Berkeley. He has published articles in *IEEE Transactions on Engineering Management, Journal of Marketing Research, Journal of Marketing, Journal of Consumer Affairs*, and *Journal of Consumer Research.*

Gerald Udell is currently associated with the Innovation Center at the University of Wisconsin. He formerly was an Associate Professor of Marketing and Director of the Experimental Center for the Advancement of Invention and Innovation at the University of Oregon. He received his B.S., M.B.A., and Ph.D. at the University of Wisconsin. Dr. Udell has published ten books and monographs, 40 articles, and 30 papers in conference proceedings. In addition, he has managed 11 funded research projects.

Karl H. Vesper, B.S.M.E., M.S.M.E., Ph.D., Stanford, M.B.A., Harvard, is jointly appointed as Professor of Business Administration and Professor of Mechanical Engineering at the University of Washington, where he has been since 1969. In the Business School he teaches and does research in business policy and entrepreneurship. In the Engineering School he teaches an interdisciplinary graduate course in systems design. His publications include *Engineers at Work, The Entrepreneurial Function* (coauthored with L. T. Hosmer and A. C. Cooper), and *New Venture Strategies,* plus a compendium on *Entrepreneurship Education,* which has been updated periodically. He has also authored cases in both engineering and business and articles which have appeared in the *Academy of Management Journal, California Management Review, Harvard Business Review, Management Science, Research Management,* and other periodicals and conference proceedings.

William E. Wetzel, Jr. is an Associate Professor in the Whittemore School of Business and Economics at the University of New Hampshire. Active in the area of venture finance, he had 11 years of experience in banking and investments and currently serves on the board of directors of two banks and two industrial firms. He has completed several funded research contracts relating to the cost and availability of risk capital and has published several papers in the same area. His publications have appeared in the *New England Journal of Business and Economics, Business Horizons,* and the *New Hampshire Review.*

This book is dedicated to

Herman W. Lay

W. W. Caruth, Jr.

Dr. Joseph F. Schoen

Foreword

Richard C. Scott

This book is a compilation of outstanding chapters on research and education in entrepreneurship. The chapters have been written by several of the most prestigious academicians laboring in this new and fast developing field of inquiry. The purpose of this volume is to collect the thoughts of these academic entrepreneurs so four things can be determined:

What do we know about entrepreneurs and the process of new venture initiation?

What is not known that needs to be determined, if curricula are to be developed and public policies promoted which will foster and encourage the entrepreneurial spirit?

What directions should future academic inquiry regarding entrepreneurship take?

Where are the gaps and what type of research will be most effective and useful in the future?

Several conclusions are immediately apparent. First, entrepreneurship is important. The introduction of new products and technologies to better satisfy consumer wants and raise productivity has been the most important force in man's long and precarious climb from underdevelopment to affluence. For that reason, the study of entrepreneurship is desirable to satisfy more than just intellectual curiosity.

Second, despite its importance, little is known about the process of entrepreneurship. Our understanding of what kindles the spark that flames into new ventures, of what factors cause some to succeed while others falter, and of what environmental conditions promote or discourage risk-taking is limited.

Third, we really don't know some of the things we thought we knew about entrepreneurship. The field is strewn with axioms and admonitions that fail the twin tests of experience and inquiry. Despite the blind alleys into which this ignorance has led us, entrepreneurship has survived in so many settings that generalizations based on casual observations, or only a few detailed cases, may be more than misleading—they may prove counterproductive.

Fourth, the environment for entrepreneurship must occupy a position of dominance in research and public policy. What can be changed that will make a difference? The evidence in this volume is that the climate for entrepreneurship in the United States is becoming increasingly negative, particularly when compared to some of the other industrial nations. Yet entrepreneurship sometimes flourishes in economies that are more controlled than our own and can be found in the underdeveloped world where tradition and taboos create additional obstacles to success.

Fifth, while innovation and venture initiation are usually associated with small business, there is evidence of entrepreneurship in larger corporations. Perhaps "big business's" greatest challenge is to create the conditions that will further "internal entrepreneurship." At the same time, public policy must recognize the disadvantages the small firm faces in the marketplace and remove the barriers which have been created and perpetuated.

Sixth, it is not clear to what extent entrepreneurship can be taught. Certainly, skills that are valuable can be communicated, but can attitudes and disposition be encouraged and even created? Less may be known about the effects and effectiveness of entrepreneurship education than any other phase of entrepreneurial study.

Seventh, research and education in entrepreneurship are in early stages. While certain facets of this field are more advanced than others, none have reached adolescence, much less maturity. This volume is not a synopsis of a developed discipline with established definitions and generally accepted theory; it is rather a sketch of where we are and where we should travel.

Preface

Humanity's progress from caves to concrete canyons has been explained in numerous ways. But central to virtually all of these theories has been the role of the "agent of change," the force that initiates and implements material progress. Today we recognize that the agent of change in human history has been and most likely will continue to be the entrepreneur.

The *Encyclopedia of Entrepreneurship* is an ambitious undertaking. It seeks to summarize and categorize existing knowledge about the entrepreneur. The entrepreneurial process is misunderstood not because of prejudice but because of ignorance—ignorance about the conditions that facilitate or retard the entrepreneurial effort, about what motivates those who initiate ventures, about appropriate programs for nurturing and strengthening the flame of innovation.

The authors of these chapters are the pioneers who have sought to bring scientific inquiry to the art of entrepreneurial study. These pages are not a codification of a well developed body of theory substantiated by systematic and rigorous research. Since inquiry in the field has just begun, some topics have been well explored and others virtually ignored. In many areas the development of research methodology has been retarded because the appropriate questions have yet to be determined.

As Thomas Jefferson so wisely observed, "The price of ignorance is too great to pay." Knowledge about the entrepreneur should lead to understanding and out of this understanding should come both public and private policy designed to strengthen and hasten the process of change. Regrettably, ignorance about entrepreneurship has led to policies that discourage rather than enhance the environment for venture initiation. This in turn has resulted in a lower standard of living throughout the world.

The chapters in this book summarize what is currently known about entrepreneurship, innovation, and the process of technological transfer—a state of the art. A common theme is that material improvement in the standard of living and a favorable climate for entrepreneurship are most likely to reinforce one another. This work seeks to synthesize our knowledge of the field in a manner which will allow it to be more easily understood and expanded.

Numerous questions remain, of course, and the importance of continued research cannot be overemphasized. To a large degree, the material well-being of mankind will be shaped by the policies based on entrepreneurship research. As Voltaire said, "From the conflict, truth is born."

Introduction and summary of entrepreneurship research

Karl H. Vesper

This book maps the frontiers of entrepreneurship research. The overall field of entrepreneurship is loosely defined as the creation of new business enterprises by individuals or small groups. Scholars who have been especially productive in each of 14 sub-areas were recruited to discuss their respective specialities. Each resulting chapter has been supplemented by one or more constructively critical reviews by other specialists in the field. The goal has been to produce a comprehensive summary of entrepreneurship research to date, including observations about the most likely directions for further research.

Three broad waves have been sweeping the subject of entrepreneurship forward recently. One has been an explosion of popular literature on the subject. In book form this includes biographies of entrepreneurs, histories of their companies, and a plethora of "How to Start Your Own Business" books, many of the "Get Rich Quick" variety. Among magazines recently introduced are *Entrepreneur* (schemes for making money without much investment or skill), *Venture* (start-up), *Inc.* (smaller firms), and *In Business* (nontraditional entrepreneurship), plus hundreds of newsletters. Among these publications the quality of journalism ranges from excellent to deplorable, but considering there were far fewer books and no such magazines a decade ago, they represent in aggregate a considerable boost to the field. They do not constitute academic research; they aim more to point out interesting bits of information about entrepreneurship than to discover the truth about it systematically. Scholars attempting to piece together the whole may nonetheless find such publications very useful.

A second wave, which actually began earlier and has continued to build, has been the spread of course offerings in entrepreneurship at the four-year college and graduate level. These are found principally in business schools but also in engineering programs. This started in the late sixties with less than a half dozen universities and has now spread to around 150 in the United States and Canada. Academics being what they are, a certain percentage of them have begun to conduct research on entrepreneurship as an adjunct to their teaching: one supervises a student independent study on some issue of the field; another begins collecting material for a book and finds that new data are needed; yet another decides as a result of his teaching to specialize in the area and then must do some research to get promoted. With such courses on the books, universities find with the inevitable faculty turnover that they need to recruit people to fill the vacated entrepreneurship teaching slots. They look for doctoral graduates, which creates a certain amount of market pull for entrepreneurship majors.

By this process the introduction of entrepreneurship courses begins to cause progressively more research on entrepreneurship. It is important to note, however, that this effect is not instantaneous. Faculty need time to become acquainted with what has gone before in entrepreneurship research and then to strengthen their methodologies and creative instincts for carrying it forward. Collaborating doctoral students may introduce a further time-lag in the process.

The third wave has been increasing federal interest in and spending on venture initiation research. Entrepreneurship itself has not become a major object of federal research, but two related areas have assumed prominence. One is the area of small business in general, of which entrepreneurship forms a part. In seeking to foster more small firms, the government studies how to help small companies get started, which is to say, how to foster entrepreneurship. A far larger proportion of the government's attention is aimed to keep small businesses from failing. This emphasis may be related to the fact that already-established firms are a more identifiable political constituency than entrepreneurs who are not yet fully started. As the total appropriation for research on small business grows, the entrepreneurship share tends to be pulled along with it.

A second related area of federal research is industrial innovation, where the importance of entrepreneurship is undenied. Authorities sometimes argue whether large companies or entrepreneurs produce more. Perhaps the fact that they argue suggests that the contributions of the two are roughly equal. In any case the search for ways to increase national industrial innovation leads inevitably to the question of how entrepreneurship operates and can be enhanced.

Curiously, the attention given to entrepreneurship has tended to be somewhat small in relation to the attention given to innovation in large companies and laboratories. But attention is there, especially in the National Science Foundation–sponsored innovation centers. The decline in U.S. industrial performance has inspired federal research support for studies of innovation processes, including those of entrepreneurship.

The combined effect of these three waves has been a marked increase in entrepreneurship research. There are seven main academic publication outlets for these research results. The first group consists of three journals, the *American Journal of Small Business*, the *Harvard Business Review* (small business and entrepreneurship articles mostly tucked at the back), and the *Journal of Small Business Management.* The second group includes the proceedings of the annual meetings of the Academy of Management, the American Institute for Decision Sciences, and the Small Business Institute Directors Association. The third group comprises professional books. Articles appear from time to time in other channels, but their representation in the field is relatively minor. Even in the seven main outlets, writings on entrepreneurship are dwarfed in number by those on small business in general.

The reasons for this lack of emphasis can be debated without resolution. Small business has a political constituency and a nameplate in the federal bureaucracy to prove it, while entrepreneurship does not. Big business has big money for consulting, research, academic endowments, student scholarships and fellowships, internships, buildings, and higher salaries to graduates. It is not surprising that large business dominates business schools to the detriment of both small business and entrepreneurship. Recently, there has been a small counter-trend in the form of endowed chairs of entrepreneurship contributed by wealthy entrepreneurs. So far this has occurred at only a few schools, and like the three waves mentioned above, its emergence has been too recent to produce major effects on the field. Thus, although present trends may be shaping a much more significant future, the balance of forces to date has left entrepreneurship with a very minor overall representation in academic research.

The chapters in this book reflect this state of affairs. The number of references is small compared to other fields, and many are repeated from one chapter to the next. Many of the sources, moreover, are not research works at all but expositions. As some of the authors point out, much of what is called the literature of entrepreneurship is either anecdotal or else judgmental without clear reference to basis in fact. The greatest abundance of research data lies in the psychology of entrepreneurship, sociology of entrepreneurship, and venture capital. Other important areas—innovation from entrepreneurship, the environment for entrepreneurship, and the technology of entrepreneurship (how to perform it well)—are lean on research. Considerable experimentation is being conducted in the area of entrepreneurship education, yet the number of published studies on that subject is very small.

The situation does not suggest, in any way, that the field is intrinsically barren. Rather, it has not been much explored. As treated by historians, the subject tends to become merged with economic and even political history. In the opening chapters, both Livesay and Martin find a need to impose definitions and limitations. The impression left by Livesay's review is that historians have not really given much systematic attention to the formation of new companies but have tended either to follow the later careers of tycoons or to stand far back from the details of individual businesses to make economic proclamations. The result seems to have been little in the way of either validated broad theory or advisable operating rules. Livesay argues that the study of business history is potentially helpful to managers. Whether and how it might be helpful to the *creators* of businesses, neither he nor Martin says.

Information about today's entrepreneurs has become much more abundant with the recent introduction of numerous biographies (for example, the life history of Armand Hammer) and a number of popular magazines, such as *Venture*, *In Business*, *Inc.*, and *Entrepreneur*. Hornaday briefly reviews these and other sources of information in his chapter on living entrepreneurs, offering schemes for classifying both entrepreneurial traits and the literature about entrepreneurs. Knight observes that the literature to date has been biased toward successful entrepreneurs and toward high-growth enterprises.

Studies on the psychology of entrepreneurs appear to be richer both in theory and findings, judging from the discussions by both Brockhaus and Gasse. Achievement motivation, locus of control, risk-taking propensity, values, experience, role models, education, age, and other variables have received both theoretical and operational attention. These factors have been examined in correlation with entrepreneurial performance. Brockhaus and Gasse summarize the difficulties of measurement as well as the findings of psychologists. Although the data does not all point to a central definitive model, the collective variables do have meaning as predictors of entrepreneurship.

The sociology of entrepreneurship has based a relatively rich theoretical framework upon the study of identifiable racial and ethnic groups in the United States and a number of foreign countries. Shapero, as Harwood points out, presents an intriguing examination of the contradictory results advanced by these studies. Weber's Protestant theory is undercut by the performance of many non-Protestant groups. Hagen's theory of entrepreneurs as social underdogs is belied by the entrepreneurs who come from elite groups. The tendency of a single discipline, Shapero argues, is to truncate analysis according to its own specialized jargon. He proposes a model which takes many "pushes and pulls" into account to explain "entrepreneurial events" and then suggests some possible means to form policy that encourages entrepreneurship.

The second section of the book, on entrepreneurial technology, begins with an overview of the nonacademic advice-giving literature. Concentrating on a ten-year period, McClung and Constantin identify some 1800 articles relating in one way or another to entrepreneurship and sort them into twenty-two categories. They find it relatively easy to exclude the infrequent academic articles from this sampling. Most common among the nonacademic articles and books are those dealing with small business management, finance and venture capital, the entrepreneur, minority entrepreneurship, and laws and public policy. No publications were found on the sociology of entrepreneurship, tycoon history, or methodologies for entrepreneurship research.

Timmons examines the practical implications of entrepreneurship literature. Based largely on textbooks, his chapter first reviews the critical ingredients for starting a business: a talented lead man, a compatible team, a good venture concept and plan, and adequate financing. Timmons then lists some adjunct factors that should help the entrepreneurial process: the development of certain skills, the use of checklists, and so forth. He also points out some unresolved issues and closes with a suggested typology for research. To Timmons's discussion, Kierulff adds some thoughts about models and the difficulty of defining success, and some doubts about the value of government intervention.

Perhaps the most data-rich sub-field within the subject of entrepreneurship is that of venture capital. Concentrating on the New England region, Wetzel points out the importance of entrepreneurship to both industrial innovation and regional job generation. The new companies that provide these benefits in turn require venture capital. A firm he characterizes as the "foundation firm" presents special problems. Its job generation potential is much greater than that of the "mom 'n pop" enterprise but not as great as that of the high-technology, high-glamour business. The foundation firm cannot be financed with personal savings alone, yet its prospective growth is not enough to appeal to established venture capital firms. To this type of firm informal risk capital sources are particularly vital. For that reason Wetzel's attention is focused on those sources.

Brophy's venture capital chapter applies formal statistical analysis to several venture capital topics. Comparative data of high-technology firms in Boston and Detroit–Ann Arbor show how the greater venture capital available in the former region leads to faster firm development after start-up. In another section, Brophy applies modern finance theory to the problem of valuing equity participation agreements. He demonstrates that complex, "high-powered" techniques are clearly applicable to venture capital studies, notwithstanding the fact that academics have not yet tended to apply them in that direction. This illustrates the important fact that entrepreneurship is intrinsically no less challenging a subject for academic inquiry than is big business.

Cooper's perspective includes not only start-up but the main venture outcomes that follow inception: discontinuance, marginal survival, growth, and sellout. High technology is the major exception to early failure. Team size; capitalization level; education, experience, and well-roundedness of the venture team; and effective use of professional help all affect success probability. Having prefaced his summary of findings with the observation that empirical literature in the field is as yet very limited, Cooper closes with suggested directions for future study. Longenecker further underscores the scarcity of sound empirical study and suggests that a better data base is needed.

Even within big business, entrepreneurship has its place. It has been suggested that some big business managers are more entrepreneurial than others, more oriented toward innovation and marshaling fresh resources. It has also been suggested that entrepreneurship can be deliberately encouraged in large companies (by setting up, for example, new and relatively autonomous units to exploit new market opportunities and new product developments). Schollhammer's chapter establishes five categories for classifying internal corporate entrepreneurship: administrative, opportunistic, imitative, acquisitive, and incubative. Drawing upon the published literature as well, Schollhammer suggests a framework for contrasting these categories according to such variables as frequency of use, effectiveness, efficiency, and limitations. The ensuing commentary by Shils differs with Schollhammer's emphasis on definitions and offers generalizations which concentrate more on entrepreneurial management than on internal entrepreneurship.

The third section of the book, Entrepreneurship and Progress, places our subject in a still broader context. First examined is the impact entrepreneurship has upon the economic system, in developing jobs, industries, innovations, exports, and the like. Second under consideration is the manner in which the economic system stimulates or inhibits entrepreneurship. These two types of interaction are, of course, closely interrelated.

Kent begins his chapter with a history of economic thought and notes that the entrepreneur has been given short shrift in the thinking of all but a very few economists: Schumpeter, Hughes, and Kirzner are the notable exceptions. Thus Kent's discussion becomes something of a general exposition of the way in which major economic theories might be construed as relating to entrepreneurship.

Broehl discusses the somewhat different problem of entrepreneurship in less industrialized countries. He examines both the sociological characteristics of such countries and the economic effects of entrepreneurship upon them. A flow-chart diagram illustrates relationships among the variables. The economic discussion, centered around the ideas of Schumpeter and the role of the entrepreneur as innovator, illustrates the differences between these countries and the more industrialized nations, and the effects of those differences upon entrepreneurship. Like Kent, Broehl finds relatively few authors in his field who explicitly talk about entrepreneurs or entrepreneurship. Only eight of the fifty-one references he cites include either of these terms in their titles.

One of the exceptions is a work by Kirzner, author of the ensuing chapter, who argues that a lack of economic equilibrium is what creates opportunity for entrepreneurship. In Kirzner's analysis, it is market imperfections that create profit opportunities and give the entrepreneur something to do. Although the entrepreneur's activities will move the economy toward equilibrium, changing circumstances will always create new profit opportunities, provided the government does not interpose rigidities and constraints.

Kirzner's arguments, like those of Kent and Broehl, are exclusively based upon theory because so little empirical study has been done on the economic effects of entrepreneurship. Wetzel's study of job generation and the industrial impact of venture capital is an attempt to remedy this lack, as are the following chapters, which treat the impact of entrepreneurship on industrial innovation.

Krasner notes from the literature that large organizations and entrepreneurs respond differently to different types of innovation. Because of their capability for financing large investments and their intrinsic organizational conservatism, large organizations perform better on process innovations and on incremental, as opposed to breakthrough, product innovations. Entrepreneurs do better on product breakthrough, less perhaps because they have formal plans for all contingencies than because they have worried about the right things. Availability of venture capital, patent protection, and ancillary industry support can also be important influences on innovation output by entrepreneurs. Brown's commentary underscores the importance of independent entrepreneurs to the national innovation level and economy. He proposes a scheme for enhancing entrepreneurial innovation through a university innovation center.

For a broader look at environmental impact on entrepreneurship, Bruno and Tyebjee examine the factors that influence entrepreneurial start-up. Although systematic empirical data is lacking, the lists of factors found in the literature overlap considerably, and Bruno and Tyebjee extract a primary list of 12. Just how and to what extent each of these factors influences entrepreneurship has never been determined. One reason is the failure to clearly define dependent variables. To remedy this, the authors propose several classifications of entrepreneurial outcome. A second reason is the failure to relate the independent variables (environmental factors and factors internal to the entrepreneurs and their enterprises) to the outcomes or dependent variables. In this realm, Bruno and Tyebjee offer some suggestions about where to begin. A third problem is the lack of systematic data concerning dependent and independent variables according to regions of the country.

Pennings suggests a contrasting approach. He classifies the view taken by Bruno and Tyebjee as a "resource-exchange" model, characterized by a high degree of self-determination on the part of the entrepreneur, in contrast to a "population-economy" model, in which environmental statistics are regarded as the determinants of entrepreneurial performance. This second model may be better suited to situations where the focus of interest is more upon (1) start-up as opposed to subsequent development, (2) firms other than those in high technology, and (3) intensely urban as opposed to suburban industrial tracts.

As research on the people and processes of entrepreneurship proceeds, we can hope that the teaching of entrepreneurship will improve as a result. The number of courses in this field has expanded very rapidly in the past few years, and with that expansion has come a variety of teaching approaches. Vesper summarizes some of the educational experimentation which, although it has not been conducted in the sort of laboratory conditions purists might prefer, has nevertheless unearthed many options for teachers in this subject area. Vesper describes the conclusions derived from some of these experiments; classifies the parameters, the independent and dependent variables; and traces trends. From single entrepreneurship courses at four-year schools and business schools, the subject is expanding into engineering programs, two-year vocational programs, and secondary schools. Whole programs and majors in entrepreneurship are beginning to appear. Loucks, in his commentary, raises the issue of basic course objectives: Should they be guided by academics or by practitioners, by the traditions of big business curricula or by the different needs of new or small companies?

Paulin, Coffey, and Spaulding provide a summary look at the literature of entrepreneurship, classified both by topics and by research methods. The organization of this book provides one classification scheme, but there can be any number of others. For instance, these authors group research into four categories: the entrepreneur, the processes of entrepreneurship, functions of entrepreneurship in society, and other supporting topics. Research on the functions of entrepreneurs is emerging rapidly and toward more systematic study.

Paulin, Coffey, and Spaulding also classify publications according to the different research methods on which they are based. In doing so, they provide a convenient review of the different types of general research strategies and tools available to scholars. Eighty percent of the literature of the field they classify as "exploratory," and note, as have several other authors in the book, that much of the available data has been anecdotal at best. Laboratory experimentation and simulation studies have not yet been employed at all for research on this field.

The reader will very likely be left with some thoughts about the future development of entrepreneurship research. In the concluding chapter, Sexton summarizes the research needs and issues and provides an overview of research opportunities in the major subdivisions of entrepreneurship.

Section One

The Entrepreneur

chapter i

Entrepreneurial history

chapter ii

Research about living entrepreneurs

chapter iii

The psychology of the entrepreneur

chapter iv

The social dimensions of entrepreneurship

chapter v

The sociology of entrepreneurship

Entrepreneurship is clearly not a uniformly distributed quality, yet the appearance of the entrepreneur is considered by most analysts to be nonrandom. If the origins of entrepreneurs, their psychological characteristics, and the sociological events that motivate them to begin new ventures could be established, then educational methods to upgrade entrepreneurial skills could be developed.

A first step in this process is a study of the history of entrepreneurship. Events can often be analyzed in retrospect and can provide the basis for projections of future events and their outcome.

The next step is to study living entrepreneurs. Concern is not only with the successes and the psychological aspects of their lives, but also with the overall economic situation and the other environmental conditions which inevitably affect the decision-making process. With regard to the psychological attributes of successful entrepreneurs, the question addressed is why particular individuals are achievement-oriented and are prepared to take the risks associated with the creation of a new venture while others are not. A number of individuals fit the psychological profile—need for achievement, a high degree of ambition, risk-taking propensity, work experience, and an appropriate role model—but do not choose an entrepreneurial career. Therefore, the social environment is considered, as it influences the decision to become an entrepreneur.

According to one school of thought, the sociological event is the major motivating factor in the creation of a new venture, and current efforts to define personal entrepreneurial characteristics are addressing a symptom rather than a cause. Those who support this approach emphasize situational conditions such as job dissatisfaction or displacement, family displacement, and the presence of desirable opportunities. They point to the phenomenon of "accidental" entrepreneurs, those people who "fall into" ventures without any plans and without the "requisite" attitudes or characteristics. On the opposite side are those who argue that psychological factors are the key to understanding the entire entrepreneurial process.

It is apparent that much remains to be learned. This section of the book examines past and current research on the entrepreneur. The chapters begin with the history of entrepreneurship and then consider living entrepreneurs, the psychology of entrepreneurs, and the social dimensions of entrepreneurship.

Livesay, in the chapter on "Entrepreneurial History," suggests that understanding the future in terms of the past is rather like driving an automobile by looking in the rear view mirror. It's an adequate means of maintaining general direction, but not always a guide to the pitfalls and obstacles that lie ahead. Business history, and especially entrepreneurial history, has produced some general lessons that deserve more attention than they have received. The progress of research in this area may frustrate those who yearn for general theories, precise formulas, and maximum rapidity. However, that which is important is seldom urgent.

Martin expands on three points discussed in the chapter on "Entrepreneurial History": the need to define the entrepreneurial function as a specific role; the need to locate the contribution of entrepreneurship to larger enterprises and the conditions that permit entrepreneurship to flourish; the need to place the history of entrepreneurship in a larger historical context.

Using the sources of "Research about Living Entrepreneurs," Hornaday summarizes the research in the field, the biographical and autobiographical publications, the need for additional research, and the ways in which living entrepreneurs can be used to supplement the educational process. This chapter addresses the problem of organizing information once it has been collected and delineates eight major areas in which highly significant questions remain.

Knight, commenting on the sources of research information about living entrepreneurs, takes issue with Hornaday's classification scheme, which is limited to highly successful entrepreneurs. Knight points out that academics in general have used the term "entrepreneur" as though it were interchangeable with "highly successful entrepreneur." Research has been directed toward high-technology firms and sophisticated, rapidly growing firms. The small non-growth firms have been categorized as "mom and pop" enterprises and have been deemed unworthy of serious research.

The chapter by Brockhaus on "The Psychology of the Entrepreneur" begins with various definitions of the term "entrepreneur." The author dis-

cusses the major psychological research, considering such factors as the need for achievement, locus-of-control beliefs, risk-taking propensities, and personal value systems. He then summarizes more environmental research, including such factors as job dissatisfaction, role models, displaced persons, and personal characteristics, and concludes with a model of the "typical" entrepreneur.

As has been pointed out, past studies have sought to determine the characteristics of successful entrepreneurs only. Until a similar amount of research on unsuccessful entrepreneurs has been conducted, we can determine neither the validity of previous findings nor their implications for the educational process. Further, most studies describe the entrepreneurial characteristics which obtain only after the venture has reached a successful status. There is a real need for a comparative longitudinal study to determine if characteristics change over time. Finally, Brockhaus affirms that the present, primarily regional studies are difficult to extrapolate on a nationwide basis. A nationwide random sample of entrepreneurs would provide data that could be categorized in a number of ways, while retaining subsets of adequate size for statistical interpretation.

Gasse maintains that McClelland's concept of the entrepreneur, upon which Brockhaus bases his discussion, is too broad. The distinctive power of the entrepreneur escapes attention when managers, salesmen, farmers, and professionals are also considered to be entrepreneurs. Further, the psychological complexity of entrepreneurs is such that most of the "typical" characteristics have not been adequately isolated or validly measured. Supporting Brockhaus, Gasse finds the major problem with psychological studies to be their degree of generalization. Since most studies are based upon specific groups of people, particular methodologies, and specific objectives and orientations, generalizations are problematic to say the least.

Although much has been said in the last 15 years about the characteristics of the entrepreneur, no clear link has yet been established between these characteristics and the success of business ventures. However, the prevalent methodology in current research holds great promise for advancement in this area.

The events that cause the entrepreneur to start a new venture are examined by Shapero in "The Social Dimensions of Entrepreneurship." Drawing upon studies of displaced groups, or refugees, and their success as entrepreneurs, the author develops a paradigm of the entrepreneurial process. Two questions are raised concerning each entrepreneurial event: (1) What brought about the action that led to a change from the former life path? and (2) Why was the particular path chosen, especially when a myriad of other actions were available?

Each entrepreneurial event occurs in real time as the result of interacting situational, social, and cultural factors. Harwood, in his commentary, takes exception to the broad definition of entrepreneurship espoused by Shapero and others. Following Schumpeter, Harwood believes that innovation is an essential part of entrepreneurship. He maintains that the primary motivating factor for an entrepreneur is not the need for achievement or self-actualization, but desire for money. To de-emphasize profit because of negative associations is a mistake. Harwood supplements our understanding of the entrepreneur by introducing the phenomena of the "artifactual" entrepreneur (who emerges as the result of an ideological decision) and the "accidental" entrepreneur (who falls into a venture without any plan or without what would normally be considered the requisite aptitudes).

The diversity of opinion expressed in these chapters is representative. Much has been accomplished in the primary stage of our understanding of the entrepreneur, but much remains to be done. The multiplicity of approach and emphasis marks a good climate for productive research.

chapter i

Entrepreneurial history

Harold C. Livesay

Overview

Mark Harris, author of *Bang the Drum Slowly*, once remarked that as he faced his freshman English classes he was invariably assailed by two contradictory feelings: On the one hand he felt wholly inadequate to the task; on the other he felt entirely too adequate altogether. Something like the same feelings beset the author in the development of this chapter on "Entrepreneurial History," or "Tycoon History" as it has been alternatively captioned.

The literature germane to entrepreneurial history, if the subject be broadly defined, is so vast and complex as to defy the mastery of any but the most indefatigably singleminded, armed with copious spare time. It ranges through or touches upon not only history and economics, but also such areas as sociology, anthropology, psychology, and, latterly, those disciplines exploring such phenomena as biorhythms and life-cycle theory. Since this author is neither monomaniacal, tireless, nor underemployed, a concise (or even a circuitous) guide to this labyrinth is beyond him.

On the other hand, the subject lends itself to a more limited but useful discussion if it is confined to the central issues that have concerned historians in the past, interest them now, and seem likely to absorb them in the future. Even this, as I shall illustrate later on, requires some high-handed paring, but the author is, if not indefatigable, gleefully high-handed, and thus approaches the topic with a confidence whose justification the audience can judge.

Historical definitions of entrepreneurship

The first problem that has always confronted entrepreneurial historians and, as far as we can see at the moment, seems likely to persist for some time is a definitional one: What is an entrepreneur? Some years ago, Arthur Cole opined that history had witnessed a succession of entrepreneurial types: rule-of-thumb, informed, sophisticated, and mathematically advised. This tidy scheme, however, does little to define the entrepreneur himself, for all of us could think of people embodying one or more of these dominant characteristics who have not a breath of a claim to entrepreneurship by any definition. Cole's accompanying observation that no one had "risen to challenge the validity of this sequence" (*The American Economic Review* 1968) implied a generally accepted definition of the entrepreneur, but in fact meant only that he himself had managed to distill one out of a "decade of almost interminable argument," over which he had presided at the Research Center in Entrepreneurial History at Harvard (*The American Economic Review* 1968).

The fox who kept the chickens clucking around the Harvard Coop was Joseph Schumpeter, whose definition of the entrepreneur as innovator furnished the pole star by which a whole school of entrepreneurial historians steered their craft. By accompanying his definition with the declaration that entrepreneurs provided the indispensable driving force that powered capitalist economic growth, Schumpeter energized the field of entrepreneurial studies by providing its practitioners with the sort of practical rationale that some historians, ever awash on the murky seas of uncertain purpose, find soothing. But Schumpeter's conclusion that capitalism spawned bureaucracy, which doomed the entrepreneur and the capitalism he had nurtured, pointed to the second major, and as yet unresolved, problem confronting entrepreneurial historians: how to relate the function of the entrepreneur to the operations of the stockholder-owned, bureaucratically managed modern firm, and to the economic society in which these firms operate (Schumpeter 1958).

No such quandary befuddled historians in the nineteenth century; indeed, the rise of entrepreneurial history as a distinct discipline is as much a product of big business as is the automobile. For generations of our predecessors, an entrepreneur was any successful businessman. His success was proof enough of his abilities. His motivations were obvious: material prosperity, public recognition and esteem, the welfare of his society. If he had any qualifications that distinguished him from his fellow citizens—and early historians were at pains to emphasize that in America such triumphs as Astor's or Vanderbilt's lay in reach of anyone—they were limited to a willingness to work hard and a measure of good luck. The vignettes of successful businessmen penned by such prolific nineteenth-century historians as J. Thomas Scharf, who spent a lifetime singing the praises of Delaware Valley communities and their leaders, bear a striking similarity to Horatio Alger's fictional portraits of Ragged Dick and Mark the Match Boy (1888).

Inherent in these early descriptions of business tycoons, whether national figures or local merchants, was the assumption that proprietorship and entrepreneurship went hand-in-hand. This notion survived the idolators and passed to the hands of their vitriolic successors, the muckrakers and Progressive historians, for whom ownership became the forge upon which the wily had wrought their wickedness. Having mentioned this vast and often entertaining literature, however, I'm now going to indulge in some high-handed paring by dismissing it from further consideration. It was, after all, not entrepreneurial history as such, but history that contained entrepreneurs. It contributed little to defining the term, though it provided source materials for latter-day lexicographers. Finally, I should perhaps add that the genre is far from dead, as uncritical business biographies continue to appear annually and have, or so my editors assure me, a devoted audience large enough to make their publication a lucrative proposition (see, for example, Olshaker 1978, and Cray 1978). In addition, we have the endless, witless sketches of business executives supplied by *Fortune* and the like, together with the equally shallow attacks mounted by the Richard Barnets and Anthony Sampsons who are the literarily inferior heirs of their muckraking predecessors (Barnet and Muller 1971, Sampson 1973).

Entrepreneurial history as a professional discipline, however, has more recent origins in the late 1920s work of N. S. B. Gras in business history at Harvard. Gras and his followers from the outset addressed the problem of relating the individual business executive to the management of the firm, whether a proprietorship such as Astor's or the brutally complex corporate bureaucracy of Standard Oil.

Gras himself had a far-ranging mind that perceived continuities in business history that stretched back to the Middle Ages, if not to the dawn of time (Gras 1939). His goal of relating business executives to the socioeconomic environments in which they operated, however, fell far short of realization in the works produced by Harvard business historians through the 1940s. What appears to have emerged instead was a stream of case studies, both book and article length, on individual business executives and firms. For the most part these works reflected scrupulous research in primary sources elaborated in grammatical, if largely uninspired, prose and a stubborn resistance to generalization. These labors provided a mountain of documented answers to the first two of the historian's set of basic questions: What happened? and, Who did it? They also carried the discipline into what might be called the "case study trap," from which it still struggles to emerge; that is, the assembled data on individual cases proved stubbornly difficult to distill into useful generalizations about entrepreneurs.

By the late 1940s, when the Entrepreneurial Center at Harvard took up the task, the problem of defining entrepreneurship had been joined at the focal point by the question of entrepreneurial survival. On the one hand stood the theoretical prophecies of inevitable doom voiced by Marx, Schumpeter, and other ravens; on the other, the massive body of empirical evidence that American industry was booming along better than ever. Either the entrepreneur had become unimportant, a proposition few historians would willingly accept (though it titillates some economists determined to rid their models of the clutter of individual human behavior), or business had found some way to bureaucratize the entrepreneurial functions.

Chief spokesman for the latter viewpoint was not a historian at all, but Alfred P. Sloan of General Motors, architect of the quintessential American business bureaucracy. Sloan believed "that the most effective results and the maximum progress and stability of the business [were] achieved by placing its executives in the same relative position . . . that they would occupy if they were conducting a business of their own account." The proper structure, Sloan thought, could provide "monetary reward" and "ego satisfaction" that generated "a tremendous driving force within the Corporation" (Sloan 1963).

Under Arthur Cole's aegis, the denizens of the Harvard Entrepreneurial Center tackled their difficult task from a number of directions, incorporating a variety of disciplinary approaches, and laboring to see businesses and business executives in their broader historical contexts. How one evaluates the results depends largely on one's perspective. For those of us who see history as a humanistic inquiry, justified by curiosity, aesthetics, and the intrinsic fascination of the human story, and capable of producing rough indexes to probable human behavior in various circumstances, post-World War II entrepreneurial history has generated a set of intriguing stories and some general lessons about business and society. For those who think history is, or ought to become, a social science, distilling from the past precise formulas for solving the riddles of the present and future, the results seem meager, yea verily, downright pathetic, for nothing has been resolved to everyone's satisfaction.

We still have, for example, no standard definition of entrepreneurship. Cole described it as purposeful activity to initiate, maintain, and develop a profit-oriented business. Modifying this slightly to "purposeful and successful activity to initiate, maintain, or develop a profit-oriented business" yields a working definition that suits me well enough and, given that the activity takes place in anything but a static social and technological environment, would seem implicitly to incorporate Schumpeter's sweeping innovative principle as well.

Using this definition, or some variation thereof, former participants at the Entrepreneurial Center and their students have carried out most (though I must emphasize by no means all) of the activity down to the present. Thomas

Cochran, for example, has persevered with analytical structures rooted in sociological and anthropological theory, arguing an ongoing relationship between cultures and economic performance (Cochran 1972). The practitioner whose ideas have been most widely incorporated into business school curricula and who has received the widest acclaim, including the Pulitzer Prize, has been Alfred D. Chandler, Jr., now Straus Professor of Business History at the Harvard Business School.

Chandler, whose work has evolved steadily from a biography of his grandfather, *Henry Varnum Poor*, to a historical analysis of American business management's strategies and structures, and now to a similar global analysis, implicitly accepts Sloan's argument that the benefits of entrepreneurial energy can be derived from the labors of corporate managers (Chandler 1979). Explicitly he restricts entrepreneurial functions to the top level of a three-tiered model of corporate administrative structures, which he posited together with Fritz Redlich in 1961 (Chandler and Redlich 1961). To Chandler, only those executives who control capital allocations and long-range strategy qualify as entrepreneurial in behavior.

At the other end of the scale, John Sawyer, among others, has argued that entrepreneurship can be found in a whole range of functions from "the purely innovative to the purely routine," not only in business, but in other organizations where "significant decisions involving change are made affecting the combination and commitment of resources under conditions of uncertainty" (Sawyer 1958). Advocates can be found for virtually every position lying between the Chandler-Sawyer poles. Small wonder, then, some authors wondered whether scholars should not discard "the term 'entrepreneur' " on the grounds that "so many different meanings" had been assigned "to the word that we are now confused."

Surveying the scene in 1968, James Soltow commented that "entrepreneurial history has done relatively little . . . to provide a comprehensive synthesis of entrepreneurial change and its relation to economic change," or, in Fritz Redlich's terms, a "history of business" that specifies the role of "business in history" (Soltow 1968). This condition still prevails. Henrietta Larson, an assiduous practitioner of business history, ascribed this situation to the lack of "an established system of theory." Business history, she declared, needed the support of a "theory that comes close to the realities of business" (Soltow 1968).

Theories of entrepreneurship

This supposed lack of articulated theory turned out to be one of the first issues seized by Visigoth economists when they invaded the field of economic history in the 1960s. For example, one of their number expressed a widespread sentiment, intoning that "historians, as usual backward in the exact definition of concepts and in the precise specification of problems, persistently avoid clarification of what they have been doing," thus producing "undefinable and unoperational" concepts.

Higgs and his ilk set about remedying these dreadful deficiencies and, unsurprisingly, many economists have turned their attention to developing theoretical concepts of the entrepreneur or, as the Hidys suggested, the "entrepreneurial functions." After nearly two decades, an enormous expenditure of effort by "the new economic historians" (as well as by present-oriented economists) has produced a lot of debate, not much factual information, and little if anything in the way of satisfactory explanatory theory.

What have been provided, however, are several demonstrations of the fact that theory is not a shortcut to the truth (even as historians loosely define it) and certainly no substitute for old-fashioned research. We have learned, moreover, that expecting economists to generate satisfactory theories of business behavior is like expecting an alchemist to produce a valid theory of particle physics. The economic literature in business history is jargonistic, boring, uninformative, and generally unread except by its own circle of practitioners. Indeed, the literature has amply borne out the observation of Albro Martin that "economists, whose propensity to reason deductively from a few general propositions involves the danger of taking leave of reality, past or present, owe more attention to economic historians, whose inductive method brings into view the wide range of human activities which—by whatever equation combined—have produced the phenomenon we seek to explain." I would add that Professor Chandler, who would seem to have produced unarguably the most respected work in the field of entrepreneurial history, is characterized by a devotion to plain English, and the entire corpus of his work can be read and understood by an intelligent undergraduate.

The plain fact is that in dealing with entrepreneurs, whether proprietary or bureaucratic, we are dealing with human beings, not blanks or interchangeable economic units. True understanding of entrepreneurial motivation and behavior awaits a more thorough understanding of human psychology. The wait may be a long one, as psychiatry struggles to get out of its own barber-surgeon era, a struggle unlikely to be much advanced by economic theory. The application of psychological concepts has thus far been disappointing. Few would concede, for example, that Anne Jardim's analysis (1970) of Henry Ford's motivations makes more sense than Alan Nevins's (1954–1963).

We thus can supply no general answer to questions such as: How does an entrepreneur *get into* business? We know how hundreds of individuals did it, but the personalities and methods involved are so diverse as to defy generalizations more precise than the following: An entrepreneur perceives a market opportunity and assembles the assets necessary to exploit it. Nor do we understand much about what sorts of people tend to be attracted to the entrepreneurial role, let alone succeed in it. We have Max Weber's hoary old "Protestant ethic" notion, of course, and we know that some identifiable groups—Quakers, Jews, Scotch-Irish—have exhibited a greater propensity for entrepreneurial activity than others. We are tantalized by such exotic tidbits as Leonard Arrington's discovery that among Mormons (another energetically entrepreneurial sect) the sons of second (polygamous) marriages have achieved disproportionate success in business (Arrington 1958).

Finding an explanatory thread that ties these groups together, or even explains any of them individually, as yet remains an unrealized *desideratum*, baffled as we are by the fact that the apparent reasons for the drive and skill of an Andrew Carnegie produced no similar behavior in thousands of individuals who, insofar as the state of the art can inform us, shared the same characteristics. Even less can we make any precise general observations on the impact of external environment upon the entrepreneur's behavior as an individual, or as a type. That we cannot provide satisfactory answers to these legitimate and fascinating questions might be an indictment of the field of entrepreneurial history, but in defense I would suggest that successful entrepreneurship is an art form as much as or perhaps more than it is an economic activity, and as such is as difficult as any other artistic activity to explain in terms of origin, method, or environmental influence. I see no reason why John D. Rockefeller and Alfred P. Sloan should be easier to analyze than Monet, Schubert, or Andy Warhol, nor is the explanatory task less urgent in the one area than in the other. I doubt that we are close to achieving a general theory of entrepreneurs or entrepreneurial functions, but if such a thing should emerge, it seems to me far more likely to result from the inductive methods of historians than from the deductive methods of economists. Indeed, I find myself in sympathy with Gerschenkron, Soltow, and others who have suggested that we abandon the search for a general theory and settle for partial, less satisfying, but more realistic results. That is, in fact, what most of us have done. Historians, I think, are more willing to admit it both because we are accustomed to dealing with reality in all its complexity without "exact definition of concepts and . . . precise specifications of problems" and because we are less sanguine about the possibilities of wringing from the past precise nostrums for current ills.

Current research efforts

Given this brief discussion of past activities, the ongoing research in entrepreneurial history takes place along predictable lines. It must be said, moreover, that only a handful of us are doing it, for economic and business history are tiny fields compared to other areas of interest in American history. Young scholars, out of professional necessity, tend to produce case studies cast in a traditional mold, though some of them follow promising lines such as the interaction between social structure, entrepreneurial behavior, and urban development.

Older practitioners hew along the lines already described. Chandler continues to explore the anatomy of managerial behavior. Vincent Carosso is working on a biography of J. P. Morgan. I am exploring the interaction between business executives and their cultural environments, using the Ford Motor Company's international operations as a springboard. Harry Scheiber carries on his research on the influence of law on economic development. Albro Martin explores the government's deleterious impact on entrepreneurial behavior (see, for example, Livesay 1979; Scheiber and Friedman 1978, and Martin 1971). A sprinkling of interest has appeared on questions involving business and the physical environment.

I am unaware of any radical departures or impending breakthroughs. All of us labor under the handicap imposed by the reluctance of businesses to open their records to historical researchers, and to a large extent, future research will be necessarily directed toward the handful of firms with more open minds. Historians will continue to focus on the behavior of individuals, while economists search for general propositions; this dichotomy reflects a broader disagreement on the question of whether individuals make history or simply reflect more general forces within society. As the American economy continues to deteriorate, research on all sides will doubtless reflect a concern with the extent to which entrepreneurial behavior did or did not influence the decline.

Summary and conclusions

As a closing observation, I would say that business history, including entrepreneurial history, has already produced some general lessons that deserve more attention than they receive in most business school curricula, at least if the behavior of corporate managers is anything to go by. I will supply two brief examples: First, even a cursory reading of nineteenth-century business history shows a distinct negative correlation between the percentage of borrowed capital in an individual enterprise and its prospects for long-run success, a principle ignored by numerous twentieth-century conglomerators with predictable results. Second, Carnegie's maxim, "Watch the costs and the profits will take care of themselves," forcefully and precisely developed by the likes of Pierre Dupont and Alfred Sloan, and elaborated in detail by several historians, would seem so fundamental as to need little repetition. Not so, it seems. At University of Michigan seminars for managers, literally dozens of them have told me of the misfortunes that befell their firms when, dazzled by the prospective wonders of computerization, they authorized greater and greater expenses without any cost-benefit analysis subsequent to the original estimate.

These and other examples suggest to me that entrepreneurial history has already generated a corpus of literature of great potential value to managers, and most of it has been written in the English language, a statement that could only generously be made about the literature of economics and management. Dealing with the present and future on the basis of the past is like driving by looking in the rear view mirror; it's an adequate means of maintaining general direction, but not always a guide to pitfalls and obstacles that lie ahead.

I believe that business history can be a highly informative tool in the training of managers and in their subsequent careers. In our idiosyncratic way we have already produced a mass of valuable material as well as fascinating history. I urge you to look to these sources, and I assure you that we will continue to generate more and better things. It will not be as fast as any of us would like, perhaps, and the results may be frustrating to those who yearn for general theories and precise formulas, but that's the way of history, and we should all keep in mind one of its more salient lessons, that what is important is seldom urgent.

commentary/elaboration

Additional aspects of entrepreneurial history

Albro Martin

There is very little fault to find with Harold Livesay's admirably concise effort to place this subject in the context of history, both as a humanistic study valuable for its own sake and as a source for better understanding the institutions people have developed to fill their material needs. This commentary expands on three important points that Livesay discussed, namely:

1. The need to define the entrepreneurial function as a specific economic role;
2. The need to locate the contribution of entrepreneurship to the large, bureaucratic, publicly owned enterprise, and, as a corollary, to define the conditions necessary for entrepreneurship to flourish in any type of social or political organization;
3. The need to place the history of entrepreneurship in the total history of mankind and, by inference, to determine what the study of entrepreneurship can contribute to our understanding of present-day institutions and to planning for the future.

Definition of entrepreneurship

The entrepreneur is not identified by formal rank or title but retrospectively, after the successful practice of innovation. Entrepreneurship is a pragmatic concept, fundamentally historical in nature, and not capable of being integrated into the static, neoclassical, micro-theory of the firm.

Innovation as in the Schumpeterian (1934) model is an adequate designation of the essential role of the entrepreneur as long as it is borne in mind that Schumpeter defined entrepreneurship broadly to cover virtually any kind of innovative function that could have a bearing on the welfare of an enterprise: product, process, market, organization of firm and of the entire industry, to name the most important. Equally important is to carefully exclude certain roles from entrepreneurship:

1. A person who owns an enterprise or gives the orders is not necessarily an entrepreneur. The Arthur D. Cole definition of entrepreneurship, especially because it was adopted widely, did a disservice to the understanding of entrepreneurship because it failed to distinguish between the innovator and the administrator.

2. A person who assumes the risk of his or her capital is not necessarily an entrepreneur but only an investor. However, one who risks his or her reputation or a portion in a large corporate organization, as a result of an innovation with which he or she is closely identified, fulfills some of the preconditions of entrepreneurship.

3. A creative person in the literary, artistic, or dramatic sense is not necessarily an entrepreneur. The entrepreneur does not innovate by creating ideas, but by recognizing their value and by exploiting them.

Primary requisites for the entrepreneurial climate

There are three primary requisites in the entrepreneurial climate, all of which can be placed under the heading of freedom:

1. Freedom to put one's ideas into effect if the resources can be procured, subject only to the laws of orderly society.

2. Freedom to enjoy the fruits of success or the penalties of failure.

3. Freedom from interposition by the government of its sovereign power to encourage or frustrate an enterprise.

This is the place to pose the popular question, Is there entrepreneurship in the Soviet Union? In the more dynamic segments of their economy, key individuals enjoy considerable entrepreneurial freedom. Observers who have been impressed by the apparent successes of basic industries in the command economies, with their unfree societies, have neglected to note that Soviet planners, for example, were not practicing innovation, but imitation, and they propose to go on doing so as long as they can.

Entrepreneurial profits, which constitute a surplus after the other factors of production are remunerated at their market rate, are the most important source of risk capital and thus the engine of growth in society. The entrepreneurial function is the major factor that distinguishes the executive from the administrator. The giant firm, with its bureaucratic structure and procedures, has its own reasons for being. It has its drawbacks, too, and one form of entrepreneurship peculiar to the large firm is the ability of the innovator to bend the bureaucratic structure or to neutralize it. As a corollary, we have long been aware that the ability to "turn the flank of government regulation" is also an important entrepreneurial function.

The place of entrepreneurship in history

How shall agreement be reached on the place of entrepreneurship in the broader history of mankind? There must first be agreement on the fundamental theme of human history, at least in the era since the rise of modern science in the Renaissance. Determinists—Marxists, laissez-faire libertarians, nihilists, apocalyptics—will not have much truck with entrepreneurial history, because they will not grant that the innovator can make much difference in the course of human history.

Humanists, by contrast, who believe that individual men and women do make a difference, are willing to accept the human story in all its messy complexity, and continually retool and refit their theories to the stored-up knowledge they have managed, however incompletely, to master. Most scholars conclude that the fundamental theme in modern history has been the vast increase in the population vaguely and rather parochially designated Western Man, and the settlement of this great mass of people in the New World of North America.

The most impressive aspect of this enthusiastic acceptance of the biblical injunction to "increase and multiply" has been the concomitant upward trend in material well-being. This is the "economic growth" that the new philistinism professes to abhor and understands so imperfectly. Its roots lie in the freedom this population has enjoyed and which has enabled its members to promulgate a long series of innovations that so far shows little sign of slackening.

The circumstances and events that produced this freedom have been a major topic of political philosophy and political history for roughly four centuries. Its broad consequences for material welfare have occupied economists since before the time of Adam Smith. The problems of marshaling the economic resources that grew with painful slowness in the first 300 of the last 400 years, and the institutions devised to handle them, are the concern of business history. The specific innovative acts by which established ways of doing things were continuously set aside in favor of new ones are the stuff of entrepreneurial history.

Summary

There is a vital relationship between the history of enterprise and the history of public policy. An attempt to solve any present-day public policy problems without competent historical study of its origins is likely to produce disastrous results for entrepreneurial freedom. I cannot here discuss the inane generalizations that have been drawn in recent years about the historical origins of our critical transportation problem. These generalizations are based on a shameful ignorance of history and have led us down many blind alleys of policy formulation. Because this nation simply cannot afford to repeat the past, it had better bend every effort to understand it.

References

ARRINGTON, LEONARD, *Great Basin Kingdom: An Economic History of the Latter Day Saints.* Cambridge: Harvard University, 1958.

BARNET, RICHARD, and MULLER, RONALD, *Global Reach: The Power of the Multinationals.* New York: Simon & Schuster, 1971.

BAUMOL, WILLIAM J., "Entrepreneurship in Economic Theory," *The American Economic Review* 58, No. 2 (May 1968).

Business History Review, Autumn 1961.

CHANDLER, ALFRED D., JR., *Visible Hand.* Cambridge: Harvard University, 1979.

CHANDLER, ALFRED D., JR., and REDLICH, FRITZ, "Recent Developments in American Business Administration and Their Conceptualization," *Business History Review,* Spring 1961; and "Comments," *Business History Review,* Autumn 1961.

COCHRAN, THOMAS, *Business in American Life: A History.* New York: McGraw-Hill, 1972.

CRAY, EDWARD, *Levi's,* Boston: Houghton Mifflin, 1978.

GRAS, NORMAN S. B., *Business and Capitalism: An Introduction to Business History.* New York: F. S. Crofts, 1939.

JARDIM, ANNE, *The First Henry Ford: A Study in Personality and Business Leadership.* Cambridge: MIT, 1970.

LEIBENSTEIN, HARVEY, "Entrepreneurship and Development," *The American Economic Review* 58, No. 2 (May 1968).

LIVESAY, HAROLD C., *American Made: Men Who Shaped the American Economy.* Boston: Little, Brown, 1979.

MARTIN, ALBRO, *Enterprise Denied: Origins of the Decline of American Railroads, 1897-1917.* New York: Columbia University, 1971.

NEVINS, ALAN, et al., *Ford.* 3 vols. New York: Scribner's, 1954-1963.

OLSHAKER, MARK, *The Instant Image: Edwin Land and the Polaroid Experience.* New York: Stein & Day, 1978.

SAMPSON, ANTHONY, *The Sovereign State of ITT.* New York: Stein & Day, 1973.

SAWYER, JOHN E., "Entrepreneurial Studies: Perspectives and Directions, 1948-1958," *Business History Review,* Winter 1958.

SCHEIBER, HARRY, and FRIEDMAN, LAWRENCE, eds., *American Law and the Constitutional Order: A Historical Perspective.* Cambridge: Harvard University, 1978.

SCHUMPETER, JOSEPH, *Capitalism, Socialism, and Democracy.* New York: Simon & Schuster, 1958.

SCHUMPETER, JOSEPH, *The Theory of Economic Development.* Cambridge: Harvard University, 1934.

SLOAN, ALFRED P., *My Years with General Motors.* New York: Doubleday, 1963.

SOLTOW, JAMES H., "The Entrepreneur in Economic History," *The American Economic Review* 58, No. 2 (May 1968).

chapter ii

Research about living entrepreneurs

John A. Hornaday

Overview

Increasing interest in entrepreneurs has resulted in a proliferation of published information about the careers and personality characteristics of living entrepreneurs. This chapter summarizes, in a general way, the research in this field, the need for additional research, biographical and autobiographical publications, and some of the ways in which living entrepreneurs can be used to supplement classroom work. The specific content of research and the ways in which it might be organized are discussed more extensively in other chapters.

Sources of research information about living entrepreneurs

The state of the art in entrepreneurship is such that the study of living entrepreneurs can provide extremely valuable information both for systematic scholars and for those who are considering entrepreneurial careers. In this study, three very broad sources of information were examined: publications, direct observations of entrepreneurs in action, and oral presentations by entrepreneurs themselves both in structured and in free-form settings.

Publications

To give some structure to the printed material dealing with entrepreneurs, publications have been divided as follows:

1. *Technical and professional journals.* These are refereed and carry articles dealing with research—either methodology, results, or application of results—that has been well designed and tightly structured. Examples: *Harvard Business Review*, which occasionally carries articles on entrepreneurship, and *Journal of Small Business Management*, which carries a larger number of articles on that subject.

2. *Textbooks on entrepreneurship.* These include the operation of small firms and nonprofit organizations. Sections or chapters of such books are frequently devoted to research on entrepreneurs. Examples: *New Venture Creation* (by Timmons, Smollen, and Dingee), which focuses entirely on entrepreneurship and start-up, *Small Business Management* (by Broom and Longenecker), and *Entrepreneurship and Small Business Management* (by Schollhammer and Kuerloff).

3. *Books about entrepreneurship.* Most are not written as texts but as practitioners' "how-to" guides. Some of these deal with the problems facing the individual who starts a business; others deal with a specific aspect of the subject. Examples: *Baumback's Guide to Entrepreneurship* (by Baumback), *Entrepreneurship: Playing to Win* (by Baty), *Fun and Guts: The Entrepreneur's Philosophy* (by Mancuso) as general books and *Business Planning Guide* (by Bangs) as a more specialized guide.

4. *Biographies or autobiographies of entrepreneurs.* Examples: *Grinding It Out: The Making of McDonald's* (by Kroc, with Anderson) and *The First Henry Ford: A Study in Personality and Business Leadership* (by Jardin).

5. *Compendiums about entrepreneurs.* These are collections that deal with several selected individuals or which present statistical information or overviews of perceived general trends. Examples: *The Entrepreneurs* (by Shook) as a compendium of information about selected living entrepreneurs and *The Enterprising Americans* (by Chamberlin) as a summary of trends.

6. *News periodicals.* A number of these feature either regular or irregular sections on entrepreneurs. Examples: *Business Week*, *Forbes*, *Fortune*, *The Economist*, and *The Wall Street Journal.*

7. *Venture periodicals.* A growing number of new magazines are specifically concerned with new business ventures so that virtually all contents are related to entrepreneurship. Examples: *Black Enterprise*, *Entrepreneur*, *In Business*, *Inc.*, and *Venture.*

8. *Newsletters. The Entrepreneurial Manager's Newsletter*, for example, is devoted exclusively to entrepreneurship.

9. *Proceedings of conferences.* Several recent conferences dealt in part or entirely with entrepreneurship. Examples: *Proceedings of the Academy of Management*, and *Proceedings of Project ISEED.*

10. *Government publications.* The government publishes on entrepreneurship, small business operations, and specific small businesses. Examples: SBA pamphlets.

To be entirely on top of developments in this field, the research-minded student of entrepreneurship should follow all ten types of publications. The bibliographical section of this chapter provides more complete lists.

For research and for academic information, groups 1, 2, and 9 are the best sources. Groups 3, 7, 8, and 10 are of special interest to the practitioner. For those interested in the study of "living entrepreneurs" as a collection of interesting people, groups 4, 5, and 6 are of special interest. Of course, none of these sources is limited to materials on living entrepreneurs alone. The actions and personal histories of past entrepreneurs can do much to further our understanding of the nature of success.

The fact is, however, that this report is primarily concerned with the living entrepreneur, and the author wishes to introduce a word of caution: While generalizations can be developed on historical grounds, "The New Entrepreneur" is to some extent a distinct phenomenon. In the free enterprise society of the United States as it is today, and as it will be in the future, successful entrepreneurship requires different behavior than it did even several decades ago. The New Entrepreneurs must be more willing to join forces with other small businesses, must be more aware of the behavioral responses of subordinates and must be somewhat less authoritarian than their predecessors could afford to be. They must be willing to change at an ever increasing pace, and be fully ready to make use of technological advances.

Direct observation

A second source of information is direct observation of entrepreneurs in action.

Observation of behavior would appear to be limited to "living entrepreneurs" indeed, but that is not entirely true. Films, audio tapes, videotapes, and photographs can supply some insight into the nature of successful entrepreneurs of the past. By the use of cases in interactive classroom settings, students can "experience" the processes by which entrepreneurs of the past wrestled with problems. Of course, with living entrepreneurs, further information can be gathered by means of standardized interviews, questionnaires, surveys, and inventories that reflect personal traits. This relatively controlled research has many obvious advantages over the effort to infer characteristics and attitudes from materials written by or about the entrepreneur.

Another way in which the living entrepreneur can contribute both to education and to research is to engage in open, free conversations with students and researchers. Educationally, there is enormous impact on students who have an opportunity to engage in dialogue with the operator of a successful local business or with a world-renowned tycoon. There is also a great deal to be learned from the entrepreneur who has failed, if he or she can be persuaded to talk undefensively about the causes of problems, the consequences of failure, and plans for the future. Whether the presentation is addressed to the full student body, to a smaller classroom, or to individual students who are queued up for the opportunity, the value of the interaction is great. If the students can conduct a series of structured, standardized, and systematized interviews, they can collect a considerable amount of material.

As an alternate approach, students might study an ICCH or CTA case in preparation for classroom discussion. It is always dramatic if the subject of the case is in the audience, unknown to the students, and is introduced after a fairly complete analysis has been made, but sufficient time should be left for evaluative comments and elaborations. This kind of "trick," if instructors are willing to stoop to playing it, may afford further insight into the nature of the subject entrepreneur. This in turn will help instructors to lead better discussions of the same case in the future and perhaps to provide better cases on entrepreneurial development than are available at this time.

Finally, Executive-in-Residence programs and departmental Boards of Visitors provide important forums for the participation of entrepreneurs in higher education.

Several of these methods are not research-oriented in the traditional sense, but if one includes the development of training and education courses under the broader definition of research, living entrepreneurs can help academicians far beyond the means of "ivy-tower" research alone. They can also provide much-needed assistance in case development. In this realm, such organizations as the Case Teacher Association, Wellesley, Massachusetts, are actively seeking entrepreneurial case material and ought to be encouraged.

Having discussed the three sources of research material, we will now suggest categories that will aid in organizing and interpreting the data. It is not our purpose here to summarize the findings of entrepreneurial research but rather to present an organized, interpretable, global view of research.

Organization of information about living entrepreneurs

How can the researcher organize the information we gather about living entrepreneurs? What cross-cuts can be made in order to categorize the data? One obvious answer is that the data can be organized in a manner roughly similar to the sections of this book. Scholars cannot learn a great deal about the history of entrepreneurship or about research methodology from living entrepreneurs, but most of the chapters constitute appropriate divisions of the data that living entrepreneurs can provide. Actually, these chapters closely parallel a breakdown of entrepreneurial studies developed by Schreier and Komives (1973) and cited by Vesper (1976). Their ten sub-fields of entrepreneurship, and the comparable topics in this book, are listed in Table 1.

Table 1   *Comparable classification topics*

Vesper 1976	*Encyclopedia of entrepreneurship*
Tycoon History	Entrepreneurship History
Psychology of the Entrepreneur	Psychology of the Entrepreneur*
Sociology of the Entrepreneur	Sociology of the Entrepreneur*
Economic Development via Entrepreneurship	Entrepreneurship in Economic Development†
Entrepreneurship Education	Education for Entrepreneurship*
Start-up Methodology	Mechanics and Strategy of Venture Initiation†
Venture Finance	Venture Finance†
Ongoing Small Business	Entrepreneurship-Small Business Interface†
Internal Entrepreneurship	Internal Corporate Entrepreneurship†
Innovation	Innovation from Entrepreneurship
	The Environment for Entrepreneurship*
	Nonacademic Literature on Entrepreneurship

*These topics lend themselves particularly well to categorization.

†These topics also constitute appropriate categories, but they subdivide into two subjects: entrepreneurial traits per se and the factors that make for successful establishment of an organization. Paulin, Coffey, and Spaulding, in their chapter on "Entrepreneurship Research," discuss the first of these topics under the heading, "The Entrepreneur," and the second under the heading, "Entrepreneurship Processes." By far the greatest amount of published work, especially in textbooks, concerns the procedures to be used in starting a business—the business plan, market survey, financing, and so forth. We focus in this chapter on what these men and women are rather than what they do to start a business. Our special concerns, then, will be the psychology and sociology of entrepreneurship, the environment of entrepreneurship, and education of entrepreneurs.

Detailed discussion of research findings within these topics will be found in other chapters of this book. The purpose here is to provide (1) a list of characteristics that distinguish entrepreneurs from people in general; (2) an overview of the factors that affect entrepreneurial success—political, economic, sociological, familial, psychological, cultural, physical, and chance; (3) a consideration of the efforts to "type" entrepreneurs; and (4) a review of the ways in which the success factors can be increased in aspiring entrepreneurs.

For McClelland (McClelland and Winter 1969) the distinction between entrepreneurial traits and those which characterize people-in-general was a simple matter. He believed that the individual entrepreneur's need for achievement (n Ach) was the differentiating factor, and to be considered even to the exclusion of other factors. In an interview in *Forbes* (McClelland 1969), McClelland stated, "We've spent twenty years studying just this—why one businessman succeeds and another fails—twenty years in the laboratory doing very careful research, and we've isolated the specific thing. We know the exact type of motivation that makes a better entrepreneur. Not necessarily a better head of General Motors; I'm talking about the man who starts a business." That specific characteristic is the individual's need for achievement.

In the early 1970s other investigators (Hornaday and Bunker 1970; Hornaday and Aboud 1971), while agreeing that n Ach is an important factor, perhaps the most important psychological factor, found that other traits bore a significant relationship to success. The findings of those investigators and of other research studies have been summarized in a variety of ways. One compilation, which included national differences, was published by the East-West Center Technology and Development Institute (1977). Table 2 illustrates the wide variety of traits cited in the East-West Center report; Table 3 extracts the 19 most frequent traits. Even if national differences are excluded, the variety of traits is large.

The factors listed in Table 4 represent the thinking of SMU's Caruth Institute, as reported in a popular article by Garza (November 1975). Several traits on the SMU list are distinct from those of the East-West Center list. The lack of agreement concerns not only the relative importance of traits but the question of whether certain traits should be included at all. In the SMU and East-West profiles, the entrepreneur is expected to take only calculated or moderate risks, yet Brockhaus (Brockhaus and Nord 1979, Brockhaus 1976) has questioned whether there is any relationship at all between risk-taking propensity and the success of the enterprise.

The point to be made, then, is that we need more definitive studies of personality traits, and such studies can best be carried out on living entrepreneurs. Good groundwork has been laid; issues and questions are no longer pure conjecture. Much is known about the physical health, mental ability, and psychological drives that make individuals more likely to become successful entrepreneurs. The effects of childhood experiences and early business experience are appreciably understood. The most conducive environmental factors have been documented—relationships with spouse and children, the average number of children (2.1), and the average age of entry (32) into a new enterprise for certain kinds of entrepreneurs (Roberts and Wainer 1971). Research must be designed to probe still more precisely into these important factors if entrepreneurs are to be properly trained for success.

Another cross-cut ordering of the data is by "types" of entrepreneurs. In a 1967 publication, Smith refers to the Craftsman-Entrepreneur and the Opportunistic-Entrepreneur. Hornaday and Bunker (1970) confirm the value of that distinction; they find the former type of entrepreneur to be characterized by a limited cultural background and limited social involvement, the latter by a broader educational background, broader social involvement, and a more aggressive approach to long-range development and expansion. There are numerous other "types": the individual who starts a business where there is none before; the individual who injects such energy and change into an existing business that it begins to "fly"; the innovator in a large and progressive business who deals with his or her own section or division in a highly creative way; an individual who is simply a risk-taker. In a recent publication Vesper

Table 2 *Characteristics often attributed to the entrepreneur*

	Reference source						
Characteristics	**SBA**	**H&B**	**IIM (a)**	**EWC Workshop**	**INED**	**Akhouri**	**IIM (b)**
1. Confidence	x	x	x	x	x	x	x
2. Perseverance, determination	x	x	x	x	x		
3. Energy, diligence	x	x	x	x	x	x	x
4. Resourcefulness	x	x	x	x	x		
5. Ability to take calculated risks		x	x	x	x	x	x
6. Dynamism, leadership	x	x	x	x			
7. Optimism	x		x	x			x
8. Need to achieve	x	x	x	x		x	
9. Versatility; knowledge of product, market, machinery, technology	x	x	x	x			x
10. Creativity	x	x	x	x		x	
11. Ability to influence others	x	x	x				
12. Ability to get along well with people	x	x	x				x
13. Initiative	x	x	x	x	x		
14. Flexibility		x	x			x	x
15. Intelligence	x		x				
16. Orientation to clear goals			x	x	x		
17. Time-competence, efficiency			x	x		x	
18. Ability to make decisions quickly			x	x			
19. Positive response to challenges			x	x	x	x	
20. Independence	x	x	x	x		x	
21. Honesty, integrity	x		x				
22. Maturity, balance	x		x				
23. Responsiveness to suggestions and criticism	x		x	x	x		x

(1980) posits 11 entrepreneurial "types," but points out that each of those could be further subdivided. His divisions include: solo self-employed individuals, team builders, independent pattern multipliers, economy-of-scale exploiters, capital aggregators, acquirers, buy-sell artists, conglomerators, speculators, and apparent value manipulators.

These overlapping lists will illustrate the fluid state of the basic concepts in entrepreneurial studies. Although researchers are well accustomed to juggling many different, sometimes overlapping, sometimes contradictory orderings of

Table 2 *(cont.)*

Characteristics	Reference source						
	SBA	H&B	IIM (a)	EWC Workshop	INED	Akhouri	IIM (b)
24. Responsibility				x	x		
25. Foresight	x		x	x		x	x
26. Accuracy, thoroughness	x		x				
27. Cooperativeness	x		x				
28. Profit-orientation		x	x	x	x		
29. Ability to learn from mistakes				x	x	x	
30. Sense of power				x		x	
31. Pleasant personality	x			x			
32. Egotism				x			
33. Courage	x			x			x
34. Imagination	x			x			
35. Perceptiveness		x		x		x	x
36. Toleration for ambiguity				x			
37. Aggressiveness	x			x		x	
38. Capacity for enjoyment				x			
39. Efficacy	x					x	
40. Commitment	x			x	x		
41. Ability to trust workers	x					x	x
42. Sensitivity to others				x		x	

Abbreviations and references:

SBA	Hal B. Pickle, *Personality and Success: An Evaluation of Personal Characteristics of Successful Small Business Managers.* Washington D.C.: U.S. Small Business Administration, 1964.
H&B	J. Hornaday and C. Bunker, "The Nature of the Entrepreneur," *Personnel Psychology* 23, No. 1 (1970), 47-54.
IIM (a,b)	Indian Institute of Management, Studies 1 and 2 as cited in Appendix B.
EWC Workshop	East-West Center Technology and Development Institute, *Entrepreneur Curriculum Development Workshop*, August 1976.
INED	Institute for New Enterprise Development, *New Venture Creation*, by Timmons, Smollen, and Dingee, p. 37.
Akhouri	See citation in Appendix B.

data, the practitioner and the student may find the array bewildering. Any single piece of research must define the kind of individual with whom it deals. Good, recent summaries of the investigation into entrepreneurial types and into the psychological and sociological characteristics of entrepreneurs can be found in Broom and Longenecker's fifth edition (1979) and in Schollhammer and Kuriloff (1979).

Another question is whether entrepreneurial characteristics, once identified, can be taught. Can students be trained and, in addition, inspired to undertake the difficult and challenging task of starting a business? What role can living entrepreneurs (successful and unsuccessful) play in this process? Can

Table 3 Most frequent characteristics in surveyed studies

1. Self-confidence
2. Perseverance, determination
3. Energy, diligence
4. Resourcefulness
5. Ability to take calculated risks
6. Need to achieve
7. Creativity
8. Initiative
9. Flexibility
10. Positive response to challenges
11. Independence
12. Foresight
13. Dynamism, leadership
14. Versatility, knowledge of product, market, machinery, technology
15. Ability to get along with people
16. Responsiveness to suggestions and criticism
17. Profit-orientation
18. Perceptiveness
19. Optimism

Source: Table 2

we utilize them as role models for students and practitioners who are just starting out?

Some authors of entrepreneurial literature (Roscoe 1973) enjoy speculating that an individual "is what he is" and that significant change is not possible. Empirical evidence, however, suggests that some aspects of human nature can be changed. Some of McClelland's work (1965) addresses this point directly. He and his associates were able to develop an educational program which, in courses of relatively short duration, increased the all-important n Ach in individuals. Following a theoretical structure suggested by Argyris (1970), the courses create in the individuals a powerful belief in their ability to change through their own efforts. The argument is most fully presented in McClelland's 1965 publication, but Schollhammer and Kuriloff (1979) give a brief, clear summary of the McClelland training process.

Zaleznik and Kets de Vries (1975) and Zaleznik (1977) follow the Freudian emphasis on early childhood influences, but both writers accept the premise that personality can be changed, specifically that the traits associated with success can be inculcated. Vesper (1976) and Kierulff (1973) support this premise.

A definitive, longitudinal study on the effects of education is much needed. A well designed piece of research, with pre- and post-measurement techniques and a carefully selected control group, could investigate both the measurable and the perceived effects of entrepreneurial education. Current efforts

Table 4 *Characteristics of the entrepreneur (Garza 1975)*

1. Good physical health
2. Superior conceptual abilities
3. The broad thinking of a generalist
4. High self-confidence
5. Strong drive
6. Basic need to control and direct
7. Moderate risk-taking
8. Great realism
9. Moderate interpersonal skills
10. Sufficient emotional stability

in this area, reported by Hornaday, Vesper, and Moore (1980), may partially fill one of the major gaps in research on living entrepreneurs.

Gaps in the research about entrepreneurs

Eight of the major projects that remain are as follows: (1) to study the effect of entrepreneurial education, (2) to study the particular characteristics of retail outlet operators (manufacturing organizations and retail-food outlets have received much more attention), (3) to study the "very small business owner" as contrasted to the tycoons, (4) to study failures, (5) to develop more effective means of measuring entrepreneurial characteristics, (6) to establish a central clearinghouse for assimilation, categorization, and dissemination of ideas and information, (7) to establish a noncommercial newsletter to supplement current commercial newsletters, and (8) to establish a professional, scientific journal to supplement the commercial publications listed elsewhere in this chapter.

Education research

The studies that have been done in this area, with the exception of McClelland's work, have been little more than casually reported. They are popular and appealing, but the field needs more systematic, quantitative studies to determine: (1) the effectiveness of specific functions in the curriculum (for example, what is the best way to teach students to write a business plan so that the principles they learn will be of maximum adaptability and effectiveness?), (2) the effectiveness of individual courses and series of courses, (3) the true effects of training and education upon the probability of success.

An example of the second kind of study is currently underway at Babson College. Using data available from six cooperating schools, all of which have offered courses in entrepreneurship for eight years or more, researchers are studying the activities of students who graduated in 1975 or earlier. The effort is to determine the effect of entrepreneurial courses on the subsequent careers of these students. Each student who took one or more entrepreneurial course is matched with a comparable student who did not take that course. The sample is large enough to support statistical analysis within each school. The alumni are being questioned about their careers, about their attitudes toward their schools and courses (especially the entrepreneurial course), and about their perception of the effects of education upon their careers. Such factors as the opportunity to enter a family business are being taken into account. Even in a study as carefully designed as this one, a problem results from the fact that entrepreneurial courses are "electives" and therefore the differences found between experimental and control groups may be the result of self-selection rather than course content.

A study of the kind described may suggest areas that might be emphasized in entrepreneurial courses, but definitive studies of effectiveness are very difficult to design under our present educational system. Longitudinal studies of the careers of all alumni of entrepreneurial courses may prove to be even more fruitful. Some schools have had entrepreneurial courses for more than ten years, and from those "older" alumni we can obtain significant histories with relative speed.

Studies of general retail outlets and micro-industries

Given the number of people who operate retail outlets and very small businesses, the amount of research in these areas is disproportionately small. We are just beginning to recognize the importance of the very small undertaking, and in conferences on entrepreneurship around the country, "micro-business" sessions are appearing with increasing frequency. Heretofore, management courses have been heavily and consciously oriented toward large corporate settings; some university members even express appreciable disdain for the small business course! In recent years, however, there has been a significant movement toward courses in small business and in entrepreneurship. The number of colleges offering such courses has increased from 8 to almost 200 over a ten-year period, and numerous non-academic seminars have developed all over the United States. As is often the case when there is a proliferation of this latter kind, one must examine the offerings closely to determine which will realistically meet the needs.

If the gaps in education and training are beginning to be filled, research on the smaller business is progressing more slowly.

Failures

Research on those who have made unsuccessful attempts to become entrepreneurs is difficult for obvious reasons: locating the subjects, getting them to cooperate in a study which does not show them at their best, avoiding the distortions that occur because of defensiveness. Some work has been published along this line (Hess 1974, Nekvasil 1972, Brockhaus 1980), but more is needed.

A recent book, devoted exclusively to its author's mistaken entrepreneurial decisions, is *How to Lose $100,000,000 and Other Valuable Advice*, by Royal Little (1979). Little made numerous investments in businesses that failed and missed other opportunities because he underestimated the degree to which an organization would later become successful. Nowhere in his book does the author mention that his other decisions on acquisitions netted $2 billion for his company, Textron.

Another type of study that would strengthen our understanding of entrepreneurial failure is the "control group" arrangement. Like the educational studies that compared alumni of entrepreneurial courses with those who had not taken the courses, these studies would compare successful entrepreneurs to those who have failed, to professional people, to those who say they want to be entrepreneurs but do not make the necessary move, and to those who have no expressed wish to launch into businesses of their own. Designing such studies and obtaining cooperation from the failure group will be difficult, but it can be accomplished by mounting effort.

Measuring entrepreneurial characteristics

This area of research involves three questions: (1) Are there characteristics (psychological, sociological, hereditary, environmental, educational, or experimental) that distinguish the successful entrepreneur from other persons? (2) If so, are these characteristics present prior to entrepreneurial experience itself? (3) If there are distinguishing characteristics and if they are present prior to entrepreneurial activity, how can they be reliably measured in advance of a new enterprise?

Strong evidence suggests an affirmative answer to the first question. Studies cited in the early section of this chapter support the contention that there are statisically significant psychological and sociological characteristics that distinguish entrepreneurs from other groups. Those most likely to succeed are well acquainted with business and with the specific product or service they will be offering. The effects of differences in education have not been established, and the question of heredity or environment is ambiguous.

Researchers have not fully determined whether those psychological and sociological factors closely associated with success produce the entrepreneurial personality or are themselves produced by the innovative, entrepreneurial experience. A definitive study on this question has yet to be carried out, but a great deal of evidence suggests that preexisting psychological characteristics play a highly significant role in affecting the selection of occupation (Strong 1955, Kuder 1970, Zytowski 1973). In numerous professional areas, it is possible to predict with accuracy an individual's selection of occupation. Although we do not have comparable studies for entrepreneurs, there is every reason to believe that similar results could be obtained, especially if "types" of entrepreneurs are dealt with as separate groups. While not denying the need to confirm the determining powers of a preexisting condition, it appears that researchers can move into predictive research at this time.

Measurement instruments like the *Strong Vocational Interest Blank* (Strong 1959) and the *Kuder Occupational Interest Survey* (Kuder 1970) are producing research that relates interests and motivation to occupational choice. Subjects respond both to activity choices and to personal-background questions. In some cases, an individual responds directly to a computer program and is then questioned further as the nature of his or her interest profile becomes more clearly defined. Thus, after an hour of interaction with the terminal, participants receive an immediate printout of specific occupations in which they would find intrinsic satisfaction. It should be noted that the program referred to here is very different from—and far more sophisticated than—others that are on the market at this time. What is not fully developed is a measure of entrepreneurial inclinations.

When computerized prediction of entrepreneurial success is undertaken, it is particularly important that the analysis be made by the "person-to-person" technique. This procedure, interestingly, is one toward which most psychological measurement will move in the next two decades. According to this technique, a participant is compared to other individuals from a pool of thousands and sees the history, characteristics, and present activities of several persons whose responses were very similar to his or her own. The sex of the individual compared is not necessarily the same as that of the participant; what is important is that the pattern of responses be similar. Especially with highly individualistic subjects like entrepreneurs, individualized analysis is crucial. This innovation in psychological evaluation has been described in the work of Kuder (1977, 1980) and of Hornaday (1979).

Clearinghouse

During the past four decades, efforts have been made to set up a central organization for the assembly and classification of entrepreneurial research. Notable among these are the efforts of Michigan State University, the Caruth Institute at Southern Methodist University, the Center for Venture

Management in Milwaukee, and the Entrepreneurship Center at Harvard. These undertakings have been characterized by a brilliant take-off period, a surprisingly quick leveling off, a decline in energy and effort after several years, and in some cases a demise of the service.

At the time of this writing, the United States is entering its seventh recession (by some economists' count) since 1940. The effects will be especially difficult for small business, and the recession may be of much greater significance than anticipated: government rules and regulations have increased drastically within recent years so that small business is being "squeezed," tax rates are higher than ever before, and the prime rate has been hovering around 20 percent. In spite of all of these factors, a new wave of small business and entrepreneurial activity in the United States may be beginning. There is reason to expect the crest to come during the 1990s, and it may extend well beyond the year 2000. If history does repeat itself, the first decade of the new millenium should be comparable to the 1960s in the shift of American value systems. Business opportunities in this free enterprise society should be as great as they were during the period following World War II. The predicted entrepreneurial activity may not develop, but there is a growing conviction by those concerned with economic development in the United States that a pessimistic outlook is not justified.

The clearinghouse should not be limited to formal research. It should serve as a collection point for biographical and autobiographical material on entrepreneurs. It should produce biographies of a standardized, structured design such that comparisons on many specific vital points can be made.

The problem with the familiar biographical and autobiographical publications on extremely successful entrepreneurs ("tycoons"), however appealing or inspirational, is that they yield little that can be studied comparatively, systematically, or quantitatively. They may convey the entrepreneur's or the writer's point of view and they sometimes stimulate self-assessment or action on the part of the reader. They cannot substitute, however, for systematically collected and analytically presented material.

In spite of the tendency to focus research and teaching on the entrepreneurs who are "household names," a great deal can be learned from moderately successful small business operators. The latter are often better for teaching and role-model purposes because they may be within the reach of the students' capabilities. Study of this group of entrepreneurs may yield important differences not only between them and non-entrepreneurs but also between them and the superstar "tycoons." It will be fruitful to extend the intensive studies to include those companies with five or fewer employees. It is such companies that will need to undergo the most extensive adjustment in the 1980s; they may need to band together more effectively in order to maximize their inbound information and their impact on municipal and federal governments.

The study of the top-level entrepreneurs has a great deal of interest and popular appeal, but as Russell Knight has pointed out, it is merely the tip of the iceberg. The greater impact can be found below the surface among the unsung and relatively unresearched smaller entrepreneurs. The balance of attention should be changed if we are to assemble a full picture of The New Entrepreneur.

Newsletter

In the United States at this time, only a few hundred research people are primarily interested in the entrepreneurial area. This is in contrast to the hundreds of thousands of students and practitioners who will be affected by their findings. The research pool is growing, however, and a strong need is developing for periodic, internal communication. Conferences such as the one at Baylor University in 1980 are helpful but are necessarily irregular and infrequent. There are numerous newsletters for practitioners: the monthly *Entrepreneurial Manager's Newsletter*, recently acquired by the American Management Association; *Invention Management* and *Copyright Management*, published by the Institute for Invention and Innovation, Inc.; *Common Sense*, published by a company with the interesting name of Upstart Publishing, Inc.; *Venture Capital*, published by Capital Publishing Company; and many others throughout the United States. There is no quarterly, professional newsletter for researchers. Previous efforts to establish a service of that kind have had a start-and-stop history, but the need for circulation of information among professionals in the field of entrepreneurship remains strong.

A journal of entrepreneurial research

The difference between this proposal and the preceding one is clear. The journal would be a refereed, professional outlet for manuscripts that report research, research methods, and application of research results to entrepreneurial problems. Well established journals in the fields of management and economics already carry occasional articles on these subjects, but the need here is for a journal devoted exclusively to the proliferating body of entrepreneurial research.

These, then, are eight areas in which development or expansion is needed in order to meet the challenges of entrepreneurial research more effectively. Good progress has been made in the areas of academic and nonacademic training; new publication outlets are particularly needed, but all the areas mentioned require attention and development.

commentary/elaboration

Additional considerations of research about living entrepreneurs

Russell Knight

Professor Hornaday provides a broader perspective about sources of research information on living entrepreneurs than do most writers on the subject. His chapter is limited neither to published studies nor to the very successful entrepreneurs. Alternate sources of information include case studies of living entrepreneurs, direct observation, and conversations with entrepreneurs. The chapter stresses a variety of pedagogical techniques.

If education is taken as the primary purpose of entrepreneurial research, this has some implications both for the research that is currently being undertaken and for topics that are not being studied but ought to be. Education-oriented research combines with traditional research to provide more applicability. Research without the educational objective is "Ivy Tower" research and threatens to become an end in itself rather than a means to an end.

Hornaday has attempted to use the same classification schemes used by others. For the most part, these are limited to the study of highly successful entrepreneurs. The vast majority of the entrepreneurs possess relatively few of the characteristics itemized in Tables 2 and 3 of Hornaday's chapter. It appears that many researchers have chosen to ignore the entrepreneur who is fighting for survival and to make the term "entrepreneur" interchangeable with "highly successful entrepreneur."

Further consideration should be given to the characteristics of all entrepreneurs—unsuccessful, marginally successful, successful, and highly successful. By considering a life cycle in which the entrepreneur moves from one stage of success to another, one may ascertain those characteristics or events that allow the entrepreneur to move along the continuum. In this respect one examines the process rather than the end result.

Hornaday is somewhat inconsistent on this matter of the small entrepreneur. In his section on entrepreneurial education, he stresses the need for research on retail and service firms and on the small business owner, yet he fails to stress the need for research assistance to unsophisticated entrepreneurs.

There is also a tendency to emphasize high-technology business, perhaps due to the rapid growth in this field and its impact on the production of higher priced goods and services. Invention and innovation, however, occur in other businesses as well. The author takes issue with those who feel that small business entrepreneurs and small, non-growth enterprises are not worthy of research. Much can be learned from the study of unsophisticated entrepreneurs. If an increase in the level of sophistication can be directly related to the profitability of the firm, then the benefits of research can be most effective in these areas.

References

ARGYRIS, CHRIS, *Intervention Theory and Method.* Reading, Mass.: Addison-Wesley, 1970.

BANGS, DAVID H., and OSGOOD, WILLIAM R., *Business Planning Guide.* Portsmouth, New Hampshire: Upstart Publishing Company, 1979.

BAUMBACK, CLIFFORD M., *Baumback Guide to Entrepreneurship.* Englewood Cliffs, N.J.: Prentice-Hall, 1981.

BROCKHAUS, ROBERT H., "Risk Taking Propensity of Entrepreneurs," *Proceedings of the Academy of Management,* 1976.

BROCKHAUS, R. H., and NORD, W. R., "An Exploration of Factors Affecting the Entrepreneurial Decision: Personal Characteristics vs. Environmental Conditions," *Proceedings of the Academy of Management,* 1979.

BROCKHAUS, R. H., "Psychological and Environment Factors Which Distinguish the Successful From the Unsuccessful Entrepreneurs: A Longitudinal Study," *Academy of Management Proceedings,* 1980.

BROOM, H. N., and LONGENECKER, JUSTIN G., *Small Business Management* (5th ed.). Cincinnati: South-Western Publishing, 1979.

Copyright Management. Arlington, Mass.: Institute for Invention and Innovation.

GARZA, DANIEL, "Going It Alone," *Texas Parade,* November 1975.

HESS, NANCY R., "Retail Strategy—How to Avoid Failure by Success," *Business and Economic Dimensions* 10 (March-April 1974).

HORNADAY, JOHN A., "Reliability of Person-to-Person Interest Measurement," New York: American Psychological Association Convention, September 1979.

HORNADAY, JOHN A., and ABOUD, JOHN, "Characteristics of Successful Entrepreneurs," *Personnel Psychology* 24, No. 2 (Summer 1971).

HORNADAY, JOHN A., and BUNKER, CHARLES S., "The Nature of the Entrepreneur," *Personnel Psychology* 23, No. 1 (Spring 1970).

HORNADAY, JOHN A., VESPER, KARL H., and MOORE, LYNN, "Effects of Entrepreneurial Courses on Careers," Working paper, Babson College, 1980.

"An Interview with Professor David C. McClelland of Harvard," *Forbes* 103, No. 11 (June 1, 1969).

Invention Management. Arlington, Mass.: Institute for Invention and Innovation.

KIERULFF, HERBERT E., "Can Entrepreneurship Be Taught?" *MBA Magazine,* June-July 1973.

KUDER, FREDERIC, *Activity Interests and Occupational Choice.* Chicago: Science Research Associates, 1977.

KUDER, FREDERIC, *Kuder Occupational Interest Survey.* Chicago: Science Research Associates, 1970.

KUDER, FREDERIC, "People Matching," *Educational and Psychological Measurement* 40 (1980).

KUDER, FREDERIC, "Some Principles of Interest Measurement," *Educational and Psychological Measurement* 30 (1970).

LITTLE, ROYAL, *How to Lose $100,000,000 and Other Valuable Advice.* Boston: Little, Brown, 1979.

MCCLELLAND, DAVID C., "Achievement Motivation Can Be Developed," *Harvard Business Review*, November-December 1965.

MCCLELLAND, DAVID C., and WINTER, DAVID G., *Motivating Economic Achievement.* New York: Free Press, 1969.

MILL, J. S., *Principles of Political Economy and Some of Their Applications to Social Philosophy.* London: John W. Parker, 1848.

NEKVASIL, CHARLES A., "Plight of the Small Businessman," *Industry Week* 173 (June 12, 1972). See also Robert H. Brockhaus, "Psychological and Environmental Factors Which Distinguish the Successful from the Unsuccessful Entrepreneurs: A Longitudinal Study," *Academy of Management Proceedings*, 1980.

RESEARCH METHODOLOGY WORKSHOP, *Entrepreneurial Discovery and Development: Progress of Action Research.* Honolulu, East-West Center Technology and Development Institute, 1977.

ROBERTS, E. B., and WAINER, H. A., "Some Characteristics of Technical Entrepreneurs," Institute of Electrical and Electronic Engineers. *Transactions on Engineering Management*, EM-18, No. 3 (August 1971).

ROSCOE, JAMES, "Can Entrepreneurship Be Taught?" *MBA Magazine*, June-July 1973.

SCHOLLHAMMER, HANS, and KURILOFF, ARTHUR H., *Entrepreneurship and Small Business Management.* New York: John Wiley, 1979.

SCHREIER, J. W., and KOMIVES, J. L., *The Entrepreneur and New Enterprise Formation: A Resource Guide.* Milwaukee: Center for Venture Management, 1973.

SMITH, NORMAN R., *The Entrepreneur and His Firm: The Relationship between Type of Man and Type of Company.* East Lansing: Michigan State University, 1967.

STRONG, EDWARD K., JR., *Strong Vocational Interest Blanks.* Palo Alto, California: Consulting Psychologists Press, 1959.

STRONG, EDWARD K., JR., *Vocational Interests Eighteen Years after College.* Minneapolis: University of Minnesota, 1955.

VESPER, KARL H., *Entrepreneur Education: A Bicentennial Compendium.* Milwaukee: Center for Venture Management, 1976.

VESPER, KARL H., *New Venture Strategies.* Englewood Cliffs, N.J.: Prentice-Hall, 1980.

VESPER, KARL, "Sub-Fields of Entrepreneurial Research," *Proceedings of Project ISEED,* 1976.

ZALEZNIK, ABRAHAM, "Managers and Leaders: Are They Different?" *Harvard Business Review*, May-June 1977.

ZALEZNIK, ABRAHAM, and KETS DE VRIES, MANFRED, *Power and the Corporate Mind.* Boston: Houghton-Mifflin, 1975.

ZYTOWSKI, DONALD G., *Contemporary Approaches to Interest Measurement.* Minneapolis: University of Minnesota, 1973.

chapter iii

The psychology of the entrepreneur

Robert H. Brockhaus, Sr.

Overview

This chapter takes a broad view of the "psychology of the entrepreneur." In addition to "pure" psychology, the research includes the effects of previous personal and business experiences as well as personal characteristics.

Various definitions of the term "entrepreneur" are followed by a discussion of the need for achievement, locus-of-control beliefs, risk-taking propensity, and personal values.

The next section summarizes factors of a more environmental nature: dissatisfaction with previous work, role models, and "displacement." Personal characteristics, such as age, education, and residency, are considered in a third section. The conclusion contains a possible psychological model of the entrepreneur and suggestions for future research.

Definitions of the entrepreneur

Webster's Third New International Dictionary (1961) defines the entrepreneur as "an organizer of an economic venture, especially one who organizes, owns, manages, and assumes the risk of a business." Funk and

Wagnall's Standard Dictionary (1958) offers a similar definition: "one who undertakes to start and conduct an enterprise or business, assuming full control and risk."

J. S. Mill is credited with bringing the term into general use among economists. Mill (1848) considers direction, control, superintendence, and risk-bearing to be entrepreneurial functions. Mill appears to believe that risk-bearing distinguishes the entrepreneur from the manager. Schumpeter (1954) stresses the role of innovation in defining the entrepreneur, and places less emphasis on risk since he believes that both entrepreneurs and managers are subject to the risk of failure.

McClelland (1961) is less restrictive and believes that an innovative manager who has decision-making responsibility is as much an entrepreneur as the owner of a business. However, Hartman (1959), in a thorough historical discussion of "entrepreneurs" and "managers," finds that a useful distinction can be made. He supports Weber's (1917) concept of the entrepreneur as the ultimate source of all formal authority within the organization. Such a definition, Weber states, distinguishes the entrepreneur from the manager.

Most presentday writers would consider the owner-manager of a business to be an entrepreneur, but not the person who provides capital without also managing the venture. Many authors, such as Collins and Moore (1970) and Hornaday and Aboud (1971), are even more restrictive in their studies and examine only successful business ventures.

Thus it should be kept in mind that a well-defined entrepreneurial population does not exist and research findings are often difficult to compare and make generalization a dangerous practice. However, despite these difficulties some psychological characteristics are reported in a relatively consistent manner.

The factors associated with the decision to become an entrepreneur can be divided into three categories: psychological influences upon the individual, effects of previous experiences (especially previous jobs), and personal characteristics.

Psychological characteristics

Cole (1942) brought into relatively sharp focus the need for definitive research into motivating forces and characteristics of the entrepreneur. In 1948 Cole established the Center of Entrepreneurial History at Harvard. The Harvard studies have been conducted primarily by David C. McClelland whose book, *The Achieving Society,* has been highly influential (McClelland 1961).

Need for achievement

McClelland's work was not only a major contribution to the literature but was also a pioneering effort in the attempt to determine whether entrepreneurs tend to hold a certain psychological set. McClelland's (1961) research was based upon the concept of a "need for achievement" (n Ach). He characterized individuals with high n Ach as those preferring to be personally responsible for solving problems, for setting goals, and for reaching these goals by their own efforts. Such persons also have a strong desire to know how well they are accomplishing their tasks. On the basis of these demonstrated characteristics, McClelland suggested that entrepreneurs should have high n Ach. He conducted empirical research on this hypothesis in three major studies.

McClelland (1961) reported relationships between n Ach scores and "entrepreneurial" behavior in young men. In the United States, Italy, and Poland, he found that school-age men with high n Ach scores exhibited a preference for business occupations of a moderately high level. He also found that these young men preferred the occupational status of a business executive rather than that of a specialist or professional. McClelland interpreted these results to suggest that high n Ach would influence a young man to select an entrepreneurial position.

In a second study McClelland (1965) attempted to confirm his findings with a longitudinal study. Eighty-three percent of men in entrepreneurial positions had demonstrated high n Ach 14 years earlier, while only 21 percent of those in non-entrepreneurial positions had demonstrated high n Ach. Using a large number of college alumni who had graduated seven years earlier, he found that 60 percent of the entrepreneurs and only 41 percent of the non-entrepreneurs had high n Ach scores as college freshmen. McClelland concluded that high n Ach does influence the decision to enter entrepreneurial occupations.

In a third study, McClelland and Winter (1969) reported that 48 percent of Indian businessmen who had participated in a program designed to increase the level of n Ach had subsequently been unusually active in entrepreneurial efforts.

All of McClelland's early studies used a rather general definition of entrepreneurial occupations. For example, in the 1965 study McClelland considered the following occupations entrepreneurial: salesman (except clerical sales), management consultant, fund-raiser, and officer of a large company, as well as actual owners of a business. Thus, he did not directly connect n Ach with the decision to own and manage a business.

Komives (1972), however, measured the n Ach values of 20 high-technology entrepreneurs who tended to be successful. Using Gordon's "Study of Personal Values," he found that these entrepreneurs were high in the achievement and decisiveness categories. However, in a study of 307 graduates of a university business school, Hull, Bosley, and Udell (1980) found that n Ach was a weak predictor of an individual's tendency to start a business.

The effectiveness of achievement training courses has been discussed in several studies. Neck (1971) reported that achievement motivation training courses were not successful when the participants' opportunities to act were stifled by the general business environment. Moreover, Timmons (1971) reported that achievement motivation training without training in business skills is not helpful. Similar evidence presented by Patel (1975) suggests that achievement training combined with business training is most effective in establishing new factories. However, Durand (1975) found inconclusive results in his attempt to examine this issue.

In a study designed to specifically examine this issue, Timmons (1973) interviewed small business owners in two cities who had four years earlier received training to increase their level of achievement motivation. He also interviewed owners who had not received the training. In Washington, D. C., the 31 who had been trained started a total of 11 new businesses with an average annual profit of $12,500; the approximately equal number who had not received training had started only one new business, and it had an operating loss. In McAlester, Oklahoma, there was no difference between trained and untrained persons in the number of businesses started. In both cities, personal income was larger for the trained. However, the owners included in these follow-up studies may not have been representative of the larger groups that took part in the training. Also, the selection criteria used to assign the participants to training or non-training groups was not random; according to Miron and McClelland (1979) the selection process could have been a major factor in the results.

Reporting on three other achievement motivation training programs, Miron and McClelland conclude that such training increases energy for establishing and improving small business. Business training improves understanding but may lead to more cautious and slower expansion. The three programs yield conflicting results on whether greater increases in profit result from the achievement training or from the business training. We cannot state with certainty that increased business activity is the result of an increased level of achievement motivation. A "Hawthorne effect" may account for conflicting results in this research.

Miron and McClelland also found that those participants with a high need for power apparently did not get as much from the training. Similarly, in their study of 51 technical entrepreneurs, Wainer and Rubin (1969) found that high need for achievement and moderate need for power are associated with high company performance. However, Schrage (1965) reported that successful research and development entrepreneurs had neither consistently high achievement motives nor consistent power motives.

The causal link between ownership of a small business and a high need for achievement is not proven. Most small business owners available for inclusion in a study are successful, and this success may contribute to their high need for achievement rather than the reverse. No research has been undertaken to determine if a correlation exists between the decision to start a business and a "natural" high need for achievement.

Locus-of-control beliefs

A responsible individual who does not believe that the outcome of a business venture will be influenced by his efforts is unlikely to expose himself to the high penalties that accompany failure. Liles (1974) suggests that it is the potential entrepreneur's perception of a specific situation, rather than the actualities involved, that influences his decision to start a business venture. Because subjective perception of both risk and ability to affect results are crucial to the ultimate decision, it follows that we ought to study the concept of perception of control.

According to Rotter's (1966) "locus-of-control" theory, an individual perceives the outcome of an event as being either within or beyond his personal control and understanding. Rotter offers a further definition of these two categories of locus-of-control:

> *When a reinforcement is perceived by the subject as following some action of his own but not being entirely contingent upon his action, then, in our culture, it is typically perceived as the result of luck, chance, fate, as under the control of others or as unpredictable because of the great complexity of the forces surrounding him. When the event is interpreted in this way by an individual, we have labeled this a belief in external control. If the person perceives that the event is contingent upon his own behavior or his own relatively permanent characteristics, we have termed this a belief in internal control.*

Rotter believed that need for achievement is related to the belief in internal locus-of-control. He felt that McClelland, Atkinson, Clark, and Lowell (1953) and Atkinson (1957) found that people who have high n Ach tend to believe in their own ability to control the outcome of their efforts. McClelland (1961) determined that an individual tends to put forth greater effort when he perceives that his actions will directly result in personal achievement. Using these studies as a basis, Rotter hypothesized that individuals with internal beliefs would more likely strive for achievement than would individuals with external beliefs. Later studies by McGhee and Crandall (1968), Gurin, Gurin, Las, and Beattie (1969) and Lao (1970) all verified that internal individuals do, indeed, have a more pronounced need for achievement.

The studies cited above have established a relationship between a high need for achievement and belief in internal locus-of-control. As noted previously, McClelland found that entrepreneurs tend to have a high need for achievement. The writings and research of McClelland, Rotter, and their followers might indicate that entrepreneurs tend to believe that events are contingent upon their behavior, that is, they hold "internal" beliefs.

McClelland and Sutton support this possibility in their writings. McClelland (1961) states:

The entrepreneurial role has also generally been assumed to imply individual responsibility.

In a somewhat similar vein of thought, Sutton (1954) writes:

The key definitions for the businessman seem to center around the concept of responsibility . . . responsibility of this sort implies individualism. It is not tolerable unless it embraces both credit for successes and blame for failure, and leaves the individual free to claim or accept the consequences, whatever they may be.

Both McClelland's and Sutton's writings are consistent with the proposition that entrepreneurs are more internal in their locus-of-control beliefs than the general population. Such an interpretation is also supported by recent research. Shapero (1975) found that the mean I-E scale scores of both 34 Italian entrepreneurs and 101 Texas entrepreneurs were more internal than mean scores reported by Rotter (1966a) for all groups except Peace Corps volunteers. Brockhaus (1975) found that ten graduate business school students who expressed strong intentions to become entrepreneurs were significantly more internal than an equal number of their classmates who did not intend to start business ventures. Borland (1974) determined that a belief in internal locus-of-control was a better predictor of entrepreneurial intentions than n Ach measurement. But Hull, Bosley, and Udell (1980) failed to find a relationship between locus-of-control scores and entrepreneurial activity on the part of business school alumni.

Brockhaus and Nord (1979) compared the locus-of-control beliefs in entrepreneurs and managers. The scores on Rotter's I-E Locus-of-Control scale did not differ significantly between the owners of new businesses and managers. The mean score for the entrepreneurs was lower than any score reported by Rotter (1966a) with the exception of the Peace Corps trainees. Managers were also more internal than the other groups discussed by Rotter. Thus, although locus-of-control beliefs did not distinguish entrepreneurs from managers, the entrepreneurs did tend to hold more internal locus-of-control beliefs than those reported by Rotter for the general population.

That the entrepreneurs were found to be more internal in their locus-of-control beliefs than all but one group reported by Rotter provides a foundation upon which to reconcile previous research findings with the results of this study. Shapero's findings are identical with those of this study. Brockhaus, it will be remembered, found that graduate business school students who intended to become entrepreneurs held more internal locus-of-control beliefs than did students who expressed less definite intentions to start business ventures. If it is assumed that those business students who did not intend to start a business venture intended to become managers, then Brockhaus's (1975) study may be interpreted as showing that these aspiring entrepreneurs were more internal than the aspiring managers. Such a suggestion would not be consistent with the conclusion reached in the 1979 study.

This apparent conflict can be reconciled if it is assumed that an internal locus-of-control is an asset to advancement in management. The finding that both groups of managers hold more internal locus-of-control beliefs than all but one of the groups reported by Rotter lends support to this assumption. Those students in the earlier Brockhaus study who tended to hold external locus-of-control beliefs may not be likely prospects for middle and upper management positions because they may not have sufficient belief in their ability to achieve such positions by their own efforts. Consequently, they are unlikely to exhibit the kind of ability and aggressiveness required for promotion. Furthermore, it is possible that many of the students with strong internal beliefs and strong intentions to start a business may never actually do so; they may not perceive a sufficiently promising venture, or they may believe that the consequences of failure are too great. However, their internal locus of control may help them achieve middle and upper management positions.

In a later study (Brockhaus 1980a), locus-of-control scores obtained in 1975 from owners of new businesses (less than three months old) were examined in conjunction with the success rates of those businesses. The owners of businesses that still existed in 1978 were found to hold more internal locus-of-control beliefs than those whose businesses had ceased to exist. The internal beliefs may have resulted in more active efforts to positively affect the results of the ventures. The more external entrepreneurs may have been more likely to accept less than desirable outcomes as beyond their control.

An internal locus-of-control belief may therefore be associated with a more active effort to affect the outcome of events. This internal belief and the associated greater effort would seem to hold true for both successful entrepreneurs and successful managers. Therefore, it fails to uniquely distinguish entrepreneurs, but holds promise for distinguishing successful entrepreneurs from the unsuccessful.

Risk-taking propensity

McClelland (1961) determined that persons with high n Ach have moderate risk-taking propensities. Such a determination is especially interesting to the study of entrepreneurs, since all the definitions of "entrepreneur" cited earlier included risk-taking. Indeed, two of the major considerations in the decision to become an entrepreneur may be the perceived degree of risk and the perceived possibility of failure associated with the financially unsuccessful venture. Palmer (1971) argues that "the entrepreneurial function primarily involves risk measurement and risk-taking."

Liles (1974) speculates that in becoming an entrepreneur an individual risks financial well-being, career opportunities, family relations, and psychic well-being. The personal financial obligation to an unsuccessful enterprise can result in major losses to the entrepreneur as an individual and can jeopardize his future standard of living. Moreover, the failure of the venture becomes, in effect, the failure of the individual and therefore can have major emotional consequences.

Realizing that the financial and emotional consequences of failure can be devastating, Liles suggests that the potential entrepreneur is well-advised to analyze carefully the risks associated with his specific business proposal and then to determine whether he is willing to undertake them. Hull, Bosley, and Udell (1980) report that a four-item risk scale distinguished business alumni with a high probability of starting a business from those with a low probability. The potential entrepreneurs were found to have a greater propensity for risk-taking.

Expectance theorists, especially Atkinson (1957), have stimulated much study of risk preferences. Atkinson's risk-taking model is derived from the relationship McClelland found between need for achievement and preference for moderate probabilities of success. Atkinson's model involves six variables: the subjective probability (expectance) of success (P_s), the subjective probability of failure (P_f), the incentive value of success (I_s), the incentive value of avoiding failure ($-I_f$), the achievement motive (M_s), and the motive to avoid failure (M_f). Atkinson assumed that I_s is a positive linear function of difficulty and can be represented by $(1 - P_s)$. He further assumed that $-I_f$ is a negative linear function of difficulty and can be represented by $-P_s$. The variables are combined multiplicatively in the following equation: Resultant Motivation $= (M_s \times P_s \times I_s) + (M_f \times P_f \times -I_f)$. The Resultant Motivation function has a maximum at P_s 0.5 if M_s is greater than M_f. Where M_f is greater than M_s, the Resultant Motivation function would be maximum either at the lowest value of P_s or the highest value of P_s.

The major prediction that follows from Atkinson's theory is that performance level should be greatest when there is greatest uncertainty about the outcome (when subjective probability of success is 0.5). This prediction should be true regardless of whether the motive to achieve or the motive to avoid failure is stronger within an individual. However, persons in whom the achievement motive is stronger should prefer intermediate risk, while those in whom the motive to avoid failure is stronger should avoid intermediate risk, preferring instead either very easy and safe undertakings or extremely difficult and speculative ones. This preference is based upon the theory that an individual with a stronger motivation to avoid failure will tend either to succeed with the safe task or will be able to explain failure of a very speculative task without assuming the personal blame he finds particularly painful.

McClelland (1961) has stated that the situations in which an individual's degree of control or skill is most important are moderately risky situations rather than very risky or very certain ones. According to McClelland, an individual needs no more than average ability to successfully perform safe functions, while no amount of skill can help in the situation of pure chance.

These three levels of risk preference—low, intermediate or moderate, and high—could affect an individual's decision to start a business venture. Mancuso (1975) states that established entrepreneurs tend to be moderate risk-takers, but he does not provide empirical support for his viewpoint, nor does he suggest what the propensity for risk-taking might be at the time the entrepreneurial decision is made. Moreover, entrepreneurial risk can be divided into three components: the general risk-taking propensity of a potential entrepreneur, the perceived probability of failure for a specific venture, and the perceived consequences of failure. Since the latter two components require intimate knowledge of the specific venture before they can be evaluated, a study based upon them would be very difficult and very likely subject to uncontrolled independent variables.

For the purpose of his study, Brockhaus (1980b) defined the propensity for risk-taking as the perceived probability of receiving the rewards associated with success of a proposed venture, which is required by an individual before he will subject himself to the consequences associated with failure; the alternative situation provides fewer rewards as well as less severe consequences than the proposed venture. Such a definition might best describe the situation that faces the potential entrepreneur when he decides to establish a new business venture.

When Brockhaus administered the Choice Dilemmas Questionnaire (CDQ) developed by Kogan and Wallach (1964), he found no significant differences between the responses of entrepreneurs and those of managers. The failure of the risk-taking propensity to distinguish entrepreneurs from managers appears to be a major deviation from the widely held theory that entrepreneurs are the more moderate risk-takers. However, the fact that no differences were found does not imply that entrepreneurs are not moderate risk-takers. In fact, both the entrepreneurs and the managers who participated in this study are best described as moderate risk-takers because their scores were clustered around the mean score reported by Kogan and Wallach in their original (1964) study.

However, when the entire range of scores obtained from entrepreneurs in this study were compared to the entire range of scores obtained in the Kogan-Wallach study an interesting result was obtained. The distribution of the risk-taking propensity scores of entrepreneurs was similar to the distribution of risk-taking propensity scores in the more general population of the Kogan and Wallach study. Thus the data indicates that the risk-taking propensity does not distinguish new entrepreneurs either from managers or from the general population.

Just as the majority of the established entrepreneurs interviewed in earlier studies (see, for example, Mancuso 1975) expressed a desire for moderate levels of risk, over 64 percent of the entrepreneurs in this current study were found to have a propensity for moderate levels of risk; their CDQ scores were within one standard deviation of the mean for the Kogan and Wallach subjects. Since, however, approximately 68 percent of the general population would by definition be expected to have scores in this range, earlier studies may have correctly found the majority of entrepreneurs to have a tendency toward moderate levels of risk, but may have overestimated the distinction of this characteristic. However, even this statement must be followed with several cautions.

This study dealt with entrepreneurs of new ventures, but it is possible that the risk-taking propensity of established entrepreneurs might differ for several reasons. First, the process of entrepreneurship may increase the desire for moderate levels of risk, thus causing a larger percentage of established entrepreneurs to appear to be moderate risk-takers. Second, those entrepreneurs who have a propensity for low or high levels of risk may cease to be entrepreneurs at a greater rate than those with more moderate propensities.

This latter aspect was investigated by Brockhaus (1980a), who used the CDQ scores obtained from owners shortly after the formation of their businesses in an attempt to distinguish those persons whose businesses still existed from those whose businesses no longer existed three years later. No significant differences were found to exist between the two groups.

It is tentatively concluded that risk-taking propensity may not be related to either the entrepreneurial decision, or to the success of the enterprise. However, it must be recognized that general risk-taking propensity, as measured by the CDQ, is only one component of risk. As mentioned earlier, two components of risk, the perceived probability of failure and the perceived consequences of failure for a specific venture, were not included in these studies.

The perception held about each of these components may be due more to specific environmental conditions than to personality-related characteristics. A given individual may alter his perceived probability of failure for a specific venture if he acquires additional information about the competition, the amount of capitalization required, the managerial skills and technical knowledge required, or other aspects of the venture. Moveover, the individual may alter his perception of the consequences of failure by learning about individuals who started ventures which subsequently failed. Therefore, the informal communication systems that Cooper (1973) found to exist among technical entrepreneurs may provide knowledge and information that affect the propensity to establish new ventures.

Webster (1976) states that the wise entrepreneur does not risk his own financial well-being but only that of innocent investors. Indeed, the "dealing" entrepreneur risks only the time spent putting together a deal that may realize no payoff. Collins and Moore (1970) arrive at a similar conclusion.

Personal values

The first major study of personal values of entrepreneurs was done by Hornaday and Aboud (1971). They employed objective tests to identify and measure certain personality characteristics of individuals who had successfully started new businesses. Forty entrepreneurs, each with at least eight employees and at least five years in business, were interviewed and tested with the Kuder Occupational Interest Survey (OIS) Form DD, Gordon's Survey of Interpersonal Values (SIV), and a questionnaire composed of three scales drawn from Edward's Personal Preference Scale (EPPS). Hornaday and Aboud found that, on the EPPS scale reflecting need for achievement and on the SIV scales for independence and effectiveness of leadership, the entrepreneurs scored significantly higher than the general population. They also scored lower on the SIV need-for-support scale. The OIS scores were not significantly different from the general population. Hornaday and Aboud concluded that these tests were objective indicators of the successful entrepreneur.

DeCarlo and Lyons (1979) obtained scores for Edwards Personal Preference Schedule (EPPS) and for Gordon's SIV from 120 minority and nonminority female entrepreneurs. The results supported the findings of Hornaday and Aboud. In addition, the scales of achievement, conformity, and benevolence seemed to most effectively distinguish the minority from the nonminority groups. The nonminority female placed higher on the scales of achievement, support, recognition, and independence. Minority females scored higher on conformity and benevolence. Perhaps of greater importance was the fact that minority and nonminority females scored higher on the EPPS achievement, autonomy, and aggression scales than did the general female population. Both groups scored higher on the SIV scales for leadership and independence and lower on the SIV scales for support, conformity, and benevolence than did the general female population. The recognition scale was significantly higher for the nonminority subjects than for the general female population.

Komives (1972) studied the personal values of approximately 20 high-technology entrepreneurs in the greater Palo Alto area. They scored significantly higher than the general population on the SIV leadership scale but significantly lower on the SIV support and conformity scales. These findings are to some extent consistent with those of Hornaday and Aboud. Komives also reported that Allport-Lindgey's "Study of Values" (which Komives administered) indicated high values of aesthetic and theoretical categories but a low religious value.

In their study of business school alumni, Hull, Bosley, and Udell (1980) found that entrepreneurs were highly creative and highly interested in recruiting key people and setting organizational objectives and goals.

All of these studies indicate that values may be effective in distinguishing successful entrepreneurs from the general population. However, they did not determine whether these scales will distinguish between the general population and the entrepreneur who has made an attempt and failed. Thus, it is not clear whether these scales would distinguish between successful and unsuccessful entrepreneurs.

Using an abridged version of the Dogmatism Scale elaborated by Rokeach (1960), Gasse (1979) concluded that the more open-minded the entrepreneur, the more he tends to be oriented toward management. Managerial orientation indicates the degree to which an entrepreneur is likely to entertain abstract concepts and to be scientific and rational in his approach to business problems.

In a related study, Gasse (1977) found that the dogmatism and business ideology of the entrepreneur are related to organizational variables such as innovation and growth rate. Moreover, certain types of entrepreneurs may be more effective in specific industrial environments. For example, open-minded entrepreneurs should be more attracted to and more effective in dynamic environments. Gasse (1977) also found that English-Canadians, as compared to French-Canadians, were more open-minded, less authoritarian, and more tolerant. Therefore, various types of industry may be more appropriate for different subcultures of a country.

Aplin and Leveto (1976) developed a conceptual model which was similar to Gasse's concept. They argued that to accurately assess the potential of minority entrepreneurs, it is mandatory to examine not only psychological profiles, but cultural backgrounds, technical and managerial competence, and organizational characteristics.

Baumback and Schoen (1979) suggested that a battery of objective and projective tests would reduce the margin of error in assessing entrepreneurial potential. Palmer (1971) made a similar statement. However, all recognized that research to date does not allow a causal connection to be specified between these tests and entrepreneurial success.

Effects of previous experiences

At the moment of decision, entrepreneurial activity is always compared to the potential entrepreneur's present situation. For that reason, several studies have examined the connection between the entrepreneurial decision and previous job experience.

In a study of high-technology entrepreneurs, Cooper (1973) discovered that

30 percent of the founders had no specific plans for the future at the time they left their previous jobs; 13 percent had left because of external factors such as plant closings, and an additional 40 percent would have left their previous positions even if they had not become entrepreneurs. Draheim (1972) and Susbauer (1972) reported similar results. Thus, a "push" seems to force potential entrepreneurs from their place of previous employment. Shapero (1971) suggested that such a push was associated with dissatisfaction with the previous position.

Dissatisfaction with previous work experience

Brockhaus (1980) studied previous job satisfaction on the part of entrepreneurs. He used the Job Description Index (JDI) developed by Smith, Kendall, and Hulin (1969) of Cornell University to measure the degree of job satisfaction. The JDI consists of five sub-scales, to measure the employees' satisfaction with the work itself, their perception of supervision, pay, opportunity for promotion, and their attitude toward co-workers.

When compared to the normative population used by the developers of the instrument, the entrepreneurs were found to be significantly less satisfied for all sub-scales except pay; in the case of the pay sub-scale, the entrepreneurs were significantly more satisfied. Their greatest dissatisfaction appeared to be with the work itself.

Possibly mere dissatisfaction with the work might not provide sufficient "push" if the co-workers and supervisors were well-liked. However, when unsatisfactory work combined with unsatisfactory co-workers and supervision, the worker remained in the position only if he perceived a likely promotion to a more satisfactory position. If promotion was not likely, even a satisfactory level of pay was not sufficient inducement to remain.

An extreme degree of dissatisfaction with the previous job seems not only to push the entrepreneur from his previous place of employment, but to convince him that no other place of employment may be a satisfactory alternative. Future research must examine the perception of the availability of alternative employment and, then, the effect of this perception on the decision to become an entrepreneur.

Fifty-nine percent of the entrepreneurs desired to start a business before they had a product or service idea compared; 14 percent had the idea first. This supports the concept of the entrepreneur being pushed from his previous place of employment rather than "pulled" into an extremely appealing business opportunity.

Prior dissatisfaction may also indirectly contribute to the success of the new venture. Brockhaus (1980a) compared successful with unsuccessful entrepreneurs and found that the former were more dissatisfied with previous jobs at the time they started their businesses. They may have been more highly motivated to avoid returning to their previous or similar jobs. Thus, they may have been more active and persistent in their efforts to develop a successful enterprise. Although such a scenario is also supported by the literature on job turnover, it is possible that the entrepreneurs were not as dissatisfied as the data indicate; it could be that cognitive dissonance (the desire to make apparently conflicting facts congruent) has affected the results of the JDI questionnaire. If the entrepreneurs were ambivalent about their previous jobs immediately prior to leaving, they may have come to consider the jobs unsatisfactory after leaving, thus resolving any conflict resulting from their decision to quit the previous job. If they continued to view the prior place of employment as satisfactory, it would be more difficult for them to believe that they had made the correct decision.

The conclusion is consistent with what Comegys (1976) terms "entrepreneurial cognitive dissonance." It is his contention that when an entrepreneur risks his life savings and quits his previous job, he becomes "supercommitted" to the belief that he will succeed. Such commitment causes him to lose analytical objectivity and to subconsciously seek only information that reinforces his decision.

Role models

Over 97 percent of the new high-technology companies studied by Cooper (1972) had at least one founder who had previously worked in the same industry. Similarly, Susbauer (1972) reported that 90 percent of the companies had a founder who had previously worked in the same industry. Cooper (1972) and Lamont (1972) both found approximately 85 percent of the new firms had initial products or services that drew on the founder's previous technical experience. Thus, it appears that established organizations serve as incubators for new companies which serve the same basic clients.

Cooper (1971) and Shapero (1971) both reported that the credibility of starting a company appears to depend somewhat upon the entrepreneur's acquaintance with others who have started their own companies. Thus, an entrepreneur who starts an organization may stimulate his employees to do the same, and employees who establish businesses encourage fellow employees to do likewise. Cooper (1971) further reported that technically-oriented entrepreneurs seem to develop informal networks of communication among new firms. This influence seems to obtain whether the entrepreneur observed has a successful or an unsuccessful business.

The literature also suggests that an unusually high percentage of entrepreneurs had fathers who were themselves entrepreneurs or farmers. (Roberts and Wainer 1971, Shapero 1971, Susbauer 1969, Collins and Moore 1970). No studies have compared the fathers of entrepreneurs and non-entrepreneurs. Brockhaus and Nord (1979) asked managers and new entrepreneurs if any close relative or friend had owned a business. There was no significant difference between the two groups.

"Displaced" persons

Of course, not all entrepreneurs leave a position because of dissatisfaction. Some are "pulled" from a satisfactory job by an extremely attractive opportunity. Others are dismissed or fired. Similar to this latter group are recent graduates, discharged servicemen, and immigrants. Shapero (1975) referred to all of those between positions as displaced persons. Displaced persons are forced to make a career decision. Unlike working people, they cannot afford the luxury of not making a change. Unlike working people, they are not giving up a regular salary or prestigious position. Thus, the restraints which prevent many employed persons from making the entrepreneurial decision do not apply. In a well-known study, Collins and Moore (1970) conducted in-depth interviews of 150 entrepreneurs in Michigan manufacturing companies established between 1945 and 1958. Almost 20 percent of the entrepreneurs were foreign-born, although the white population of the United States in 1960 was less then 6 percent foreign-born. The foreign-born, with more limited opportunities, may have regarded ownership of small businesses more favorably than did the native-born, who were able to choose from a wider range of occupations.

In summary, research strongly suggests that dissatisfaction with previous work experience is closely related to the entrepreneurial decision. Moreover, the person who is unemployed is more likely to decide to start a business than if he were employed. Finally, entrepreneurs serve as role models who indirectly increase the likelihood of friends, employees, and family members deciding to establish a business.

Personal characteristics

A number of studies have attempted to determine the personal characteristics and experiences associated with entrepreneurs. Age, education, and residency have frequently received attention.

Age

The years between 25 and 40 have frequently been mentioned as the age when the entrepreneurial decision is most likely to be made (Shapero 1971, Mayer and Goldstein 1961, Cooper 1973, Howell 1972).

According to Liles (1974), an individual has at this time obtained sufficient experience, competence, and self-confidence but has not yet incurred financial and family obligations or a position of prestige and responsibility in a large company. Thus, Liles concludes, this is a "free choice period."

Susbauer (1969) advises against placing too much emphasis on this age interval. He found that the age of high-technology entrepreneurs at the time of company formation closely paralleled the distribution of the general population between the ages of 25 and 60. Before 25, education and military service tend to reduce the number of entrepreneurs; after 60, decreased energy and other physical limitations tend to reduce the number of entrepreneurs.

Education

Brockhaus and Nord (1979) used a multidiscriminant analysis procedure to compare owners of new businesses to managers. The "personal or environmental characteristics" in the discriminant functions included the number of previous employers, the level of education attained, and the number of years of residence in a given geographical area.

On an average, the entrepreneurs had worked in slightly more than three organizations—approximately one less organization than the average for managers. One possible explanation is that managers were more employable than entrepreneurs and therefore able to leave one place of employment for another when dissatisfied. This assumption is congruent with the fact that the average entrepreneur had spent almost six years at his previous place of employment, while the average manager had spent slightly more than three years at the previous place of employment.

The level of education was found to be significantly less for entrepreneurs than for managers; the entrepreneurs averaged 13.57 years of education, while the managers averaged 15.74 years. This lower level of education for entrepreneurs may have limited their ability to obtain challenging and interesting jobs. Having found that the work itself was not sufficiently challenging, the entrepreneurs may have desired work more suitable to their own assessment of their abilities. Lacking opportunities for promotion to more desirable jobs, the entrepreneurs in this study chose to start their own businesses.

The managers, due to their higher level of education, may have been able to obtain more satisfying jobs. If their jobs proved unacceptable, their level of education allowed them to obtain more desirable employment elsewhere. It should be noted that the education of the entrepreneurs in this study did exceed that of the "average person." This finding is consistent with previous research by Howell (1972).

Collins and Moore (1970) reported that in Michigan the number of college graduates among business executives was higher than among manufacturing entrepreneurs. However, the percentage of manufacturing entrepreneurs who had graduated from college was three times that in the adult Michigan population. Roberts (1969) and Susbauer (1969) reported that the founders of high-technology companies had at least one college degree; one-half of them held at least a Master of Science degree.

Thus entrepreneurs appear to be better educated than the general population but less so than managers. Moreover, there is a wide variation in the educational level of different types of entrepreneurs.

Residency

In their study, Collins and Moore (1970) reported that despite the normally large percentage of foreign-born entrepreneurs, almost two-thirds of the manufacturing entrepreneurs were natives of Michigan. They suggested that these natives did not want to leave family and friends and had consequently chosen small business ownership as a means of remaining at home.

Brockhaus and Nord (1979) found that the mean period of residence in the local area for the entrepreneurs, 29.30 years, was significantly longer than the 22.04 years reported by the managers. The data from this study did not allow confirmation of possible explanations. However, the entrepreneurs had perhaps started their own businesses so that they would not be subject to relocation demands by their employer. Also, the entrepreneurs who did not have college degrees might have been less likely to seek jobs in the national job market than the managers who were college graduates. The more limited one's education, the more job opportunities in one metropolitan area tend to be similar to those in other metropolitan areas; therefore, the entrepreneurs were more likely to remain in the home area, seeking jobs that did not necessarily require a college degree and did not require competition in the national job market.

Conclusions

An entrepreneurial model

A plausible scenario, consistent with most of the research findings, is now proposed. It should be noted that other scenarios may also exist. Only future research can provide confirmation.

Research has indicated that although entrepreneurs are better educated than the general population, the large majority of them do not have college degrees. The lack of college education may limit their job possibilities to lower-level, local positions. In the case of the college educated entrepreneur, of course, this portion of the scenario does not apply.

The values held by the entrepreneurs include need for achievement, independence, and effective leadership. Many hourly workers without college educations lack this set of values and are less likely to become dissatisfied with the work available to them.

College trained managers have values similar to those of the college trained prospective entrepreneurs. Those who remain managers tend not to have experienced the disappointing and dissatisfying events the prospective entrepreneurs encounter. Therefore, the managers are able to fulfill their values and needs by means of their work.

Prospective entrepreneurs both with and without college educations tend to have values and expectations which eventually lead to dissatisfaction with their jobs. Although they consider the pay adequate for the work performed, they are dissatisfied with the actual work and with promotion opportunities. They eventually decide that there is little likelihood of finding more satisfactory positions in other organizations.

Entrepreneurial acquaintances and family members serve as role models who make the starting of a business a plausible act to the prospective entrepreneur. Moreover, these role models need not have been successful in their ventures.

The internal loci-of-control of the prospective entrepreneurs allow them to believe that they could effectively influence the results of a business if they personally own it. Typically, it is only after deciding to start a business that they determine on a product or service to offer.

They are naive about the low probability for success and about the consequences of failure. Therefore, the venture appears to have an acceptable level of risk when compared to the alternative of continuing to be employed.

Both effort and the probability of success are increased by the degree of dissatisfaction with the previous job and by the strength of the internal locus-of-control beliefs. Entrepreneurs who lack these characteristics are more likely to favorably reevaluate their employment by others.

Although such a scenario is consistent with the reported research on entrepreneurs, it cannot be confirmed by the present study. Future research is necessary for confirmation and elaboration.

Future research needs

What is needed most is a comprehensive longitudinal study of a comparative nature. Ideally, information should be obtained from a population of potential entrepreneurs before the entrepreneurial decision is made. The magnitude of such an effort is staggering if the sample is to be large.

A second, more feasible alternative would focus on persons who had just received business licenses from their local county or similar entity. The information obtained could be of three major types: characteristics of the owner (race, previous business experience, psychological traits, etc.); the nature of the enterprise (type of industry, number of employees, sales, etc.); and external factors (federal assistance programs, impact of government regulations, etc.).

The initial bank of data could be supplemented at a later time and compared to other data obtained in a similar manner. Indeed the specific small businesses contacted for the original study could be contacted on a periodic basis for updated information. In this manner, the effects of government policies, programs, and regulations could be measured in a comparative fashion. Before and after information could reveal the effects of a specific program on its participants, and a large control group would automatically exist.

This macro approach to data gathering would allow non-psychological variables to enter a statistical analysis of the factors associated with the entrepreneurial decision and with the frequency of success. With a large, random, nationwide sample of new entrepreneurs, the data could be categorized in many ways and still provide subsets significant enough for statistical interpretation.

commentary/elaboration

Elaborations on the psychology of the entrepreneur

Yvon Gasse

Overview

It is difficult to deny that entrepreneurship is a matter of individuals: Most of the historical scholarship about this phenomenon consists of biographies of extraordinary business executives; more abstract formulations are typically couched in terms that are applicable to individuals, such as ability to make new combinations, perception of opportunities, risk-taking, inventiveness, sense of efficacy, and achievement motivation. As can be seen from Robert Brockhaus's summary of the literature on the major psychological attributes of entrepreneurs, this literature is often exploratory and not well integrated. The purpose of our comments will be to document some of the reactions and additions to the major concepts presented by Brockhaus.

Psychological characteristics

Need for achievement

Certainly the most widely cited characteristic of entrepreneurs, the need for achievement, as defined by McClelland (1961), has much appeal and surface validity. To say that an entrepreneur tends to set his own objectives, to accept responsibility, to be a moderate risk-taker, and to look for immediate feedback is also convincing. However, there are major methodological shortcomings in the achievement motivation approach.

First, it does not take into account the historical and holistic structure in which motivation takes place. According to McClelland, the economic, social, and political determinants of the distribution of power and the direction of achievement are negligible. As Gunder (1969) and Kunkel (1965) have suggested, this theory is inadequate because it cannot identify the determining social and historical structures. Both Weber (1950) and Tawney (1947) have stressed the point that the rational decisions of entrepreneurs are inevitably restrained and colored by the cultural milieu. Their motivations and profit-orientation are socially derived; their decisions, though rational, are influenced by the values and restraints society places upon risk, risk-taking, and freedom of economic choice. The entrepreneurial role itself, with its behavioral expectations, enjoys a status not fully derived from the power of wealth or capital manipulation but from traditional prestige values and traditional concepts of the "good life" and the individual's proper relationship to society. Some societies appear to breed entrepreneurs more readily than others.

The second shortcoming of the achievement motivation approach concerns the nebulous aspect of the concept itself. For McClelland, achievement motivation (and hence entrepreneurship) is a way of thinking. The field for research is nothing more than the following:

> *If I can tap into someone's brain and get the content of their* [sic] *thought process, what they* [sic] *go around through life thinking about, and what kinds of things are there; entrepreneurs tend to think in a certain way about certain kinds of things. (Berlew 1969, p. 49)*

In fact, the different results obtained in achievement motivation research might very well be due to a lack of consensus regarding the interpretation and measurement of the data. The Thematic Apperception Test does not lead to a precise identification of the major motivational dimensions or of their relative distribution. There is a good deal of agreement about the attitudes and motives that characterize the entrepreneur: independence, desire for prestige, desire for power, internal locus-of-control belief, drive, high involvement, strong self-actualization, and moderate risk-taking. If these attributes are indeed representative, it is necessary to assess the relative importance of these factors in the entrepreneurial profile.

Finally, McClelland restricted his studies to economic activity as the proper channel for the achievement drive. Other areas of professional endeavor, such as arts, politics, religion, or education, may also constitute proper channels for achievers. People devoted to these various sectors may easily be characterized by McClelland's entrepreneurship characteristics. Even within economic activities, this concept of entrepreneurship may be applied to managers, farmers, salespeople, professionals, and others. Therefore, the specificity and the distinctive power of the concept is largely lost.

Locus-of-control

Entrepreneurs have been characterized as "internals"; that is, they believe their behavior to be relatively decisive in determining their fate. This concept, though closely related to the need for achievement, may be more promising than achievement motivation for identifying entrepreneurs.

Studies have shown that internals seem to have better control over their own behavior than do externals; they are more likely to be activists on political and social issues and more successful at persuading other people. On the other hand, they are less easily persuaded themselves (Phares 1973). One study (Seeman and Evans 1962) found that internals more actively seek strategic information and knowledge relevant to their situation. Valecha (1972) found that internals were better informed about their vocations; Organ and Greene (1974) found they experienced less ambivalence about their jobs.

Internals perform better on tasks that are presented as skill-related, but do less well when the same tasks are said to depend on luck or chance (Watson and Baumol 1967). A number of studies have found internals to be more efficient at processing information (Wolk and DuCette 1974). Other correlates of locus-of-control include anxiety (externals are more anxious and emotional), clarity of self-concept (internals are more subjectively certain, though not necessarily more accurate), trust (internals are more trusting), reactions to failure (internals are more likely to black out remembrance of failure), style of supervision preferred (externals prefer a more structured, directive style), and conditionability (internals are more sensitive to organizational attempts to shape behavior). Not all of these relationships are conclusive, however, since attempts to replicate original findings have not always been successful (Hamner and Organ 1978).

Because the entrepreneurs' decisions have a direct influence on their business performance, they must believe in the efficacy of their actions. As a contrary example, some writers have claimed that a fatalistic attitude is embodied by others, such as Latin American social values:

A reluctance to recognize the possession of money as a result of hard work, thrift, good management or intelligence. It is more a matter of chance. Fate has been kind to such people. . . . A fatalistic outlook, the assumption that whatever happens is the will of God . . . is the best adjustment the individual can make to an apparently hopeless situation. (Foster 1962)

Uncertainty about the future and a pessimistic economic outlook may impede investment and cause entrepreneurs to turn down opportunities. Optimism, on the other hand (which seems deeply ingrained in American culture), restrains the perception of uncertainty. Also, when uncertainty is perceived, it may be viewed as an exciting stimulus rather than a severe threat.

Before we leave the topic of locus-of-control, we should voice a note of caution. The abilities and behavioral patterns that correlate with internal locus-of-control (as measured by Rotter's instrument) seem to suggest that "more internal" necessarily means "better." But as Hamner and Organ point out, one could argue that extreme internals are perhaps less well adjusted than their counterparts. If we live in a world with forces beyond the control of the individual, then the extreme internal may be over-rigid, defensively overestimating his ability to control events in his life.

Risk-taking

Risk-taking has long been the subject of study among economists in entrepreneurial research. A major proponent of this tendency has been Frank Knight in his famous book *Risk, Uncertainty and Profit* (1921). Although Knight's theory has resulted in a reformulation of the old risk-bearer theorem of entrepreneurship, it does not distinguish clearly between ownership, control, decision-making, and management. Redlich (1957) has advanced a theory of risk which better takes into account the difference between those who bring a specific risk into existence and those who bear that risk. He sees the entrepreneur as the man who will bear risk, at least in business terms. This distinction between creating risk and risk-bearing fundamentally distinguishes between entrepreneurs and managers; Doctors and Juris (1971) have pointed out that the individual with entrepreneurial drive is willing to take high risks to achieve his goals, while stability, security, and a predictable environment are more commonly desired by the manager.

Large-scale business managers are usually powerful enough to select transactions involving relatively small risk, and to reject or shift the risk involved. Small-scale businesses involve both higher risk and a higher death rate. James H. Strauss (1944) argues that entrepreneurs unable or unwilling to shift risk engage in the strategy of "risk-conditioning." James D. Thompson (1967) proposes a similar strategy for reducing uncertainty in organizations. Baumol (1968), after pointing out that the entrepreneur must bear risks, goes on to suggest that economic theory should consider how the marginal costs of risk-bearing can be reduced and should analyze the entrepreneur's attitudes to risk. Leibenstein (1968) sees in the entrepreneur "the ultimate uncertainty and/or risk bearer." Schumpeter's particular definition of the entrepreneur as an innovator confuses this attribute a bit: "[I]f he [the entrepreneur] contributes the means of production belonging to his business, the risk falls on him as capitalist or as possessor of goods not as entrepreneur" (1934). In his study of small industries, Stepanek (1960) identifies the entrepreneur-manager as willing to take risks: "[H]e stands to lose not only his capital but reputation and prestige." In the same manner Reuss (1970) qualifies "venture spirit and willingness to take risks" as a major trait of entrepreneurship. Finally, Lipman's (1969) interesting study on the Colombian entrepreneur shows that much of the entrepreneur's efforts are devoted to minimizing risk and uncertainty. Thus, the evidence in this realm is highly varied, if not downright contradictory.

Entrepreneurs may see risks differently and may encounter many kinds of risk: business risk, social risk, psychological risk, family risk. As business executives, entrepreneurs take risks that directly affect the future of the firm and often of the community in which they operate. This type of risk-taking may also have a direct influence on their careers and personal lives. Unwillingness to take personal risks may lead entrepreneurs to be unwilling to take business risks. Fearing bankruptcy and financial loss or loss of status and prestige, entrepreneurs may be unwilling to take any risks.

Finally, we do not possess an appropriate instrument for measuring the various aspects of entrepreneurial risk-taking, or for distinguishing among the various contributing motives. We need instruments specifically designed for these purposes.

Personal values

Value orientation might be defined as a generalized and organized conception, influencing behavior, of nature, of man's place in it, and of man's relation to man. In other words, it is a set of beliefs about various aspects of the world. More specifically in terms of entrepreneurship, it means the cognitive functioning of entrepreneurs. Cognitive content refers to the individual's ideas about persons and things. Only certain objects, among all objects that are "out there," enter into a selectively organized conception of the external world. These perceptions need not be objectively confirmed. Starbuck (1976) pointed out that environmental uncertainty is an inevitable component of ideology or systems of belief. Entrepreneurs' conceptions of the environment and their reactions will, then, largely depend on their prior beliefs about business matters.

Business ideology is mainly shaped by the role of the individual within an organization; on this matter the role of the entrepreneur can be compared to the role of the executive, despite differences. The entrepreneur, that is, the person in effective control of a business unit, contrasts to the adaptive manager in the small firm. His or her enterprise, opportunism, individuality, and intuition contrast to the organization, planning, professionalism, rationality, and prediction of the manager and the executive. Our studies (Gasse 1977, 1978) have shown that the small business owner-manager or entrepreneur has both a different function from the large firm manager or executive and a different set of attitudes or beliefs about the nature of the management process and business in general. On a continuum of business ideology we have identified two poles: a rational-managerial pole and an intuitive-entrepreneurial pole. Of course in actuality people only tend toward one of these types.

We found that as one moves from complex belief systems (open-mindedness) downward on a cognitive-complexity scale, several important things occur. Even the simpler forms of knowledge decrease. The net result, as one moves downward, is that integration and interdependence decline across the universe of beliefs, and the range of relevant belief systems becomes narrower and narrower. As Converse (1964) has suggested, one moves from a few wide-ranging belief systems that organize large amounts of specific information to a proliferation of idea clusters with little integration, even in instances of logical interdependence.

At the same time, moving from top to bottom of this complexity dimension, the objects of belief become increasingly simple, concrete, or "close to home." Where business and management objects are concerned, this progression tends to be from abstract, "ideological" principles to the most fundamental management principles or business practices and finally to such objects of immediate experience as family, job, and immediate employees. Most of these changes have been suggested in one form or another by a variety of researchers (Deeks 1976, Litvak 1971, Carroll 1965). "Limited horizons," "foreshortened time perspective," "concrete thinking," and "day-to-day details" have been singled out as notable characteristics of the ideational world of the small firm owner-manager. Such observations have impressed even those investigators who deal with entrepreneurs' immediate worlds: their families, their attitudes toward people more wealthy than they, their attitudes toward leisure time and work regulations, and the like. Most of the matters of management and organization, particularly those related to medium-sized and large enterprises, are remote and abstract. Where business management is concerned, therefore, such ideational changes begin to occur rapidly below the stratum of large or medium scale entrepreneurs. In other words, these changes in belief systems are not limited to the bottom layer of little business operators; they are immediately relevant to the majority of small firm owner-managers. In summary, we found that a rational-managerial business ideology tends to be associated with more complex, integrated ways of thinking than an intuitive-entrepreneurial ideology, where simple cognitive structures would be more prevalent.

Effects of previous experiences

In his chapter Brockhaus talks about dissatisfaction with previous work experience and the decision to start a business, the role model as a stimulant for entrepreneurship, and the effects of displacement on career choice. The effect of previous experience on entrepreneurial performance has not been directly considered and will be dealt with briefly here.

Experience may have two different and even opposite effects on entrepreneurial performance. On one hand, it can provide the entrepreneur with a set of guidelines and knowledge conducive to increased performance; on the other hand, it may create habits that are hard to change and that may act as obstacles to adaptation and better performance. The net effect of experience upon the entrepreneur's performance will depend on a lot of factors, including the personality characteristics of the entrepreneur and the transferability of experience to the new job.

Experience in one type of activity can be transferred to another type of activity under two conditions. First, the activities may share similar components. Second, the entrepreneur may have learned methods, techniques, principles, systems, or shortcuts of universal applicability.

There are very few studies dealing specifically with the relationship between entrepreneurs' experience and their performance. Carroll (1965) pointed out that the experience gained in previous ventures had probably been one of the most important factors in the ultimate success of manufacturing entrepreneurs. An American study by Mayer and Goldstein (1961) has shown that previous business experience rather than formal schooling provided the most significant training for business ownership; it is fairly common for an owner-manager to own and to run several different businesses during the course of his lifetime. Whereas experience as an employee in a given line of business did not ensure success as an owner in the same line, previous experience as an owner was important, particularly so if in the same line of business. Similar findings have been reported by Lamont (1972) and by Cooper (1970). In his study of technology-based enterprises, Lamont (1972) pointed out that entrepreneurs with previous experience in founding and developing a company exhibit substantial learning when they start another business; more often than not, their experience was reflected in superior corporate performance. Also, the second business tended to have a product orientation, substantial initial financing, and a balance of essential business skills among its employees. Cooper's (1970) research on technical enterprise formation suggested that past entrepreneurship generates experienced entrepreneurs who often stay with their firms as they grow. Without exception, these men stated that it was easier to start a company the second time, both in regard to making the decision and in knowing how to launch and run a firm. In sum, the relative importance of experience on entrepreneurial performance seems to be related to the technological complexity and size of the business.

Personal characteristics

Age

The age at which entrepreneurs make the decision to start a business is widely distributed. Some differences seem to exist, however, among entrepreneurs of different cultures. For instance, Taylor (1960) has shown that 23.5 percent of the French Canadian male owners, managers, and officials in

Québec manufacturing were below the age of 35; 2.7 percent were under 25. This compared with 19.5 and 2.0 percent for English Canadians in Ontario. According to Taylor, this haste to become one's own boss, with insufficient experience, capital, and know-how, explains in large part the high rate of business mortality in Québec.

Education

A common belief about entrepreneurs is that they are less educated than the general population. Many of the better known books on entrepreneurship and small business management refer to the low education of the entrepreneur. However, studies of entrepreneurs who found high-technology firms have indicated a different educational picture. Technical entrepreneurs seem to have at least a B.S. degree, often in engineering, and frequently hold M.S. degrees (Cooper 1973, Mancuso 1975, Litvak and Maule 1971). Douglass (1976) has recently compared earlier studies to census data and revealed that entrepreneurs have more education than the general population, and that the gap is increasing. Thus, statements about the uneducated entrepreneur hardly seem justified.

More interesting is the influence of education on entrepreneurial performance. Here again the evidence is not clear, perhaps because education is most influential where the organization is complex.

At different stages in the development of their businesses, small firm owner-managers require different mixes of entrepreneurial and administrative skills. The relative emphasis on these two kinds of skills is different in larger firms because of differences in the scale of operations, in the complexity of the organization, in the degree of specialization, and in the professionalism of management. When top managers or entrepreneurs engage in planning and decision making, controlling, organizing, staffing, and directing, their effectiveness may depend in large part on their knowledge of applicable techniques, tools, and principles. Many of these functions can be handled by owner-managers without any special training if the firm is small enough, but as it grows, more knowledge of the techniques and principles may be required. The administrative job of planning and controlling requires a more rational approach to management and more special training.

In his study of manufacturing entrepreneurs Carroll (1965) has reported that their education was related to the size of their firm. D'Amboise (1974) has shown that more educated entrepreneurs tend to use more control techniques and related this to positive performance results in small and medium sized firms in the furniture industry. In their study of entrepreneurs in high-technology firms, Robidoux and Garnier (1973) have shown that the more educated the entrepreneur, the higher the rate of growth of the firm; however, they found no differences between the performance of those with a management background and those with engineering training. On the other hand, Douglass (1976) found no significant correlation between educational background and success measures (rate of growth) among 153 owner-operators of firms with 30 or fewer employees. Furthermore, he has shown that business majors were less successful than non-business graduates.

Education may have an influence on other crucial variables like open-mindedness, business ideology, information processing, and general performance.

Methodological considerations

Studies on entrepreneurship are difficult to generalize. Most studies involve specific groups of people, particular methodologies, and specific objectives and orientations.

Other problems involve the difficulties of doing research on small businesses. The management process in the small firm is not a readily visible process, nor is it a consistent process based on formal principles and rigorous conceptualizations. It is a process elaborated by the owner-manager himself on an ad hoc basis to meet specific needs in particular circumstances. Its application is rather sporadic and depends more on the contingencies of the environment and the perceptions of the owner-manager than on an overall pattern or model of management. Since the research process consists in discovering and observing regularities and constants in phenomena in order to formulate generalizations, it is not always possible when studying small business management to arrive at precise generalizations.

A related difficulty is encountered when dealing with the owner-managers of the small businesses. Their level of management sophistication is often low, and the language they use and understand is not always that found in the traditional management literature; neither do they understand very well the subtleties and complexities of modern management. By nature, the entrepreneur is often skeptical and apprehensive about the research process. Although usually cooperative, they often try to provide the answers they think the researcher is looking for or those that will best accord with the image they would like to project.

In some situations entrepreneurs just cannot answer certain questions because they do not possess the relevant information; this applies to matters within the firm as well as to those outside it. One way to alleviate this type of difficulty would be to collect the information from other sources. But in small businesses, entrepreneurs are often the only source of information. Small firms are often not public on financial matters. Therefore, it is not possible to get this information other than from the entrepreneur himself.

Because of these problems and because many studies deal with so-called "sensitive" issues where the information is meager and hard to get, they suffer from certain weaknesses in the research process and lack of rigor in the analysis. Although empirical, they are often at best exploratory. The body of knowledge and the state of the art in the field of small business research is not yet systematic to the point where conceptual frameworks can be adequately mastered. Of course, this does not apply equally to all areas in the field; some areas are particularly affected by a scarcity of previous research, conceptualizations, and frameworks.

Data gathering methods and instruments vary greatly, from archival data to participant observations. The choice of the gathering instruments must reflect the objectives of the study and the research field. In our studies, we chose to work with interviews for practical reasons.

We discarded the mailed questionnaire because entrepreneurs often consider themselves too busy to answer them. Most Canadian studies on small business enterprises conducted through mailed questionnaires received an average response of only 15 to 25 percent. This implies a self-selected sample that may introduce a biased representation. Also, with only 20 percent of the sample responding, huge sample sizes are needed for statistical purposes. Another major reason to dismiss mailed questionnaires was the possibility that entrepreneurs might ask secretaries or assistants to fill out the questionnaires. For a study that includes matters of attitude and opinion, these would be absolutely useless and misrepresentative. Finally, questionnaires may engender misunderstanding of questions, a tendency to guess at difficult questions, haste, and incompleteness.

Since no interview is devoid of observation, the opportunity to visit the firm is highly attractive, despite the difficulty of analyzing this information in a systematic way. Provision must be made in the questionnaire for recording the observations and impressions of the observer. Sometimes phenomena are explicable only by such "outside" information. Furthermore, the so-called "standard information" concerning the business operation must be compared with what can be observed by the interviewer.

Conclusion

Although much progress has been made in the past 15 years, no clear link has yet been established between the personality characteristics of entrepreneurs and the success of their business ventures. However, present research and research methodology holds great promise for the advancement of our knowledge of entrepreneurship and small business management.

References

APLIN, J. C., and LEVETO, G. A., "Factors That Influence the Business Success of Minority Entrepreneurs," *American Journal of Small Business* 1, No. 2 (October 1976).

ATKINSON, J. W., "Motivational Determinants of Risk Taking Behavior," *Psychological Review,* 1957.

BAUMBACK, C. M., and SCHOEN, J. E., "Assessing Entrepreneurial Potential," *Proceedings for the 24th Annual Conference International Council for Small Business.* Québec City: Laval University, June 1979.

BAUMOL, WILLIAM J., "Entrepreneurship in Economic Theory," *American Economic Review* 58 (May 1968).

BERLEW, DAVID, in *First Annual Karl A. Bostrum Seminar in the Study of Enterprise.* Milwaukee: Center for Venture Management, 1969.

BORLAND, C., *Locus of Control, Need for Achievement and Entrepreneurship* (Doctoral dissertation, The University of Texas at Austin, 1974).

BROCKHAUS, R. H., "The Effect of Job Dissatisfaction on the Decision to Start a Business," *Journal of Small Business Management,* 1980.

BROCKHAUS, R. H., "I-E Locus of Control Scores as Predictors of Entrepreneurial Intentions," *Proceedings.* New Orleans: Academy of Management, 1975.

BROCKHAUS, R. H., "Psychological and Environmental Factors Which Distinguish the Successful from the Unsuccessful Entrepreneur: A Longitudinal Study," submitted for the Academy of Management Meeting, 1980a.

BROCKHAUS, R. H., "Risk Taking Propensity of Entrepreneurs," *Academy of Management Journal,* September 1980b.

BROCKHAUS, R. H., and NORD, W. R., "An Exploration of Factors Affecting the Entrepreneurial Decision: Personal Characteristics vs. Environmental Conditions," *Proceedings of the National Academy of Management,* 1979.

CARROLL, J. J., *The Filipino Manufacturing Entrepreneur.* New York: Cornell University, 1965.

COLE, A. H., "Entrepreneurship as an Area of Research," *The Task of Economic History* (supplement to *Journal of Economic History),* December 1942.

COLLINS, O. F., and MOORE, DAVID G., *The Organizational Makers: A Behavioral Study of Independent Entrepreneurs.* New York: Meredith, 1970.

COMEGYS, C., "Cognitive Dissonance and Entrepreneurial Behavior," *Journal of Small Business Management,* January 1976.

CONVERSE, P. E., "The Nature of Belief Systems in Mass Publics," *Ideology and Discontent,* ed. D. E. Apter. New York: Free Press, 1964.

COOPER, A. C., "Entrepreneurial Environment." *Industrial Research* 12 (September 1970).

COOPER A. C., *The Founding of Technologically-Based Firms.* Milwaukee: Center for Venture Management, 1971.

COOPER, A. C., "Technical Entrepreneurship: What Do We Know?" *Research and Development Management* 3 (February 1973).

D'AMBOISE, G. R., "Personal Characteristics, Organizational Practices, and Managerial Effectiveness: A Comparative Study of French- and English-Speaking Chief Executives in Québec" (Doctoral dissertation, University of California, Los Angeles, 1974).

DECARLO, J. F., and LYONS, P. R., "A Comparison of Selected Personal Characteristics of Minority and Non-Minority Female Entrepreneurs." *Journal of Small Business Management* 17, No. 4 (October 1979).

DEEKS, J., *The Small Firm Owner-Manager: Entrepreneurial Behavior and Management Practice.* New York: Holt, Rinehart & Winston, 1976.

DOCTORS, SAMUEL I., and JURIS, HERVEY A., "Management Technical Assistance for Minority Enterprise." Working paper No. 89-71, Northwestern University, 1971.

DOUGLASS, M. E., "Entrepreneurial Education Level Related to Business Performance," *Academy of Management Procedings,* 1976.

DRAHEIM, K., "Factors Influencing the Rate of Formation of Technical Companies," *Technical Entrepreneurship: A Symposium,* eds. A. Cooper and J. Komiver. Milwaukee: Center for Venture Management, 1972.

DURAND, D. E., "Effects of Achievement Motivation and Skill Training on the Entrepreneurial Behavior of Black Businessmen," *Organizational Behavior and Human Performance* 11, 1975.

FOSTER, GEORGE M., *Traditional Cultures and the Impact of Technological Change.* New York: Harper & Row, 1962.

GASSE, Y., "Characteristics, Functions and Performance of Small Firm Owner-Managers in Two Industrial Environments" (Doctoral dissertation, Northwestern University, 1978).

GASSE, Y., *Entrepreneurial Characteristics and Practices: A Study of the Dynamics of Small Business Organizations and Their Effectiveness in Different Environments.* Sherbrooke, Québec: René Prince Imprimeur, Inc., 1977.

GUNDER, FRANK ANDRE, "Sociology of Development and Underdevelopment of Sciology." *Catalyst,* eds. N. Howel et al., 1969.

GURIN, P., GURIN, G., LAS, R., and BEATTIE, M. M., "Internal-External Control in the Motivational Dynamics of Negro Youth," *Journal of Social Issues,* 1969.

HAMNER, W. C., and ORGAN, D. W., *Organizational Behavior.* Dallas: Business Publications, 1978.

HARTMAN, H., "Managers and Entrepreneurs: A Useful Distinction?" *Administrative Science Quarterly* (March 1959).

HORNADAY, J. A., and ABOUD, J., "Characteristics of Successful Entrepreneurs," *Personnel Psychology* 24 (Summer 1971).

HOWELL, R. P., "Comparative Profiles: Entrepreneurs Versus the Hired Executive: San Francisco Peninsula Semiconductor Industry," *Technical Entrepreneurship: A Symposium,* Milwaukee: Center for Venture Management, 1972.

HULL, D. L., BOSLEY, J. J., and UDELL, G. G., "Renewing the Hunt for the Heffalump: Identifying Potential Entrepreneurs by Personality Characteristics," *Journal of Small Business* 18, No. 1 (January 1980).

KNIGHT, FRANK, *Risk, Uncertainty and Profit.* New York: Harper & Row, Pub. 1921.

KOGAN, N., and WALLACH, M. A., *Risk Taking.* New York: Holt, Rinehart & Winston, 1964.

KOMIVES, J. L., "A Pulminary Study of the Personal Values of High *Technical Entrepreneurship: A Symposium,* Milwaukee: Center for Venture Management, 1972.

KUNKEL, JOHN H., "Values and Behavior in Economic Development," *Economic Development and Cultural Change,* April 1965.

LAMONT, L. M., "The Role of Marketing in Technical Entrepreneurship," *Technical Entrepreneurship: A Symposium,* eds. Arnold C. Cooper and John L. Komives. Milwaukee: Center for Venture Management, 1972.

LAMONT, L. M., "What Entrepreneurs Learn from Experience," *Journal of Small Business Management,* July 1972.

LAO, R. C., "Internal-External Control and Competent and Innovative Behavior among Negro College Students," *Journal of Personality and Social Psychology* 14 (1970).

LEIBENSTEIN, HARVEY, "Entrepreneurship and Development." *American Economic Review* 58 (May 1968).

LILES, P. R., *New Business Ventures and The Entrepreneur.* Homewood, Ill.: Richard D. Irwin, 1974.

LIPMAN, AARON, *The Colombian Entrepreneur in Bogota.* Coral Gables, Fla.: University of Miami, 1969.

LITVAK, I. A., and MAULE, C. J., *Canadian Entrepreneurship: A Study of Small Newly Established Firms.* Ottawa: Department of Industry, Trade and Commerce, 1971.

McCLELLAND, DAVID, *The Achieving Society.* Princeton: D. Van Nostrand, 1961.

McCLELLAND, DAVID, "Achievement Motivation Can Be Developed," *Harvard Business Review,* November-December 1965.

McCLELLAND, DAVID, and WINTER, D. G., *Motivating Economic Achievement.* New York: Free Press, 1969.

McCLELLAND, DAVID, ATKINSON, J. W., CLARK, R. A., and LOWELL, E. L., *The Achievement Motive.* New York: Appleton-Century-Crofts, 1953.

McGHEE, P. E., and CRANDALL, V. C., "Beliefs in Internal-External Control of Reinforcement and Academic Performance," *Child Development,* 1968.

MANCUSO, J. R., "The Entrepreneurs' Quiz," in C. M. Baumback and J. R. Mancuso, *The Entrepreneurship and Venture Management.* Englewood Cliffs, N.J.: Prentice-Hall, 1975.

MAYER, K. B., and GOLDSTEIN, S., *The First Two Years: Problems of Small Firm Growth and Survival.* Washington, D.C.: Small Business Administration, U.S. Government Printing Office, 1961.

MILL, J. S., *Principles of Political Economy with Some of Their Applications to Social Philosophy.* London: John W. Parker, 1848.

MIRON, D., and McCLELLAND, D., "The Impact of Achievement Motivation Training on Small Businesses," *California Management Review* (Summer 1979).

NECK, P., "Report on Achievement Motivation Training Program Conducted in Uganda" (1971).

ORGAN, D. W., and GREENE, C. N., "Role Ambiguity, Locus of Control, and Work Satisfaction," *Journal of Applied Psychology* 59 (1974).

PALMER, M., "The Application of Psychological Testing to Entrepreneurial Potential," *California Management Review* 13, No. 3 (1970–1971).

PATEL, V. G., "Venture Assistance Experiments in India," *Proceedings: International Symposium on Entrepreneurship and New Enterprise Development* (Summer 1975).

PHARES, E. J., *Locus of Control: A Personality Determinant of Behavior.* Morristown, N.J.: General Learning Press, 1973.

REDLICH, FRITZ, "Towards a Better Theory of Risk" *Explorations in Entrepreneurial History* 10, No. 1 (October 1957).

REUSS, GERHART E., "Entrepreneurship in the Area of Management," in T. H. Bonaparte and J. E. Glaherty, *Peter Durcker.* New York: New York University, 1970.

ROBERTS, E. B., "Entrepreneurship and Technology," *Factors in the Transfer of Technology,* eds. W. Gruber and D. Marquis. Cambridge: M.I.T., 1969.

ROBERTS, E. B., and WAINER, H. A., "Some Characteristics of Technical Entrepreneurs," *I.E.E.E. Transactions on Engineering Management,* Vol. EM-18, No. 3 (1971).

ROBIDOUX, J. and GARNIER, G., *Facteurs de succés et faiblesses des petites et moyennes entreprises manufacturieres au Québec, spécialement des entreprises utilisant des techniques de production avancée.* Sherbrooke, Québec: Faculté d'Administration, 1973.

ROKEACH, M., *The Open and Closed Mind.* New York: Basic Books, 1960.

ROTTER, J. B., "Generalized Expectancies for Internal Versus External Control of Reinforcement," *Psychological Monographs,* 1966a.

SCHRAGE, H., "The R & D Entrepreneur: Profile of Success," *Harvard Business Review,* November-December 1965.

SCHUMPETER, JOSEPH A., *The Theory of Economic Development.* Cambridge: Harvard Economic Studies, Harvard University, 1934.

SCHUMPETER, J. A., *History of Economic Analysis.* New York: Oxford University, 1954.

SEEMAN, M., and EVANS, J. W., "Alienation and Learning in a Hospital Setting," *American Sociological Review* 27 (1962).

SEXTON, D. L., "Characteristics and Role Demands of Successful Entrepreneurs," *Academy of Management Proceedings,* 1980.

SHAPERO, A., "An Action Program of Entrepreneurship." Austin: Multi-Disciplinary Research, 1971.

SHAPERO, A., "The Displaced, Uncomfortable Entrepreneur," *Psychology Today,* November 1975.

SMITH, P. C., KENDALL, L. M., and HULIN, C. L., *The Measurement of Satisfaction in Work and Retirement.* Chicago: Rand McNally, 1969.

STARBUCK, W. H., "Organizations and Their Environments," *Handbook of Industrial and Organizational Psychology,* ed. M. D. Dunnette. Chicago: Rand McNally, 1976.

STEPANEK, JOSEPH E., *Managers for Small Industry.* Glencoe, Ill,: Free Press, 1960.

STRAUSS, JAMES H., "The Entrepreneur: The Firm," *Journal of Political Economy* 52 (1944).

SUSBAUER, J. C., "The Technical Company Formation Process: A Particular Aspect of Entrepreneurship" (Doctoral dissertation, University of Texas at Austin 1969).

SUSBAUER, J. C., *The Technical Entrepreneurship Process in Austin, Texas. Technical Entrepreneurship: A Symposium,* eds. A. Cooper and J. Komives. Milwaukee: Center for Venture Management, 1972.

SUTTON, F. X., "Achievement Norms and the Motivation of Entrepreneurs, in Entrepreneurship and Economic Growth." Cambridge: Social Science Research Council and Harvard University Research Center in Entrepreneurial History, 1954.

TAWNEY, RICHARD H., *Religion and the Rise of Capitalism.* New York: Penguin, 1947.

TAYLOR, NORMAN W., "L'Industriel Canadien-Francais," *Recherches Sociographiques,* No. 11 (1960).

THOMPSON, JAMES D., *Organizations in Action.* New York: McGraw-Hill, 1967.

TIMMONS, J. A., "Black is Beautiful—Is it Bountiful?" *Harvard Business Review* (November-December, 1971).

TIMMONS, J. A., "Motivating Economic Achievement: A Five Year Appraisal," *Proceedings of the Fifth Annual Meeting, American Institute of Decisional Sciences,* 1973.

VALECHA, G. K., "Construct Validation of Internal-External Locus of Reinforcement Related to Work-Related Variables," *Proceedings of the 80th Annual Convention of the American Psychological Association* 7 (1972).

WAINER, H. A., and RUBIN, I. M., "Motivation of R & D Entrepreneurs: Determinants of Company," *Journal of Applied Psychology* 53, No. 3 (1969).

WATSON, D., and BAUMOL, E., "Effects of Locus of Control and Expectation of Future Control upon Present Performance," *Journal of Personality and Social Psychology* 6 (1967).

WEBER, MAX, *General Economic History.* New York: Free Press, 1950.

WEBER, MAX, *The Theory of Social and Economic Organization,* eds. and transl. A. M. Henderson and Talcott Parsons. New York: Oxford University Press, 1947.

WEBSTER, F. A., "A Model for New Venture Initiation: A Disclosure on Rapacity and the Independent Entrepreneur," *The Academy of Management Review* 1, No. 1 (January 1976).

WOLK, S., and DUCETTE, J., "International Performance and Incidental Learning as a Function of Personality and Task Dimensions," *Journal of Personality and Social Psychology* 29 (1974).

chapter iv

The social dimensions of entrepreneurship

Albert Shapero

Lisa Sokol

Overview

Which groups (social, cultural, ethnic, institutional, economic, regional, etc.) produce entrepreneurial events? Which groups produce more entrepreneurial events than others and why? For example, why do Jews start companies? What kinds of social and cultural factors and environments result in entrepreneurial events? Which factors and environments produce more entrepreneurial events than others and why? For example, why do refugees in the United States start more new companies than do similar refugees in France? The questions posed are central to a discussion of the social dimensions of entrepreneurship. Drawing upon data from a wide range of disciplines, we will address them in terms of a paradigm that describes the formation of the entrepreneurial event.

Grouping of social variables

That the questions posed are reasonable can be established by appeal to a range of familiar and lesser-known examples. Among the groups that are more strongly associated with entrepreneurship than others in America are the Jews and the Lebanese. Sombart (1913) went so far as to attribute almost all modern capitalistic institutions to the Jews. Less familiar entrepreneurial groups include the Ibos in Nigeria, the Antioqueños in Colombia, Parsis in India, Gujerati Indians in Africa, Bataks in Indonesia, Ilocanos in the Philippines, and Gorokas in the New Guinea highlands. In addition, we find regional groups identified with entrepreneurship: the Smalanders in Sweden, the central Saudis as compared to the western Saudis, the Mendocinos in Argentina. We find that the remote island of Oinusa in Greece, which once had 5000 inhabitants and now has 400, is the source of half a dozen "great shipping clans, numbering about 30 millionaire shipping families" who control one-fourth of the Greek merchant fleet, the largest in the world (*New York Times* May 6, 1979).

Certain refugee groups are readily identified with entrepreneurship. The Cubans in the United States have founded several thousand businesses and transformed the economy of Florida. The *pieds noirs* or "black feet," the displaced French colonists from Algeria, Tunisia, and Morocco, have founded thousands of businesses in France, as have East Germans in West Germany. We can already discern the entrepreneurial efforts of the latest wave of refugees, the Indochinese, in the United States.

The workers in certain industries are noted for their company formation propensities: those in the garment industry, advertising, construction, and high technology (semiconductors, instrumentation, and computer software). There are economic explanations in the latter instances, but a case can also be made that historical, regional, and ethnic factors influence the emergence of entrepreneurship as well.

Social and cultural factors

Company formation rates are far higher in the United States than in France and Italy; this is partially attributable to social and cultural variations. The historical record demonstrates that refugees are more likely to start businesses than they would have been had they remained in their home countries. Refugees in the United States are more likely to form companies than are those in France.

There are also many clear, historical examples of social and cultural environments that have been antipathetic to entrepreneurship. Medieval society in Europe maintained fixed social relationships. Everyone was identified with a particular group (nobility, clergy, peasantry, craftsmen) and each group had a "charter" that defined its role, its relationships to the other groups, the manners its members ought to adopt, even the colors they could and could not wear. The violation of group boundaries and relationships was frowned upon and usually forbidden by law. Innovation was proscribed by the guilds. Advertising was forbidden. Social mobility was wrong and was legislated against. One's place in life was prescribed, and one's reward was to be found in heaven. Though the nobility spent much of their lives breaking all of the rules, they went to elaborate lengths to legitimize their activities within the norms and values of their society. There was social climbing, but it was rare and historically noticeable. A merchant might enter the lower gentry by financing a noble's ransom or providing an enormous dowry for his daughter's politically useful marriage.

The world is essentially "messy," and will not conform to the particular rigidities of a given cultural period. Hence, entrepreneurial activity during the Middle Ages was left by default to groups that did not fit into any of the established "classes." The Jews did not fit, and took over many unclaimed or unsanctioned activities: moneylending, dealing in waste materials, innovating (the guilds forbade the use of new techniques, and the Jews were not permitted to join the guilds), advertising, cutting prices (forbidden by guilds but welcomed by customers, including the nobility), giving credit. The "outsiders" could only survive by performing new roles, roles considered to be outside or beneath the domain of established groups, or roles that were illegal but necessary (and therefore tolerated).

Efforts to answer the questions that have been posed about the social aspects of entrepreneurship lead, almost perforce, to an approach innocent of academic categorization. No single discipline is sufficient to the task; it is necessary to cast one's net widely beyond the obvious choices of economics, economic history, and the literatures that cluster under the omnibus heading of "business administration." Some relevant materials are found in the disciplines which explicitly deal with entrepreneurship, and are found under such diverse headings as "entrepreneurship," "entrepreneurs," "entrepreneurial," "business leaders," "innovators," "capitalists," "adventurers," "factors of production," "self-employed," and even "undertakers" (a direct translation of the German term *unternehmer*). However, the trail soon leads to the literature of other disciplines, to such areas as social stratification and social mobility, occupational psychology, demography, ethnicity, mobility, migration, cultural anthropology, economic geography, bureaucracy, industrialization, the sociology of religion, personality psychology.

Standing back from the profusion of literatures and references, it becomes apparent that "entrepreneurship" is a label for a profound and pervasive human activity that is of interest to many disciplines but is not encompassed by any one of them. Academic disciplines are accidents of history; each is bounded and consequently Procrustean. Discipline-centered approaches to the subject of entrepreneurship almost always define away parts of the subject or oversimplify it to fit existing theoretical structures.

Take McClelland's definition of entrepreneurs. David McClelland is one of the most frequently quoted writers on the subject of entrepreneurship. His framework is psychological theory. For years I accepted McClelland's theory rather uncritically but was uncomfortable with his emphasis on the need for achievement. I had studied too many entrepreneurs who were in no way driven by a need for achievement, whose behavior and attitudes would have to be tortured out of shape or ignored to make them concur with McClelland's frame of reference. McClelland simply defines segments of the data away:

I am not using the term "entrepreneur" in the sense of "capitalist": in fact, I should like to divorce "entrepreneur" entirely from any connotations of ownership. An entrepreneur is someone who exercises control over production that is not just for his personal consumption. According to my definition, for example, an executive in a steel-production unit in the U.S.S.R. is an entrepreneur. (McClelland 1971)

I have no objection to McClelland defining "entrepreneurship" in any way that makes sense for him. In fact I am quite relieved to find that he and I are talking about different things.

Weber's view

Weber's view on the key role of the Protestant ethic in the development of capitalism and entrepreneurial drive is one that nicely explains the economic development of the North Atlantic community, but does little to explain events in other cultures. Fleming (1979), on the entrepreneurs of Mendoza Province in Argentina, points out that they were part and parcel of the Latin American, Roman Catholic culture. How do we explain them in terms of Weber or the Japanese entrepreneurs? As Hill and Tawney point out with regard to what is a limited part of the world,

There is nothing in Protestantism which leads automatically to capitalism; its importance was rather that it undermined obstacles which the more rigid institutions and ceremonies of Catholicism imposed. (Hill 1961) The capitalist spirit is as old as history, and was not, as has sometimes been said, the offspring of Puritanism. But it found in certain aspects of Puritanism a tonic which braced its energies and fortified its already vigorous temper. (Fleming 1979)

Hagen's theory

Another widely quoted theory is that of Hagen, who explains entrepreneurship in terms of a lower status group seeking to overcome their social grievances by means of economic creativity and venturing. Hagen draws upon historical cases from Japan, Colombia, England, and Russia, but more recent historical research leads one to question his conclusions:

Drawing upon the cases of Japan, Colombia, England, and Russia, Hagen argued that the leaders of the development process (ENTREPRENEURS) always come from a subdominant group or groups seeking redress of social grievances (withdrawal of status respect) through the exercise of creativity in the economic realm. (Fleming 1979)

Fleming points out that it was the elite in Mendoza Province in Argentina who were the major entrepreneurs. Similarly, recent historical research on the development of Japan throws cold water on the rather romantic view of displaced Samurai who selflessly led entrepreneurial development for God and country. Yamamura (1978) points out that many of the so-called Samurai bought their positions so that they could get jobs in the bureaucracy (something I would consider very entrepreneurial) or were peasants only later considered to be Samurai. And in Dahmen's study of Sweden (1970) the educated upper class and upper middle class were highly represented at the beginning of Sweden's industrialization. In Russia, another Hagen example, there were entrepreneurs who started out as members of the elite. Kaser (1978) identifies three categories of Russian entrepreneurs: members of the nobility, serfs, and religious outsiders. In England some of the leading nobility engaged in entrepreneurial events to supply monies for their lordly extravagances (Gough 1969).

Another example of the way in which the conventions and categorizations of a discipline constrain the data on entrepreneurship can be found in a study of migration and social stratification in Monterrey, a leading entrepreneurial center in Mexico (Balan et al. 1973). Because the sociologists carrying out the study start with a discipline-constrained view of class, they lump corporate managers and owners together—after all, they are in the same class, aren't they? They dismiss street hawkers as of no interest, as do most economists and sociologists, and they state, without support, that street hawkers would take jobs if they were skilled and could get them. (Would they? Not according to hawkers in one Indian city who state that it is their independence that is of greatest value to them [*New York Times* May 6, 1979]). The authors state flatly that the well-paid workers in industrial plants obviously have security, good wages, and good fringe benefits, and so would not start businesses, yet their own data show that the small entrepreneurs of Monterrey are relatively more satisfied with their lot. Nor can the investigators explain why so many of their respondent business people started businesses in their forties when they were burdened with responsibilities. The conclusions reached are in harmony with the theoretical and ideological assumptions of tenured sociologists, rather than with their data.

A possible frame of reference— a paradigm of entrepreneurial event formation

In the discussion that follows, the process by which an entrepreneurial event takes shape is conceptualized as a paradigm. The effort is to explain the phenomena rather than to find generalizable laws, to include the situational and persisting social variables and to avoid the premature closure that so often accompanies lawlike generalization.

Definitional

The particularities of McClelland and Hagen have been mentioned, but any cursory review of the literature finds a very large diversity of definitions or implied definitions of entrepreneurs and entrepreneurship.

Gough (1969) points out that the *Oxford English Dictionary* defined "entrepreneur" in 1897 as "the director or manager of a public musical institution: one who 'gets up' entertainments, especially musical performances." It was not until 1933 that the term included a broader reference to business, as in "one who undertakes an enterprise: especially a contractor." To early Schumpeter the entrepreneur is the individual whose function is to carry out new combinations called enterprise. To later Schumpeter the innovator is concerned with doing new things or doing old things in a new way. To Cole (1959) the entrepreneur is the individual who undertakes "to initiate, maintain, or aggrandize a profit-oriented business unit for the production, or distribution of economic goods and services." To others, the entrepreneur is variously a risk-taker, an organization builder, and a decision-maker. In one writer's eyes the firm itself is the entrepreneur (Strauss 1944). As economics has become more formalized, others have either ignored the subject or treated it as part of a

catch-all residual factor. The latter residual, variously termed "technical change" or "coefficient of ignorance," includes, among other things, technology, education, institutional organization, and entrepreneurship. (Kilby 1971)

The historian Gras is quoted in Gough (1969) as suggesting that the entire concept of the entrepreneur is "largely a figment of the imagination." Gras essentially assumes that the corporate managers are today's dominant figures and not risk-takers at all. We might round out our survey of definitions by pointing out that in France, whence came the term, it means a building contractor.

In variance with past conceptualizations, I've chosen to define the unit of interest as the "entrepreneurial event" rather than the entrepreneur. This avoids such questions as whether an individual who has carried out one entrepreneurial act is or is not an entrepreneur. It permits one to consider the one-time entrepreneur and the part-time entrepreneur as well as the repetitive or full-time entrepreneur, and to consider a large variety of activities without being tied to a particular kind of individual. The event becomes the dependent variable while the individual or group that generates the event become the independent variables, as do the social, economic, political, and cultural contexts.

Operationally, the entrepreneurial event is denoted by

1. *Initiative-taking.* An individual or group takes the initiative.
2. *Consolidation* of resources. An organization is formed or restructured to accomplish some objective.
3. *Management* of the organization by those who took the initiative.
4. *Relative autonomy.* Resources are disposed of and distributed with relative freedom.
5. *Risk-taking.* The organization's success or failure is shared by the initiators.

Though innovation is widely associated with entrepreneurship, it is not included here as part of the definition of the entrepreneurial event. In the early Schumpeterian (1935) sense, the entrepreneurial event itself is the innovation, and there is no necessity to tie the event to new technology.

As defined here, every entrepreneurial event comprises all of the characteristics listed above. It may be performed by the one-time entrepreneur, the hawker, or the promoter; it may take place in an intra-corporate or a civic setting, or in a planned economy. Many managers take initiative, innovate in the technological sense, and even bring together resources, but if they do not personally share the risk of success or failure, if they do not manage the organization with a considerable degree of autonomy, they have not generated a genuine entrepreneurial event.

A suggested paradigm of entrepreneurial event formation

The criteria guiding design of the paradigm are comprehensiveness and reasonableness. The paradigm attempts to include all versions of the entrepreneurial event, from the one-time promotion to civic organization, and to include all of the variables, situational, social, and individual, that might be identified with the event. The paradigm also attempts to accommodate the diverse data on the subject while making sense to those who take part in the events described and to nonacademic observers in business and government.

There are two questions to be answered concerning each entrepreneurial event: (1) What brought about the action that led to a change in the entrepreneur's former life path? and (2) Why this particular path, the generation of an entrepreneurial event, and not one of the myriad other actions available? From the viewpoint of this discussion, the questions will focus on how group membership and how social and cultural environment affected the choice of an entrepreneurial path.

Each entrepreneurial event is the endpoint of a process and the beginning of another. The most obvious entrepreneurial event is the formation of a new company: in the United States there are approximately 800,000 to one million new company formations each year. Each new company formation is generated by an individual or a group of individuals who choose this particular path over many feasible alternatives open to them. Seldom can we find a case where starting a new company was the only possible alternative; no psychological framework suggests that there is a particular need or drive for company formation even though company formation may be linked to more generalized needs for achievement or expression.

Though each formation is a unique event, data from a large number of studies of company formation in different countries, economic sectors, and time periods suggest a general pattern. It is important to understand that the formation process is overdetermined; that is, no single variable or factor can account for the outcome of the process. A number of factors are necessary, but no one is sufficient.

The roads to action

What brings an individual, or a group, to take any action? At one extreme there are persons driven by overwhelming events such as war, political or religious persecution, loss of employment. At the other extreme there are individuals with no evident reason for change who opt to make a major shift in life path.

The process of change in an individual's life path can be described in terms of vectors, directed forces that keep the individual moving in a given direction at any given time. The great majority of individuals are held on a given path by the sum of vectors in their lives: a job, family situations, the powerful force of inertia, the daily pushes and pulls that make up the bulk of each individual's life. It takes a powerful force in a new direction or the accumulation of many detracking forces before an individual is pushed to or consciously opts for a major change of life path.

Research data show that individuals are much more likely to take action upon negative information rather than positive, and the data on company formations support that conclusion. Negative displacements are found to precipitate far more company formations than do positive possibilities, but, adhering to our notion of vector summation, it is the combination of both positive and negative forces that accounts for most major changes in life paths. Though displacement is a prevalent antecedent, being out of place or between things is also common.

The most extreme displacements are externally imposed, as in the case of political and religious refugees. The refugees have little or no choice, are knocked from their previous paths, and it is not surprising that refugees are highly identified with new company formation. Each wave of political refugees has produced its own special history of company formations in the country of refuge. The refugees from Tunisia, Algeria, and Morocco who resettled in France (Bonifay et al. 1977), the East German refugees in West Germany, the East Indians forced out of East Africa have been responsible for the formation of a large number of new companies in their new home areas. In recent years the waves of Hungarian, Cuban, and Vietnamese refugees into the United States have made their mark. A special report by the Bureau of the Census on minority-owned businesses in the United States (Bureau of Census 1972) indicates that by 1972, 13 years after they started arriving from Cuba, the Cubans in the United States were responsible for 4664 existing companies, 1266 of which had paid employees and 848 of which were in construction and manufacturing. More recent reports indicate far greater numbers. A study of entrepreneurs in Lebanon (Sayigh 1962) found that several were Palestinians and presumably refugees. Derossi's (1971) study of Mexican entrepreneurs shows that a noticeable percentage were refugees from Germany and Lebanon. Similar phenomena were found in Bogota by Lipman (1969). Papanek (1962) reported whole groups of Memon Muslims who were in Pakistan as refugees from India and were very entrepreneurial. More recently, Indochinese refugees in the United States have begun to form companies. Though less well-known, the almost one million Iranian immigrants, many of them quasi-refugees, have been responsible for many company formations, often the only means for obtaining immigrant visas (*New York Times* December 9, 1979).

Job-related displacements are far more frequent though less dramatic. Being fired is a major externally-imposed displacement. Others include being demoted or not promoted due to organizational changes or being transferred to an undesired location. All of the foregoing are situations found in abundance as antecedent to large changes in life paths. In studies of 109 company formations in Austin, Texas (technical companies, accounting firms, publishing firms), 65 percent of the influences leading to start-up were classified as negative: "I was fired," "boss sold the company," "organizational changes," "transferred but did not want to leave the city," "no future," "didn't like the job" (Shapero 1975).

Other studies in a great diversity of environments provide strong support for the importance of negative displacement. Studies of manufacturing entrepreneurs in the Philippines (Carroll 1965), industrial entrepreneurs in Pakistan (Papanek 1962), industrial entrepreneurs in Madras (Berna 1960), industrial and technical entrepreneurs in northern Italy (Shapero et al. 1974), small businessmen in the United Kingdom (Boswell 1972), industrial entrepreneurs in Turkey (Alexander 1960) and in Marseilles (Bonifay et al. 1974) all report anecdotal and statistical evidence of displacement. Carroll documents severe import controls that triggered merchants to enter manufacturing. Papanek, Berna, and Alexander found similar effects of import controls on industrial formations. Carroll quotes several instances of Filipino entrepreneurs being launched on their careers by negative displacements: one had a taxi horse taken away by the Japanese; one lost a government job because of the war; one had a family business argument; one saw the closing down of a plant. Boswell identifies "the emigration of frustrated men from corporations" as a prime generator of new engineering and hosier/knitwear firms in the United Kingdom.

Job dissatisfactions of many kinds are mentioned with great frequency by company formers; they include boredom and what might be called technical frustration. A noticeable percentage of technical companies are formed after a technical professional has proposed a particular product or service or project to an employer and has failed to find acceptance. Creative frustration is one of the most frequently mentioned causes for the spinout of technical companies in Japan (Kiyonari 1976). Benoit (1974) tells of a French engineer, 73 years old, who became frustrated with the use of his patents by an employer and who thereupon formed a company with two of his college classmates! The well publicized story of Ross Perot is that, as an IBM salesman, he had earned the highest possible annual bonus within the first two months of a year, and because IBM was adamant in its policies, he quit to form his own company and compete with IBM.

Some displacements are internal to the entrepreneur in that they are generated without reference to anything but the passage of time. One recurring precipitator of entrepreneurial activity can best be referred to as "traumatic birthdays" or "magic numbers." The entrepreneur describes his motive in the following terms: "I realized I was going to be 40 years old (or 30, or 50) within three months. It was now or never." This has been also described as the midlife crisis, a period in middle life, defined differently by different writers, characterized by large disaffection and the phenomenon of "dropping out" or significantly altering life paths. The power of this crisis is witnessed by a variety of evidence.

The state of being out of place or between things often precedes the formation of a company. One is more likely to start a new venture upon discharge from military service, on completion of studies, or upon completion of a project. There is one study of 22 ex-offenders who started their own companies when they were paroled from prison (Jansyn et al. 1969). Another such semi-displacement is popularly identified as the "empty-nest" syndrome, experienced by the mother whose children have grown and left home. Every U.S. city has numerous middle-class, middle-years former housewives acting as real estate brokers (Shapero 1980).

Voluntary migrants rank high as company founders. Derossi's (1971) Mexican entrepreneurs included a high percentage of first generation immigrants and their heirs. Similar findings are also reported from other Latin American countries (Lipman 1965, Zalduendo 1963). Whether migrating to escape some negative situation or to exploit perceived opportunities, the voluntary migrant is out of place for some time period. The data mildly support a speculation that the more migrants are out of place in their new environment, the more likely it is that they might start an independent venture. Derossi's study shows little or no entrepreneurship displayed by refugees who fled the Spanish Civil War to Mexico; their education in the liberal professions and their common language found them easily in place in Mexican society.

The migrants among the Bogota entrepreneurs in Lipman's study (1969) made up 69 percent of his sample. Migrants made up 35 percent of the Marseilles entrepreneurs in Bonifay's study (1974), 28 percent of the Lebanese entrepreneurs in Sayigh's study (1962), more than 90 percent of Liberian entrepreneurs in Ross's study (1971), a high percentage of Mendozan entrepreneurs in Fleming's study (1979) and of Indian entrepreneurs in Koppel and Peterson's study (1975).

Though negative displacements predominate, there are many positive pulls that lead to the start-up of a business. The offer of financial support or the offer of a contact by a would-be customer are not unheard of. Typically, in the latter case, the contract is offered to a technical person for research, to a competent professional or technician for services, or even to a salesperson for a product. Another major pull is an offer of partnership by a friend, a colleague, or even a customer. In many instances the subjects of positive pulls report that they had no idea of going into business when the offer came.

It should be noted that in this author's field research only one of the hundreds of entrepreneurs interviewed claimed to have planned a step-by-step process leading to the formation of a business, though many reported that they had often thought of it. It is highly likely that a very large percentage of Americans have thought of being in business for themselves. A survey in France reported that well over 30 percent of all those surveyed, regardless of political affiliation, would like to be in business for themselves.

Not everyone perceives events in the same way or takes an equal amount of initiative. On becoming a refugee or being fired from one's job, one encounters unequivocal displacement. In most other circumstances the events are matters of individual perception and interpretation, and it is here that psychological differences may help to explain subsequent responses. However, the psychological attributes of entrepreneurs are discussed elsewhere in this volume.

The action taken

Why is one action taken rather than the many other conceivable actions that are available to the individual? Perceptions of desirability and of feasibility are products of cultural and social environments and help determine which actions will be seriously considered and subsequently taken.

The particular action taken by an individual in a major shift from one life path to another is a product of the situation and of socially and culturally implanted predispositions. Another way to put it is as follows: Individuals have varying perceptions of desirability and feasibility. A college graduate may know that plumbers earn more than do social workers; however, be-

Table 1 *Entrepreneurial event formation*

Life path change			
Negative Displacements:			
Forcefully emigrated			
Fired			
Insulted			
Angered			
Bored	*Perceptions of Desirability*	*Perceptions of Feasibility*	
Reaching middle age	Culture	Financial support	
Divorced or widowed	Family	Other support	*Company Formation*
Between Things:	Peers	Demonstration effect	
Out of army	Colleagues	Models	
Out of school	Mentor	Mentors	
Out of jail		Partners	
Positive Pull:			
From partner			
From mentor			
From investor			
From customer			

cause of socially determined values, the former career does not seem to be a possibility. One may find it desirable, but not feasible, to have a career as a professional athlete. Of course, feasibility may influence our notions of what is desirable, but for purposes of explanation the two factors will be treated separately in the discussion that follows. (See Table 1.)

Perceptions of desirability (values)

The social and cultural factors that enter into the formation of entrepreneurial events are most felt through the formation of individual value systems. More specifically, in a social system that places a high value on the formation of new ventures, more individuals will choose that path in times of transition. More diffusely, a social system that places a high value on innovation, risk-taking, and independence is more likely to produce entrepreneurial events than a system with contrasting values. To examine concepts of the desirable as they influence company formation, we will use data on the families, peer groups, ethnic groups, educational and professional contexts of entrepreneurs.

Family

The family, particularly the father or mother, plays the most powerful role in establishing the desirability and credibility of entrepreneurial action for an individual. Fifty to 58 percent of company founders in the

United States had parents who were company owners, free professionals, independent artisans, or farmers, yet a census from the same period revealed that less than 12 percent of the U.S. population was self-employed. In a Northern Italian study conducted by the author in 1973, 56 percent of entrepreneurs had parents who were self-employed. In Carroll's study of Filipino manufacturing entrepreneurs, the percentage was 74; in Marris and Somerset's study of Kenyan entrepreneurs, 80 percent; in Harris's study of Nigerian entrepreneurs, almost 89 percent (Marris and Somerset 1971; Harris 1970).

The data follow the same pattern in study after study and in culture after culture. Of Lipman's (1969) Bogotan entrepreneurs, 61 percent had independent fathers; of Roubidoux's (1975) Québecois, 68 percent; of Sayigh's (1962) Lebanese, 74 percent; Hammeed's (1974) Sudanese, 70 percent. Finney's (1973) Gorokan entrepreneurs of New Guinea show a high incidence of fathers who are relatively independent in terms of tribal position. Borland (1974) found that the variable most commonly associated with a business student's declared entrepreneurial expectations was the professional independence of the student's father. Only one of 75 girls in Borland's sample expected to start a company.

The credible model is not necessarily consciously followed. Susbauer (1969) asked technical entrepreneurs whose fathers had been self-employed if their fathers had been models or had encouraged them to start a company. Most often, their fathers had told them never to start a company or their fathers had themselves been unsuccessful.

Peers

Though parents stand out as the major credible examples of entrepreneurship, there are many other potential examples. The larger the number and variety of entrepreneurs in a particular culture, the greater the probability that the individuals in that culture will form companies. This may well explain differences in the proportionate role of the parental example in different countries such as 50–58 percent in the United States and 80–89 percent in African countries.

Other credible examples include relatives, colleagues, and classmates. When a corporate vice president breaks away to form a new company, this does not necessarily affect his many subordinates. However, when a group of engineers, far down in the organizational line, breaks away to form a company, their colleagues are much more likely to follow the example (Draheim et al. 1966).

Previous work experience

In Cooper's study of technical company formations in the San Francisco area (Cooper 1971), he found that new companies were more likely to originate from small corporate divisions than from large ones. Cooper calls the small divisions "incubators." A small firm provides a close view of the man who formed or heads it, a man who in many cases is very much like his employees. It becomes possible for the potential entrepreneur to envision a comparable role for himself.

Cooper found that many of the entrepreneurs he studied had formed more than one company, and many had experienced previous business failures. Failures apparently do not shake the credibility of the company formation act, but may even reinforce its credibility and serve as a learning experience.

Ethnic groups

It is no accident that entrepreneurship is highly identified with certain ethnic groups: Jews, Lebanese, Ibos in Nigeria, Jains and Parsis in India, Gujeratis in East Africa. Each of these ethnic groups contains a large number of examples to establish the credibility of company formation. In the case of the Jews, 2000 years of refugee status and large numbers of credible examples make the entrepreneurial act almost an expected role.

Approximately 40 percent of the Chinese-Americans are in business for themselves, as are a similarly high percentage of the Japanese-Americans. Overseas Chinese are heavily engaged in business wherever they are found; this is considered a political problem in Indochina, Malaysia, and the Philippines. Strong feelings against Chinese merchants have created a similar issue in some developing countries. The descendants of 10,000 Chinese brought into Peru to build the railroads have produced one of the two mainstreams of restaurant cuisine in Lima.

Classmates, colleagues, mentors

Entrepreneurs in South Africa, Italy, Brazil, and the United States have often commented about others like themselves, "If he could do it, I knew I could too!" These comments have replicated in many interview contexts. "I saw the boss every day. I did everything he did but take home the profits. If he could do it . . ." "I had this classmate in high school who has a prosperous company. Why he was stupid! If he could do it . . . ." The same was heard with regard to work peers, relatives, and observed strangers. It would seem that it helps to see someone lesser than oneself establish the credibility of the act.

Another powerful influence on the perceptions of the nascent entrepreneur is that of a mentor. The mentor plays the part of convincing, assuring, and instructing. Unlike the peer whom one can look down on, the mentor is respected and looked up to. When I asked a South African black businessman how he happened to go into business, he told me he had worked for a Jewish businessman who had encouraged him. The same was heard from an Ohio college graduate who was encouraged by an elderly, respected friend. In the New Guinea cases discussed by Finney, the pattern is clearly perceived:

Gorokans had served during World War II on lonely outposts with white men who had subsequently served as mentors. Extension agents, teachers, and respected elderly friends can all play this powerful role.

Perceptions of feasibility

Perceptions of desirability and perceptions of feasibility necessarily interact. If one perceives the formation of a company as unfeasible, one may conclude it is undesirable. If one perceives the act as undesirable, one may never consider its feasibility.

The general or specific availability of financial support for entrepreneurial activities directly influences the propensity to form companies. More companies form in times when financial resources are readily available in a given community. The particular way in which financial support is made available also plays an important role. The data shows that the great majority of all company start-ups use capital from personal savings and borrowings, particularly from relatives. After personal sources, private individuals from the local community are the major source of finanical support. The influence of family and ethnic group is manifest in the relative readiness to provide financial support. Some ethnic groups have developed financial institutions to support the formation of new businesses. Chinese immigrants to the United States used an institution known as *hui* (Peterson 1978); the Japanese brought with them a similar institution known as *tanomoshiko* or *moujin,* in which workers subscribed monies on a monthly basis to be loaned to their compatriots or raffled off until each contributor had had an opportunity to start a business (Light 1972). American Jewish communities often formed free loan associations to help new immigrants.

In many ethnic groups there is a practice of hiring a new immigrant and then helping him to move on and start his own similar business. Greek restaurateurs in the United States and Portuguese greengrocers in South Africa are two such examples. In nineteenth-century New Mexico, German-Jewish traders took new immigrants as employees, helped them learn the trading post business, and then helped finance them in a new trading post "further on" in the Indian territory.

Would-be partners often transform vague possibilities into action. They may pull a nascent entrepreneur into the act by providing funding, moral support, labor, a necessary skill, and shared risk. They may even originate the entire notion of starting a business. The companionship offered by a partner who is a friend may provide a further element of desirability to a new business. In a study of executive mobility I found far more group formations among technical companies (on the order of 26 percent) than among other kinds of companies. There is far less apparent risk in starting a company to carry out well-known manufacturing or service processes than there is in a high-technology field; hence the greater need for associates to provide support where uncertainty is high.

Many kinds of agencies provide support for starting a new business. The many efforts of the Small Business Administration, including advice, consultation, education, and financial support, make the act feasible to the potential entrepreneur. Popular journal articles and press items may impart knowledge that removes some of the perceived uncertainty.

Examining the central questions in terms of the paradigm

The paradigm suggests that entrepreneurial formations are the result of interacting situational and cultural factors. The utility of the proposed paradigm is in its application to questions of policy and to questions of historical example. In terms of policy, the paradigm suggests that efforts to make the entrepreneurial event should even precede the usual offers of financial support. It suggests that exposure to those near oneself is more important than exposure to great successes. It suggests that educational programs that pride themselves on discouraging the "wrong" candidates are misguided to ignore the extent to which desirability and feasibility can be modified.

The proposed paradigm provides a way of explaining entrepreneurial diversity among ethnic subgroups. Why are West Indian blacks in the United States so highly entrepreneurial? They come from the same areas of Africa as blacks who are much less likely to start businesses of their own. In New York the children of West Indians are more highly entrepreneurial than the peers who have the same educational advantages (Sowell 1978). One explanation is that in the West Indies, where slaves constituted 90 percent of the total population, they grew their own food and marketed their surplus. They did not compete with a white working class and were thus able to develop in all trades and to provide visible examples of entrepreneurship. By contrast, blacks in the United States were surrounded by a white population and competed with a white working class. The price of a slave was equivalent to that of a house, and slave owners allowed little room for independent action. In the deep South, laws forbad the presence of free blacks and forbad education for slaves, thus deliberately removing sources of credibility and feasibility.

Many more questions can be used as starting points for research.

How will equal opportunity legislation for minorities and women affect the rate of entrepreneurial formation? Will the laws initially decrease formations among these populations by siphoning off the most capable into large corporations and government? There is some evidence that young Chinese-Americans are going into government rather than business; government positions have always had a high value in the Chinese culture. Will there be some years of integration and gaining of experience to be followed by displacement-induced company formations?

What is the effect of business school education on entrepreneurship? Does it convey the idea that small business is not desirable or doomed to failure?

Does a business school education, particularly a "good" one from a major business school, decrease the probability that an individual will start a business?

Why do the children of entrepreneurs become professionals in large organizations rather than in the family business, and why do many entrepreneurial parents encourage the shift? Is there a general cultural bias in favor of the professions?

References

ALEXANDER, ALEX P. "Industrial Entrepreneurship in Turkey: Origins and Growth," *Economic Development and Cultural Change* VIII, No. 4 (July 1960).

BALAN, J., BROWNING, H. L., and JELIN, E., *Men in a Developing Society.* Austin: University of Texas, 1973.

BENOIT, J. L., *Venture Capital Investment Behavior: The Risk-Capital Investor in New Company Formation in France* (Doctoral dissertation, The University of Texas at Austin, 1974).

BERNA, JAMES J., *Industrial Entrepreneurship in Madras State.* Bombay: Asia Publishing House, 1960.

BONIFAY, P. H., EON, J. F., LABRE, H., and MELER, J., *La Creation D'Enterprise* (Doctoral dissertation, The University of Texas at Austin, 1974).

BORLAND, CANDACE, *Locus of Control, Need for Achievement and Entrepreneurship* (Doctoral dissertation, The University of Texas at Austin, 1974).

BOSWELL, JONATHAN, *The Rise and Decline of Small Firms.* London: George Allen and Unwin, 1972.

CARROLL, JOHN H., *The Filipino Manufacturing Entrepreneur.* Ithaca: Cornell University, 1965.

COLE, ARTHUR H., *Business Enterprise in Its Social Setting.* Cambridge: Harvard University, 1959.

COLLINS, ORVIS F., and MOORE, DAVID G., *The Organization Makers—A Behavioral Study of Independent Entrepreneurs.* New York: Meredith, 1970.

COOPER, ARNOLD C., "Spin-offs and Technical Entrepreneurship," *IEEE Transactions of Engineering Management,* Vol. EM-18, No. 1 (February 1971).

DAHMEN, ERIK, *Entrepreneurial Activity and the Development of Swedish Industry, 1919-1939.* Homewood, Ill.: Irwin, 1970.

DEROSSI, FLAVIA, *The Mexican Entrepreneur.* Paris: OECD, 1971.

DILLARD, DUDLEY, *Economic Development of the North Atlantic Community.* Englewood Cliffs, N.J.: Prentice-Hall, 1967.

DRAHEIM, KIRK, HOWELL, RICHARD P., and SHAPERO, ALBERT, *The Development of a Potential Defense R & D Complex: A Study of Minneapolis-St. Paul.* Menlo Park, Ca.: Stanford Research Institute, 1966.

FINNEY, B. R., *Big Men and Business: Entrepreneurship and Economic Growth in the New Guinea Highlands.* Honolulu: University of Hawaii, 1973.

FLEMING, W. J., "The Cultural Determinants of Entrepreneurship and Economic Development: A Case Study of Mendoza Province, 1861-1914," *Journal of Economic History* XXXIX, No. 1 (March 1979).

GOUGH, J. W., *The Rise of the Entrepreneur.* New York: Schocher Books, 1969.

GRIGGS, JACK, *The Commercial Banker and Industrial Entrepreneurship: The Lending Officer's Propensity to Make Loans to New and Different Companies* (Doctoral dissertation, The University of Texas at Austin, 1972).

HAMMEED, K. A., *Enterprise: Industrial Entrepreneurship in Development.* London: Sage Publications, 1974.

HARRIS, JOHN R., "Entrepreneurship and Economic Development," in *Business Enterprise and Economic Change,* eds. L. P. Cain and P. J. Eselding. Kent, Ohio: Kent State University, 1973.

HARRIS, JOHN R., "Nigerian Entrepreneurship in Industry," in *Growth and Development of the Nigerian Economy,* eds. C. Eicher and C. Lieholm. East Lansing: Michigan State University, 1970.

HART, GILLIAN P., *African Entrepreneurship.* Occasional Paper #16. Grahamstown: Institute of Social and Economic Research, Rhodes University, 1972.

HILL, C., "Protestantism and the Rise of Capitalism," in *Essays in the Economic and Social History of Tudor and Stuart England: In Honour of R. H. Tawney,* ed. F. J. Fisher. London: Cambridge University, 1961.

HOFFMAN, CARY A., *The Venture Capital Investment Process* (Doctoral dissertation, The University of Texas at Austin, 1972).

HOFFMAN, CARY A., and SHAPERO, ALBERT, *Providing the Industrial Ecology Required for the Survival and Growth of Small Technical Companies.* Austin: MDRI Press, 1971.

"Iranian Immigrants, Totaling Perhaps a Million, Bring Wealth and Diversity to the U.S.," *New York Times,* December 9, 1979.

JANSYN, LEON, KOHLHOF, E., SADOWDKI, C., and TOBY, J., *Ex-Offenders as Small Businessmen: Opportunities and Obstacles.* Final Report under Office of Manpower Contract, Project #27-4900, Rutgers University (July 1969).

KASER, M. C., "Russian Entrepreneurship," in *The Cambridge Economic History of Europe* VII, Part 2, eds. P. Mathias and M. M. Postan. Cambridge: Cambridge University, 1978.

KILBY, PETER, ed., *Entrepreneurship and Economic Development.* New York: Free Press, 1971.

KIYONARI, TADAO, "Conditions of Venture Businesses in Japan," 1976.

KOPPEL, B., and PETERSON, R. E., "Industrial Entrepreneurship in India: A Re-evaluation," *The Developing Economies,* September 1975.

LIGHT, I. H., *Ethnic Enterprise in America.* Berkeley: University of California, 1972.

LIPMAN, AARON, *The Columbia Entrepreneur in Bogota.* Coral Gables, Fla.: University of Miami, 1969.

LIPMAN, AARON, "Social Background of the Bogota Entrepreneur," *Journal of Inter-American Studies* VII, No. 2 (April 1965).

LJUNGMARK, LARS, *Swedish Exodus.* Carbondale, Ill.: Southern Illinois University, 1979.

MCCLELLAND, DAVID, *The Achieving Society.* Princeton: D. Van Nostrand, 1961.

MCCLELLAND, DAVID, "Entrepreneurship and Achievement Motivation," *Approaches to the Science of Socio-Economic Development,* ed. P. Lengyel. Paris: UNESCO, 1971.

MARRIS, P., and SOMERSET, A., *African Businessmen: A Study of Entrepreneurship and Development in Kenya.* London: Routledge and Kegan Paul, 1971.

PAPANEK, GUSTAV F., "The Development of Entrepreneurship," *American Economic Review* 52 (May 1962).

PETERSON, W., "Chinese Americans and Japanese Americans," *American Ethnic Groups,* ed. T. Sowell. Washington, D.C.: The Urban Institute, 1978.

ROSS, D. F., "The Tribal Entrepreneur in the Emerging Liberian Economy," *Liberian Studies Journal* III, No. 2 (1970-1971).

ROUBIDOUX, J., "Profil Electif D'Entrepreneurs des Enterprises à Success au Québec" (Unpublished paper). Lyon: University of Laval, 1975.

SAYIGH, YUSIF A., *Entrepreneurs in Lebanon.* Cambridge: Harvard University, 1962.

SCHUMPETER, JOSEPH A., *Capitalism, Socialism and Democracy.* London: George Allen & Unwin, 1947.

SCHUMPETER, JOSEPH A., *History of Economic Analysis.* New York: Oxford University, 1954.

SCHUMPETER, JOSEPH A., *The Theory of Economic Development.* Cambridge: Harvard University, 1934.

SHAPERO, ALBERT, "Entrepreneurship and Economic Development," *Entrepreneurship and Enterprise Development: A Worldwide Perspective.* Milwaukee: Proceedings of Project ISEED, 1975.

SHAPERO, ALBERT, "Have You Got What It Takes to Start Your Own Business?" *Savvy,* April 1980.

SHAPERO, ALBERT, BARCIA-BOUZA, JORGE, and FERRARI, ACHILLE, *Technical Entrepreneurship in Northern Italy.* Milano: IIMT, 1974.

SHAPERO, ALBERT, HOFFMAN, C., DRAHEIM, K. P., and HOWELL, R. P., *The Role of the Financial Community in the Formation, Growth and Effectiveness of Technical Companies.* Austin: MDRI Press, 1969.

SOMBART, WERNER, *The Jews and Modern Capitalism.* London: T. Fisher Unwin, 1913.

SOWELL, T., "Three Black Histories," *American Ethnic Groups.* Washington, D.C.: The Urban Institute, 1978.

STRAUSS, JAMES H., "The Entrepreneur: The Firm," *Journal of Political Economy* LII (June 1944).

SUSBAUER, JEFFREY D., "The Technical Company Formation Process: A Particular Aspect of Entrepreneurship" (Doctoral dissertation, The University of Texas at Austin, 1969).

TAWNEY, R. H., *Religion and the Rise of Capitalism.* London: Harcourt Brace Jovanovich, 1926.

"A Tiny, Remote Island Spawns Dynasties of Greek Ship-owners," *New York Times.* May 6, 1979.

YAMAMURA, KOZO, "Entrepreneurship, Ownership and Management in Japan," in *The Cambridge Economic History of Europe* VII, Part 2, eds. P. Mathias and M. M. Postan. Cambridge: Cambridge University, 1978.

ZALDUENDO, E. A., "El Empresario Industrial en American Latina," Buenos Aires: CEPAL, 1963.

chapter v

The sociology of entrepreneurship

Edwin Harwood

Overview

Almost all empirical studies on entrepreneurs relate to individuals engaged in profit-making activity in competitive markets. Scholarly interest has focused primarily on successful business innovators. Yet insistent pressures to broaden the concept of "entrepreneur" beyond these definitional boundaries create problems for the sociology of entrepreneurship. Schumpeter's demarcations of the entrepreneur (1961) are doubtless too restricted today because of historical changes in the advanced capitalist countries and because of the emergence of legitimate research interest in underdeveloped and centrally planned economies, where venturing takes forms very different from mature industrial capitalism. Further, the more inclusive concept of entrepreneur which Arthur Cole (1965) and David McClelland (1969) adopted 20 to 30 years ago has led to a certain dilution. The working definition of entrepreneurship for scholars should not be too far removed from either contemporary popular usage (as in the business press) or from its historical foundation in profit-generating enterprise.

The problem of definition

What is entrepreneurship and who are the entrepreneurs? There are some questions that are never laid to rest, perhaps because social scientists relish semantic jousting or because a sense of what scientific inquiry requires drives them to keep hunting for the perfect fit between the definition of a phenomenon and the phenomenon itself. Thus to the question, "Who becomes entrepreneurial and why?" one is tempted to reply, "But didn't Peter Kilby take care of all that in his classic essay 'Hunting the Heffalump'?" While Kilby (1971) may not have spotted the Heffalump directly, he did apparently find his habitat and range, somewhere between the valley of macroeconomic supply-demand functions, the riverbank of childhood socialization experiences, the desert of social marginality, and the treacherous canyons of political constraints on economic decision-making. After so much has been written on this subject, one might fairly conclude that it is not really so important to know what or who the entrepreneur is, rather, one ought to examine the habitat of this mysterious creature. Let the definition hunters abandon their futile pursuit after these elusive animals! Know them instead by the environmental variables that mold their behavior and determine their range! That would seem to be the current consensus on this topic.

Yet definitions remain important because they make research manageable. A concept loose enough to give ample breathing space for all the concrete phenomena everyone might want to include can make explanation very unwieldy. Thus at one extreme "entrepreneur" might refer to any business people whenever it can be shown that they take some risk, assemble resources, show some initiative, or exhibit some independence of action. In this case "entrepreneur" is almost synonymous with "businessperson." But if that's the case, why should schools of business administration draw boundaries between programs of small business management and new venture management (entrepreneurship), and why should writers for *Time, Forbes, The Wall Street Journal, Venture*, and other periodicals find "entrepreneur" and "entrepreneurial" more appropriate labels for some business people and undertakings than others? Practical people need workable distinctions.

Professor Shapero's concept of the "entrepreneurial event" is more liberal still since it includes any role, regardless of the occupational or social context, that can be associated with initiative, risk-taking, resource aggregation, and autonomy. By such expansion, a "venture" can come to include almost any new accomplishment. Professor Shapero's definition would allow street hawkers, promoters, civic organizers, even the organizers of events in socialist countries to enter Joseph Schumpeter's pantheon in which the major commercial and industrial barons hold center stage. (It must be noted that Schumpeter's definition did not exclude types of people; but the examples he refers to most frequently show that his conceptualization was anchored in industrial and technological innovation more than, say, financial or marketing innovation, not to mention the non-business areas that Shapero's concept would allow.)

In America there have always been pressures for occupational upgrading and status enhancement. Because "entrepreneur" has considerable appeal now, it is not surprising that so many should covet the designation for themselves, whether they have read Joseph Schumpeter's *Theory of Economic Development* (1961) or have heard of the Harvard project in entrepreneurial history. Only the academic entrepreneurs, who may combine federal grantsmanship, private consulting, and perhaps a real estate sideline with teaching and writing may still encounter the slings and arrows of outrageous snobbery among their professional peers. And a new species, the "paper entrepreneur," has recently been added to our growing taxonomy by Robert Reich, a Federal Trade Commission policy planner. These "paper entrepreneurs" might be thought of as a kind of malign antibody in the bloodstream of advanced capitalism since the mission of many is to promote "innovative" regulations that undermine and frustrate private sector entrepreneurs or to engage in financial and legal legerdemain that diverts productive flows of capital. Shall we call this new type "counterpreneurial"?

In a liberal definition of entrepreneurship, even Lenin might qualify as an entrepreneur since he took considerable risk, showed a high degree of independence, and applied to Russian society innovative ideas that led to new organizational forms in many sectors of Soviet life. (Never mind the economic chaos, inefficiency, and decline in Soviet living standards that resulted! For the political entrepreneur, economic costs and deficits are rarely more than an off-the-books externality.) Should the Russian Revolution be considered an "entrepreneurial event"? Should the foes of capitalism be credentialed in this manner and grouped with those who are, to Schumpeter's thinking, not only the fulcrum of economic progress in the western world but also (if you read between the lines) a kind of Knighthood of the Capitalist Social Order?

Risk, profit, and innovation

The problem of the broad definition of entrepreneurship (regardless of whether we are talking about entrepreneurs or entrepreneurial events) is that the temptation for an expanding list is great. Take, for example, Professor Shapero's criterion of "risk-taking." Marketing managers who err in a new product promotional strategy take career risks; professors who start entrepreneurial training programs in liberal arts colleges with antibusiness faculties expose themselves to tenure risks; civil servants can find their programs caught in congressional crossfire that may engulf their careers. Intellectual innovators may find themselves outcasts in their own professions because they jeopardize entrenched dogmas.

If, on the other hand, risk-taking is restricted to contributions of capital (assets), our definition of "entrepreneur" comes much closer to the popular understanding and to the reality of private sector venturing. True, some entrepreneurs may escape having to make money asset (equity) contributions. It should be noted, too, that this was not an essential criterion for Schumpeter (1947), who distinguished entrepreneurs (organizers of resources for novel combinations) from capitalists (suppliers of venture capital). However, the equity or asset risk-taking criterion might exclude many worthy candidates who risked time, energy (sweat equity), and perhaps career or family tranquility to organize a venture. At a minimum the definition should include those who have a share in the outcome of a venture whose magnitude is unknowable from the start.

A category of venture organizers who contribute time, skills, and energy in exchange for a share of hoped-for equity and earning gains rather than a fixed salary or fee would allow us to include the ex-division manager, for example, who acquires the unwanted subsidiary of the parent company through a leveraged buy-out financed by others. It certainly allows us to include those who become part of the entrepreneurial teams that we find in the high-technology and high-growth fields even though some contribute skills and sweat rather than seed capital.

The "gamesmen" described by Michael MacCoby (1976) build teams, push projects, and shoot craps with a slice of the corporate cash flow. The "venture managers" found in the new ventures divisions of companies like 3M and Monsanto, whether because they desire to be trendy or because they feel nostalgia for the earlier, less routinized days of the firm's birth, have also caught the entrepreneurial bug. These and others like them may all have an entrepreneurial temperament or flair and may validly, in Shapero's terms, be involved in "entrepreneurial events" (Copulsky and McNulty 1974). But should they be included in the genus "entrepreneur"? Perhaps they should be, if they have more than a token stake in the financial outcome. If they do not, they are creative managers, "water walkers," men and women on a "fast track," but managers still for all of that.

Those who get to the top in most large corporations must have, besides demonstrated competence in technical specializations, interpersonal skills of considerable magnitude. Such skills allow them to build up "assets" in the form of social networks, a phenomenon noted by Rosabeth Kanter in her mid-1970s study of a large industrial supply corporation. Kanter notes that the ability to take risks and be venturesome depends crucially on the organizational network supports available to managers. Indeed, it has been suggested by Edward Banfield (1964), a political scientist, that the most successful politicians in a political machine are those like the late Mayor Daley of Chicago, who knew how to accumulate an enormous reserve of obligations and personal favors. Large corporations operate in many respects like political machines. Entrepreneurs are too often better at doing things than working their social networks for all the interpersonal advantages the traffic will bear. Not surprisingly, they tend to find bureaucratic environments not at all to their taste. As Shapero and others have rightly noted, it is often precisely these irritants of organizational routine, reduced autonomy, and hand-pumping that lead the black sheep out of the fold to go their own way.

Innovation, as another essential property in the definition, poses some difficulties. For Professor Shapero the entrepreneurial event is by definition the innovation. Merely starting something becomes an innovation if the other criteria Shapero lists are also present. But why should the decision to set up a street stall and hawk goods be considered innovative? Again, without innovativeness or novelty as part of the working definition of entrepreneurship, the distinction between run-of-the-mill small business and new venture organization is difficult to justify. But even if academics choose to disregard it, the writers in the business press will doubtless wish to continue to discriminate between people who open nondescript dry cleaning establishments, sandwich shops, and gas stations and those who market Pet Rocks, plastic skis, hula-hoops, and micro-processors.

Since innovativeness varies on a continuum without clear-cut partitions, there may well be difficulties of application. All new businesses have something different about them. When is that something enough of a something to call it "entrepreneurial"? Surely Ray Kroc's pioneering changes in the short order food industry qualify as innovation by any standard. As Ted Levitt pointed out in a 1972 *Harvard Business Review* article, Kroc applied the techniques of the assembly line to the production of McDonald's hamburgers and the servicing of customers, creating an organizational revolution in fast food service that was to be copied by many others. This was not a striking technological innovation but a "novel combination" according to Schumpeter's definition, and clearly different from the case of the business person who increases volume in a luncheonette merely by creating a new sandwich. Call both "entrepreneurial events" if you like, but courses in new venture start-ups are more likely to focus on the example of Kroc and of others who broke new ground in their industries in dramatic and visible ways.

Updating Schumpeter

Schumpeter's concept of entrepreneurship was certainly flexible enough to allow for less dramatic cases, even though his prototype appears to have been the nineteenth-century industrial magnate rather than the less visible dry goods dealers who created the first emporiums with attractive merchandising, sarsaparilla counters, and a strict fixed price policy to make shopping a more dignified experience. Schumpeter gave more emphasis to the dramatic innovations that fostered long-run economic growth.

Schumpeter also acknowledged that entrepreneurs remain entrepreneurs while they are organizing new ventures and become owner-managers when the business gets going. New innovations and adaptations of earlier ones can return the owner-manager to his earlier entrepreneurial role. Thus Schumpeter's definition does approach Shapero's concept of the entrepreneurial event, but it still remains more restricted because Schumpeter insisted on innovation (which requires more than just starting something that hadn't physically existed before) and on an incalculable profit coupon which it is privilege of the successful entrepreneur to clip.

It is the last item, in particular, that is restrictive and requires that entrepreneurship remain anchored in the private sector of free enterprise economies. Assuredly in a society such as the Soviet Union there are many "expediters" who function as entrepreneurs and who are tolerated because they can aggregate resources in the face of bureaucratic rigidity. They would not earn "profit" in the conventional sense but would receive under-the-table kickbacks, in-kind payments, and privileges that would constitute their qualification for our pantheon.

When we move from the issue of who or what is entrepreneurial to the problem of why some people are more likely than others to seek independence, take initiative, accept risk, and engage in innovation, we realize immediately that our answer to this set of issues relates crucially to the concept of entrepreneurship we accept. If the concept is too broad and inclusive, one must begin to wonder if the hunt for causal factors has much meaning; surely very large numbers of people in a society such as our own must have engaged in "entrepreneurial" events at one point or another in their lives. Personality, parental occupation, social background, and other correlates of entrepreneurs have been studied largely in relation to independent, private-sector business persons. Those correlations would probably weaken if the concept of entrepreneur were to include civil servants, Soviet factory managers, or civic organizers.

Professor Shapero's chapter is useful in alerting students of entrepreneurship to the "accidental" nature of much venturing. Unpredictable contingencies can lead many into entrepreneurship who might otherwise have pursued more secure and established careers. Although much of the literature has tended to assume that certain personality types are inevitably "pulled" toward autonomous roles as venturers, Professor Shapero notes that the negative aspects of an individual's life situation can be equally if not more important. Displacement due to religious and political oppression or the loss of a job may be as important as the desire for high income or independence. One might assume that "accidental" entrepreneurs who owe their roles largely to displacement factors would represent a broader range of individual factors than would the "inevitable" entrepreneurs posited in other parts of the literature.

Artifactual entrepreneurs

The sociology of entrepreneurship should also consider the fact that entrepreneurship is becoming professionalized. There is now a discipline of entrepreneurship thanks to the many new centers, institutes, and graduate training programs. While the new professional entrepreneur represents a minuscule percentage of American entrepreneurs, and is likely to do so for decades, his emerging presence on the scene may require some adjustments of established explanatory models. MBA students now may perceive an option that, in the absence of a professional program, might not have occurred to them. Undergraduates find increasing numbers of entrepreneurship training seminars available at their colleges and universities. Certainly a sociology of entrepreneurship will want to examine the new professionally trained entrepreneurs and compare them with those who launch ventures without formal business educations. Are they equally successful? Considering the fact that many of their students self-select, do professional training programs in new venture start-ups really make much of a difference?

Whereas the "accidental" entrepreneur falls into a venture because of contingencies to some extent beyond his control, the professionally trained entrepreneur may have made a self-conscious decision to assume this role even before knowing what his business will be. This suggests yet another species of the genus Heffalump: the "artifactual entrepreneur." The artifactual entrepreneur adopts a self-conscious identification with the role even before putting the venture to the test in the marketplace.

How many Heffalumps?

How many species of the genus Heffalump are there? Doubtless many, very many under a broader definition than the Schumpeterian one. The "entrepreneurship" of many of India's business families is to know government officials and their regulations and to shrewdly work around bureaucratic and political obstacles. The Madras textile manufacturer who, when informed his firm was too big to qualify for government clothing orders intended for smaller firms, painted lines around each of his looms and turned each into a separate firm was an eminent example. The "entrepreneurship" of many commercial traders and speculators consists of discerning arbitrage possibilities before their competitors and developing quasi-monopolistic channels of information to this end. Richard Cantillon coined "entrepreneur" in the eighteenth century for just such traders (Kilby 1971). And high-technology venturers who scoop the market possibilities with technological breakthroughs require considerably more financial sophistication than trading entrepreneurs and most small business people usually possess.

In summary, if it takes initiative, assumes considerable autonomy in the organization and management of the resources, shares in the asset risk, shares in an uncertain monetary profit, and innovates in more than a marginal way, it is probably a Heffalump of the kind found ranging over the United States and Western Europe. Granted, Schumpeter's concept may have been too restrictive, and it is clearly less applicable today to both centrally planned and less developed economies where entrepreneurs are clearly present. On the other hand, the current trend to accept a very broad definition may take the subject matter too far beyond its original anchorage in business enterprise in free market economies, which is after all the place where the research studies claim to find the Heffalump foraging for nutrients most of the time.

References

BANFIELD, EDWARD C., *Political Influence.* New York: Free Press, 1964.

COLE, ARTHUR, "An Approach to the Study of Entrepreneurship," *Exploration in Enterprise,* ed. Hugh G. J. Aiken, Cambridge: Harvard University, 1965.

COPULSKY, WILLIAM, and MCNULTY, H. W., *Entrepreneurship and the Corporation.* New York: AMACOM, 1974.

KANTER, ROSABETH MOSS, *Men and Women of the Corporation.* New York: Basic Books, 1977.

KILBY, PETER, ed., *Entrepreneurship and Economic Development.* New York: Free Press, 1971.

LEVITT, THEODORE, "Production-Line Approach to Service," *Harvard Business Review,* September-October 1972.

MCCLELLAND, DAVID C., and WINTER, DAVID G., *Motivating Economic Achievement.* New York: The Free Press, 1969.

MACCOBY, MICHAEL, *The Gamesman.* New York: Simon & Schuster, 1976.

SCHUMPETER, JOSEPH A., *Capitalism, Socialism and Democracy.* New York: Harper and Brothers, 1950.

SCHUMPETER, JOSEPH A., *The Theory of Economic Development.* New York: Oxford University, 1961.

Section Two

Entrepreneurial Technology

Entrepreneurship, broadly defined, is the act of organizing, managing, and assuming the risks of a business enterprise. In the United States, approximately 8400 new firms are started each week. While not all of these new firms are entrepreneurial ventures, many possess at least some of the aspects of entrepreneurship. In this section, the direction is away from the more esoteric aspects of the entrepreneur to consideration of those factors which affect the entrepreneur on an almost daily basis.

As part of the decision-making process leading to the creation of a new venture, the would-be entrepreneur may read books and articles that describe, in layman's terms, the many successes of other entrepreneurs (and less frequently their failures), their problems with new ventures, and all the mechanics of starting ventures. Included in the literature will be "how to" articles on every aspect ranging from how to obtain a franchise to how to make a million dollars. The would-be entrepreneur will also read about entrepreneurs who started small businesses and those who were involved in spin-offs from large corporations. At this stage it may be unclear whether an entrepreneur is one who starts a business, runs a small business, or serves as a corporate executive.

This section begins with a review of the nonacademic literature in this field and its recent proliferation. Next the methodologies of new venture creation and risk capital are considered. Then the entrepreneurship–small business interface and finally internal corporate entrepreneurial activities are examined.

The would-be entrepreneur may ask, "How can people be entrepreneurs if they do not assume the risk of a business enterprise?" There are several risks involved in entrepreneurship. In addition to the obvious financial risks, there are the psychological and social risks of failure. There are also the risks that the family cannot adjust to the time pressures or the lower initial income often associated with new ventures.

McClung and Constantin begin their chapter, "Nonacademic Literature on Entrepreneurship: An Evaluation," with a search of the literature over roughly a ten-year period. The objective of the chapter is to determine if the literature adequately covers the topical areas most important to researchers. In periodicals ranging from The American Legion Magazine *to* U.S. News and World Report, *the paucity of the literature and the almost total lack of topical coverage disclosed many opportunities for research and journalistic coverage. It is interesting to note that during the ten years in which the articles appeared, the number of academic institutions with courses in entrepreneurship or small business grew from eight to almost 2000. Clearly, the importance of entrepreneurship in colleges and universities is in a rapid growth stage.*

Mancuso, in the commentary, discusses the possible misrepresentations associated with the topical classification of the articles. He further discusses the impact of three recent periodicals directly related to entrepreneurship, namely: Venture, Inc., *and* In Business. *These periodicals are expected to provide the entrepreneur with a higher quality of journalistic reporting on a variety of topics.*

Timmons begins the chapter on "New Venture Creation: Models and Methodologies" with the frequently asked question: "Is there more art than science in the creation of a new enterprise?" In this light he considers a number of approaches to new venture creation. Disagreements may occur about whether entrepreneurs are born or made, whether psychological characteristics or social dimensions are more important, and whether innovation is really the central issue in entrepreneurship. As Timmons points out, while the approaches differ, they also share common threads.

The 1970s have produced a remarkable burst of interest in entrepreneurship and venture creation. New models have appeared and new methods are being evaluated. The 1980s are expected to bring a continued growth in interest accompanied by the development and testing of new methodologies. As more is discovered about what is and is not learnable, then we can refine our understanding of venture creation.

Kierulff's discussion of the chapter begins with the Chinese proverb, "To open a business, very easy. To keep it open, very difficult." Accordingly, he takes issue with the broad-based, esoteric discussions which permeate much of the study of new venture creation. While some generalization can and must be done, enough data must be catalogued before patterns can emerge. The study of effective entrepreneurial methods would be valuable not only to teachers but to entrepreneurs now practicing their trade. Kierulff ends with the thought that it is time for academicians to move from watching a ray of sunlight coming through a window to actually feeling the heat of the rays.

Cooper's chapter on the "Entrepreneurship–Small Business Interface" introduces the process by which an entrepreneur moves from the general desire to start a new venture to owning and managing an established firm. The succession of challenges in achieving this step and the problems associated with growth are also discussed. The chapter focuses on what happens to the new ventures after they have been created: (1) To what extent are the new ventures successful? (2) What factors, known at the time of starting the new venture, contribute to success, and what factors contribute to failure? (3) How does the venture survive and grow, and what are the problems to be solved in each stage?

Longenecker points out that an operating small business is an end product, or at least an intermediate stage, through which inferences can be made about the entrepreneurial process. The data normally cited with regard to success or failure of the small business are derived from the Dun and Bradstreet Failure Record. Many people have questioned the validity and accuracy of this data on the basis of the way it is gathered. Though many authors have expressed a need for longitudinal studies, only six such studies have been reported, and only two of them were completed since 1964. Four of the studies were in manufacturing operations which bias the results. There is definitely a need for a comprehensive data base from which more definitive and statistically significant studies about the entrepreneurship–small business interface can be made.

Schollhammer's chapter on "Internal Corporate Entrepreneurship" broadens the concept to include entrepreneurial strategies in large business organizations. Following Cole's perspective, entrepreneurship can be viewed as a combination of properties that characterize individuals as members of an organization. Internal entrepreneurship expresses itself in a variety of modes or strategies that firms adopt in the pursuit of technological and organizational innovation, competitive advantage, market standing, and profitability. Five internal corporate entrepreneurial strategies are examined: administrative, opportunistic, imitative, acquisitive, and incubative. The impact of the organizational climate on internal corporate entrepreneurship is also explored.

Shils feels that too much time is spent on definitions and too little time on the real aspects of internal corporate entrepreneurship. He points out that internal corporate entrepreneurship depends upon the design and structure of the organization, its general objectives, and the corporate environment. The environment can either support creativity or stifle it. The environment which fosters entrepreneurship is one in which the earnings opportunities enable internal managers to operate as though they were autonomous owners.

chapter vi

Nonacademic literature on entrepreneurship: an evaluation

Jacquetta J. McClung

James A. Constantin

Overview

This chapter reports on a literature search in the broad area of entrepreneurship over roughly a ten-year period. That search disclosed 1296 articles in 359 periodicals, 330 books, and 226 miscellaneous publications for a total of 1852 items in 22 bibliographical categories. It lists by year the number of articles, books, and miscellaneous publications in each of the 22 categories. The objective was to determine which of the topics in this book are considered most important by researchers. The paucity of the literature and the almost total lack of topical coverage disclose many opportunities for academic research and journalistic coverage.

Scope of the search

This chapter is the result of a literature search that identified 1852 entries distributed by subject and by year as shown in Table 1. The authors make no claim to having read the articles. Most of the data was derived

Table 1 *Summary of types of publications (by year)*[a]

	1980 & Misc.[b]	1979	1978	1977	1976	1975	1974	1973	1972	1971	Before 1971	Total
Articles (359 periodicals)	2	232	139	142	117	86	39	73	65	56	345	1296
Books	1	3	10	11	13	18	16	32	20	48	158	330
Pamphlets, Miscellaneous Publications	NA	0	0	7	9	2	4	24	16	4	28	94
Dissertations & Theses	NA	NA	4	3	3	4	7	4	5	10	35	75
Symposiums, Presentations, & Research Institute Publications	NA	0	0	3	1	1	0	4	6	3	39	57
Total	3	235	153	166	143	111	66	137	112	121	605	1852

[a]See Appendix 1 for year and month of last entry.
[b]1—1980 book
2—Dummy used to make the books balance because we couldn't always locate minor errors in tabulation and/or counting

through a series of indexes. The 359 periodicals ranged from *The American Legion Magazine* to *Working Woman* and included *The American Journal of Sociology* and *U.S. News and World Report*. *Inc.* and *Venture* began publication in 1979. The *Entrepreneur* was received too late to classify.

After discussing the nonacademic literature on entrepreneurship, we relate the articles discovered to the topics discussed in this book in order to emphasize gaps in the literature. We can then identify those areas where additional research appears to be needed and suggest directions for future journalist endeavors. Concerned about the anesthetic possibilities of the effort, the authors present something of a bibliographical travelogue and discuss some of the high spots of potential interest. Accordingly, they cast themselves in the role of prospector–tour guide–promoter. The audience is cast in the role of explorer–entrepreneur. The chapter is cast as a potential limited partnership whose members are making the trip to determine if the territory promises rewarding development.

Here is the scenario for the travelogue: First, in an aerial view of the point of departure, the authors describe how the task was accomplished and present tables with a suggestion that they be reviewed in more detail at a later date. Second, the charts are used to describe the nature and scope of the periodical literature, the books, and miscellaneous publications. Third, the territorial imperative of this book is compared with the spoor of the literature. The chapter concludes with a few impressions of the nonacademic literature.

Emerson once said that there is no force more powerful than that exerted by an idea whose time has come. Business schools, authors, researchers, and journalists have focused primarily on the final stage of the innovation–entrepreneurship–small business–big business continuum. They have acknowledged that small business is there, ignored the entrepreneurs, and nodded to innovation.

Entrepreneurship and its frequent companion, innovation, are ideas whose time has come, especially for the academic community. This book is a plateau which represents a decade of work by a number of authors. Almost exactly a decade ago, Vesper made his first study to determine what was being done in entrepreneurship and who was doing it. If memory serves, he found four schools with programs of some sort that were over two years old. He found 12 other schools with programs. In a 1974 follow-up, he found 59 schools with existing programs and 12 more with programs planned.

In roughly that same period, the 1852 items considered here were published. The analysis of data includes: (1) consideration of the time period involved; (2) the number of periodicals and the number of issues; (3) the importance of entrepreneurship to productivity improvement, significant innovations, job creation, and the development of big business; (4) the importance of small business to the total work force and GNP; (5) small business domination of wholesaling, retailing, and construction; and (6) the position of small business in the innovation–entrepreneurship–small business–big business continuum.

Methodology

This project began as a modest effort to update certain entries in the entrepreneurship bibliography published by The Center for Venture Management (1973). We used the bibliographical categories of CVM and added two additional categories: (1) Laws, Legislation, and Public Policy, and (2) Marketing for Small Business. Several indexes were used to bring the listings up-to-date. Appendix 1 contains a note on the dates of volumes used, which explains why certain listings (especially for 1979) are not complete. Table 1 shows the annual distribution of entries in each of several categories. All citations were coded for sorting by year into the CVM bibliographical categories.

The second step was to reduce the number of articles to manageable proportions. The 359 periodicals with 1296 articles were reduced to those which published at least five articles in the five-year period starting in 1975. That brought the list to 32 periodicals (8.9 percent of 359) with 597 articles (46.0 percent of 1296). Table 2 lists those periodicals, the number of articles published since 1975, the number published in the entire search period, and the number published each year. Of the 597 articles published in the entire period, 432 (72.4 percent) appeared in the past five years. These 432 articles represent 33.3 percent of the 1296 total and 60.3 percent of the 716 published since 1975 by all 359 periodicals.

The third step was to itemize the subject categories of the articles. This information appears in Table 2 for periodicals and Table 3 for books and miscellaneous publications.

The fourth step was to further refine the data for the five-year period 1975–1979.

Table 4, a source table for others, shows the number of articles published in each of the 22 bibliographical categories. In Table 5 the 22 bibliographical categories are ranked by the number of articles written in each; only the top ten periodicals appear. Out of 32 periodicals, eight accounting journals (25.0 percent) published 68 of the 432 articles (15.7 percent). Table 6 reflects that professional concentration.

The fifth step was to prepare a comparable table for books, dissertations and theses and cassettes, pamphlets, and symposia proceedings. (See Table 7.) The data on dissertations and theses is presented as a matter of interest though of course it is outside our category of nonacademic literature.

Table 2

Periodicals	1975–1979	Total	1979	1978	1977	1976	1975	1974	1973	1972	1971	Before 1971
Accountant	5	5	3	0	1	1	0	0	0	0	0	0
Advertising Age	5	6	5	0	0	0	0	0	0	1	0	0
Antitrust Law & Economic Review	5	5	1	3	1	0	0	0	0	0	0	0
Engineer	5	5	0	0	0	3	2	0	0	0	0	0
International Management	5	6	4	0	0	0	1	0	0	0	0	1
Journal of Contemporary Business	5	6	0	0	0	5	0	0	0	0	0	1
Long Range Planning	5	6	2	1	0	0	2	1	0	0	0	0
National Public Accountant	5	7	0	0	2	3	0	1	0	0	1	0
Organic Gardening & Farming	5	5	0	1	1	1	2	0	0	0	0	0
Ebony	6	7	1	0	4	0	1	0	1	0	0	0
Electronic News	6	7	3	3	0	0	0	0	0	0	0	1
Money	6	7	0	5	1	0	0	0	1	0	0	0
Newsweek	6	10	2	1	0	1	2	1	0	0	0	3
Office	6	6	3	3	0	0	0	0	0	0	0	0
Woman CPA	6	12	0	0	1	3	2	5	1	0	0	0
Accountancy	7	7	2	2	3	0	0	0	0	0	0	0
Changing Times	7	13	1	1	1	2	2	2	0	1	2	1
Mini-Micro System	7	7	7	0	0	0	0	0	0	0	0	0
Inc.	8	8	8				Publication began April, 1979.					
Management Accounting (NAA)	8	9	1	0	2	1	4	0	0	1	0	0
CA Magazine (Chartered Accountant)	9	9	2	1	2	3	1	0	0	0	0	0
Harvard Business Review	12	42	3	0	1	2	6	1	0	1	2	26
CPA Journal	13	13	1	3	4	3	2	0	0	0	0	0
Forbes	15	35	3	7	2	1	2	3	0	0	1	16
Journal of Accountancy	15	15	0	3	6	4	2	0	0	0	0	0
U.S. News & World Report	15	24	1	1	6	6	1	3	1	1	1	3
Fortune	18	31	5	5	4	1	3	1	4	1	2	5
Business Week	32	62	11	5	5	3	8	0	3	6	4	17
Nation's Business	34	51	14	10	3	5	2	0	1	7	7	2
Venture	45	45	45				Publication began April, 1979.					
Black Enterprise	51	51	21	20	5	5	Indexing began August, 1979.					
Journal of Small Business Management	55	75	11	13	17	7	7	3	3	6	1	7
32 Total	432	597	160	88	72	60	52	21	15	25	21	83

See Appendix 1 for year and month of last entry.

Table 3 *Number of articles in bibliographical categories (by year)*[a]

Bibliographical categories	1975–1979	Total	1979	1978	1977	1976	1975	1974	1973	1972	1971	Before 1971
The Entrepreneur	64	79	35	16	4	3	6	2	0	0	1	12
The Female Entrepreneur	8	8	2	1	3	1	1	0	0	0	0	0
The Minority Entrepreneur	59	72	24	19	7	7	2	0	2	3	2	6
Entrepreneurship in Other Cultures	1	4	1	0	0	0	0	0	0	1	0	2
Biographical	7	21	3	0	1	2	1	0	4	2	1	7
Historical	0	1	0	0	0	0	0	0	0	0	0	1
Psychological	1	6	1	0	0	0	0	0	0	0	0	5
Sociological	0	0	0	0	0	0	0	0	0	0	0	0
Small Business Start-up	21	30	5	2	6	4	4	1	0	2	4	2
Small Business Management	62	82	24	15	5	10	8	8	1	2	2	7
Small Business Overview	19	25	7	4	3	5	0	0	0	0	1	5
Financial	42	62	7	8	12	6	9	3	2	4	4	7
Venture Capital	25	50	16	2	4	2	1	1	4	3	2	15
Business Terminations or Failures	2	3	0	0	1	0	1	0	0	0	0	1
Counseling Small Business	9	13	4	1	0	4	0	0	0	2	0	2
Innvation, Technology, R & D	3	6	1	0	0	1	1	0	0	0	0	3
Economic Development	2	2	0	0	2	0	0	0	0	0	0	0
Management Concepts	7	11	4	0	0	1	2	0	0	0	0	4
Small Business Administration	9	12	4	1	1	1	2	0	0	0	2	1
Schools, Continuing Programs	3	3	0	0	2	1	0	0	0	0	0	0
Laws, Legislation, Public Policy	51	54	15	13	12	6	5	1	1	0	1	0
Marketing for Small Business	37	53	7	6	9	6	9	5	1	6	1	3
Total	432	597	160	88	72	60	52	21	15	25	21	83
Percent of 597 articles	72.4	100.0	26.8	14.7	12.1	10.1	8.7	3.5	2.5	4.2	3.5	13.9
Cumulative Percent	72.4	100.0	26.8	41.5	53.6	63.7	72.4	75.9	78.4	82.6	86.1	100.0

[a]See Appendix 1 for year and month of last entry.

Table 3 (cont.) *Number of books and miscellaneous publications in bibliographical categories (1975–1979 and entire period)*[a]

		Books		Miscellaneous publications	
	Category	1975–1979	Total	1975–1979	Total
The Entrepreneur	1	3	18	2	9
The Female Entrepreneur	2	3	4	0	0
The Minority Entrepreneur	3	0	13	0	4
Entrepreneurship in Other Cultures	4	7	41	1	31
Biographical	5	0	7	0	0
Historical	6	0	17	0	0
Psychological	7	0	11	0	0
Sociological	8	0	4	0	0
Small Business Start-up	9	7	30	0	5
Small Business Management	10	20	55	4	13
Small Business Overview	11	0	13	3	5
Financial	12	7	24	2	13
Venture Capital	13	1	15	0	9
Business Terminations or Failures	14	0	5	1	8
Counseling Small Business	15	1	3	0	0
Innovation, Technology, R&D	16	1	28	1	17
Economic Development	17	0	8	0	5
Management Concepts	18	0	21	0	1
Small Business Administration	19	0	1	1	1
Schools, Programs, Miscellaneous	20	1	1	0	5
Laws, Legislation, Public Policy	21	1	2	0	0
Marketing for Small Business	22	4	9	8	25
Totals		56	330	23	151

[a]See Appendix 1 for year and month of last entry.

Table 4 *What periodicals published what kinds of articles (1975–1979)[a] bibliographical category (codes)*

Periodicals	1	2	3	4	5	6	7	8	9	10	11	12	13	14	15	16	17	18	19	20	21	22	Total
Accountant	0	0	0	0	0	0	0	0	0	0	2	2	0	0	0	0	0	0	0	0	1	0	5
Advertising Age	1	0	1	0	0	0	0	0	0	0	0	0	0	0	0	0	0	0	0	0	0	3	5
Antitrust Law & Economic Review	3	0	0	0	0	0	0	0	0	0	1	0	0	0	0	0	0	0	0	0	1	0	5
Engineer	0	0	4	0	0	0	0	0	0	0	0	0	0	0	0	0	0	0	0	0	1	0	5
International Management	2	0	0	1	1	0	1	0	0	0	0	0	0	0	0	0	0	0	0	0	0	0	5
Journal of Contemporary Business	0	1	0	0	0	0	0	0	0	0	1	0	0	0	0	1	0	1	0	0	0	1	5
Long Range Planning	0	0	0	0	0	0	0	0	0	3	0	1	0	0	0	0	0	1	0	0	0	0	5
National Public Accountant	0	0	0	0	0	0	0	0	0	0	2	0	0	0	0	0	0	0	0	1	2	0	5
Organic Gardening & Farming	1	0	0	0	0	0	0	0	4	0	0	0	0	0	0	0	0	0	0	0	0	0	5
Ebony	0	2	4	0	0	0	0	0	0	0	0	0	0	0	0	0	0	0	0	0	0	0	6
Electronic News	0	0	0	0	0	0	0	0	0	2	0	0	0	0	0	0	0	0	1	0	3	0	6
Money	3	0	0	0	0	0	0	0	1	1	0	0	1	0	0	0	0	0	0	0	0	0	6
Newsweek	1	0	0	0	0	0	0	0	0	0	0	2	1	0	1	0	0	0	0	0	1	0	6
Office	0	0	0	0	0	0	0	0	0	6	0	0	0	0	0	0	0	0	0	0	0	0	6
Woman CPA	0	0	0	0	0	0	0	0	0	2	0	2	0	0	1	0	0	0	0	0	0	1	6
Accountancy	1	0	0	0	0	0	0	0	0	2	1	2	0	1	0	0	0	0	0	0	0	0	7
Changing Times	1	1	0	0	0	0	0	0	4	1	0	0	0	0	0	0	0	0	0	0	0	0	7
Mini-Micro Systems	0	0	0	0	0	0	0	0	0	7	0	0	0	0	0	0	0	0	0	0	0	0	7
Inc.	2	0	0	0	0	0	0	0	0	1	1	1	0	0	0	0	0	3	0	0	0	0	8
Management Accounting (NAA)	0	0	0	0	0	0	0	0	0	5	0	3	0	0	0	0	0	0	0	0	0	0	8

CA Magazine (Chartered Accountant)	0	0	0	0	0	0	0	0	0	4	0	1	1	0	1	0	0	0	1	0	1	0	9
Harvard Business Review	0	0	1	0	0	0	0	0	0	3	1	2	0	0	0	0	0	1	0	0	0	4	12
CPA Journal	0	0	0	0	0	0	0	0	0	3	0	5	1	1	1	0	0	0	0	0	2	0	13
Forbes	5	0	0	0	1	0	0	0	1	2	0	1	4	0	0	0	0	0	1	0	0	0	15
Journal of Accountancy	0	0	0	0	0	0	0	0	1	4	0	2	1	0	0	0	0	0	0	0	7	0	15
U.S. News & World Report	1	1	1	0	0	0	0	0	3	3	2	2	0	0	0	0	0	0	1	0	0	1	15
Fortune	10	0	0	0	1	0	0	0	2	1	0	0	0	0	0	0	0	0	0	0	4	0	18
Business Week	8	0	4	0	1	0	0	0	0	1	1	3	2	0	0	1	0	0	2	0	4	5	32
Nation's Business	5	3	1	0	0	0	0	0	0	4	7	1	3	0	1	0	0	0	2	0	6	1	34
Venture	17	0	1	0	3	0	0	0	5	0	0	1	10	0	1	1	0	0	1	0	4	1	45
Black Enterprise	0	0	41	0	0	0	0	0	0	0	0	1	0	0	0	0	0	0	0	0	8	1	51
Journal of Small Business Management	3	0	1	0	0	0	0	0	0	7	0	10	1	0	3	0	2	1	0	2	6	19	55
32 Total	64	8	59	1	7	0	1	0	21	62	19	42	25	2	9	3	2	7	9	3	51	37	432

[a]See Appendix 1 for year and month of last entry.

Table 5 Subjects of articles of top ten periodicals[a]

rank	Bibliographical Categories	Journal of Small Business Management	Black Enterprise	Venture	Nation's Business	Business Week
1	Small Business Management	7	0	0	4	1
2	The Minority Entrepreneur	1	41	1	1	4
2	The Entrepreneur	3	0	17	4	8
3	Laws, Legislation, Public Policy	6	8	4	5	4
4	Financial	10	1	1	1	3
5	Marketing for Small Business	19	1	1	1	5
6	Venture Capital	1	0	10	3	2
7	Small Business Start-up	0	0	5	0	0
7	Small Business Overview	0	0	0	9	1
8	The Female Entrepreneur	0	0	0	3	0
9	Counseling Small Business	3	0	1	1	0
9	Biographical	0	0	3	0	1
10	Small Business Administration	0	0	1	2	2
10	Management Concepts	1	0	0	0	0
11	Innovation, Technology, R&D	0	0	1	0	1
11	Schools, Continuing Programs	2	0	0	0	0
12	Business Terminations or Failures	0	0	0	0	0
12	Economic Development	2	0	0	0	0
13	Psychological	0	0	0	0	0
13	Enterpreneurs in Other Cultures	0	0	0	0	0
14	Historical	0	0	0	0	0
14	Sociological	0	0	0	0	0
	Total	55	51	45	34	32

[a]See Appendix 1 for year and month of last entry.

Fortune	U.S. News & World Report	Journal of Accountancy	Forbes	CPA Journal	Total No.	Total %
1	3	4	2	3	25	40.3
0	1	0	0	0	49	83.1
10	1	0	5	0	48	81.4
4	0	7	0	2	40	78.4
0	2	2	1	5	26	61.9
0	1	0	0	0	28	75.7
0	0	1	4	1	22	88.0
2	3	1	1	0	12	57.1
0	2	0	0	0	12	57.1
0	1	0	0	0	4	36.4
0	0	0	0	1	6	66.7
1	0	0	1	0	6	85.7
0	1	0	1	0	7	77.8
0	0	0	0	0	1	14.3
0	0	0	0	0	2	66.7
0	0	0	0	0	2	66.7
0	0	0	0	1	1	50.0
0	0	0	0	0	2	100.0
0	0	0	0	0	0	0
0	0	0	0	0	0	0
0	0	0	0	0	0	0
0	0	0	0	0	0	0
18	15	15	15	13	293	67.8

Table 6 *Subjects of articles in accounting periodicals (1975–1979)*[a]

	(Code)	*Journal of Accountancy*	*CPA Journal*	*CA Magazine*	*Management Accounting*
The Minority Entrepreneur	(3)	0	0	0	0
The Entrepreneur	(1)	0	0	0	0
Small Business Management	(10)	4	3	4	5
Laws, Legislation, Public Policy	(21)	7	2	1	0
Financial	(12)	2	5	1	3
Marketing for Small Business	(22)	0	0	0	0
Venture Capital	(13)	1	1	1	0
Start-up	(9)	1	0	0	0
Small Business Overview	(11)	0	0	0	0
The Female Entrepreneur	(2)	0	0	0	0
Counseling Small Business	(15)	0	1	1	0
Small Business Administration	(19)	0	0	1	0
Biographical	(5)	0	0	0	0
Management Concepts	(18)	0	0	0	0
Innovation, Technology, R&D	(16)	0	0	0	0
Schools, Continuing Programs	(20)	0	0	0	0
Business Terminations or Failures	(14)	0	1	0	0
Economic Development	(17)	0	0	0	0
Psychological	(7)	0	0	0	0
Entrepreneurs in Other Cultures	(4)	0	0	0	0
Historical	(6)	0	0	0	0
Sociological	(8)	0	0	0	0
Total, 1975–1979		15	13	9	8
Total before 1970–1974		0	0	0	1
Grand Total		15	13	9	9

[a]See Appendix 1 for year and month of last entry.

Accountancy	*Woman CPA*	*National Public Accountant*	*Accountant*	1975–1979 Total
0	0	0	0	0
1	0	0	0	1
2	2	0	0	20
0	0	2	1	13
2	2	0	2	17
0	1	0	0	1
0	0	0	0	3
0	0	0	0	1
1	0	2	2	5
0	0	0	0	0
0	1	0	0	3
0	0	0	0	1
0	0	0	0	0
0	0	0	0	0
0	0	0	0	0
0	0	1	0	1
1	0	0	0	2
0	0	0	0	0
0	0	0	0	0
0	0	0	0	0
0	0	0	0	0
0	0	0	0	0
7	6	5	5	68
0	6	2	0	9
7	12	7	5	77

Table 7 *Divisions of this book and the literature (1975–1979)*[a]

	Chapter topics
I. The Entrepreneur	
A. In General	———
B. Female	———
C. Minority	———
II. Foundations for Entrepreneurship	
A. Historical	1. Entrepreneurial History
1. Biographical	———
2. Living Entrepreneur	2. Living Entrepreneurs
B. Behavioral	
1. Psychological	4. Psychology of Entrepreneur
2. Sociological	5. Sociology of Entrepreneur
C. Environmental	6. Environment of Entrepreneur
D. Educational & Facilitating	13. Education for Entrepreneurs
1. Counseling	———
2. S.B.A.	———
3. Schools, Continuing Programs	———
III. Enterprise Development	
A. Venture Initiation	9. Venture Initiation
B. Financing	
1. Financial	———
2. Venture Capital	10. Venture Finance
C. Stages in Venture Development	11. Stages in Venture
D. Small Business Management	———
1. Management Concepts	———
2. Small Business Marketing	———
3. Laws, Public Policy	———
4. Small Business Overview	———
E. Terminations or Failures	11. Stages in Venture
F. Corporate Entrepreneurship	12. Corporate Entrepreneurs
IV. Results of Entrepreneurship	
A. Innovation, Technology	8. Innovation
B. Economic Development	7. Economic Development
V. Research Methodology	14. Research Methodology
TOTAL	

[a]See Appendix 1 for year and month of last entry.

	Number		
Bibliographic categories	Articles	Books	Dissertations & Theses
1. The Entrepreneur	64	3	1
2. The Female Entrepreneur	8	3	0
3. The Minority Entrepreneur	59	0	4
6. Historical	0	0	0
5. Biographical	7	0	0
———	0	0	0
7. Psychological	1	0	1
8. Sociological	0	0	0
4. Entrepreneur in Other Cultures	1	7	0
———	0	0	0
15. Counseling Small Business	9	1	2
19. Small Business Administration	9	0	0
20. Schools, Continuing Programs	3	1	1
9. Start-up	21	7	0
12. Financial	42	7	1
13. Venture Capital	25	1	0
———	0	0	0
10. Small Business Management	62	20	0
18. Management Concepts	7	0	0
22. Marketing for Small Business	37	4	0
21. Laws, Public Policy	51	1	2
11. Small Business Overview	19	0	0
14. Termination or Failures	2	0	0
———	0	0	0
16. Innovation	3	1	0
17. Economic Development	2	0	2
———	0	0	0
	432	56	14

The literature

Periodicals

In the opinion of the authors, there are significant opportunities for periodicals in the field of entrepreneurship. No market studies, however, have been conducted to assess these opportunities. The search found 32 bibliographical periodicals that had published at least five articles in the five-year period between 1975 and 1979. Also, 432 articles were published in the five-year period, for an average of 2.7 articles for each periodical each year.

Table 5, presented earlier, lists the ten periodicals that published the highest number of targeted articles. Those periodicals published 293 articles in the five-year period, 5.9 articles per journal per year, or 0.29 per issue. Those are misleading averages, however, for *Black Enterprise* wasn't indexed until sometime in 1976, *Venture* didn't start publishing until the spring of 1979, and the *Journal of Small Business Management* is an academic journal. The seven remaining periodicals published only 142 articles—about the same as in the period from before 1970 through 1974. This translates to an average of 20.3 articles per periodical, 4.1 per periodical per year, and 0.15 per issue.

The search is undoubtedly incomplete, since not all articles are indexed. The categories are complete, however, including several "catch-all" categories such as "Small Business Overview," and "Management Concepts."

So far as is known by the authors, only *The Entrepreneur, Inc.,* and *Venture* have attempted to specialize in this area. *The Entrepreneur* analyzes opportunities for new businesses and provides a prolific source of emerging and established concepts. *Inc.* (The name, according to the publisher, reflects one of the most significant steps in building an enterprise—incorporation) began in response to the vain search of a smaller publishing house owner for articles about managing a small company. Its 2–6 page articles focus on the management aspects of small to mid-size companies. News, trends, legal developments, and ideas on small business supplement the seven to eight articles published monthly. *Venture* articles are sort of kissin' cousins to many *Forbes* articles. Eight to twelve articles from one to four pages long focus on news, developments, and entrepreneurs. These can help academics keep up-to-date and can provide insights on both success and failure situations.

Table 3 lists the topics covered for the entire period and for the five years 1975–1979. The bibliographical categories covered most frequently relate to the financial aspects of entrepreneurship (including "Venture Capital"), the entrepreneur in general, the minority entrepreneur in particular, small business management, laws and public policy, and marketing for small business. The top ten periodicals seen in Table 5 essentially follow in the same pattern. Other topics appear much less frequently.

Books and miscellaneous publications

Books and miscellaneous periodicals are classified in this section for two reasons: professional cowardice and professional uncertainty. No attempt was made to separate the books and miscellaneous publications into academic and nonacademic categories. Some of the books are clearly nonacademic but are useful to academics. For example, both the Albert (1977) and White (1977) books have been very valuable in class discussion as an orderly approach to discovery of opportunities. On the other hand, certain books could be labeled academic. If Mancuso's book (1978) had no other attraction, his discussion of the business plan and the sample plans that appear in the Appendix would make it worthwhile. Both academics and nonacademics have much to learn from Schollhammer and Kuriloff's (1979) distinction between entrepreneurial and managerial aspects.

Then there are the inspirationals and the potboilers, the analytical and the superficial, whose authors will remain nameless. Suffice it to say that in potboiler authorship equality may at last be coming to entrepreneurship; sex discrimination in the superficial may be moribund. Commissioner Ewald B. Nyquist of the New York State Education Department said, "Equality is not when a female Einstein gets promoted to assistant professor; equality is where a female schlemiel moves ahead as fast as a male schlemiel." Perhaps these authors, male and female, and their books serve some useful function—they make it possible for people like us to look virtuously down our noses at them and say, "There, but for the grace of God, go I."

The books and miscellaneous publications and the bibliographical categories assigned to them are presented in the second part of Table 3. Here is where professional uncertainty enters. Only 56 books and 18 miscellaneous publications were found in the 1975–1979 period; the coverage may be incomplete. Books were assigned to only 12 of 22 categories, the largest of which was "Small Business Management." The 18 miscellaneous publications (pamphlets, proceedings, cassettes) were concentrated in "Marketing for Small Business" (8), "Small Business Management" (4), and "Small Business Overview" (3). There may be some arbitrariness in these category assignments.

Divisions of this book and the literature

Coverage

The research and writing of college professors are typically—and properly—on the cutting edge of the field, and multiple-author surveys typically reflect those exploratory and pioneering efforts. In that light the designers of this book did their work well, for there is almost no relationship between the topics covered here and those covered in the nonacademic periodicals.

Book topics and bibliographical categories have been distilled into an outline that appears in Table 7. Of 13 chapter topics, only six articles on nine of these topics were considered. (Two topics were represented by two articles, two by one article, and four by none.) Two of the topics, "Venture Initiation" and "Venture Finance," were represented by 21 and 25 articles respectively. "Education for Entrepreneurship" was the subject of 21 articles.

One task of journalists is to ferret out the new and to detect development which is of potential interest to their readers. In that sense their work is similar to the efforts of this chapter. Also, there is or should be something of a symbiotic relationship between professors and journalists, since one function of the latter is to popularize and present the developments of the former to appropriate publics. The paucity of literature on the subjects of this book should present both groups with many varied opportunities.

Perhaps one explanation of this paucity is the lack of academic and public interest in the innovator–entrepreneur–small business continuum until that continuum stretches out to embrace big business. Some straws in the wind now indicate that entrepreneurship is a subject whose time has come for academics, journalists, and their respective publics. Among these signs are: (1) such nonacademic periodicals as *Black Enterprise, The Entrepreneur, Inc.*, and *Venture*; (2) the number of professors, academic programs, and new Ph.D.s with active interests in the area; and (3) the Innovation Centers, bills pending in Congress, and the White House Conference.

Where are the gaps?

The simplest way to identify the gaps is to point to the topics covered in this book and the bibliographical categories as shown in Table 7. Once again, caution must be considered in the assignment of articles and books to certain bibliographical categories. Some articles could have been classified differently.

The gaps in the literature are viewed as directions for future research, in a topical sense and in broad terms. The most significant gaps are in the categories dealing with innovation, economic development, and terminations, including failures.

The authors are concerned with the literature gap in three aspects of innovation. First, innovation usually connotes new products. These in turn imply increased productivity from a new machine, new jobs from a new concept, or increased customer satisfaction from a new product that performs an old function better. Second, innovation may include adaptation of an existing product to a new use such as adaptation of materials handling devices for use in trucks and truck terminals. Third, innovation may result from managerial activities that introduce new concepts to an industry or transfer them to new markets.

There is also concern about the lack of published information on the role of entrepreneurship in economic development, especially the development of small towns and rural areas. If more were written on this, and if economic development officials could see the articles, they would have a much better understanding of this particular aspect of entrepreneurship. The potential job creation in those areas is probably much greater from entrepreneurship than from attracting expanding firms.

The third literature gap is in terminations, including failures. It is of very little help to academics, to entrepreneurial advisers, or to entrepreneurs to say that four out of five business failures are caused by bad management. It would be very helpful if more were written about the specific management practices that lead to failures and about their cure. Not all terminations are failures: Some are profitable liquidations; others merely terminate the founding entrepreneur's connection or cast the founder in new role. More information is needed about why and how businesses are terminated and what factors determine the selling price when a business is sold.

Although no articles were found on entrepreneurial history and living entrepreneurs, both topics should be of interest to academics because of lessons to be learned from history and the inspiration provided by live role models. Journalists should also be interested, if for no other reason than the Horatio Alger effect.

Venture management as a strategic management tool in corporations is about where strategic planning was in 1960. *Innovation* used to deal with this topic before it ceased publication. The concept holds so many advantages for corporate growth and managerial training that it deserves much more emphasis by the nonacademic press.

Urban renewal, ghetto entrepreneurship, and small town economic development should have spawned a rash of both academic and nonacademic articles on the "Sociology of Entrepreneurship." However, no articles relating to that particular topic were found.

While the authors are sensitive to the possibility of misclassification of articles, gaps would still exist if the articles were redistributed. The 32 periodicals are all that had at least five articles from 1975 to 1979, and the 32 had an average of 10.2 issues per year. The nonacademic press would not be interested in publishing articles on bibliography and research methodology. Thus, in the five-year period, if each published one article per issue on one of the 12 remaining topics, each periodical would cover each topic 4.25 times. All together, 1632 articles would have appeared, 3.8 times as many as the 432 actually located. Even an average of one article per year on each of the 12 topics would have left a significant gap in the innovation–entrepreneurship–small business portion of the continuum. Yet small business accounts for 4.3 percent of GNP and employs 58 percent of the work force. There should be demand for many more articles, in fact, for more periodicals that emphasize entrepreneurship. These periodicals could have unimaginative names such as *The Nation's Small Business, Small Business Week, Fortune, Jr.*, and the like.

Conclusions

1. So few academically oriented articles are published that little effort was required to separate them from the nonacademic. When the list was reduced from 329 periodicals to a more manageable number, all academic journals but one fell out. *The Journal of Small Business Management* was the only one that had published five articles in five years.

2. The coverage of the field is very skimpy. Even including a variety of bibliographic topics that would pick up "small business," only 432 articles in 32 publications were found.

3. While there are many uncovered areas for academics and journalists to publish in, the outlets for publication are few and far between. Even the university-based periodicals, such as *HBR*, *Business Horizons*, and *Business Topics*, that publish articles in the field are few in number.

4. There is a great opportunity for existing periodicals to expand their coverage of the field.

5. Although entrepreneurship is flourishing as an area for teaching, it is languishing as an area of research and publication. Perhaps one cure—or palliative—is for some of the newer magazines in this area to follow the approach taken by other business publications and cement the symbiotic relationship of business and academia. Several trade papers do two things to this end: (1) They encourage written articles and place academics on their board of editors or advisers; (2) they offer to assist with research projects and suggest areas for academic investigation.

6. Entrpreneurship is an idea whose time has come in the colleges. The recent introduction of at least two periodicals specializing in the field may indicate that its time has also come in the communications world.

7. Perhaps more nonacademic articles ought to be written by academics. When an entrepreneur begins to think of going public, he or she should be concerned about losing the entrepreneurial spirit. Caution is urged that academics do not lose the entrepreneurial spirit when writing nonacademic articles.

Appendix 1 *Indexes consulted*

Index	Index date	Ending article date	Latest (1) only (2) available	Description
Business Periodical Index	1970–January 1980	September 1979	(1)	*BPI* is a cumulative subject index to the English language

Index	Index date	Ending article date	Latest (1) only (2) available	Description
				periodicals relating to business. It is published by H.W. Wilson on a monthly basis (except August) with a bound cumulation through each year.
Accountants Index	1972-1977	December 1977	(2)	*AI* is a standard reference guide published by the American Institute of Certified Public Accountants as a service to the accounting profession. It is published in three quarterly issues plus a cumulative year-end volume covering all four quarters.
Reader's Guide to Periodical Literature	March 1970-December 1979	December 1979	(1)	The *Reader's Guide* is a cumulative author and subject index to periodicals of general interest published in the U.S. It is published eight times each year by H.W. Wilson Co.
Sociological Abstracts	1970-August 1979	1978-early 1979	(1)	*SA* is published five times a year by Sociological Abstracts. Each reference includes a short abstract.
Comprehensive Dissertation Index	1972-1978	December 1978	(1)	This annual index lists almost every dissertation accepted for academic doctoral degrees at North American educational institutions, and the 1972 cumulative index (1861-1972) includes some foreign universities.

commentary/elaboration

Commentary on nonacademic literature on entrepreneurship

Joseph Mancuso

Professors McClung and Constantin have reported on a significant effort to locate and categorize the nonacademic literature on entrepreneurship. Even with the indexes available, considering nearly 1900 entries is a yeoman's effort.

The data, however, may or may not represent the true picture in this area. The authors express concern, as do I, that classification of the data, especially when many of the articles could conceivably be classified in two or more categories, could result in erroneous conclusions. The authors make no claim to having read the material. This is understandable, given the volume, but implies that classifications were made by a number of different people whose perception of the categories may have been less definite than that of the authors. Hence the classification scheme must be considered with a certain amount of trepidation.

In general, there seems to be an underriding assumption, especially among academics, that nonacademic literature has not the quality or level of sophistication that academic literature possesses. Granted, journalists do not concern themselves with sophisticated methodologies and do not enhance the validity of their reporting by citing references. As pointed out by McClung and Constantin, much that is written falls into the inspirational, potboiler, and superficial categories. At the same time, there certainly exists among academicians a considerable amount of literature that could be assigned to similar realms.

Further, a substantial amount of data has not been indexed. While it is recognized that obtaining this information is a nearly impossible task, we must recognize the implications of the data that were not included in the study.

All studies must be reduced to manageable proportions. The authors have chosen to limit their study primarily to periodicals and books. This precludes the articles written in major newspapers such as the *Wall Street Journal*, the *New York Times*, and the *Chicago Tribune*. Most of these newspapers have assigned members of their staffs to areas such as small business and entrepreneurship. Many of their feature articles represent high quality journalism. The planned second front page of the *Wall Street Journal* will feature articles in these areas on a regularly scheduled basis.

The authors mention the creation of new nonacademic periodicals: *Black Enterprise, Inc.*, and *Venture.* Conspicuous by its absence is *In Business.* This periodical is unique in that it is directed toward and managed by the counter-culture forces of the 1960s. While a number of the people involved in this movement have been assimiliated into the big business environment, others have utilized, as an outlet for their creativity, the entrepreneurial path to business ownership.

Further, the authors mention the creation of Innovation Centers through the National Science Foundation, legislation pending in Congress, and the White House Conference. Another phenomenon that exemplifies interest in the area is the number of centers that have been established both within and outside of universities. These include the Center for Entrepreneurial Management in Boston, the Center for Venture Management in Milwaukee, and the Center for Private Enterprise and Entrepreneurship at Baylor University.

The authors identify a number of gaps in the nonacademic literature. It would be interesting to see the results of a similar study of academic literature. Would the same gaps exist? Do academicians consider other areas to be of more importance? If studies of both academic and nonacademic literature were combined, would there still be gaps in the literature? Such areas would be the prime candidates for further research, provided of course that topics are significant to begin with.

Finally, as the authors opine, much more needs to be written. However, too much of what has been written does nothing more than consume great volumes of paper and ink. While volume solicits attention, poor quality turns attention in the other direction. The entrepreneurial spirit is awake and growing among both practitioners and academicians. It is our charter to nourish this spirit through the academic development of would-be entrepreneurs into successful new venture creators.

References

ALBERT, KENNETH J., *How to Pick the Right Small Business Opportunity.* New York: McGraw-Hill, 1977.

MANCUSO, JOSEPH R., *How to Start, Finance, and Manage Your Own Small Business.* Englewood Cliffs, N.J.: Prentice-Hall, 1978.

SCHOLLHAMMER, HANS, and KURILOFF, ARTHUR H., *Entrepreneurship and Small Business Management.* New York: John Wiley, 1979.

SCHREIER, JAMES W., and KOMIVES, JOHN L., *The Entrepreneur and New Enterprise Formation: A Resource Guide.* Milwaukee: Center for Venture Management, 1973.

WHITE, RICHARD M., JR., *The Entrepreneur's Manual.* Radnor, Pa.: Chilton Books, 1977.

chapter vii

New venture creation: models and methodologies

Jeffry A. Timmons

Overview

Is there more art than science in the creation of new enterprises? What methods, models, and approaches have emerged from the academic community to foster venture initiation? This chapter discusses the works of over two dozen authors published during the 1970s. While the field is eclectic and fast-changing, the author concludes that: (1) There are several common threads among entrepreneurial methods; and (2) there is a major need for funding and support of research in the 1980s. In the following pages, I discuss a framework for exploring research issues and consider some future directions for research.

Start-up and entry methodologies

In the past decade a variety of entry methods and models have emerged from the academic literature on venture creation. What are some of these models? What ingredients are believed to be necessary for launching an enterprise? What variables seem to be central to these discussions of the entrepreneurial process? What assumptions seem to underlie the prevailing entry models? Are there any common denominators in the process? How much consensus exists among various academic writers?

The following summary of academic contributions from the past decade is not exhaustive. It is intended rather to describe the territory, providing some boundaries and benchmarks. The nonacademic literature is not included here, since it is dealt with in the preceding chapter.

In his latest book, Vesper (1979) builds on work presented earlier with Cooper and Hosmer (1977) which contends that five key ingredients are needed to build a new firm: (1) technical know-how; (2) product or service idea; (3) personal contacts; (4) physical resources, including capital; and (5) customer orders. In the most frequent start-up sequence according to Vesper, the entrepreneur: (1) acquires technical know-how; (2) crystallizes the venture idea to capitalize on past know-how; (3) develops connections; (4) obtains manpower and physical resources; and (5) obtains customer orders. While this is the most common sequence, Vesper points out that theoretically over 100 possible sequences exist (Vesper 1979).

In another recent book, Schollhammer and Kuriloff (1979) indicate that venture creation has a logic and a sequence of its own:

The plan of the book is keyed to a rational, step-by-step procedure in starting a new business.

They go on to present "four key requirements that make a broad base for the entrepreneurial adventure": (1) know yourself; (2) know the business you want to enter; (3) know marketing; and (4) know financial management." For example, the common characteristics of successful entrepreneurs may provide one with a basis for analyzing one's own entrepreneurial potential. Schollhammer and Kuriloff provide detailed lists and charts as a framework for analysis of the marketing, financial, and technical aspects of start-up and for the development of a prospectus. Implicit in the approach is the notion that the creative act of venture initiation is definable and rational enough to surrender to the demands of step-by-step analysis.

Another flow-chart model is espoused by Hollingsworth and Hand (1979). These authors contend that chances for success can be improved through an honest and thorough analysis of 16 key questions: Am I personally prepared to start my own business? Do my qualifications and characteristics suggest I have a high chance of success? Are my market survey and forecast of income consistent with my needs and expectations? The approach places great emphasis on the individual entrepreneur and the development of a business plan.

In the latest edition of their book on small business management, the oldest in the field, Baumback and Lawyer (1979) do not propose a model or sequence of steps. They do, however, indicate that the justification for a new enterprise is needed in the marketplace. Thus market analysis is central to the business plan. Further guidelines are not suggested by the authors.

Based upon his years of experience, Steinhoff (1978) proposes another method—the desired income approach—for planning a new business. Here the entrepreneur must follow 14 basic steps in a comprehensive business plan:

1. Determine the profit you want to earn and complete a pro forma income statement.
2. Survey the market to ascertain if the necessary sales volume can be generated.
3. Prepare a statement of assets to be used.
4. Prepare an opening day balance sheet.
5. Study the location.
6. Prepare a layout for the entire space.
7. Choose your legal form of organization.
8. Review all aspects of your merchandising plan.
9. Analyze your estimated expenses in terms of their fixed and variable nature.
10. Determine the firm's break-even point.
11. Establish credit policy.
12. Review the risks and how you plan to cope with them.
13. Establish a personnel policy at the outset.
14. Establish an adequate system of accounting records.

As one can see, Steinhoff's coverage of the mechanical steps involved in launching a new enterprise is relatively extensive.

In a recent revision of their text on small business management, Tate and his fellow authors (1978) state that the chapter on starting a new business has

The purpose . . . to aid you in successfully planning a new small business . . . [and] should enable you to move in an orderly fashion from the idea stage to making the new business a reality (Tate, Megginson, Scott, and Trueblood 1978).

They suggest nine steps to follow:

1. Develop a timetable.
2. Establish your business objectives.
3. Set up your organizational structure.
4. Determine your personnel requirements.
5. Determine your physical plant needs.
6. Plan your approach to the market.
7. Prepare your budget.
8. Locate sources of funds.
9. Implement your plans.

They do not specifically order these events but seem to advocate the sequence as presented.

In his discussion of starting a new enterprise, Naumes (1978) contends,

Virtually anyone can mechanically proceed through these steps to become the founder, owner, and manager of a new business . . . . All this is relatively easy, and can be inexpensive, but having the company operate, transact profitable business, and produce income is something else again—and much more difficult. (Hosmer, Cooper, and Vesper 1977)

Webster (1976) contends that an attractive venture typically has six stages: (1) a pre-venture stage in which the entrepreneur searches for, evaluates, and negotiates rights for a venture idea; (2) an organization stage in which the founders energetically set up operations; (3) financial jeopardy while prototypes are debugged and sales channels established; (4) the introduction of the product; (5) the rapacious act of the entrepreneur who gains control by squeezing out partners; and (6) an outcome stage, either survival or failure.

The core of a start-up, according to Pickle and Abrahamson (1976), is the feasibility study, which should include investigation of (1) location, (2) market, (3) physical facilities, (4) operations and personnel, and (5) projected financial information. The authors suggest some guidelines for subcategories, but suggest no particular sequence and examine no issues beyond the basic feasibility study.

Central to nearly all models of venture creation is the individual entrepreneur as catalyst, energizer, project champion, innovator, creator, and team leader. Osgood and Wetzel (1976) propose a novel and unconventional alternative to this pattern by replacing the lead entrepreneur with a team of business initiation specialists to improve on the random and inefficient nature of venture initiation. In their scheme, the 57 steps of Swain and Tucker, the 14 steps of Steinhoff, or Vesper's five key ingredients would be parceled out to different specialists—market researchers, technical and financial analysts—who would each complete a piece of the puzzle and additively construct the whole, a proposal. Venture capitalists would then fund the start-up, and the team of specialists would find an administrator to run the venture once it was stabilized (Osgood and Wetzel 1976). Apparently this approach has not yet been tried in real world conditions.

At the heart of the entrepreneurial act, according to Welsh (1974), is the venture plan:

The plan . . . is far more than the usual volume of prose, with some numbers, floating in over the transom. The entrepreneur's career path is part of it. Knowledge about the innate personality characteristics of the entrepreneur and his team rank equally with financial forecasts and market plans. The business concept is also ranked equally, but it is not just a good idea described well by an enthusiast. It is a mathematical abstraction calculable and measurable. The forecasts of intended activity involve the entrepreneur in learning as well as planning.

Welsh contends that a venture plan can be developed by applying four techniques: (1) emulating the career paths of successful entrepreneurs; (2) matching the composite personality profile of the management team with the profile of the successful entrepreneur; (3) analyzing the business concept and experience curve; and (4) producing detailed financial forecasts. Welsh observed presentations by 40 successful entrepreneurs at the Caruth Institute and concluded that there are seven sequential steps to success: the entrepreneur (1) conceives the idea; (2) gains product and market knowledge; (3) develops the business concept; (4) decides to forge ahead; (5) makes it work once; (6) perceives growth opportunity; and (7) expands nationwide. Clearly, Welsh gives central importance to the entrepreneur and the venture plan.

Using flow-charts with decision trees, Swain and Tucker (1973) detail three stages—concept, planning, and implementation—whose 57 specific steps provide a road map by which one should be able to start any business. These steps include such things as personal goals, strengths, and weaknesses; customer and market analysis; financial goals and requirements; production, personnel, and policy requirements. The authors also devote considerable attention to the make-up of entrepreneurs (personality, self-confidence, goal-orientation, risk-taking, thick skin, selective curiosity) and their management philosophies. The authors do not specify a sequence to these 57 steps beyond the implicit notion that one first conceptualizes, then plans, and finally implements.

Early notions of a systematic approach to venture creation were suggested by Timmons (1971), later developed with his colleagues (Timmons, Smollen, and Dingee 1977, 1981) and continue to be refined (Timmons 1979, 1980). This model builds on research with successful entrepreneurs and the investment criteria of venture capitalists. Four ingredients appear to characterize high-potential, growth-oriented ventures: (1) a talented lead entrepreneur with a balanced and compatible team; (2) a technically sound and marketable idea for a product or service; (3) thorough venture analysis leading to a complete business plan; and (4) appropriate equity and debt financing.

The approach places major emphasis on the characteristics, commitment, experience, and skills of the lead entrepreneur and his team and their fit with the requirements of the venture. Rather than insisting on some necessary sequence of steps, these authors suggest that the venture creation process, while susceptible to logic and careful thinking, also requires iterations and trial and error as the inherently uncertain and creative entrepreneurial event unfolds. An earlier proposal for a business opportunity idea bank rapidly emerged as the model's woolly mammoth—entrepreneurs were not particularly interested in over 5000 ideas of others.

Through 1979, this model has been applied in pragmatic form in the United States, Nova Scotia, and Sweden to spawn over 30 new firms requiring $4.5 million in venture capital. Their combined 1979 sales approached $90 million, and the ventures were valued at $70–80 million. Further application of this approach is now underway in England, Scotland, and Sweden.

Project ISEED— representative conclusions (ISEED 1975)

The proceedings of this international conference seem to support the variety of models and approaches just discussed. For example:

There is agreement that multiple (team) entrepreneurship holds great promise for increased success of new ventures. (p.33)

Entrepreneurs can be defined by their personalities, their background, and/or the functions they perform. (p. 34)

Venture capitalists differ substantially in their investing propensity and practices when responding to the same set of investment situations. [Their] investment decisions are based more on investor-centered and nonfinancial factors . . . rather than on financial factors. (Hoffman p. 204)

The major criteria for a venture capital proposal include: (1) management team, (2) financability of firm, (3) market, (4) return on investment, (5) business concept. (Liles p. 209)

There is no consensus on the appropriate tools for entrepreneurial training. [Training] should move away from academic training and be practically oriented. (p. 247)

Government programs exist to assist small business, . . . but little exists to assist in developing entrepreneurs and entrepreneurship. (p. 323)

A range of private, public, nonprofit, and university sources contribute numerous concepts, programs, and models for training which are also reported in the ISEED proceedings and dealt with in the Vesper chapter.

A synthesis

It appears that many of the approaches ISEED reports are quite similar to those discussed here; they share or contest various assumptions, emphases, and ingredients. Judging by the rapid growth of interest and action in venture creation during the 1970s and since ISEED, it is apparent that no simple consensus of opinion exists. But several themes and assumptions persist:

1. The entrepreneurial act, creative and innovative by nature, does have some logical, rational, even learnable components.

2. Some agreement seems to exist as to which of these components might constitute a more general model.

3. While no single model or sequence of events prevails, many writers argue that there are certain steps to follow and that some ought to precede others.

4. The process itself is complex, subtle, and interactive, requiring some trial and error.

5. Nuts and bolts survival skills—such as break-even and cash flow management—are learnable and significant in the start-up.

6. Rather elaborate checklists, procedural steps, and flow-charts can aid mastery of the mechanical steps in a start-up.

7. None of the procedures come with success guarantees; the approaches can improve one's chances for success, reduce failure, and make risks more understandable and manageable. (This caution would not characterize much of the nonacademic material).

Common threads and controversies

What emerges from this tentative effort to synthesize various methodologies in venture creation? Do any boundaries appear? Are any directions shared by several writers? Where do these approaches seem to be heading? In examining some twenty books and articles, I found substantial variations in content, assumptions, and emphasis, and little theory to anchor the variety of viewpoints. It would be presumptuous to assert that a consensus exists. Nonetheless, there appear to be some common threads to theories of new venture formation.

First, there appear to be recurrent ingredients in discussions of successful venture creation:

The importance of a talented, creative, committed lead entrepreneur who has realistic knowledge about his or her talents and the needs of the venture.

The importance of attracting and molding a team with complementary skills and talents if the venture is to grow beyond roughly $1 million in sales.

The importance of a triggering idea for a product or service.

The importance of a business plan to determine effective strategies, market potential, financial requirements, technical feasibility, and team needs.

The importance of outside contacts, a network of people, and resources.

The importance of appropriate financing.

Secondly, there appear to be some enduring issues concerning the nature of venture creation. These might be summarized as assumptions, explicit or implicit, as to whether the process is:

- iterative, interactive, inductive
- non-logical, non-rational, non-generalizable
- innate to the individual and non-learnable
- susceptible to logic, planning, rational analysis

- a sequence of steps based on replicable patterns
- a combination of all or some of the above characteristics.

Thirdly, and perhaps commanding the largest agreement, are the mechanical or procedural elements of start-up. They are the necessary, though insufficient, conditions for launching most new enterprises. Some of these mechanical elements have greater or lesser relevance to a given venture, but all ought to receive the entrepreneur's attention. The following is a reasonable summary, if not an exhaustive list, of the elements an entrepreneur must decide upon when launching a new venture:

- Legal structure of the organization
- Location
- Company name and logo
- Licenses and insurance
- Recordkeeping and bookkeeping methods
- Tax strategies
- Physical facilities and equipment
- Personnel policies
- Merchandising plan
- Cash flow projections
- Pro formas P/L & B/S
- Desired income and profit levels
- Breakeven analysis
- Credit policy
- Timetables
- Checklists

Controversies

In the absence of much theory and empirical evidence, a number of controversies about new venture creation endure:

1. Entrepreneurs are born; therefore it's presumptuous to teach approaches to success.

vs.

Entrepreneurial success has identifiable patterns of a cognitive nature and can be learned.

2. Each individual is unique; measures of personality are inadequate; efforts to assess and predict entrepreneurial success are fruitless.

vs.

An emerging body of knowledge about the behavior and characteristics of successful entrepreneurs, while in an embryonic stage, can yield useful insights about who might succeed or fail.

3. One can't really change creativity or intelligence, which, in the final analysis, are the most crucial personal variables.

vs.

Entrepreneurs can realistically assess their strengths and weaknesses and can compensate for these through partners, outside resources, contacts, and planning.

4. There is a discrete series of steps or procedures one can follow to ensure entrepreneurial success.

vs.

Many of the risks and trade-offs involved in entrepreneurship are identifiable and manageable; discovering these is an iterative process.

5. Since entrepreneurial characteristics cannot be adequately measured and since people can't be totally honest and objective about themselves, self-assessment methods aren't useful.

vs.

The realistic assessment of self may be one of the most important characteristics of a successful entrepreneur. Various means of assessment can be useful for clinical rather than predictive purposes.

6. The idea is the crucial factor in venture creation; other factors are secondary.

vs.

A combination of factors and a variety of strategies can lead to successful start-ups.

7. Motivation, commitment, risk-taking—these crucial factors come from within and can't be changed.

vs.

Comparing one's own behavior to entrepreneurial role models and mentors can foster both understanding and development.

8. Everyone has a private definition of success; there aren't any common denominators.

vs.

Different criteria for entrepreneurial success can alter the relative importance of different factors, and it is useful to understand these.

9. Since anyone can start a business, you can't generalize.

vs.

It is useful to differentiate entrepreneurs according to the size, performance, and stage of their ventures; it is important and feasible to distinguish them from inventors, promoters, and managers. Performance requirements differ among these various roles, and, in the words of a Chinese proverb: To open a business, very easy. To keep it open, very difficult!

Future directions for research

The opportunities and needs for research about new venture formation are limitless. Table 1 suggests one of many possible typologies for focusing research issues and investigating hypotheses. There is startling evidence and increasing awareness about the job creating capacity of new enterprises. New, small enterprises are the apparent wellspring for significant technical innovations. Entrepreneurial enterprises may make other important economic and social contributions in a comparably disproportionate fashion. The possibilities for examining such contributions are immense. Can similar patterns be found? What influences them: size, technological intensity, capital requirements, stage of development, founder profiles, strategy? These questions have major policy implications for the role of venture creation and entrepreneurship in our society. They are just beginning to be taken seriously.

Research in the 1980s might include such issues as:

The economic and social contributions made by new and growing firms;

A comparison of these contributions with the venture variables noted in Table 1:

Table 1 *Possible typology for research*

Venture Variables:
Nature of Technology
Size Aspirations
Capital Requirements
Stage of Growth
Number of Founders
Financial Performance
Founder Profiles
Start-up Strategy
10th Year Status
Economic and Social Contributions:
• Job Creation
• Innovation R&D
• Productivity
• Capital Formation
• Technology
• Alternative Careers
• Inflation Deterrent
• Competitive Vibrancy

Longitudinal research to track the start-ups over time;
Methods for pursuing the elusive human variables, particularly of founder teams;
The influence of public policy and resource allocation on the social contributions of new ventures;
The relative effectiveness of various models, methods, training and assistance for venture creation.

Conclusion

The 1970s spawned a remarkable burst of interest and activity in entrepreneurship and venture creation. New models have appeared; at least two dozen academic books, a stream of articles and papers, and an untold number of authors have emerged; methods are being tried in the United States, Sweden, the United Kingdom, Canada, the Philippines, Malaysia, India, Korea, and other countries too numerous to mention.

If one can speculate about the 1980s, one would expect a continued growth of interest, accompanied by testing and acceptance of selected methodologies. Theoretical and empirical research may focus on some of the issues noted earlier. Evidence is likely to confirm the significant contributions of new enterprises, but will also contain contradictions to remind us that the territory is complex and clear solutions elusive. As data bases evolve, major breakthroughs could occur in macro-modeling and behavior analysis of successful entrepreneurs. We will discover a great deal more about what is and what is not learnable. Entrepreneurship and new venture creation are coming of age as important areas of inquiry and pedagogy.

commentary/elaboration

Additional thoughts on modeling new venture creation

Herbert Kierulff

In the academic environment there is room for both pure and applied research. Pure research in venture creation would seek truth for its own sake regardless of its apparent usefulness.

However, most academic researchers in this field have in mind some practical and reasonably immediate application of their work. The output must in some way lead to the encouragement of successful business formations. Thus, much research tends to concentrate on identifying and evaluating (1) the variables that influence venture formation, and (2) the factors that cause these variables to have an impact upon venture creation.

If the subject under study is successful venture creation, then the "common threads" described by Timmons may be the primary facilitating variables. These "common threads" include the talented lead entrepreneur, the team with complementary skills, the idea, the business plan, outside contacts, and the plan for obtaining financing.

Identifying the factors that cause these threads to have a positive impact on entrepreneurship represents a second tier of research. In this area, the personality of the entrepreneur and the sociopolitical environment are being investigated. Extensive checklists or step-by-step procedures for start-ups are being developed by many researchers, usually with specific application to a given business plan.

It seems apparent that the desired end of this effort is the development of a predictive and causal model or set of models that can increase entrepreneurial success when the independent variables are manipulated in appropriate ways. The policy implications—both macro and micro—are extremely important. A workable model at the macro level could lead to a more predictable level of successful starts and could have a profound effect on the socioeconomic environment in which we live. At the micro level, a working model could improve an individual's chances for success as an entrepreneur or as a financier who must design a portfolio of investments.

The foregoing, of course, is the grand view of research in this complex area. Whether models can ever be sufficiently explanatory and predictive to serve the practical needs of policy-making is another matter. In large measure, the outcome will depend on how well the goals and the independent variables can be defined and correlated.

One broad challenge to researchers is measuring the successful start-up. Total number of start-ups per period and net start-ups (start-ups less discontinuances) say nothing about the nature of venture creation. In such methods of calculation, a retail shoe shop employing one man and his family is counted as heavily as a high-technology venture with a potential work force of thousands. Macroeconomic policy-makers interested in the impact on GNP, price levels, employment, and balance of payments will find this measure less than adequate.

Sales volume or net worth generated may seem to be more satisfactory statistics but can lead to numerous pitfalls if not examined properly. For example, the retail shoe store should display sales and profits during its first year of operation, while an R & D company developing an advanced technology may show significant losses over its first months or even years of operation.

Successful short-term economic policy-making depends heavily upon accurately predicting when the impact of a policy decision will be felt in the general economy. Entrepreneurial models will have to compute the time variable to be useful to short-term policy-makers.

On the other hand, is it desirable to measure success in strictly quantitative terms when entrepreneurship has so many subjective implications for quality of life? Not everyone would be happy or most productive as an entrepreneur, and not all would define success in terms of sales and profits. Isn't an entrepreneur who starts and runs a shoe store that employs her husband and children (that keeps the family together in an atmosphere of mutual support) a successful person? Or must an entrepreneur start up a high-potential venture with hundreds of employees and sales in the millions? Practical modeling will require careful attention to the ways of measuring success.

A second major task is that of relating independent variables to the process of successful venture creation, to each other, and to the mediating factors. Traditionally, American entrepreneurs have not worked closely with government in developing start-ups. Is it better for a government to actively encourage new venture formations, or to stay out altogether?

What about the negative influences of government? In this country, high taxes are seen as a negative inducement to entrepreneurship. In Sweden where taxes are high, however, entrepreneurship is flourishing. Further, if entrepreneurs can avoid or evade taxes on a large scale, as appears possible in many countries, apparent difficulties are mitigated.

Government may also create a society of observers, federal officials, educators, and others who look for ways to encourage entrepreneurship. This idea entails the danger that the society of observers will be only marginally successful in its primary mission and will seek to perpetuate itself regardless of usefulness.

Models and methodologies of venture creation should take the government equation into account somehow. The maze of fact and fancy surrounding this variable remains a problem. And, as mentioned, the government factor is only one of many. The subject remains a vital and viable field for research in the 1980s. The first steps have been taken, but major challenges lie ahead.

References

BAUMBACK, CLIFFORD M., and LAWYER, KENNETH, *How to Organize and Operate a Small Business* (6th ed.). Englewood Cliffs, N.J.: Prentice-Hall, 1979.

HOLLINGSWORTH, A. THOMAS, and HAND, HERBERT H., *A Guide to Small Business Management.* Philadelphia: Saunders, 1979.

HOSMER, LARUE T., COOPER, ARNOLD C., and VESPER, KARL H., *The Entrepreneurial Function.* Englewood Cliffs, N.J.: Prentice-Hall, 1977.

NAUMES, WILLIAM, *The Entrepreneurial Manager in the Small Business.* Reading, Mass.: Addison-Wesley, 1978.

OSGOOD, WILLIAM R., and WETZEL, WILLIAM E., "Systems Approach to Venture Initiation." Presented to the Academy of Management, Annual Meeting, Kansas City, August 1976.

PICKLE, HAL B., and ABRAHAMSON, ROYCE L., *Small Business Management.* New York: John Wiley, 1976.

Proceedings of Project ISEED, ed. James W. Schreier et al. Milwaukee: Center for Management, 1975.

SCHOLLHAMMER, HANS, and KURILOFF, ARTHUR H., *Entrepreneurship and Small Business Management.* New York: John Wiley, 1979.

STEINHOFF, DAN, *Small Business Management Fundamentals* (2nd ed.). New York: McGraw-Hill, 1978.

SWAIN, CHARLES B., and TUCKER, WILLIAM R., *The Effective Entrepreneur.* Morristown, N.J.: General Learning Press, 1973.

TATE, CURTIS E., MEGGINSON, LEON C., SCOTT, CHARLES B., and TRUEBLOOD, LYLE R., *Successful Small Business Management,* rev. ed. Dallas: Business Publications, 1978.

TIMMONS, JEFFRY A., "Black is Beautiful—Is it Bountiful?" *Harvard Business Review,* November-December 1971.

TIMMONS, JEFFRY A., "Careful Analysis and Team Assessment Can Aid Entrepreneurs," *Harvard Business Review,* November-December 1979, and "A Business Plan Is More than a Financing Device," *Harvard Business Review,* March-April 1980.

TIMMONS, JEFFRY A., SMOLLEN, LEONARD E., and DINGEE, ALEXANDER L. M., *New Venture Creation,* rev. ed. (in progress). Homewood, Ill.: Richard D. Irwin, 1981.

VESPER, KARL H., *New Venture Strategies.* Englewood Cliffs, N.J.: Prentice-Hall, 1979.

WEBSTER, F., "A Model for New Venture Initiation," *Academy of Management Review* 1, No. 1 (January 1976).

WELSH, JOHN A., *Investing in the Entrepreneur.* Vail, Col.: Caruth Institute Proceedings, March 1974.

chapter viii

Risk capital research

William E. Wetzel, Jr.

Overview

Sound risk capital research is founded upon an understanding of the entrepreneurial process, the role of risk capital in that process, and the diverse forms, functions, and sources of risk capital. This chapter attempts to lay that foundation. Entrepreneurship is defined in the context of an economic policy for New England. Capital problems are identified in areas affecting inventors, start-up firms, and established growing firms, and the limited body of existing research is referenced. The chapter describes the University of New Hampshire's current research on the cost and availability of informal risk capital in New England and concludes with observations on research problems and opportunities in the risk capital area.

Economic development strategy

Designing an effective economic strategy for a mature economy is the economic challenge currently confronting New England. Despite the continuing attention of such influential organizations as the New England Regional Commission, the Council for Northeast Economic Action, the New England Council, and the Coalition of Northeastern Governors, a coherent regional strategy has yet to emerge. Clearly, the problem is complex and solutions difficult to identify.

An assessment of New England's competitive advantages and disadvantages provides many more explanations for the area's stagnation than suggestions for its revitalization. This imbalance does not necessarily imply that effective economic strategies for New England are unattainable. The explanation, and part of the solution, lies in the distinction between tangible and intangible resources. The former are clearly limited in New England. The tangible disadvantages under which the area must operate are familiar and include:

1. limited natural resources, other than timber
2. inefficient transportation systems
3. high energy costs
4. industrial plants and equipment 35 percent older than the U.S. average
5. heavier tax burdens than in southern and western regions

The region's only apparent tangible advantage is a skilled, stable labor force and an average wage in the manufacturing sector that is 10 percent below the national average.

New England's intangible resources include a regional pool of professional venture capital centered in Boston. Only New York and the San Francisco Bay area offer comparable concentrations of professional risk capital and investment expertise. New England also appears to contain a potential pool of risk capital in the hands of informal investors, essentially individuals of means. A reservoir of technological know-how is concentrated in New England's educational institutions, consulting firms, inventors, and technology-based businesses. Finally, New England's tradition of Yankee entrepreneurship, ingenuity, and self-reliance has created the social climate and an entrepreneurial base to provide a catalytic effect on the formation of new firms.

In the first part of this chapter I discuss those characteristics of the New England economy that bear on the development of regional economic strategy. I assert that an entrepreneurial component based upon the exploitation of New England's intangible resources and skilled labor force must be an integral part of a regional economic policy. In the second part of the chapter I discuss the single most serious barrier to an effective entrepreneurial strategy, the shortage of risk capital for technology-based inventors, for new firms without access to professional venture capital sources, and for established, growing firms without access to the public equity markets. Firms without access to venture capital or the public equity markets represent a significant foundation for employment in the United States in general, and in New England in particular. These "foundation firms" typically generate sales between $1 million and $20 million, employ between 20 and 600 people, are expanding at 10 percent to 30 percent per year, are unlikely to qualify for a public stock offering or merger with a larger firm in the next ten years, and often require risk capital of $50,000 to $500,000.

I also summarize the results of a 1978 pilot research effort designed to test the hypothesis that informal investors, essentially individuals of means and successful entrepreneurs, represent a relatively unknown and under-utilized source of risk capital for inventors, entrepreneurs, and dynamic small firms. In October 1979, based on the results of this pilot effort, the Office of Economic Research of the U.S. Small Business Administration funded a 13-month inquiry into the cost and availability of informal risk capital in New England.

Entrepreneurship, risk capital, and New England economic policy

New England economy

The economic stagnation of New England is common knowledge. Since the turn of the century the rate of employment growth in New England has lagged behind that of the U.S. as a whole. Between 1970 and 1975 employment in the U.S. economy grew by 6.9 percent, while employment in New England increased by only 2.8 percent. The regional unemployment rate between 1970 and 1974 averaged almost 1 percent above the national average. During the recession years of 1974 and 1975 the gap was almost three percentage points. Coupled with higher unemployment rates, New England's average hourly earnings for manufacturing workers are 12 percent below the national average, $5.91 per hour vs. $6.71 per hour as of July 1979.

Although the region's employment problems are well documented, little is known about the changing profile of employers in the region—a factor that determines the direction and rates of employment change. Consequently, attempts at developing regional economic strategies have been built upon limited empirical data. At least four recent studies shed light on the profile of New England firms and the dynamics of New England's business population. The strategic implications of these studies are summarized below.

In 1976, Price Waterhouse and Company prepared an analysis and profile of New England business for the New England Regional Commission (*New England Business: Profile and Analysis,* 1967). The primary objectives of the study were to help determine the feasibility of a New England Capital Corporation, as recommended by the Commission's Task Force of Capital and Labor Markets (*Report of the Task Force of Capital and Labor Markets,* 1975), and to provide statistical and financial information on businesses based in New England for economic planning and analysis purposes. Highlights of this report include conclusions that New England still has a relatively high proportion of manufacturing businesses and that New England–based businesses tend to be smaller than the nation's as a whole.

A second analysis of New England with strategic implications is Hekman's study entitled "What Attracts Industry to New England" (Hekman 1978). He points out that analyses of inter-regional differences in factor costs influencing industrial location traditionally deal with labor, raw material, energy, transportation, state and local taxes, and similar tangible resources. While traditional analyses suggest that New England's industry will differ from that of other regions in terms of product mix, since it is less energy and transport cost intensive, they ignore the most important reason for industrial location in New England, i.e., available technology. Two salient characteristics of New England industry, today as 150 years ago, are the high degree of skilled, specialized work done and the large number of relatively new technologies or processes used.

Hekman points out that for a wide range of products New England is not really in competition with other regions. It has a unique attractiveness to new firms responding to changes in production processes. During the early stages of product development new firms benefit from their New England location by making use of the region's skilled labor force and specialized services, including a range of high-technology suppliers and consultants. As innovative processes become routine or mechanized, the substitution of low-skill for high-skill labor lessens a firm's dependence on New England's unique resources. Thus it is important that the region not lose its ability to attract high-technology firms and to develop new ideas and products. Strategic implications clearly involve an emphasis on entrepreneurs, technology, and the capital required to create new ventures.

In an analysis of the New England economy using Dun and Bradstreet rated firms as their data base, Jusenius and Ledebur (1977) found that in the five-year period from 1969 to 1974, 54,000 New England firms shut down; these represented 33 percent of the firms that had existed in 1969. In a growing economy, the firms that die are replaced by new ones. However, this replacement process in New England was not complete. Only 36,000 new firms were born over this period, 22 percent of the 1969 base. The net result was a loss of over 360,000 jobs.

New England historically has specialized in two industries: manufacturing and finance, and insurance and real estate. Over the 1969–1974 period, the manufacturing sector of New England experienced particularly severe economic difficulties. Jusenius and Ledebur (1977) point out that almost 3000 Dun and Bradstreet rated manufacturing firms closed, 31 percent of the 1969 base, while only 4386 such firms opened, 17 percent of the 1969 base. While the mortality rate was slightly below the average for all industries (31 percent versus 33 percent), the birth rate of manufacturing firms was well below the average for the region (17 percent versus 22 percent). The loss of manufacturing firms was a particularly serious blow to the economy of the region since these firms generate employment not only directly, but also in other industries via the employment multiplier. If New England is to rely on new manufacturing enterprises for its revitalization, especially those utilizing innovative technology, it would not appear to be doing well so far.

Some insights into the nature of the structural adjustment within the manufacturing sector are contained in a study cited in the New England Regional Commission's *Report of the Task Force of Capital and Labor Markets* (1975). The unidentified study revealed that the dynamics of industrial change in New England are increasingly dominated by more sophisticated manufacturing processes as the region's more labor-intensive, low-technology industries are phased out. Of 45 New England plant closings during the two-year period ending July 1974, 20 (44 percent) were in labor-intensive industries, and only eight (18 percent) were high-technology firms, while 94 of 211 new plant openings (44 percent) were concentrated in high-technology or high-technology supporting industries. The study also noted that 61 of 87 expansions of existing plants were concentrated in these high-technology, capital-intensive industries.

The creativity of New England's technological know-how is demonstrable. On a per capita basis, more patents have been issued to inventors in New England than in other economic regions of the United States (O'Neil 1971). While New England represents about 6 percent of the U.S. population, 15 percent of the energy-related inventions recommended for development by the National Bureau of Standards through 1979 originated in New England (Orton 1979). Finally, of the 117 Phase I and Phase II awards made by the National Science Foundation's Small Business Innovation Research Program through February 1980, over 30 percent were won by New England firms (National Science Foundation news releases, April 1979 and October 1979).

Analysis of the available data leads to the following conclusions:

1. New England depends on small manufacturing firms for a larger proportion of its employment than does the United States as a whole.

2. New England's competitive economic advantages include a skilled, stable, and relatively low paid labor force, a reservoir of technological know-how, a substantial pool of professional venture capital, and a tradition of Yankee entrepreneurship.

3. In recent years, New England has not combined these resources to spawn new ventures fast enough to replace ventures that have disappeared or moved elsewhere.

Entrepreneurship, risk capital, and new jobs

The recommendation for a New England economic strategy based upon entrepreneurship, technology, skilled labor, and risk capital is grounded upon an analysis of New England's competitive advantages and disadvantages. A complementary line of reasoning, based upon broader data developed over the past ten years, demonstrates that sales growth and job creation occur more rapidly in small, young firms and in innovative, high-technology companies than in more mature organizations.

The unique contribution of new technical enterprises was examined in 1967 by the Technical Advisory Board of the U.S. Department of Commerce and led to subsequent research conducted by the MIT Development Foundation. Results of this research were published by the Commerce Technical Advisory Board in a January 1976 "White Paper" entitled "The Role of New Technical Enterprises in the U.S. Economy" (Morse and Flender 1976). The authors compared the performance of six "mature companies," five "innovative companies," and five "young technology companies." During the five-year period 1969–1974 the average annual percentage growth rates of these companies were:

	Sales	*Jobs*
Mature companies	11.4%	0.6%
Innovative companies	13.2%	4.3%
Young technology companies	42.5%	40.7%

The young technology companies, whose sales were 2 percent of the mature industry sales, created 34,369 jobs, or 34 percent more than the 25,555 jobs created by the mature companies. The innovative companies, whose sales were 58 percent of the mature industry sales, created 106,598 new jobs, or over four times as many as the mature firms. Morse and Flender also point out that in the late 60s and early 70s adverse changes in the business environment reduced the rate at which new companies were started and restricted the development of many small companies that were established. "Probably the most important change in the environment for starting and developing new high technology companies during the recent past has been the decline in the supply of risk capital for small companies" (Morse and Flender 1976).

A more recent and more comprehensive analysis of the contribution of young, technology-based firms to the creation of employment opportunities was prepared by the American Electronics Association (U.S. House of Representatives 1978). A sample of 269 member firms was divided into four categories: "Mature" (more than 20 years old), "teenage" (between ten and 20 years old), "developing" (five to ten years old), and "start-up" (less than five years old). Employment growth in 1976 for the "teenage" companies was 20–40 times the growth rate in employment for "mature" companies. The "developing" companies had an employment growth rate in 1976 that was nearly 55 times the employment growth rate for the "mature" companies. The AEA data in absolute terms are also revealing. Although the mature companies founded before 1955 had, on the average, 27 times more employees than the companies founded since 1955, the young companies created an average of

89 jobs per company versus an average of only 69 new jobs per mature company.

Both the AEA study and the MIT study identified obstacles to new firm formation, including environmental factors that have curtailed entrepreneurs' access to risk capital. The AEA study contained evidence that the scarcity of risk capital has not only stifled formation and growth of young companies but, by compelling increased reliance on debt, it has made those companies that have been able to get started more vulnerable to economic fluctuations.

A third and yet broader study entitled "The Job Generation Process" was prepared in 1979 by David Birch of the MIT Program on Neighborhood and Regional Change for the Economic Development Administration of the U.S. Department of Commerce. According to this report, firms employing 20 or fewer employees provided 66 percent of all new jobs generated by small business. Birch summarizes his data as follows:

A pattern begins to emerge in all of this. The job generating firm tends to be small. It tends to be dynamic (or unstable, depending on your viewpoint)—the kind of firm banks feel very uncomfortable about. It tends to be young. In short, the firms that can and do generate the most jobs are the ones that are the most difficult to reach through conventional policy initiatives. (Birch 1979)

Birch observes in his conclusion that:

It is not clear what to offer job-replacing firms. Some have argued persuasively that small businesses need, use well, and cannot easily get, capital. Beyond that, however, the answers are less clear. (Birch 1979)

Each of the three studies discussed above confirms the likelihood of significant benefits for New England from an entrepreneurial economic policy. Such a policy would deal with slow employment growth and simultaneously reinforce New England's technological, entrepreneurial, labor, and capital advantages.

Entrepreneurship, risk capital, and technological innovation

Research dealing with the contribution of independent inventors and small firms to the pace of technological innovation is less extensive and less academically rigorous than research dealing with job formation but is nevertheless provocative. The following examples confirm the conventional wisdom that young, small firms and independent inventors are more efficient generators of technological innovation and improvements in industrial productivity than are the established, mature firms:

1. Firms with less than 1000 employees accounted for almost one-half of major U.S. innovations during the period 1953–1973. The ratio of innovations to R & D employment is four times greater in firms with less than 1000 employees than in large firms. (U.S. Office of Federal Procurement Policy 1977)

2. Of 61 important inventions and innovations in this century, over one-half came from small firms and independent inventors. In the 1946–1955 decade, over two-thirds of the major inventions resulted from the work of independent inventors and small companies. Seven of 13 major innovations in the American steel industry came from independent inventors. Of seven important inventions in the aluminum industry, major producers accounted for only one. All seven major inventions in the refining and cracking of petroleum were made by independent inventors. The contributions of large firms were primarily in the area of improvement inventions. (U.S. Office of Federal Procurement Policy 1977)

3. In a sample of major innovations introduced to the market between 1953 and 1973, small firms (with up to 1000 employees) were found to produce about 24 times as many major innovations per R & D dollar as large firms (over 10,000 employees) and four times as many as medium-sized firms. (National Science Board 1977)

4. A comparison of the performance of high-technology versus low-technology industries in the United States over the period 1950–1974 revealed that employment in high-technology industries grew almost nine times as fast as in low-technology. Prices increased at only one-sixth the rate. Our balance of trade in high-technology products rose to a surplus of $25 billion a year, while in low-technology products it declined from break-even in 1950 to a $16 billion deficit in 1974. (*The Role of High Technology Industries in Economic Growth* 1977)

Each of these studies reinforces the expectation of substantial benefits for New England from an entrepreneurial economic development policy. New England's strengths include a broad base of innovative, technological know-how, a skilled, stable labor supply, a regional pool of risk capital, and a record of Yankee ingenuity and self-reliance. These ought to be the ingredients for entrepreneurial success. That they have been less than adequate to date seems to be due, at least in part, to the difficulty of raising risk capital. The studies already cited agree on this point. The discussion that follows summarizes the results of recent research in the risk capital markets and describes the University of New Hampshire's current investigation of the cost and availability of informal risk capital in New England.

Capital gaps and risk capital research

Risk capital defined

Given the fragmented, informal character of the risk capital markets, it is difficult to measure the volume and type of transactions, the level of available funds, or the number of viable business opportunities that never get started due to lack of financial backers. Although efforts to measure the depth of "capital gaps" have yet to yield convincing results, there is evidence that the single most important change in the environment for starting and developing new companies, including high-technology firms, during the 1970s was the decline in the supply of risk capital for small companies.

The nature and function of risk capital need to be identified before factors affecting the supply of such funds can be completely understood, or research designed. Venture capital is not "expansion" capital; it is, for lack of a better term, "creative" capital. The distinction involves differences in function, degrees of risk, and form of reward. Expansion capital is invested in existing ventures for the purpose of expanding facilities to meet demand, to add product lines, to enter new markets. Expansion opportunities must meet capital market risk and reward criteria, but in established, efficient capital markets seldom exceed such criteria by wide margins. Evidence of this fact, though imperfect, is found in a comparison of market values and book values of industrial shares. If allowance is made for the accounting system's disregard of the effects of inflation upon historical costs, it is clear that market values are close to or below book values in most cases. To the extent that book values approximate invested capital, either through direct investment or retained profits, it is clear that little if any new capital has been "created"; that is, the funds are worth little more invested in income-producing assets than they were prior to the investment. Holders of securities received in return for "expansion" funds earn their rewards primarily in current income, that is, in interest yields on debt, and dividends and capital gains yields on stocks (the proportion depending on dividend payout policies). In the case of equity, although dividend payout policy for "expanding" firms would shift returns between dividend yields and capital gains, the return on assets would only maintain market values at book values. In these cases, capital gains arise solely as a result of foregone dividends.

Risk capital, on the other hand, exploits asset market imperfections. It is the cutting edge that, together with entrepreneurs, exploits opportunities to put together apparently neutral or sterile resources to create firms with capitalized earning power, or market value, well in excess of the cost of invested funds. Risk capital creates capital—in the market value or capitalized earning power sense of the term. Its function is to find investment opportunities that when proven will yield returns in excess of those demanded in the market for comparable risks. It rewards the twin functions of finding and providing opportunity, for economic creativity and risk-bearing.

The creative, risk-bearing function of venture capital also determines its source of reward. Risk investors receive their return exclusively from capital gains, from the difference between the cost of resources invested and the market value of firms created. In this case the source of capital gains is not foregone dividends. The potential for this type of "economic creativity" is generally exhausted within ten years of the birth of a firm. By that time, venture investors ordinarily liquidate their investment to recycle it in new opportunities. The risk capital process is therefore a dynamic, circular process with a life cycle between five and ten years in duration. Exit mechanisms for venture investors are limited to essentially three techniques: (1) public sale of the firm's shares, (2) merger with or sale to a larger established firm, or (3) repurchase of shares by the firm or its management.

The characteristics of risk capital that affect its cost and availability can be summarized in five points. First, risk capital performs the creative function of financing the formation and growth of commercial ventures. Second, it bears the extreme risks that creative, innovative processes involve and therefore requires the prospect of high returns. Third, its cost is not a cash burden to the firm. Risk capital creates its own reward in the form of market values based on capitalized earning power. Fourth, the creative, risk-bearing function is a short-term, specialized activity. Risk capital investors anticipate recapture of their original advances within five to ten years. Finally, from the firm's point of view risk capital is permanent capital that undergoes a transformation to traditional equity capital as operating performance confirms profit expectations, as risk or uncertainty is reduced. From an investor's point of view, risk capital investment in small firms typically exhibits the following characteristics:

1. Substantially higher risks than equity investments in large, established firms.

2. Substantially greater potential returns than equity investments in large, established firms

3. Limited or nonexistent marketability (liquidity) of investments

As a consequence of the nation's economic problems, particularly as they relate to productivity, technology transfer, and new firm formation, the performance of the risk capital markets has received considerable attention in the past six to eight years (U.S. House of Representatives 1977). However, recent studies of venture and equity capital for small firms have paid more attention to the problems of firms seeking public capital than to the problems of firms without access to the public markets. The latter tend to be stereotyped as small, individual proprietorships almost totally dependent on debt (U.S. Senate 1979). From New England's point of view the stereotype is inaccurate and the emphasis is misplaced.

Investigations of the risk capital markets must be based on a clear understanding of the differences between these two classes of firms. The stereotype reflects the popular image of small businesses as essentially "life style firms," with annual sales under $1 million, less than 20 employees, and an owner/manager with a successful life style. At the other extreme are the "high-potential" ventures, those with annual sales in excess of $20 million, after-tax profits in excess of $1 million, and 400 to 600 employees, or the potential to reach those levels within five to ten years. Access to the public equity markets or merger with a larger firm is seldom feasible for smaller, slower-growth firms. Between the "life style" ventures and the "high-potential" firms are a group of privately held "foundation firms" upon which New England depends for much of its technological innovation and new job formation. Foundation firms seldom have access to traditional venture capital sources or the public equity markets. New or growing foundation firms typically require risk capital in amounts ranging from $50,000 to $500,000, are expanding at rates between 10 percent and 30 percent per year, are unlikely to qualify for a public stock offering or merger with a larger firm within five to ten years, employ from 10 to 600 people, and generate annual sales between $1 million and $20 million. Given the predominance of firms in New England with sales under $20 million, New England's reliance on manufacturing employment, and its need to develop new technology-based manufacturing firms to capitalize on its competitive advantages, the risk capital problems of foundation firms deserve more attention than they have received.

Capital gaps—inventors

The creativity of New England inventors has been documented. In recent years several organizations have been established in New England to assist inventors in the commercial application of new technology. These organizations include the New England Industrial Resources Development Program, Northeast Solar Energy Center, Massachusetts Technology Development Foundation, Connecticut Product Development Corporation, and the New England Innovation Group.

Despite the regional interest in inventors as a source of commercially useful technology, their projects remain among the most troublesome to finance. Informal investors, in particular successful technological entrepreneurs, represent a potential source of funds:

Venture capitalists, in general, are not interested in inventors. Focusing on inventors uses enormous amounts of time and results in very little money being invested, since so few ideas turn out to be worth pursuing. It is very difficult to finance and to staff a venture company to work with inventors. Individual investors, particularly successful entrepreneurs, are often the most helpful to inventors. (McMurtry 1978)

Inventors as a group appear to be receptive to cooperation with outside investors. In a recent Canadian survey of private investors, 88 percent would sell some equity in a business that produced their invention, and 75 percent were willing to take a minority equity position in a business that produced their invention (Grasley 1976).

Informal investors, essentially individuals of means and successful entrepreneurs, are a diverse and dispersed group with a preference for anonymity. Creative techniques are required to identify and reach them. Currently, inventors and entrepreneurs must find their own way through the maze of channels leading to informal risk capital with few guidelines or sources of assistance to call upon. The problems involved in bringing a new invention or innovation to commercial reality were summarized by James R. Bright, Associate Dean of the Graduate School of Business at the University of Texas, in a series of ten propositions and accompanying conclusions. The financial problems facing an invention were summarized in Proposition 10:

Proposition 10. *A major weakness in our national support of the innovative process is the financing of innovations during progress after Stage 3—Verification of Theory, up through Stage 5—Full Scale or Field Trial.*
Conclusion. *We do not fund this activity (invention) as an act of faith. Furthermore, we leave this search for financial support of the innovation in the hands of the inventor. During this crucial time, in effect, society expects the inventor to drop his real forte (invention) and to become promoter, entrepreneur, and financier. Why should the inventor, dedicated to a technological struggle and probably already under financial stress, be expected to be an effective fund raiser? Psychologically and intellectually, he is not usually a good candidate for this job. Is it any wonder that social and economic progress is delayed? (Bright 1969)*

Capital gaps—start-up and early stage financing

The recent literature on capital gaps cites shortages of start-up funds as a major capital market problem. Investors who formerly provided funds to an interesting new enterprise now shun a start-up situation.

The National Venture Capital Association commissioned a two-year study by Professor A. Ofer, Northwestern University, on the flow of venture capital. Ofer studied the investment activity of 143 venture capital firms during 1974 and 1975. His studies indicated that the flow of venture capital investment was slowing materially and that very little money was being directed into start-up or barely emerging companies. His report included the following data:

	1975 (millions)	*1974 (millions)*
Total funds invested	$111.3	$181.9
Amount invested in start-ups	15.6 (14%)	12.9 (7%)
Amount invested in "first-round" financing	8.1 (7%)	37.5 (21%)
Amount invested in somewhat more seasoned "second-round" financings	17.7 (16%)	36.3 (20%)
Subtotal	41.4 (37%)	87.0 (48%)

The report of the SBA Task Force on Venture and Equity Capital for Small Business cited the nationwide shortage of risk capital for start-ups.

Most venture capital firms have adopted a policy of staying away from startups and have put their available capital in safer and more liquid investments. (U.S. Small Business Administration 1977)

"Seed capital of any nature for new and interesting innovative products or processes" was among the capital gaps in New England identified by T. A. Associates in their 1976 report to the New England Regional Commission (*Verification of Capital Gaps in New England* 1976).

While the 1978 reduction in capital gains tax rates and a modest revival in the public new issues market attracted several hundred million dollars into professional venture capital portfolios within the year, less than 10 percent of these funds appear to have been available for start-ups and then only for firms with the prospect of a public share offering within five to ten years. Minimum investment standards established by professional venture capital firms are in the neighborhood of $500,000, while equity-oriented SBICs typically consider $250,000 as a minimum. The average investment per business, as of March 31, 1975, by the nine largest equity-oriented SBICs was $450,000. Seven of the nine had established at least $250,000 as minimum investment (Report of the Comptroller General of the United States 1978).

New foundation firms requiring venture capital in amounts between $50,000 and $250,000 are exceptionally difficult to finance. Informal investors are one of the few potential sources of such financing.

Providing seed capital or startup financing to an inexperienced management team is also enormously time consuming, but it can be very rewarding. More venture companies are needed to specialize in this area. It is, however, difficult to find staff both qualified and interested, and it is difficult to finance such venture companies since they can invest relatively little money but need strong staff. Individual investors and groups of individuals are frequently the most likely sources of such financing. (McMurtry 1978)

Capital gaps—external equity for established foundation firms

The T. A. Associates report cited above identified a second capital gap in New England: "junior debt and equity for small companies growing at a rate too slow to attract venture capital." This gap is particularly troublesome for New England due to the region's relatively heavy reliance on foundation firms. These firms cannot raise funds in the public equity markets and, in the absence of alternative equity sources, growth rates are constrained to the growth in internally generated equity. These firms might earn 15 percent per year without distorting the debt/equity proportions of their balance sheets, whereas growth rates in excess of 30 percent per year are typically necessary to attract the interest of professional venture investors. The troublesome firm to finance is the established foundation firm growing faster than retained earnings can support but not fast enough to attract venture capital. These attractive growth rates tend to fall between 10 percent and 30 percent per year.

Informal investors are a potential source of equity financing for sound, growing foundation firms.

For companies with modest growth prospects, private individuals are by far the most likely financing source. The same may also be true for many service businesses. A great deal of time can be wasted talking with institutional venture capital sources about deals which they are very unlikely to do. (McMurtry 1978)

Capital gaps—high-potential ventures

The venture capital problems of high-potential firms lie primarily in the start-up stage. Here they share the start-up financing problems already cited. In the case of high-potential ventures, a partial explanation of the shortage of seed capital is found in investment recapture problems resulting from limited markets for new stock issues and SEC restrictions on the sale of shares in secondary markets.

As defined, high-potential ventures provide early investors with the prospect of a public stock offering within five to ten years of a private risk capital financing. Changes in the public equity markets for shares of emerging companies have foreclosed all but a handful of ventures from qualifying as high-potential ventures. The following quotation summarizes conditions as they existed in 1977:

Speaking directly as an investment banker, I can tell this committee that we are unable to provide start-up capital for new enterprises. The marketplace has caused us to substantially increase our criteria for providing capital for existing businesses. In short, capital in meaningful terms is available only for medium sized companies—those with annual after-tax earnings in excess of $2.8 million. (U.S. House of Representatives 1977)

The National Association of Small Business Investment Companies cited similar criteria: "Smaller underwriters are currently insisting that a company have a minimum of $500,000 to $1,000,000 of after-tax earnings to undertake a public offering while the larger underwriters generally look for a minimum of $2,000,000" (National Association of Small Business Investment Companies 1977). Between 1969 and 1975 the market for stock issues by companies for which there was no prior market (new issues) virtually disappeared, declining from 1298 new issues in 1969 to 29 in 1975. Since 1975 there has been a modest revival in new issues, with 58 offered in 1978.

Effective public markets for successful emerging innovative companies serve a twofold purpose. First, they provide external equity capital to companies at a time of significant growth in sales and employment. This follows their successful emergence from the very high risk start-up and early development stages funded privately by founders, friends of founders, other informal sources and, in many cases, venture capitalists. Second, they permit the early investors and venture capitalists with locked-in private investments to sell a portion of their holdings and thereby "recycle" funds from their more successful early stage investments into new, private, emerging companies that require capital. Even in active secondary markets, SEC regulations (Rule 144) restrict the rate at which unregistered shares held by venture investors can be sold. For a comprehensive analysis of the market for shares in small firms, and for recommendations designed to improve access to public markets, see *Small Business Financing, the Current Environment and Suggestions for Improvement*, prepared by the Joint Industry/Government Committee on Small Business Financing of the National Association of Securities Dealers (1979).

Capital gaps—summary

One can infer from this discussion that there are no generally accepted, operational definitions of small business or of risk capital; that very limited data is available and much of what does exist is fragmented and anecdotal; and that, consequently, our conclusions are tenuous at best. The only known attempt at an aggregate measure of the small business capital gap was undertaken by the Small Business Administration in 1976 using data supplied by government agencies. Mitchell Kobelinski, then Administrator of SBA, reported: "We estimate that small business faces a shortfall in venture and working capital that will average from $7 billion to $8 billion a year over the next decade" (U.S. House of Representatives 1977).

Informal investors, essentially individuals of means, are one of the limited sources of venture and equity capital for inventors and foundation firms. However, very little is known about the extent of informal risk capital, its investment criteria, or the means by which it might be located. The essence of the problem is captured in the following excerpts from the report of the Commerce Technical Advisory Board to the Secretary of Commerce, January 1976:

1. "Probably the most important change in the environment for starting and developing new high technology companies during the recent past has been the decline in the supply of risk capital for small companies." (Morse and Flender 1976)

2. "Both the public issues data and the private financing data reflect the declining number of financings by clearly identifiable segments of the financial community. There are no data regarding the individual and truly private sources of seed money." (Morse and Flender 1976)

The risk capital problems of foundation firms, firms without access to traditional venture capital sources and without access to public equity markets, have been largely overlooked in recent years as attention has focused upon problems created by the demise of the new issues market and other problems affecting the secondary market for shares in small firms. Informal investors (individuals of means and successful entrepreneurs) represent an alternative source of risk capital for inventors, entrepreneurs, and established foundation firms.

Informal risk capital—1978 pilot research

"Does the shortage of seed capital for foundation firms preclude an effective New England economic policy based on developing technology-based manufacturing ventures?" This question prompted a pilot research project in the fall of 1978 conducted by the Whittemore School of Business and Economics at the University of New Hampshire. The research undertook to test two hypotheses related to the seed capital question:

1. Informal venture investors, essentially individuals of means, represent a potentially significant source of seed capital for foundation firms.
2. Informal investors employ investment criteria that differ in material ways from the criteria employed by professional venture capital firms.

Both hypotheses grew out of past experience with New England entrepreneurs and out of the experience of individuals involved in technology transfer and regional economic development.

The pilot research was based on a comprehensive questionnaire distributed to 100 individuals with a known interest in venture investment situations. Their names were obtained through the cooperation of the Smaller Business Association of New England (SBANE) and the New England Industrial Resources Development Commission (NEIRD). Questionnaires were also mailed to 50 chief executive officers of manufacturing firms with over 100 employees and $5 million in annual sales. As an experiment in reaching investors indirectly, through likely referral sources, the questionnaire was mailed to 250 bank presidents and CPAs in New Hampshire, Vermont, and Maine.

A total of 48 completed questionnaires were returned. The most significant results of the survey are summarized below:

1. The average age of respondents was 48; over half had had previous experience as entrepreneurs or investors in start-up situations.
2. The average desired investment in any one situation was $32,000; 10 percent preferred to invest over $50,000, and another 10 percent preferred to invest under $10,000. The total potential pool of venture capital represented by respondents exceeded $1 million per year over the next three years.
3. Respondents in general were interested in participating with others in venture investments. Preferred partners included other financially sophisticated individuals, banks, and venture capital firms.
4. Required rates of return were lower than those typically required by professional venture capitalists, ranging from 22 percent per year for start-ups to 16 percent per

year for investments in established, growing firms. On the average, exit horizons appeared to be longer than those required by venture capital firms.

5. Over half of the respondents indicated that they would accept a lower rate of return on investment in exchange for some form of nonmonetary return. The creation of local job opportunities in an area with high unemployment was an acceptable substitute for 59 percent of respondents with an average ROI reduction of approximately 20 percent or nearly four percentage points. Other trade-offs were also cited.

6. Respondents have been offered approximately three venture investment opportunities per year, most of which were directed to them by friends or business associates, not from sources such as bankers, accountants, lawyers, or investment firms. Over 60 percent indicated an interest in a regional service that would screen and refer venture capital investment opportunities to them.

Experience and the results of this pilot research suggest that the informal venture capital markets represent a substantial potential pool of funds and are relatively inefficient in bringing entrepreneurs and investors together. Private market makers are unable, by and large, to reap the substantially public benefits of improving the efficiency of the informal capital market. Therefore, entrepreneurs can expect to find little guidance in preparing sound investment proposals and in identifying potential individual investors. Investors themselves will continue to rely largely on random events to bring investment opportunities to their attention.

In view of New England's need for small amounts of seed capital to spawn new foundation firms, and in view of the compelling rationale for adopting an entrepreneurial development policy, it is recommended that New England experiment with publicly funded efforts to improve the efficiency of the informal capital market. By eliminating the inefficient and redundant effort of entrepreneurs inexperienced in the search for investors, this service alone should materially improve the effectiveness of the marketplace. Given the mobility of capital (66 percent of research respondents were interested in investments anywhere in New England) an experimental market clearing mechanism should be regional in scope.

Informal risk capital—current research

Based upon the analysis and data presented in this paper and the suggestive results of the 1978 pilot research, the Office of Economic Research of the U.S. Business Administration funded in October 1979 a 13-month expanded study of the cost and availability of informal risk capital in New England. The research is designed to test three hypotheses concerning informal investors as a source of risk capital.

1. Informal investors represent a potentially significant source of risk capital for inventors and for new and growing foundation firms. "Significant" is defined in relative terms to mean on the same order of magnitude as the funds available from small business investment companies. The limited investigation conducted in the fall of 1978 identified potential risk capital in excess of $1 million per year in the portfolios of 48 informal investors located primarily in northern New England.

2. Informal investors employ investment criteria that differ in material ways from criteria employed by professional venture investors. "Material differences" are differences that result in investment opportunities that are attractive to informal investors but unattractive to professional venture investors, including equity-oriented SBICs, and vice versa.

3. Opportunities exist for facilitating the flow of risk capital from informal investors to inventors, entrepreneurs, and established foundation firms. The absence of established channels of communication between informal investors and entrepreneurs, the diverse and dispersed character of informal risk capital sources, the random emergence of entrepreneurs, and the almost total absence of data concerning informal investors contribute to market inefficiencies. The proposed research should yield techniques for increasing the efficiency of the informal risk capital markets, with potential public benefits well in excess of costs.

The research is expected to yield the following specific results:

1. Biographical profiles of informal investors

2. Profiles of the investment criteria employed by informal investors

3. Analysis of the most efficient methods of gaining access to informal investors

4. An estimate of the volume of risk capital potentially available from informal investors

5. Analysis of successful venture founders (a subset of informal investors) as a source of risk capital and management expertise for inventors and new foundation firms

6. Recommendations for public policy initiatives designed to increase the availability of informal risk capital

7. Analysis of the potential role of Small Business Development Centers in facilitating the flow of risk capital from informal investors to inventors, entrepreneurs, and established foundation firms

8. Analysis of entrepreneurial assistance organizations as a source of investment opportunities, including analysis of their ability to facilitate the flow of informal risk capital by providing services that enhance the probability of successful enterprise development. Examples of entrepreneurial support groups in New England include:

a. Maine Development Foundation
Maine Capital Corporation
Augusta, Maine

b. New Enterprise Institute
Portland, Maine

c. New England Industrial Resources Development Program
Durham, New Hampshire

d. Northern Community Investment Corporation
St. Johnsbury, Vermont

e. Massachusetts Technology Development Foundation
Wakefield, Massachusetts
f. Northeast Solar Energy Center
Cambridge, Massachusetts
g. Smaller Business Association of New England
Waltham, Massachusetts
h. New England Innovation Group
Providence, Rhode Island
i. Connecticut Product Development Corporation
Hartford, Connecticut
j. New England Research Application Center
Storrs, Connecticut

9. Analysis of the potential contribution of informal risk capital to the federal programs designed to facilitate the commercialization of innovative technologies. Examples of federal technology development programs include:

a. Department of Energy
(*1*) Northeast Solar Energy Center
(*2*) Small-Scale Appropriate Technology Grants Program
b. National Science Foundation
(*1*) Innovation Centers Experiment
(*2*) Small-Scale Business Innovation Research Program
c. Department of Commerce—Experimental Technology Incentive Program
d. National Bureau of Standards—Energy Related Inventions Programs

10. Assessment of the feasibility of a pooled investment fund (SBIC) designed to meet the investment objectives of informal investors and, at the same time, to offer an opportunity to participate in a diversified, professionally managed portfolio of venture investments

11. A data base for designing and testing a market intervention project to increase the efficiency of the informal risk capital markets in New England. This application of the data could be the single most important outcome of the proposed research.

The SBA's Office of Economic Research is a division of the new Office of Advocacy and, therefore, is concerned with public policy initiatives to improve the small business environment. The current research is expected to contribute to public policy in the following areas:

1. The research is designed to identify the investment criteria employed by informal investors. Once these criteria are understood, appropriate incentives can be designed to meet these criteria and thereby stimulate the flow of informal risk capital to inventors, entrepreneurs, and established foundation firms.

2. The survey questionnaire has been designed to include questions dealing with investor attitudes toward current public policy proposals, e.g., capital gains tax modifications, SEC regulations, and IRS Sub-Chapter S provisions.

3. The research will explore the feasibility of creating an SBIC, publicly held by informal investors, designed to provide the type of risk capital now provided directly by individual investors. Such an SBIC could develop working relationships with organizations established to assist entrepreneurs and inventors, and would offer informal investors the opportunity to place part of their funds in a diversified portfolio under professional management. Potential public benefits may justify the development of special incentives to stimulate the formation of SBICs serving informal investors on the one hand, and inventors, entrepreneurs, and growing foundation firms on the other.

4. The research will assess the feasibility of creating a mechanism to increase the efficiency of the informal risk capital markets and thereby increase the flow of risk capital from informal investors and entrepreneurs. Such an activity could be part of the services provided by SBA-sponsored Small Business Development Centers and could be the single most significant outcome of the research. By providing access to the risk capital essential to the commercialization of new technology, such a program would complement public programs established to stimulate the development of technology and its transfer to the marketplace.

This research faces two major challenges: identifying informal investors and collecting and analyzing useful data. Informal investors are defined to include sources of risk capital other than professionally managed venture capital firms and SBICs. Wealthy individuals constitute the primary component of the group. Also included are local investment clubs and smaller corporations pursuing expansion or diversification strategies. Wealthy individuals include practicing and retired executives and other professionals, successful entrepreneurs, and representatives of families with inherited wealth. In view of their diversity and their preference for anonymity, creative techniques will be required to identify and reach these investors. Lessons learned in the search process alone will be useful in providing guidelines for inventors and entrepreneurs seeking informal risk capital. In addition to the collection of descriptive data, a major benefit will lie in the creation of channels of communication which will facilitate the flow of investment opportunities to informal investors and the flow of risk capital to inventors and entrepreneurs.

During the first three months of the project, a range of techniques for reaching informal investors was explored. Sources included the following:

1. Files of regional organizations providing entrepreneurial support services (New England Industrial Resources Development Program, Smaller Business Association of New England, Massachusetts Technology Development Foundation, etc.). This approach was used successfully in the 1978 pilot research.

2. State files of plane, boat, and automobile registrations

3. Cooperative arrangements with securities dealers, business brokers, and venture capitalists

4. Purchased mailing lists

5. Professional society membership lists (bar associations, medical societies, state CPA societies, etc.)

6. Cooperative arrangements with commercial banks and trust companies

7. Fraternal and civic organizations

8. College and university alumni directories

The search for informal investors will pay particular attention to the identification of successful entrepreneurs, who tend to be linked by an informal network of social and professional contacts. The research project will solicit the interest and cooperation of these individuals, many of whom financed their own ventures through informal sources of risk capital.

An investment capital questionnaire was developed and tested, primarily in northern New England, during the fall of 1978. During the first three months of the current research project, the original questionnaire was revised and expanded on the basis of the 1978 research and the cooperation of the entrepreneurial assistance organizations and federal programs. The revised questionnaire is constructed to collect six categories of information from informal investors: risk capital investment history, current investment objectives, rate of return objectives, White House Conference recommendations, investment referral sources, and biographical information. As of March 1, 1980, the machinery for distribution of the questionnaire was largely in place, and the project was awaiting clearance from the U.S. Office of Management and Budget.

Observations and suggestions

These examples of recent risk capital research are offered within the broader context of the emerging body of knowledge about entrepreneurship and its contribution to job creation, technological innovation, and competitive economic advantages. The relationship between risk capital and entrepreneurship in New England has served as a unifying theme. Following are a number of observations and suggestions for future risk capital research.

Observations

First, an analytical framework is needed to serve as the basis for the future risk capital research. Risk capital performs a unique role in financing high-risk, innovative activities and in earning its reward through the creation of new wealth based on capitalized earning power. In a sense, risk capital investments in new firms are the ultimate in discounted cash flow capital budgeting decisions. Some of Joseph Schumpeter's views on capital formation in emerging industries and capital destruction in declining industries may be helpful in developing such an analytical framework.

Second, there must be a careful definition of terms. For example, the stages in the development of new technology range from the extreme risks associated with the financing of inventors to the more moderate risks associated with the financing of proven businesses with expansion opportunities.

These varying degrees of risk require definition, as do the stages in the development of commercial enterprises. Each stage offers different risk and reward opportunities and consequently attracts investors with different propensities. On the investment side, the diverse types of risk capital investors must be identified before hypotheses can be tested or generalizations attempted.

Third, we must assemble data that describes the functioning of risk capital markets. The diverse, dispersed, and confidential nature of most risk capital transactions presents a real obstacle to rigorous research. Any significant research effort will face a challenge in collecting relevant data. Compromises will be necessary and frustrations frequent. Nevertheless, the potential contributions to the free enterprise system will be substantial. At least initially, many of the niceties of research will be sacrificed in return for practical results. Innovation is a sloppy process and, until better data bases are available, risk capital research will be a sloppy but rewarding process. This is not an excuse for abandoning intellectual rigor. It is an observation about the environment within which intellectual rigor must function.

Fourth, the opportunities for risk capital research are enormous. This field of finance is virtually unexplored. Recent theories of portfolio management in efficient markets, the behavior of stock prices, and the capital asset pricing models have been based on assumptions that ignore many of the significant characteristics of the risk capital markets, including imperfect information, high transaction costs, and increasing market segmentation.

Research on the relationship of risk capital to entrepreneurship, and the contribution of entrepreneurship to job formation, technological innovation, tax revenue, productivity, price stability, and international payment balances has created a growing national interest in capital formation, particularly in risk capital formation. The Office of Economic Research within SBA's new Office of Advocacy provides in excess of $1 million per year to fund an extramural small business economic research program on policy-oriented topics: (1) the effects of government programs, policies, and regulations on small business; (2) the contribution of small business to the economic and social welfare of the United States; and (3) the development of theories or methodology for studying small business problems.

The growing interest in entrepreneurship is international in scope. The World Bank has begun to create jobs by assisting small enterprises in developing countries. World Bank lending to small enterprises is expected to reach $300 million by 1981, a six-fold increase over 1978.

Research suggestions

Several directions for risk capital research seem promising. The national interest in capital formation and so-called "supply side" economics has led to legislative proposals for a variety of tax incentives for capital formation. An examination of the impact of 1978 reductions in capital gains taxes would be timely and could provide a basis for evaluating current proposals for capital gains rollovers and tax credits for direct investment in small firms.

Cooperation with trade associations such as the National Association of Securities Dealers, the National Venture Capital Association, and the National Association of Small Business Investment Companies should be productive. Those associations are concerned with industry performance and support research that contributes new insights. Their assistance in collecting industry data can be invaluable. Possible cooperative projects include measurement of the past performance of risk capital investors, the current cost of risk capital, and risk/reward trade-off functions. These organizations are concerned with the effect of institutionalized savings (pension fund growth and investment policy, for example) upon the availability of risk capital and would probably cooperate in research on this phenomenon. The vitality of regional securities underwriters, the new issues market, and secondary, over-the-counter markets for shares in small firms also offer cooperative research opportunities.

Risk capital and entrepreneurship contributions to job creation, technological innovation, tax revenues, productivity, price performance, and international payment balances ought to be broadly and precisely quantified. Such research should contain useful implications for regional and national economic policy. The creative character of risk capital could be instructive for examining the creation of economic wealth. Researchers might use a "net present value" capital budgeting model to contrast the level of risk capital invested in new firms with the going-concern value of the ventures created. As a starting point, a comparison of book values and market values for publicly traded shares in young companies would be of interest. The difference between incremental book values and market values over a comparable period for established "Fortune 500" firms would provide a contrast to illustrate the relative capital creativity of risk capital.

A provocative characteristic of individual, as opposed to institutional, risk investors appears to be the partial substitutability of non-financial for financial rewards on a risk capital investment. The concept of "psychic income," often of a *pro bono publico* nature, could be usefully explored.

Finally, the high cost and low quality of communication between entrepreneurs and risk capital investors appear to be among the major barriers to the flow of risk capital. Methods for reducing the cost and raising the quality of information could result in public policies designed to improve the performance of the risk capital markets. These observations and suggestions are offered with the hope that they will spark interest in risk capital research. It is a large and exciting field with attractive opportunities for collaborative research efforts.

References

BIRCH, D. L., *The Job Generation Process.* MIT Program on Neighborhood and Regional Change, Economic Development Administration. Washington, D.C.: U.S. Department of Commerce, 1979.

BRIGHT, J. R., "Some Lessons from Technological Innovations Research," *Les Nouvelles* (Journal of Licensing Executives) 4, No. 5 (November 1969).

Emerging Innovative Companies—An Endangered Species. Washington, D.C.: National Venture Capital Association, 1976.

HEKMAN, J. S., "What Attracts Industry to New England?" *New England Economic Indicators.* Boston: Federal Reserve Bank of Boston, 1978.

JUSENIUS, C. L., and LEDEBUR, L., *Where Have all the Firms Gone?* Economic Development Administration. Washington, D.C.: U.S. Department of Commerce, 1977.

MCMURTRY, B. J., "Institutional Venture Associates" (Unpublished working paper prepared for Conference on Innovations and Invention in Canada, Ottawa, 1976).

MORSE, R. S., and FLENDER, J. O., *The Role of New Technical Enterprises in the United States Economy.* Washington, D.C.: U.S. Department of Commerce, 1976.

NATIONAL SCIENCE BOARD, *Science Indicators 1976.* Washington, D.C.: National Science Foundation, 1977.

NATIONAL SCIENCE FOUNDATION news releases, April 1979 and October 1979.

New England Business: Profile and Analysis. Boston: Price Waterhouse and Company, September 30, 1976.

New England Business: Verification of Capital Gaps in New England. Boston: T. A. Associates, September 1976.

O'NEIL, J. E., "The New England Entrepreneurial Experience" (Unpublished M.B.A. research paper, University of New Hampshire, Whittemore School of Business and Economics, 1971).

ORTON, RUSSELL, Director, New England Industrial Resources Development Program. Interview in June 1979.

Report of the SBA Task Force on Venture and Equity Capital. Washington, D.C.: U.S. Small Business Administration, January 1977.

Report of the Task Force of Capital and Labor Markets. Boston: New England Regional Commission, November 12, 1975.

SBA Size Standards for the SBIC Program (Position Paper). Washington, D.C.: National Association of Small Business Investment Companies, 1977.

Small Business Financing: The Current Environment and Suggestions for Improvement (Report of the Joint Industry/Government Committee on Small Business Financing). Washington, D.C.: National Association of Securities Dealers, Inc., May 22, 1979.

"Small Firms and Federal R & D" (Report to the Office of Federal Procurement Policy). Washington, D.C.: Office of Management and Budget, Executive Office of the President, March 10, 1977.

Technological Innovation: Its Environment and Management. Technical Advisory Board. Washington, D.C.: U.S. Department of Commerce, 1967.

The Role of High Technology Industries in Economic Growth. Cambridge, Mass.: Data Resources, Inc., 1977.

The Small Business Company Program: Who Does It Benefit? Washington, D.C.: Comptroller General of the United States, March 1978.

U.S. House of Representatives, *Hearings, Small Business Access to Equity and Venture Capital.* Washington, D.C.: Committee on Small Business, Subcommittee on Capital Investment and Business Opportunities, May 12 & 18, July 16, 1977.

U.S. House of Representatives, *Hearing, Small Business Investment Company Program.* Washington, D.C.: Committee on Small Business, Subcommittee on Capital Investment and Business Opportunities, May 8, 1978.

U.S. Senate, "Statement of William R. Hambrecht before the Senate Committee on Small Business." Washington, D.C.: Select Committee on Small Business, May 22, 1979.

chapter ix

Venture capital research

David J. Brophy

Overview

The purpose of this chapter is to discuss research needs and opportunities in venture capital investment and to review appropriate methodologies. Examples are derived from research carried out by this author. They are designed to address some of the observations put forth by Wetzel in the preceding chapter. It is hoped that the several projects reported below will encourage others to explore the economics of entrepreneurship.

Background

The summary in the preceding chapter of risk capital research fairly represents the main current issues in the field. An analytical framework, with both theoretical and empirical components, must be developed if serious research is to progress. Concerning the theoretical component, Wetzel states that much of the recent research ignored significant characteristics of the risk capital markets. Regarding the empirical component, he argues for a careful definition of terms and for a willingness to compromise in developing basic data. Wetzel concludes that opportunities for risk capital research are enormous and he indicates several avenues for future research. Among them:

- an analysis of the impact on venture capital investment of the 1978 revision of the capital gains tax;
- a "net present value" analysis of the relationship between the initial investment in new firms and their present going-concern value.

In this chapter no definitive treatment of the state of research in the venture capital investment field is attempted. The research presented addresses, in whole or in part, the topics suggested by Wetzel for future research.

The first study discussed compares the performance and financing experience of matched samples of high-technology firms in the Cambridge–Boston area and the Ann Arbor–Detroit area. Offering a useful and rigorous analytical framework for venture capital research, this study addresses issues raised by Wetzel—the functioning of the market, flow of information, and productivity of venture capital investment. It also addresses several that were not raised—geographic differentials, life cycle financing patterns, and the roles of various funds sources at different stages of the firm's development.

The second study applies modern finance theory to the coordination of equity participation agreements and bank loans to new and small firms. It demonstrates, in this writer's view at least, that micro-finance theory can be usefully applied to venture capital investment and small business finance.

These examples are offered in the interests of future productive research.

A study of venture capital investment: the financing of new, technology-based firms

New, technology-based firms (NTBFs) are corporate vehicles through which technological entrepreneurs mobilize resources to develop and market an innovation, with profits accruing to the firm and its investors (Roberts 1969). They are often formed by people who "spin off" from larger organizations or other NTBFs, transferring technology in the process (Cooper 1971). It is generally argued that the formation and development of NTBFs should be encouraged by public and private sector policy-makers both because of beneficial effects on the national rate of technological innovation and because of direct contributions to national and regional economic development (U.S. Department of Commerce 1967).

NTBFs tend to be concentrated geographically. Environmental factors commonly associated with successful NTBF clusters are (Spiegelman 1964, Clark 1972, Cooper 1971):

1. A supply of technological entrepreneurs
2. A local culture conducive to the formation and development of new, small firms by technological entrepreneurs
3. The existence of technology-intensive sources of employment which serve as "incubators" for NTBFs
4. The presence of firms and institutions which offer support of various kinds to NTBFs
5. The existence of a local customer base (a home market)
6. Local access to financing of the type needed by NTBFs

Particular attention has recently been directed to the availability of finance (Robinson 1968, U.S. Department of Commerce 1970). The perceived local access to finance as well as the actual access may influence NTBF development in particular areas, given the presence of other factors usually associated with NTBF clustering (Deutermann 1966, Hodgins 1972, Shapero et al. 1969). However, little research has been done to determine the relative weight of the finance factor or to determine regional differences in its influence.

Problem statement and methodology

The following analysis compares NTBFs incorporated and operating from 1965 to 1970 in the Ann Arbor–Detroit area and the Greater Boston metropolitan area. It assesses the availability and terms of local financing and their effects on NTBF performance.

Ann Arbor–Detroit was chosen as a study group because its NTBF cluster is in the early stages of development, and there does not appear to be a well developed venture capital network in the area. Boston was chosen as the control area since it has a well developed NTBF cluster and outstanding access to venture financing, as reflected in this comment:

The Panel accepts the proposition that our economy can best be served through a level of venture capital activity comparable to that which is found in the Boston area. (U.S. Department of Commerce 1970)

First, performance measures for the first four years of firm life were compared using sales and assets as indicators. The analysis tests the hypothesis that sales performance in the early years of NTBF life is significantly related to the volume of total assets the firm is able to acquire.

Second, financing experiences were analyzed in terms of the amount of required capital raised, the sources of funds, the type of financial instruments used, and the cost of funds. The analysis tests the hypothesis that the availability of financing, as reflected by the percentage of desired funds obtained, significantly affects the relationship between the volume of assets obtained and subsequent level of sales.

Information for the study was developed through intensive interview analysis of 26 NTBFs located in the Ann Arbor–Detroit area and 26 comparable firms in the Greater Boston area. All firms were founded in the period between 1965 and 1970. Firms were selected so as to provide reasonably representative and comparable cross sections.

Performance characteristics of the samples

Along with sales and asset size, two other indicators of performance were measured: the time required to develop the firm's first proprietary product working prototype, and the time required from date of incorporation to realization of first operating revenues.

Sales growth

Sales growth is an important indicator of success since it reflects acceptance of the firm's product or service, provides cash flow, and is viewed positively by equity investors and creditors. Due partly to the youth of the firms and the small number of observations, I found quite variable sales growth within each geographic region. Table 1 shows the median sales of the Ann Arbor–Detroit and Boston firms during the first four years after incorporation. The Boston group median sales exceeded those of the Ann Arbor–Detroit group in years 1, 2, and 4. In the third year after incorporation the Ann Arbor–Detroit firms had median sales of $315,000 compared to $300,000 for the Boston sample. This small difference is due in part to the special circumstances of two Boston firms which were undergoing major product changes in their third year after incorporation.

The regression equation for growth in sales over time for the Boston firms is:

$$\underset{(32{,}134)}{\text{Sales} = \$216{,}170\ (\text{Age})} \qquad R^2 = 0.37 \qquad \text{Sig.} = 1\%$$

For Ann Arbor–Detroit the regression equation is:

$$\underset{(30{,}786)}{\text{Sales} = \$211{,}830\ (\text{Age})} \qquad R^2 = 0.38 \qquad \text{Sig.} = 1\%$$

The addition of the variable total assets lagged by one year also helped to explain sales variation. The regression equation for the Boston area is shown as:

$$\text{Sales} = \underset{(0.12)}{0.21}\ (\text{Lagged Assets}) + \$192{,}590\ (\text{Age})$$

$R^2 = 0.40$ Sig. = 1%

Partial R^2 Age: $R^2 = 0.26$ Sig. = 1%

Lagged Assets: $R^2 = 0.06$ Sig. = 10%

For the Ann Arbor–Detroit area the regression equation is shown as:

$$\text{Sales} = \underset{(12)}{0.72}\ (\text{Lagged Assets}) + \underset{(36{,}412)}{\$115{,}300}\ (\text{Age})$$

$R^2 = 0.61$ Sig. = 1%

Partial R^2: Age: $R^2 = 0.16$ Sig. = 5%

Lagged Assets: $R^2 = 0.39$ Sig. = 1%

These data show a higher rate of growth in sales for the Boston sample than for the Ann Arbor–Detroit sample and a substantial difference in the association between assets lagged one year and sales. The partial R^2 for the asset variable was considerably higher for the Ann Arbor–Detroit sample than for the Boston group. Unless explained by other factors, this suggests that the availability of assets (and the means to acquire them) was particularly important to the sales growth of Ann Arbor–Detroit firms; their lower growth rate, compared with the Boston firms, may be linked to asset deficiency.

Table 1 *Median values of sales and assets in each sample*

		Ann Arbor–Detroit		Greater Boston	
	Year	$(000)	n*	$(000)	n*
Sales	1	51.5	26	62.5	26
	2	174.0	26	240.0	24
	3	315.0	22	300.0	21
	4	400.0	11	641.5	12
Assets	1	59.0	26	84.0	26
	2	153.0	26	208.0	24
	3	193.0	21	557.0	22
	4	435.0	11	600.0	12

Asset growth

For the combined samples, the asset growth over time is expressed by:

$$\text{Assets} = \$243{,}720\,(\text{Age}) \qquad R^2 = 0.24 \qquad \text{Sig.} = 1\%$$
$$(35{,}607)$$

The growth of assets was faster for the Boston firms, as shown in Table 1. For Boston, the growth is expressed by:

$$\text{Assets} = \$270{,}000\,(\text{Age}) \qquad R^2 = 0.22 \qquad \text{Sig.} = 1\%$$
$$(58{,}364)$$

For Ann Arbor–Detroit, asset growth is expressed by:

$$\text{Assets} = \$216{,}740\,(\text{Age}) \qquad R^2 = 0.27 \qquad \text{Sig.} = 1\%$$
$$(40{,}140)$$

It is difficult to interpret the productive efficiency of these firms using only the relationship between assets and sales. Not only are qualitative differences omitted, but no measure is taken of capacity utilization. However, the median turnover of assets lagged by one year suggests some difference in asset utilization between the two samples.

These data suggest that while growth rates of sales and assets were higher for the Boston group, the Ann Arbor–Detroit group made better use of assets for producing sales one year away. This cannot be readily explained by differences in accounting for assets (capitalization of costs vs. expenses) or in the use of leased facilities, since differences of this type were found to be minor.

These relationships apparently reflect the more rapid asset growth among the Boston firms and suggest that the Ann Arbor–Detroit firms were forced to increase sales from smaller asset bases. The rate of asset growth was most probably a constraint on sales growth, despite a comparatively high rate of

Table 2 *Median turnover of total assets lagged one year*

	Years from incorporation		
Sample	**2**	**3**	**4**
Boston	2.79	1.52	1.18
Ann Arbor-Detroit	2.97	2.05	2.02

asset utilization. Clearly, in the absence of qualitative information, such conclusions must be be treated with caution.

Other measures of performance

Three additional measures of early NTBF performance were compared for the firms in the two geographic areas. These comparisons appear in Table 3.

When the firm has developed a first working prototype, it has something to offer for sale. The time required to develop a prototype is one indication of the firm's ability to activate its potential for generating capital internally through sales and retained earnings. Ann Arbor–Detroit firms, as measured by the median, attained this stage earlier in life than did the Boston firms.

The number of months from incorporation to the first revenues from operations is another measure of firm performance. The Boston firms took a median of three months and a mean of 4.4 months to generate revenues from operations; the Ann Arbor–Detroit firms took a median of four months and a mean of 5.5 months.

We also timed the point at which the founders come to believe the firm will survive. The median number of months from incorporation to identified survival point was 31 months for the Ann Arbor–Detroit firms and 27 months for the Boston group. The mean statistics were 35.3 months and 31.1 months, respectively. There were also important differences in the survival indicators used by founders. Of the 24 Ann Arbor–Detroit founders who answered the question, six said that the most important indicator of survival was the first large contract or purchase order. Six others said that repeat sales gave them confidence of their survival. Only one Michigan founder answered that the completion of a large financing had indicated to him that the firm would survive. Twenty-five Boston founders specified the indicators that had persuaded them of survival. Nine named their first large contract or repeat sales, while seven named the completion of a large financing.

Table 3 *Other measures of new, technology-based firm performance*

	Boston		Ann Arbor–Detroit	
Measures of performance	**Median**	**Mean**	**Median**	**Mean**
Number of months from incorporation to first proprietory product prototype	9	9.2	8	10.5
Number of months from incorporation to first revenues from operations	3	4.4	4	5.5
Number of months from incorporation to first survival point	27	31.1	31	35.3

Summary

The evidence indicates that the Boston group was able to increase sales and assets more quickly than was the Ann Arbor–Detroit group. Smaller differences were apparent in the time it took to develop a prototype, to obtain revenues from operations, and to attain perceived survival points.

Sales growth was found to be significantly associated with the asset level of previous years. I conclude from this that the availability of financing for asset growth is of particular importance to the development of the firms. Further evidence and discussion of this point follows.

Capital support characteristics of the samples

The following equation shows the relationship of sales to capital raised for all the firms in our sample:

$$\text{Sales} = \underset{(55{,}500)}{\$164{,}200}\,(\text{Age}) + \underset{(0.172)}{0.42}\,(\text{Capital Raised})$$

$R^2 = 0.37$	Sig. = 5%	
Partial R^2:	Age: $R^2 = 0.20$	Sig. = 5%
Capital Raised:	$R^2 = 0.22$	Sig. = 5%

The relationship between the amount of capital previously raised and the level of sales is positive and significant, although not very strong in terms of R^2. This indicates that success in obtaining funding does influence the rate of asset growth and therefore the rate of sales growth.

The relationship of sales to capital raised differs between the two geographical groups. Among the Boston firms it is:

$$\text{Sales} = \underset{(68{,}722)}{\$174{,}300}\,(\text{Age}) + \underset{(0.12)}{0.23}\,(\text{Capital Raised})$$

$R^2 = 0.35$	Sig. = 5%	
Partial R^2:	Age: $R^2 = 0.29$	Sig. = 5%
Capital Raised:	$R^2 = 0.15$	Sig. = 10%

Within the Ann Arbor–Detroit group it is:

$$\text{Sales} = \underset{(43{,}315)}{\$150{,}400}\,(\text{Age}) + \underset{(0.22)}{0.62}\,(\text{Capital Raised})$$

Partial R^2:	Age: $R^2 = 0.17$	Sig. = 5%
Capital Raised:	$R^2 = 0.65$	Sig. = 1%

These statistics suggest that the link between capital raised and sales performance was more important among the Ann Arbor–Detroit firms than among the Boston firms. Since growth of sales and assets was also lower for the Ann Arbor–Detroit group than for the Boston group, finance may have been a constraining force on sales within the Michigan group.

Tables 4 through 7 summarize pertinent aspects of the financial support obtained by both groups over the first four years of life. Table 4 shows that a greater proportion of the Ann Arbor–Detroit firms expressed a need for funds each year. There was little difference between the two groups with respect to the number of firms which obtained at least some of the needed capital. Expressed capital need was greater in each of the first two years for the Ann Arbor–Detroit firms than for the Boston firms; the reverse was true for the third and fourth years. For the total and mean amounts, the Boston sample raised a greater proportion of needed funds in each year, although the differences between the two samples were negligible in years two and four. The variance suggests that larger firms may have been more successful in obtaining capital than smaller firms.

Only in the fourth year did the percentages of the two areas coincide; the "success rate" of the Ann Arbor–Detroit group, as measured by the median values, was substantially below that of the Boston group for the first three years.

The samples also differ in the amount of financing provided by sources within the home state. In terms of total financing, the Boston group raised substantially more in Massachusetts in years one and three than the Ann Arbor–Detroit firms raised in Michigan; in years two and four the differences were negligible. When the median values are considered, the differences increase appreciably.

To the extent that the median value is more representative of the "typical firm," it may be inferred that Michigan has been considerably less hospitable to its NTBF group than Massachusetts has been to its group of new firms.

Table 7 shows the sources of financial support for each group year by year. The pattern observed in previous studies is also apparent in these data (Donaldson 1955, Baty 1963, Rubenstein 1958). Founders, friends and relatives, and private individuals contributed significantly in the first year and in decreasing proportions thereafter. In the Ann Arbor–Detroit sample, these populations evidence a slightly higher rate of contribution and a slightly longer tenure as active contributors. Investment by limited partnerships differed little between the areas. The Ann Arbor–Detroit group raised a larger percentage of its funds from these informal sources in each of the four years than did the Boston sample.

Major differences are also apparent in the institutional sources of funds utilized by the two samples. Whereas SBIC and private venture capital firms have been significant in number and size in Massachusetts, they have been scarce and only modestly capitalized in Michigan; presently only one SBIC and one private venture capital firm operate in Michigan. The absence of these facilities may account in part for the relative importance to the Ann Arbor–Detroit group of public issues, financing through investment banking houses, and financing through private firms (large nonfinancial corporations).

Table 4 *Summary of financial support during first four years*

NTBF Financial support	Boston First year	Boston Second year	Boston Third year	Boston Fourth year	Ann Arbor–Detroit First year	Ann Arbor–Detroit Second year	Ann Arbor–Detroit Third year	Ann Arbor–Detroit Fourth year
Number of firms	26	24	22	12	26	26	21	11
Number of firms needing capital	26	19	18	10	26	22	20	10
Number of firms obtaining capital	26	17	18	8	26	20	18	8
Total capital needed	$7,134,900	$7,160,100	$12,100,000	$5,797,700	$7,550,100	$12,250,000	$9,850,700	$5,104,300
Total capital raised	5,297,900	6,192,400	5,872,000	4,543,000	4,869,100	10,021,000	6,720,700	3,950,000
Percentage of needed capital raised	74%	86%	82%	78%	64%	81%	68%	77%
Mean capital needed*	$ 274,400	$ 376,800	$ 672,200	$ 620,000	$ 292,700	$ 556,800	$ 392,500	$ 475,000
	(105,300)	(271,300)	(336,100)	(381,900)	(162,800)	(272,000)	(322,700)	(279,400)
Median capital needed*	175,000	313,300	525,000	450,000	200,000	500,000	420,700	400,000
Mean capital raised*	203,800	325,900	548,400	454,300	187,300	455,500	492,500	475,000
	(91,400)	(146,500)	(268,400)	(213,300)	(92,200)	(468,600)	(279,900)	(406,500)
Median capital raised*	146,700	275,000	465,500	370,000	120,000	240,000	317,500	325,000
Total capital raised instate	4,175,000	4,892,000	7,775,500	2,843,000	3,369,000	4,700,000	4,120,000	3,050,030
Percentage of capital raised instate	89%	79%	79%	63%	69%	50%	61%	77%
Mean capital raised instate*	$ 160,600	$ 257,500	$ 432,000	$ 284,300	$ 129,600	$ 213,600	$ 206,000	$ 305,000
	(65,100)	(160,000)	(215,700)	(51,900)	(51,900)	(290,500)	(215,500)	(285,000)
Median capital raised instate*	150,000	220,000	425,000	256,700	135,000	200,000	200,000	217,500

*Means and medians calculated for all firms needing capital during the year.

**Indicates that the difference in means for Boston and Ann Arbor–Detroit firms was significant at the 5% level.

Table 5 *Percentage of median needed capital raised*

Sample	Years from incorporation 1	2	3	4
Boston	84%	88%	89%	82%
Ann Arbor-Detroit	60%	48%	75%	81%

In the first two years commercial banks constituted the second-largest source of financing for the Boston firms; this is in sharp contrast to the experience of the Ann Arbor–Detroit group. Due perhaps to the lack of bank participation, the Ann Arbor–Detroit firms utilized a larger volume of lease financing than did the Boston firms.

Table 8 shows the distribution of capital raised by type of financing instrument, as well as the average cost of funds raised in each category. The data show that the Boston sample was able to finance very heavily with straight debt (almost entirely from banks) in the first two years and was able to delay the sale of equity until those years in which its performance was comparatively strong. The Ann Arbor–Detroit firms relied much more heavily on equity-related instruments in the first two years; the proportion of their funds accounted for by straight equity financing was lower in years three and four than in year two and than in the Boston sample.

The difference in the use of straight debt (bank credit) does not show up in the average interest rates paid by the two groups. Inferences about supply conditions may be made on the basis of Table 8. In the first year the average and median amount of capital raised via straight debt was twice as large among the Boston group as among the Ann Arbor–Detroit group. The difference gradually declined until, in year four, the relationship was reversed. This tendency, along with the gradual extension of maturities, suggests that Ann Arbor–Detroit banks are averse to start-up firms but willing to extend

Table 6 *Percentage of needed capital raised in home state*

Sample	Years from incorporation 1	2	3	4
Boston	86%	70%	81%	57%
Ann Arbor-Detroit	68%	40%	48%	54%

Table 7 *Sources of financial support during first four years percentage of total capital raised*

	Boston				Ann Arbor–Detroit			
Source of capital*	**First year (26 firms)**	**Second year (24 firms)**	**Third year (22 firms)**	**Fourth year (12 firms)**	**First year (26 firms)**	**Second year (26 firms)**	**Third year (21 firms)**	**Fourth year (11 firms)**
Founders	24.2% (25)	6.6% (8)	2.3% (3)	2.0% (1)	27.5% (26)	7.2% (9)	4.5% (5)	3.5% (2)
Friends and relatives	4.1% (7)	0.0% (0)	0.0% (0)	0.0% (0)	5.4% (7)	0.0% (0)	2.5% (2)	0.0% (0)
Private individuals	14.3% (10)	7.1% (4)	0.4% (1)	1.2% (2)	15.7% (14)	4.1% (7)	1.9% (2)	3.6% (1)
Limited investment partnerships	6.4% (5)	0.8% (2)	6.8% (2)	5.3% (1)	4.9% (3)	7.1% (4)	3.0% (2)	5.5% (2)
SBICs and private venture capital firms	15.1% (4)	34.2% (5)	18.2% (5)	19.9% (4)	2.3% (3)	5.0% (2)	7.3% (2)	6.0% (2)
Investment banks	12.0% (2)	1.5% (1)	8.6% (2)	10.0% (3)	15.3% (3)	9.6% (3)	26.4% (3)	21.5% (3)
Commercial banks	16.1% (14)	31.8% (9)	8.9% (7)	11.4% (6)	7.6% (11)	4.2% (6)	9.4% (6)	10.8% (4)
Private firms	4.1% (4)	9.3% (3)	9.7% (4)	8.2% (3)	11.2% (3)	19.8% (7)	22.3% (6)	20.0% (3)
Public offerings	0.0% (0)	4.6% (1)	42.6% (4)	38.0% (3)	0.0% (0)	41.1% (2)	21.0% (3)	25.7% (2)
Insurance companies	0.0% (0)	2.7% (1)	0.0% (0)	2.2% (1)	0.0% (0)	0.0% (0)	0.0% (0)	0.0% (0)
Other (including leasing companies)	3.7% (7)	1.4% (4)	2.5% (4)	1.8% (3)	10.1% (8)	1.9% (4)	1.7% (3)	3.4% (3)
Total firms obtaining capital	100.0% (26)	100.0% (19)	100.0% (18)	100.0% (8)	100.0% (26)	100.0% (22)	100.0% (20)	100.0% (8)

*In parentheses are the number of firms receiving capital from that source.

credit in large amounts at competitive rates to firms that have survived beyond early threshold points.

Roughly one-quarter of the firms seeking capital used equity-related debt instruments, either convertible debt or debt with warrants. The interest rate on debt averaged significantly lower (150–300 basis points) when the rate on the average short-term straight debt was used. While the average maturity was quite short, typically three years, it was longer and characterized by greater dispersion among the Boston firms.

The cost of financing was determined by relating the cash raised to the percentage of the company's stock it purchased either directly or conditionally. The dollar figures shown in Table 8 represent the price paid by the purchaser for 1 percent of the company stock. For both samples, the price of the equity paid by purchasers of equity-related debt increased as the company matured; the low fourth year figures represent only two observations and may be inadequate for comparative purposes. The cost of financing via equity-related debt was clearly lower for the Boston firms in all years. The cost spread steadily declined from a ratio of 1.74 in year one to a ratio of 1.17 in year four.

All of the firms studied raised capital through sale of straight equity (common stock) in year one; about two-thirds of the firms raising funds in each of the other years financed through sale of equity. This amounted to the largest single means of raising funds, both year by year and cumulatively.

According to our measure, the cost of funds was higher through the sale of stock than through the sale of equity-linked debt. As might be expected, the average cost of funds decreased over time. The price paid per 1 percent of equity purchased increased at a compound annual rate of 40 percent for the Boston group and 41.5 percent for the Ann Arbor–Detroit group. While decline in the cost of equity was comparable between the two samples, the cost level was consistently higher within the Ann Arbor–Detroit group.

An important qualitative dimension of capital support is the referral by financial institutions to other potential sources of capital. The most important difference in referral networks was the link between commercial banks and SBICs, which was quite evident in Boston and almost totally absent in Ann Arbor–Detroit. In Boston 12 bank referrals led to actual financings; in Ann Arbor–Detroit only five bank referrals led to financing (see Table 9). This link may explain much of the difference between the bank and SBIC support in the two areas. Not every NTBF is bankable early in its life; many need equity capital before they can obtain loans.

The persons or institutions making the referral for first NTBF bank loans are shown in Table 10. Seven of 20 first bank loans made to the Ann Arbor–Detroit group involved a specific referral by another institution or person; 11 of 22 first bank loans made to the Boston group involved a referral from another financial institution.

Table 8 *Amount of capital raised by type of financial instrument used and cost of capital*

Amount of capital, instruments used, and cost of capital	Boston First year (26 firms)	Boston Second year (24 firms)	Boston Third year (22 firms)	Boston Fourth year (12 firms)	Ann Arbor–Detroit First year (26 firms)	Ann Arbor–Detroit Second year (26 firms)	Ann Arbor–Detroit Third year (21 firms)	Ann Arbor–Detroit Fourth year (10 firms)
Straight debt								
Number of firms that received capital	17	15	9	7	13	9	7	5
Total amount	$1,776,700	$2,132,000	$1,590,000	$1,225,000	$ 752,100	$ 820,000	$1,150,000	$1,100,000
Mean amount	104,500	142,100	176,000	175,000	57,900	91,100	164,300	220,000
	(52,000)	(135,500)	(166,700)	(123,900)	(38,800)	(56,600)	(101,810)	(187,700)
Median amount	75,000	107,000	150,000	175,000	35,000	75,000	140,000	125,000
Mean maturity	95 days	106 days	6.2 months	8.9 months	85 days	92 days	6.2 months	6.1 months
	(32 days)	(54 days)	(3.2 mos.)	(7.1 mos.)	(24 days)	(60 days)	(2.5 mos.)	(4.8 mos.)
Mean interest rate*	8.9%	8.2%	9.3%	8.5%	9.2%	8.5%	8.7%	8.8%
	(0.45%)	(0.62%)	(0.50%)	(0.55%)	(0.73%)	(0.45%)	(0.75%)	(0.50%)
Convertible debt or debt with warrants								
Number of firms that received capital	8	6	5	2	5	5	4	2
Total amount	$1,100,000	$1,440,000	$1,452,000	$ 400,000	$1,255,000	$1,255,000	$1,800,000	$ 525,000
Mean amount	137,500	240,000	290,400	200,000	251,000	251,000	450,000	262,500
	(83,200)	(155,500)	(262,100)	(100,000)	(113,300)	(221,900)	(344,400)	(62,500)
Median amount	100,000	186,700	159,100	200,000	167,000	200,000	375,000	262,500
Mean maturity*	5.2 Years	3.3 Years	3.8 Years	2.5 Years	3.1 Years	2.9 Years	3.3 Years	3.5 Years
	(6.4 Years)	(2.6 Years)	(1.8 Years)	(0.25 Years)	(3.0 Years)	(0.6 Years)	(2.4 Years)	(0.25 Years)
Mean interest rate*	6.2%	5.8%	6.9%	7.2%	6.2%	6.6%	7.2%	7.5%
	(0.21%)	(0.36%)	(0.75%)	(0.20%)	(0.33%)	(0.35%)	(0.47%)	(0.50%)

Mean control cost ($ Cost per 1% of firm convertible to debt)	27,000	32,700	35,000	22,300	15,500	18,500	25,000	19,000
	(15,000)	(21,600)	(32,100)	(2,500)	(7,900)	(14,200)	(12,000)	(1,000)
Straight equity								
Number of firms that received capital	26	13	13	7	26	16	14	7
Total amount	$2,421,200	$2,620,400	$6,830,000	$2,918,000	$2,862,000	$7,946,000	$3,770,700	$2,325,000
Mean amount	93,100	201,600	525,400	416,900	110,100	496,600	296,300	332,100
	(82,000)	(141,600)	(311,200)	(252,900)	(86,500)	(471,100)	(263,310)	(345,000)
Median amount	85,000	127,500	414,500	350,000	75,000	237,500	215,000	260,000
Mean control cost ($ Cost per 1% of equity purchased)	7,800	14,600	26,500	30,000	5,500	12,300	18,500	22,000
	(4,800)	(3,700)	(15,500)	(27,200)	(2,200)	(6,700)	(11,800)	(21,000)

*The arithmetic means and standard deviations are weighted by the amounts of capital involved.

Table 9 *Successful bank referrals to other capital sources*

	Boston	Ann Arbor–Detroit
Private individuals	1	0
Limited investment partnerships	0	2
SBICs and private venture capital firms	5	0
Investment banks	1	2
Insurance companies	1	0
Other commercial banks	1	0
Private firms	2	0
Other (including major leasing)	1	1
Total bank referral to successful financings	12	5

Table 10 *Source of referral to bank for first bank loan*

	Boston	Ann Arbor–Detroit
General knowledge of bank	5	10
Previous business foundings	6	3
Previous investors	7	4
SBIC or private venture capital firm	2	0
Business or financial consultant	2	1
Attorney or accountant	0	1
Investment banks	0	1
Total firms with one or more bank loans	22	20

Summary

This evidence suggests that there is a significant relationship between the availability of capital support for asset acquisition and the performance of firms as measured by growth in sales. Because the relationship appeared to be stronger for the Ann Arbor–Detroit firms, and since their growth in assets and sales was substantially below that of the Boston group, it is inferred that availability of finance may have been an important constraint on the performance of these firms. In the absence of qualitative data, this inference must be treated with caution.

Important differences were apparent in the capital support received by the two samples. Financing from informal sources was more important for the Ann Arbor–Detroit group than for the Boston group. The Boston group had more financing from commerical banks, SBICs, and private venture capital firms in years one and two than did the Ann Arbor–Detroit group. In this same period, the Ann Arbor–Detroit firms financed more through sale of equity to investment banking houses, large nonfinancial corporations, and the public.

The Boston group obtained a larger portion of its capital needs within its home state than did the Ann Arbor–Detroit group. While straight debt interest costs did not differ markedly between samples, Boston firms clearly enjoyed a lower component cost of funds in each of the years surveyed.

Information regarding referrals suggests that the venture financing communication network available to the Boston group was more active and more highly developed than that available to the Ann Arbor–Detroit firms.

Conclusions and implications

Because of the lack of published data and the need to obtain information by personal interview, the sample size in this study is small. Furthermore, the data observation points are few (four years). Because of these constraints, the relationships observed in the analysis, while significant in most instances, are not as strong as we would wish for purposes of inference. Nonetheless, the results illuminate the ways in which availability of finance may affect the performance of NTBFs in different sub-areas of the country.

The evidence demonstrates the importance of early financial support to subsequent sales performance in these firms. In the first two years of life, financing from commercial banks and from venture capital specialists was used less by the lower-performing group (Ann Arbor–Detroit) than by the Boston group. In general, the Ann Arbor–Detroit group used more equity financing over the four-year period, even though the cost of such financing was considerably higher than it was for the Boston group.

In short, institutional finance was available in greater volume and variety to firms in Boston, which therefore had less need to seek out-of-state financing. Also, the cost of capital was demonstrably lower for firms in the Boston group. Since it was not possible to identify those qualitative characteristics which may have made the sampled firms attractive to potential investors, we are unable to determine whether the Boston firms received more favorable financing earlier in their lives because they were in some sense "better" than the Ann Arbor–Detroit firms, or whether they turned out to be better because they received this level of financing. Since all the firms survived the first four years, however, there were probably no major qualitative differences among them. We recognize that the differences important to investors are often subtle, and our current research attempts to identify these factors and their effect on investors.

I would contend that the different financing methods observed represent fundamental differences in the venture capital supply systems in the two areas studied. While Michigan has a large population, a high level of personal income, and substantial wealth, it lacks a supply of venture capital investment specialists. There are presently two such firms operating in the state: one SBIC and one private venture capital firm. As a result, NTBFs in Michigan have had to rely on informal sources (individuals, joint ventures, "finders") and on commercial banks for their early financing. In contrast, Boston has many venture capital investment specialists, both individual and institutional. Commercial banks in Massachusetts and surrounding states have ownership ties with SBICs and private venture capital firms, and the venture capital network is well established and active.

Application of modern finance theory to a venture capital problem

In a recent paper, I addressed the potential use of equity participation agreements (EPAs) in connection with bank loans to new and small business firms (Brophy 1980). While the use of EPAs is consistent with U.S. banking laws and regulations, the valuation of EPAs and the establishment of an analytical framework within which to make EPA decisions must also be addressed. The analysis of valuation appears below as an example of how modern finance theory might be applied to the subject of private investment in new or small firms.

Technical considerations regarding the equity participation vehicle

A review of applicable statutes and cases indicates that EPAs are permissable under law and banking regulations and that they may be fitted into S.E.C. and usury law requirements. Two questions now arise:

1. What kind of EPA vehicles are likely to be used?
2. How can the value of the EPA be estimated by lender and borrower?

The answers to these questions are sufficiently complex when the object of discussion is a large corporate borrower whose common stock is widely traded and perhaps listed on an exchange. In this chapter, of course, we are concerned with the small firm borrower, usually characterized by privately-held stock or the lack of a substantial public market in the common shares. In this case, the valuation problem is both important and difficult.

Types of EPA vehicles

Two major types of EPA vehicles are used: the stock purchase warrant and the cash override conditional payment. The important characteristics of each are described below.

Stock purchase warrants

Under this arrangement, the bank, at the time the loan is closed, acquires warrants which give the bearer an option to buy from the borrowing firm a certain number of shares at a certain price for a certain period of time. The bank does not possess stockholders' rights (voting and dividend rights) when it holds warrants. It does, however, have an interest in those factors which affect the value and marketability of the warrant and the underlying stock. Accordingly, the bank must try to negotiate in the warrant agreement those terms that protect this interest. The warrant agreement should provide for adjustment in case of recapitalization and for continuity of the claim in case of merger. Also, it should provide for notification about actions that might affect the company and the value or outstanding amount of its stock.

Typically, at the time of issue, the exercise price of the warrants will exceed the current price of the stock. The price may be fixed over time or may rise with time or the number of warrants exercised. The warrants will normally be detachable to allow for separate sale by the bank. Their expiration date is a matter of negotiation and may run beyond the maturity date of the loan. The borrower may be able to bargain for a call feature on the warrants or for a "flush out" clause which permits the borrower to trigger exercise of the warrant by lowering the exercise price at its discretion. Both of these devices give the issuer flexibility in future financing.

In determining warrant terms, the bank and the borrower must negotiate the length of the exercise period and the distance of the exercise price from the current market price. These characteristics influence whether the warrant will reach a high premium early in its life, given a high expected value for the stock and protection from dilution.

Cash overrides

A cash override is an incremental cash payment, over and above the regular interest payment, made by the borrower to the lender. The major distinction between this device and the warrant approach is that the cash compensation comes directly from the borrower rather than from some third party. The increment is taxed as ordinary income when received and does not afford the bank the capital gains tax advantage provided by warrants.

The amount of the increment is typically dependent upon the operating performance of the borrower or the project being financed. One approach bases the performance-related supplement on some current flow variable, such as total sales or net profits of the firm. If the loan is not tied to some specific, revenue generating program, but is expected to increase the total net profit of the firm, this device offers certain advantages. The bank's cash income accrues in direct proportion to increases in the performance indicator, thus removing the intermediate factor of stock prices. This removes the problem of secondary sale of warrants.

As is well-known, the market value and theoretical value of this warrant need not be (and probably will not be) the same at a particular moment. In general, the relationship between market value and theoretical value may be represented as shown in Figure 1.

The highest value of the warrant resides on the X curve, which represents the value of the stock. The value would approach this limit if the warrant had a very long life and was not exercised until far in the future.

The lowest value of the warrant (as a function of current stock prices) is shown as zero up to the exercise price and as the Y curve thereafter. This represents theoretical value at the time of execution.

Typically, the value relationship lies between these two parameters, as described by the three convex curves. The gap between the market line and the theoretical value line is greatest at the exercise price. It is also larger for the warrant with longer expiration time (line 3) than for those with shorter expiration time (lines 1 and 2). Over the life of the warrant, as the expiration time declines, the relationship shifts downward toward the instantaneous theoretical value.

The dominant factor in determining market value of a warrant is the volatility of the underlying stock, that is, the range of possible stock prices until the expiration date. Assume that warrants are available in two stocks, A and B. The expected value of the stock at the end of the period is the same ($40 per share), and the warrant exercise price for each is the same ($38). The probability distribution of the two stock prices is as follows:

Probability	*Stock A*	*Stock B*
0.10	$30	$20
0.25	$36	$30
0.30	$40	$40
0.25	$44	$50
0.10	$50	$60

$$
\begin{aligned}
\text{Value of Option A} &= 0(0.10) + 0(0.25) + (\$40-\$38)(0.30) \\
&\quad + (\$44-\$38)(0.25)(\$50-\$38)(0.10) \\
&= \$3.30
\end{aligned}
$$

$$
\begin{aligned}
\text{Value of Option B} &= 0(0.10) + 0(0.25) + (\$40-\$38)(0.30) \\
&\quad + (\$60-\$38)(0.25)(\$60-\$38)(0.10) \\
&= \$5.80
\end{aligned}
$$

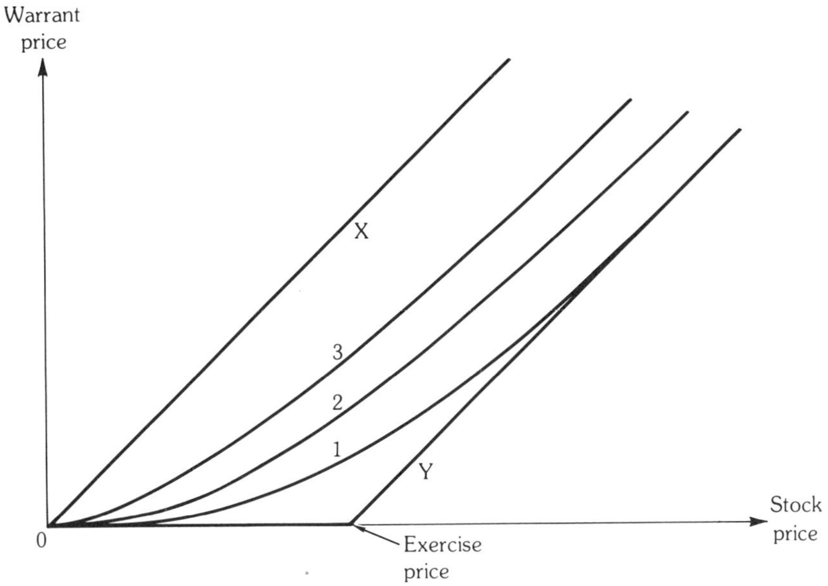

Figure 1

Thus, the expected value of the warrant is higher for the stock with the greater variance in possible stock price. This reflects the greater opportunity for more favorable outcomes under B than under A. Since the warrant cannot have a negative value, and its minimum value is zero under both A and B, the risk-return relationship B is more favorable than in A.

In the (efficient) marketplace, the value of the warrant is kept in equilibrium with the underlying stock price through arbitrage. To understand this, let us assume that a stock that sells for $50 a share has the probability distribution shown below:

Probability	***Percentage change***	***Ending value***
0.666	+20%	$60
0.333	−10%	$45

Expected value = (0.666)($60) = (0.333)($45) = $55

If each warrant permits the purchase of one share at an exercise price of $50, the expected value of the warrant at the end of the period is:

(0.666)($10) + (0.333)(0) = $6.667

The purchaser of the stock can hedge the risk by writing options (issuing warrants) against the stock and selling those claims to interested investors.

The number of options (warrants) to write is determined by the "hedge ratio" (*HR*):

$$HR = \frac{uV_o - dV_o}{uV_s - dV_s} = \frac{\$10 - 0}{\$60 - \$45} = 2/3$$

where uV_o = end-of-period value of option when stock is \$60
dV_o = end-of-period value when stock is \$45

For each two shares of stock purchased, the investor should write options to buy three shares of the stock. The hedge has the following characteristics:

Ending stock price	***Value of stock held***	***Value of short position***	***Value of combined positions***
$60	$120	−$30	$90
$45	$90	0	$90

From the stock purchaser's point of view, hedging reduces the risk of the stock purchase to zero. The initial value of the option may be determined by assuming that the investor will price it to earn the risk-free rate expected to prevail over the holding period. Assume this is the Treasury Bill rate and its value is 5 percent:

$$[\$100 - 3(V_o^{3})]1.05 = \$90$$
$$3.15(V_o) = \$105 - \$90$$
$$V_o = \frac{\$15}{\$3.15}$$
$$V_o = \$4.762$$

The overall investment at the beginning of the period is:

$100 − 3 ($4.762) = $85.714

and the return on this position is:

($90 − $85.714)/$85.714 = 5%

The expected return from the stock for the period is:

($55 − $50)/$50 = 10%.

For the option, the return is:

(\$6.667 − \$4.762)/\$4.762 = 40%

In efficient markets the price of the option (given the specified relationships) will tend toward an equilibrium value of \$4.762. Above this price, the option writer would be able to achieve a riskless hedge and earn a return above the risk-free rate. The yield on this combination of stock, option, and risk-free investment would exceed the risk-free rate. Knowledge of either of these opportunities attracts arbitragers who will transact until excess profits are competed away.

A very important advance in the valuation of conditional equity claims is the Black-Scholes option pricing model. While greater degrees of complexity could be introduced, we will examine the formula for a "European" option (one that can be exercised only at maturity) on a stock that pays no dividend. The accompanying assumptions are:

1. There are no transactions costs; options and stocks are infinitely divisible; information is available to all without cost.
2. No imperfections exist in selling short on option or stock.
3. The short-term interest rate is known and constant throughout the duration of the option contract.
4. Stock prices follow a "random walk" in a continuous time pattern.

The product of the Black-Scholes model is the equilibrium value of the option or, in this case, the EPA warrant. The formulation of the model is as shown below:

$$V_o = V_s N(d_1) - \frac{E}{e^{rt}} N(d_2)$$

where V_s = the current price of the stock
E = the exercise price of the option
r = the short-term interest rate continuously compounded
t = the length of time in years to the expiration of the option
e = 2.71828
$N(d)$ = the value of the cumulative normal density function

$$d_1 = \frac{1n(V_s/E) + (r + 1/2\delta^2)t}{t}$$

$1n$ = natural logarithm

The theoretical value of a warrant can be determined by the relationship:

$$V_t = NP_s - E$$

where N = the number of shares that can be purchased with one warrant
E = the option price associated with the purchase of N shares
P_s = the current market price of one share of the stock

To illustrate this relationship in numbers, assume that the XYZ Corporation has warrants outstanding for which $N = 1$ and $E = \$14$. On a day when the company's stock price closes at \$17, the theoretical value of the warrant (if it were exercised) is:

$$(17) - \$14 = \$3$$

Essentially, this model is useful because it expresses the value of the option as a function of the short-term interest rate, the time to expiration, and the variance rate of return on the stock but *not* as a function of the expected return on the stock.

The necessary input variables are five: the current stock price, the time to expiration of the option, the exercise price, the short-term interest rate, and the standard deviation of the stock price. The first four of these are observable for traded stocks, and the fifth is readily calculated from past stock performance data. Empirical tests of this model have produced satisfactory results and, as indicated above, its use has been extended to more complex conditions.

Valuation of a small firm EPA option (warrant or override) is complicated if the stock is not privately or closely held. One solution is suggested below:

δ^1 = standard deviation of the annual rate of return on the stock continuously compounded

Where the credit advanced is identified with a particular project or asset, the flow variable may relate to the project rather than the firm as a whole. The advantage of this device is that the expected value of the project's flow variable may be more predictable than that of the borrower's firm as a whole. The lender may have particular expertise for estimating the success of, say, a real estate development. A project-based EPA may have a higher expected value than an EPA based on the borrower's total performance.

Valuation of the EPA vehicle

A valuation of the EPA vehicle is important to both borrower and lender since it reflects part of the trade-off against some accommodation offered in the loan: a reduced interest rate, easier repayment terms, greater acceptance of risk, or some other financial concession. Valuation is important, not only at the time the loan is made, but during the entire life of the EPA. The lender, over this time period, faces the constant question of whether to sell, exercise the warrants, or exercise the right to the conditional cash override. The borrower faces the question of exercising a call on the EPA (if such an option is available) and must predict the lender's exercise of the EPA, with its attendant financial implications.

As a starting point, we will define the "theoretical" value of an EPA and show how it might relate to the underlying assets of the borrower. For simplicity, we shall use the conventional relationship between a warrant and the stock to which it is related. This concept may also be applied to the cash override vehicle.

A non-market valuation model

In the absence of a public market for the stock, valuation must be based on the value of the assets underlying the stock. Parties to the negotiation must accept some measure of net worth, either book value, replacement value, or an appraised value. The shares of stock are set against this value to determine price per share and exercise price. Variance in the observed cash flows (from proper accounting records) can be used as a proxy for the variance of stock price, inasmuch as cash flows affect the value of the net worth. In this fashion the model can be adapted to the circumstances of a small firm with no public market for its stock or to a component division or product line of a firm.

In 1968 Ball and Brown hypothesized that the change in income over period τ for business unit j is linearly related to the change in income over the same period for the market. This relationship can be expressed as:

$$\Delta I_{j,t-\tau} = \alpha_{1jt} + \alpha_{2jt}\,\Delta I_{m,t-\tau+\hat{\epsilon}}$$

where $I_{j,t-\tau}$ = the change in income for entity j at time t over the period τ,
$\Delta I_{m,t-\tau}$ = the change in income for the market at the time t over period τ,
α_{1jt} = the intercept,
α_{2jt} = the slope, and $\hat{\epsilon}$ is the error term.

Empirical studies verified the high correlation between changes in income for a business unit and changes in income for the market as a whole. Furthermore, the slope α_{2jt} can be a measure of the systematic risk of the business cycle.

This concept was modified and expanded by Gordon and Halpern (1974), who contend that the growth in earnings for a business unit is correlated to the growth in earnings for the market as a whole. Let $\gamma_{j,t}$ be earnings per share for quarter t, $\gamma_{j,t-4}$ be earnings per share for the same quarter one year earlier, $g_{j,t} = ln[\gamma_{j,t}/\gamma_{j,t-4}]$ be the rate of growth in earnings per share as of quarter t. To measure the growth in market earnings, a similar calculation was performed, where $\gamma_{m,t}$ is the total profits after taxes for quarter t as reported in the National Income and Product Accounts, U.S. Department of Commerce, Survey of Current Business.

Quarter *t* was compared to the same quarter the previous year to eliminate changes in earnings due to cyclical sales patterns. Also, company earnings may lead or lag market earnings, and measuring growth over a year's time tends to reduce this lead or lag effect. Finally, taking the natural log of the earnings ratio eliminates the absolute magnitude of earnings as a factor in determining the rate of growth.

For each business unit *j*, there is a linear relationship between its growth in quarterly earnings and the growth in quarterly earnings for the market:

$$g_{j,t} = \alpha_{jt} + c_j g_{m,t} + t$$

where c_j is a non-market measure of the systematic risk of the business unit.

Gordon and Halpern found a high degree of correlation between $\hat{\beta}_j$ and $\hat{c}_j$ for a publicly traded form *j*. From a sample of 17 public utilities and 32 industrials over the period 1957–1968, they calculated a product moment correlation coefficient of 0.66 between $\hat{\beta}$ and $\hat{c}$. Initially they had expected a higher correlation, but concluded that earnings may lead or lag the market, whereas changes in stock prices instantly reflect the firm's current expected earnings.

It seems clear that modern finance theory and practice are useful in placing a value on the EPA, even when the borrowing firm is one with privately held or thinly traded stock. Such estimation is by no means a trivial problem, but neither is it an insurmountable one, given existing financial technology.

Conclusions and recommendations

The research on venture capital investment illustrates several points. First, good information can be obtained about the development and financing history of small firms. In the comparative study of high-technology firms, the personal interview technique was used. This approach produces the most comprehensive and reliable data but is, of course, the most expensive and time-consuming method available. Since it is clear from a study such as this that firms are able and willing to supply necessary information, the challenge to the researcher is a reasonable methodological one: Develop an efficient and inexpensive method for obtaining data from firms, financial institutions, and private investors.

A major deficiency in research on small business finance has been the absence of reliable data for longitudinal, rather than episodic, studies. Without such data, research is unlikely to be generally accepted and published in leading scholarly journals. Accordingly, serious researchers prefer to work in a field where the arguments are well established and the data are universally recognized and available for use.

If venture capital investment is to engage serious researchers, we must not compromise on data quality or methodological rigor. This means that a little entrepreneurship and a lot of scholarship must be applied to the development of data bases. The payoff will come when the quantity, quality, timeliness, and comprehensiveness of the data allow for the testing and resolution of important questions.

Our second research example establishes the applicability of modern finance theory to small business finance. Research in this field will progress only upon a strong theoretical base. Even a casual observation of the development of financial theory over the past 20 years suggests that research has been impelled by fairly practical considerations. Researchers have tried to determine how financial markets work, how financial claims are priced under various circumstances, how capital structure and investment decisions are intertwined, and how investment decisions are made. By and large these questions have been approached in a general equilibrium framework, based on an assumed link between the firm in question and the market in general. As long as the discussion is theoretical, there need be no limit to the size of the firm. When theoretical propositions are empirically tested, however, the bias toward large firms develops.

This bias derives from the fact that the link between small firms and organized financial markets is neither as well established nor as easily observed and measured as that between large firms and the market. The researcher quite naturally notes that many unresolved problems in finance can be feasibly approached with the available "large firm" data.

Opportunities clearly exist for the application of financial theory to the problems of small firm finance. On the one hand, we can more thoroughly specify and measure processes, flows, and transactions costs. On the other hand, we can select theoretical concepts which better suit the small firm. We can apply the agency concept to the firm with a single owner-manager; incorporate non-marketable assets (the equity in a closely held firm) into portfolio theory; extend the concept of "human capital" to encompass the time and effort of an entrepreneur.

Vast opportunities reside in modeling processes at the microeconomic level. This offers as much rigor and generality as any other aspect of financial research and yet has the important characteristics of feasibility and empirical verification. This approach should be used as a point of departure for this type of research.

The meaningful questions about venture capital are at last becoming of interest to more than the handful of researchers who have pursued them over the years. Researchers should be very bullish on venture capital in the years ahead.

References

BALL, RAY, and BROWN, PHILIP, "An Empirical Evaluation of Accounting Income Numbers," *Journal of Accounting Research* 6 (Autumn 1968).

BATY, GORDON, *Financing the New, Research-Based Enterprises in New England* (Master's thesis, Sloan School of Management, MIT, 1963).

CLARK, N. G., "Science, Technology, and Regional Economic Development," *Research Policy* 1, No. 3 (1972).

COOPER, ARNOLD C., *The Founding of Technology-Based Firms.* Milwaukee: Center for Venture Management, 1971.

DEUTERMANN, ELIZABETH, "Seeding Science-Based Industry," *Business Review* (Federal Reserve Bank of Philadelphia), May 1966.

DONALDSON, GORDON, *Financial Management in the New, Small Manufacturing Enterprise* (Doctoral dissertation, Graduate School of Business Administration, Harvard University, 1955).

Financing New Technological Enterprise. Washington, D.C.: U.S. Department of Commerce Panel on Venture Capital, 1970.

GORDON, MYRON J., and HALPERN, PAUL J., "Cost of Capital for a Division of a Firm," *Journal of Finance* 29, No. 4 (September 1974).

HODGINS, JOHN W., *Entrepreneurship in High Technology.* Hamilton, Ontario: Cromlech Press, 1972.

ROBERTS, E. B., "Entrepreneurship and Technology," in *Factors in the Transfer of Technology,* eds. W. H. Gruber and D. G. Marquis. Cambridge: MIT, 1969.

ROBINSON, ROLAND, *Financing the Dynamic Small Firm.* Belmont, Ca.: Wadsworth, 1968.

RUBENSTEIN, ALBERT, *Problems of Financing and Managing New Research-Based Enterprises in New England.* Boston: Federal Reserve Bank, 1958.

SHAPERO, ALBERT, DRAHEIM, KIRK, HOFFMAN, CARY A., and HOWELL, RICHARD P., *The Role of the Financial Community in the Formation, Growth and Effectiveness of Technical Companies.* Austin: Multi-Disciplinary Research, 1969.

SPIEGELMAN, ROBERT G., "A Method for Determining the Location Characteristics of Footloose Industries: A Case Study of the Precision Instruments Industry," *Land Economics* XL, No. 1 (February 1964).

Technological Innovation: Its Environment and Management. Washington, D.C.: U.S. Department of Commerce, 1967.

chapter x

The entrepreneurship–small business interface

Arnold C. Cooper

Overview

This chapter examines the patterns of success and failure for small firms. Relative profitability and the great variability in performance are considered. Longitudinal studies are reviewed for the relationship of success to factors known at the time of founding. New venture development is examined for its relationship to characteristics of the entrepreneur.

After small firms are founded, the following are of interest:

1. To what extent are the firms successful?

2. What factors, known at the time of founding, seem to be associated with success and failure?

3. What stages of development do growing firms pass through? How does the founding process influence this development?

Classification of the literature

The entrepreneurship–small business literature might be classified in a number of ways. For example, there are three primary audiences:

1. Entrepreneurs or small business managers with little or no formal training in management;

2. Relatively sophisticated entrepreneurs or small business managers, already knowledgeable about basic management techniques, interested in the special problems, opportunities, or practices of small firms;

3. Policy-makers and scholars interested in the field as a whole, in its implications for government policy, in the development of better theory and understanding.

If the literature is classified according to the nature of research or the process by which conclusions and recommendations are developed, four categories emerge (based in part upon a 1975 paper by Douds and Rubenstein): (1) discursive writings; (2) case studies; (3) field surveys; (4) field research. The literature might also be classified according to the kinds of management problems: raising venture capital; developing control systems for growing firms; developing strategies for businesses with small market shares.

Our primary focus will be upon the literature intended for policy-makers and scholars; we will draw particularly upon field surveys and field research. The largest literature is discursive and wisdom-based and intended to teach basic concepts and techniques. Since many entrepreneurs have little formal training or management experience, the need for this kind of literature is vast. It is, however, inappropriate to the research emphasis of this chapter.

We will examine what happens to new firms after founding and will relate these developments to characteristics of the entrepreneur and the entrepreneurial process. The performance of new firms has its roots in earlier events.

Discontinuances, survival, and profitability

After a firm is founded, it might follow a number of alternative paths. It might discontinue, with or without financial loss to creditors or founders. It might survive as a marginal business because it is part-time in nature or because the founder is willing to accept a substandard return. The new business might also grow, demonstrating varying degrees of success. At some point it might be acquired by an established firm or by another entrepreneur.

A number of previous studies have examined the survival, discontinuance, and failure of new or small firms. Some of these are cross-sectional studies, which examine a variety of firms during a particular period; others are longitudinal, and follow the performance of a group of firms over time. The cross-sectional studies, based primarily upon governmental data, will be considered first.

Cross-sectional studies

In our society, every person, qualified or not, is free to be an entrepreneur. This is reflected in the enormous number of new firms started every year. Each week in the United States, about 8400 new corporations and a much greater number of new partnerships and proprietorships are started (Statistical Abstract of the United States 1979). There are almost an equal number of discontinuances; thousands of businesses close their doors every week, often indicating that the dreams of their entrepreneurs were not realized. Many of these are relatively new firms; Dun & Bradstreet has found that only about one of three new firms survive the first four years (*Patterns for Success in Managing a Business* 1967).

Not all discontinuances are failures in economic terms. Many occur because of an owner's illness, a lack of heirs, or the attractiveness of other opportunities. Of course, many businesses also continue on a marginal basis and are not really "successful," even though they continue to survive. It should be noted also that in only a small portion (less than 5 percent) of all discontinuances do the creditors lose money.

How do existing small firms perform? Are small firms as profitable as larger ones? Available data on manufacturing firms shows that, when all firms within a given size class are averaged, profitability increases with size as indicated in Figure 1. There are, of course, difficulties in using reported profitability figures for closely held small corporations, many of which seek to minimize taxable income through large salaries or perquisites to the owners.

Figure 1 *Profitability of manufacturing corporations by size class.* Source: Statistics of Income 1972, Corporation Income Tax Returns 1977.

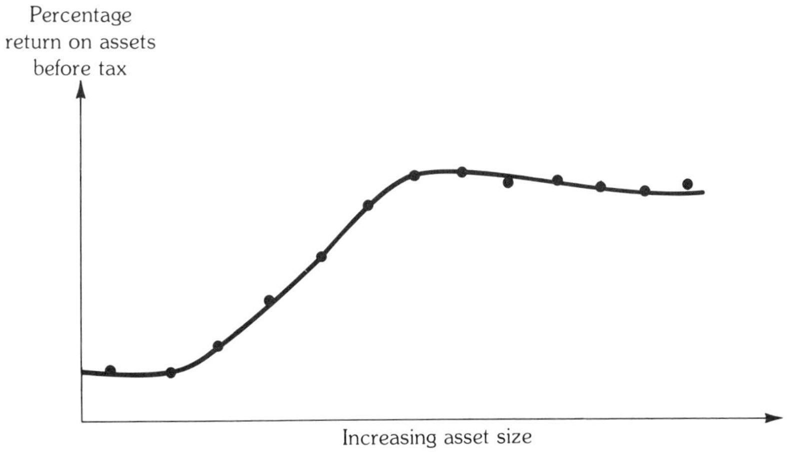

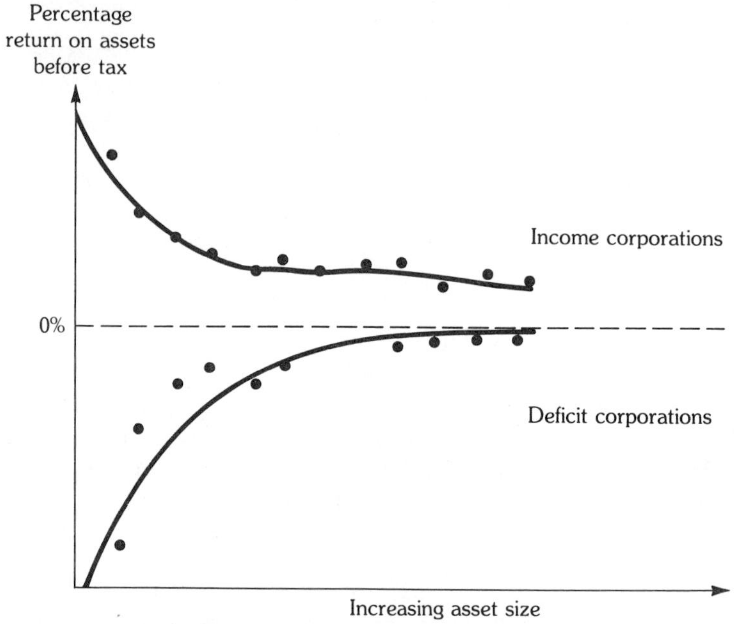

Figure 2 *Profitability of manufacturing corporations: income and deficit corporations by size class.* Source: Statistics of Income 1967–1968, Corporation Income Tax Returns.

The performance variability among firms also deserves special attention. In Figure 2, certain manufacturing corporations in a given size category show a loss, while other firms in the same size category show a profit.

For the larger firms, both profitable and unprofitable, performance represents an averaging of many product lines, many facilities, and many people. Outstanding performance for some products and markets is often balanced by poor performance for others. As a result, even the large corporations that show a loss are less unprofitable as a group than the smaller corporations showing losses.

For the smaller firms, there seem to be great variations in performance. In the $0–25,000 asset class, 43 percent of the firms reported losses in 1972 (Statistics of Income 1972, 1977), and their losses as a percentage of net worth were very high. Included in these unprofitable firms are new companies, some of them well managed, that show expected losses as they get started. Unfortunately, there are also thousands of companies that should never have been started—firms with little chance of success which run through their founders' capital and are replaced by others that do the same.

For the profitable small firms, return on net worth is higher than for the profitable larger firms. These companies, well conceived and well managed, earn the highest returns in American industry. The performance of individual firms may fluctuate, for they typically concentrate risk in a few products, a few markets, and a few key people. Nevertheless, these firms demonstrate the kinds of economic returns that are possible for well prepared entrepreneurs.

Do some types of firms have better survival records or superior performance? Are certain factors associated with success or failure? The longitudinal studies, following individual firms through time, cast light upon these questions.

Longitudinal studies

We will consider six specific studies in which new firms were monitored for a period of time. First, we will review the patterns of survival and discontinuance, and then we will focus on those studies which relate characteristics of the entrepreneur or the founding process to later performance.

Specific studies include the following:

1. A Department of Commerce study of all operating businesses started or transferred to new ownership during the eight years ending in 1954 (Churchill 1955);

2. A study of 278 new manufacturing businesses started or transferred to new ownership during a five-year period (Kinnard and Malinowski 1960);

3. A two-year study of 81 new service and retail firms in Rhode Island (Mayer and Goldstein 1961);

4. A three-year study (Hoad and Rosko 1964) of 95 new manufacturing firms in Michigan;

5. A study of 234 high-technology firms in the Boston area over a four-to-five-year period (Roberts 1972);

6. A study of 250 high-technology firms in the Palo Alto area over about a ten-year period (Cooper and Bruno 1977).

Survival patterns of firms from the first four studies are given in Table 1. It is clear that a high percentage of these firms fail to survive the first few years. Discontinuance rates for the first two years ranged from 17 percent for the Connecticut manufacturers to 49 percent for the Rhode Island retail and service firms. After 4.5 years, 71 percent of the 6.3 million firms in the Department of Commerce study had been discontinued or sold.

Acquisition of these new firms was not examined explicitly in most of these studies. The acquisition rate was apparently negligible for the Michigan manufacturing firms, with only one merger mentioned. Of the 81 Rhode Island businesses, 17 were "sold" before the end of the second year, usually at a loss. In almost all instances these were marginal businesses and were regarded as unsuccessful by the authors of the study; the founder sold the assets of his unincorporated business to a buyer who then tried to make a success of it (Mayer and Goldstein 1961).

Table 1 *New firm discontinuance rates*

	Rhode Island retail and service firms[a]		Michigan manufacturing firms[b]	Connecticut manufacturing firms[c]	All new operating firms 1947–1954[d]
Number of new firms*	81*		95	276	6,294,000*
Percentage discontinued	**	***			**
First year	28%	—	17%	6%	(0.5 years) 23%
First two years	49%	28%	32%	17%	(1.5 years) 46%
First three years	—	—	35%	24%	(2.5 years) 59%
First five years	—	—	—	44%	(4.5 years) 71%

*In the Rhode Island and "all new operating firms" studies, new firms included businesses transferred to new ownership. In the Michigan and Connecticut studies, the new firms had no predecessors.

**"Discontinued" includes all firms discontinued or sold.

***"Discontinued" does not include unsuccessful firms which were sold.

[a]Mayer and Goldstein 1961

[b]Hoad and Rosko 1964

[c]Kinard and Malinowski 1960

[d]Churchill 1955

A very different picture emerges in the longitudinal studies of high-technology firms. The discontinuance rate is much lower, as shown in Table 2. Of 229 high-technology firms studied in the Boston area, only 20 percent discontinued in the first four to five years (Roberts 1972). Of 250 Palo Alto area firms, only 29.2 percent had discontinued by 1976, when the median firm in the sample was ten years old (Cooper and Bruno 1977).

There were also major differences in the rate of acquisition or merger. Of the Palo Alto firms, 18.8 percent had been acquired or had merged by 1969, 22.8 percent by 1973, and 23.2 by 1976 (Cooper and Bruno 19-7). The nature of acquisition or merger also differed from that of the retail and service companies described earlier. Physical assets were not so important as product lines and technological capabilities. Even a group of founders unable to develop a viable business were usually worth something to an acquiring firm. This helps explain the low discontinuance rate; acquisition was an "escape route" for marginal or unsuccessful firms.

Some of the longitudinal studies provide employment, sales, or profit data and thus permit some judgments about degrees of success among surviving firms (see Table 3). Profitability as such was not determined for the Rhode Island retail and service firms, most of which had neither accrual accounting nor a separation of the financial affairs of the owner and the business. However, the typical surviving company in this sample was very small at the end

Table 2 New firm discontinuance rates, high-technology firms

	Boston area[a]	Palo Alto area[b]
Number of new firms	229	250
Percentage discontinued		
First 3 years*		5%
First 4-5 years*	20%	
First 7 years*		24%
First 10 years*		29%

*Age of median firm in sample
[a]Roberts 1972
[b]Cooper and Bruno 1977

of two years; only two of 41 survivors had more than four employees. Some of the Michigan manufacturing firms experienced modest growth in their first three years, but 21 of the 59 survivors had fewer than four hired employees, and only two of the firms had more than 40 employees. The owner's salary plus profit for the median firm was only $10,000 per year (Hoad and Rosko 1964).

For the high-technology firms, performance was substantially better. In his study of 229 Boston area firms, Roberts reported that the typical firms

Table 3 Performance of surviving new firms

Second year performance of surviving Rhode Island firms[a]		Second year performance of surviving Michigan firms[b]			
Sales	Number of firms	Sales	Number of firms	Profit plus salaries	Number of firms
Under $5,000	5	$ 5,000 or less	7	Loss	5
$ 5,000-9,999	4	5,100-10,000	2	$ 0-5,000	9
10,000-19,999	7	10,100-20,000	5	5,100-10,000	9
20,000-29,999	5	20,100-50,000	18	10,100-20,000	7
30,000-39,999	3	50,100-100,000	11	20,100-40,000	7
40,000-49,999	3	Over 100,000	10	Over 40,000	5
50,000-99,999	6	Not reported	6	Not reported	17
100,000 and over	1		59		59
Not reported	7				
	41				

[a]Mayer and Goldstein 1961
[b]Hoad and Rosko 1964

achieved annual sales of $1.5 million after four to five years. Employment generated was also impressive. Of 250 Palo Alto firms, 27 had sales over $5 million, and 20 had sales over $10 million by the time the median firm was seven years old. Profitability, however, was modest, with median return on equity at 0–3.0 percent for most years of the study.

The cross-sectional studies suggest a high rate of discontinuance for new firms. The longitudinal studies suggest modest growth and economic return for most of those which survive. However, there appears to be considerable variation in staying power according to the type of firm. Retail and service firms had the highest discontinuance rates and the lowest average employment among survivors. Manufacturing was next, and high-technology firms had the highest survival rates and the highest average growth among surviving firms.

Performance and founding characteristics

The studies show a constantly changing sea of firms, companies starting, discontinuing, and being acquired, some outstanding performers, many with only modest success. In the midst of this turbulence, some survive and some succeed outstandingly. What characterizes the successful firms? Are there attributes of the entrepreneur or actions taken at the time of founding which are associated with the later performance of the firm?

A new business revolves around the entrepreneur so that his or her strengths and weaknesses become those of the firm. Presumably, the education and the prior experience of the founder are related to company success. Several studies examine these correlations.

For the Michigan manufacturing firms, the combination of education (one or more years in college) and prior industry experience was associated with the greatest success. Education or experience alone was better than the combination of inexperience and little education. Surprisingly, researchers found that the entrepreneur's prior experience might be in managerial or non-managerial work with equal benefit to the firm. However, a variety of experience seemed to correlate with greater success (Hoad and Rosko 1964).

The study of the founders of 81 Rhode Island retail and service establishments revealed similar findings about the role of education but contrasting findings about experience. For these entrepreneurs, less than 10 percent of whom had completed college, greater education was associated with success. Surprisingly, those who had previously worked in the same industry were not more successful. Prior experience as an owner, however, led to a higher success rate (Mayer and Goldstein 1961).

Founders of high-technology firms tend to be highly educated. In one study, entrepreneurs with M.S. degrees proved to be more successful than those with B.S. or Ph.D. degrees (Roberts 1972). If the entrepreneur had previously worked in a firm with similar technology and similar markets, the new firm tended to be more successful (Roberts 1972, Cooper and Bruno 1977). Interestingly, entrepreneurs who had spun off from larger organizations (more than 500 employees) did better (Cooper and Bruno 1977).

A number of studies of manufacturing and high-technology start-ups suggest that teams tend to be more successful than single founders (Hoad and Rosko 1964; Roberts 1972, Cooper and Bruno 1977). Multiple founders usually have a broader base of skills and experience and are also able to give one another psychological support. However, since the pressures on a team may be substantial, firms may survive when teams do not (Collins and Moore 1970, Cooper and Bruno 1977).

Success also seems to be related to the amount of initial capital; firms that have more initial capital tend to be more successful (Roberts 1972, Mayer and Goldstein 1961; Lamont 1969). Presumably, the greater capital gives the new firm a longer period in which to work out its problems and survive. The ability to raise a large amount of initial capital may also reflect a more impressive strategy and management team.

The process by which entrepreneurs get started, including the extent to which they consult with professional advisors such as lawyers, bankers, and consultants, would seem to be important. The successful founders of Michigan manufacturing firms were somewhat more likely to have sought information and advice from professionals, although consultants per se were not an important source of help (Hoad and Rosko 1964). In another study (Woodworth 1969), the more successful entrepreneurs seemed to have more skills in using professionals. They knew where to seek advice, knew what specific advice they needed, and sought professional help in anticipation of problems.

The overall pattern of relationships is consistent with conventional wisdom. Despite some mixed findings, success generally attended those entrepreneurs who were better educated, who had relevant managerial and industry experience, who had owned previous businesses, who started businesses similar to those they had left, who were involved in a founding team, who had more initial capital, and who had systematically sought the advice of professional advisors as they started their firms.

Stages of development

The longitudinal studies just considered followed firms through time to determine their overall performance and the relationship of that performance to factors known at the time of founding. There is a related body of literature, primarily discursive and wisdom-based, which examines surviving firms as they change through time, the stages of development they pass through, and the implications of these changes for management.

States of development may be classified in a number of ways; some of these focus on the challenge or major problem characteristically encountered at each stage. Table 4 illustrates only some of the many classification systems that have been used. We have chosen a model (based in part upon a 1979 paper by Vesper) that focuses upon the life of a venture from the earliest hope of the entrepreneur to later growth:

1. Pre-start-up;
2. Start-up;
3. Early growth;
4. Later growth.

Of particular interest are those activities and decisions associated with each stage and the relationship between early and later stages. Of course, the process might stop at any stage: A business might stabilize after early growth and experience no later growth.

The pre-start-up stage includes those events which lead a specific entrepreneur to a specific venture opportunity. It can involve varying degrees of deliberate planning, development of contacts and resources, and systematic search for entrepreneurial opportunities. Alternatively, it can also involve what seems to be an unplanned sequence of events. The sociological and psychological background of the entrepreneur, the nature of the organization for which he or she works, and various environmental influences determine whether a potential entrepreneur considers a specific venture opportunity.

A second stage involves the start-up, the decision to found a particular business at a particular time and place. To varying degrees, the entrepreneur will analyze the rewards and risks associated with the decision to go ahead. For every business that is started, how many are conceived, analyzed, and dropped? How many are put on hold as a dream that might some day be

Table 4 *Stages of development models*

Miller (1963)	Buchele (1967)	Parks (1977)	Baumback and Mancuso (1975)
1. Survival	1. Starting Crisis	1. Start-Up	1. Idea Stage
2. Growth	2. Cash Crisis	2. Cash Flow	2. Start-Up Problem
3. Shaping	3. Delegation Crisis	3. Delegation	3. Venture Financing
4. Maturity	4. Leadership Crisis	4. Idea	4. Growth Crisis
	5. Finance Crisis	5. Leadership	5. Maturity Crisis
	6. Prosperity Crisis	6. Capitalization	6. The Impossible Transition
	7. Management Succession Crisis	7. Complacency	
		8. Diversification	
		9. Management Succession	
		10. Involvement	
		11. Value	

realized? No studies of new business "stillbirths" have been reported, but we suspect there are many firms that never get beyond the dream stage. The decision to start a new firm has almost always been studied through businesses that have actually been started. Negative decisions are usually not very visible, and the processes at work are often informal, but the area merits research.

A third stage, that of early growth, occurs as the firm becomes an operating business. The original venture idea is tested as the entrepreneur receives feedback from the marketplace. While the organization is small, the founder is involved in all decisions and possibly all activities of the firm. Success may thus depend greatly upon the strengths and weaknesses of this individual. As an organization develops, its organization chart may look something like a wheel, with the founder at the hub of reporting relationships. Control is typically maintained through direct contact with operations, rather than through formal processes. Although these methods may appear to lack sophistication, they can give the founder a "feel" for the realities of the marketplace and for operational problems, a feel that can hardly be duplicated through formal reporting systems. The small firm can also be extremely flexible, ready to change not only operations but also strategy if the founder becomes convinced that this is necessary. Of course, even though there is potential flexibility, many small firms do not change much, either because environmental pressures are lacking, or because the owner is unable or unwilling to change.

Most small firms stabilize at this stage and experience little additional growth. About 79 percent of all companies have fewer than five employees, and most might be classified as "mom and pop" businesses (1972 Enterprise Statistics 1977). These firms are heavily dependent upon the talents of the owner and are usually limited in growth potential: the owner and the firm may grow old together and the firm may still stay small, incidentally disproving the often-encountered statement that a firm "must grow or die." Subsequently, a second generation may take over, or the owner may dissolve the business or sell out to others.

The next stage, that of later growth, is associated with the building of a management team. Initially, there is delegation of operating duties and of some decision-making. Then increased formality develops, including policies and specific procedures. Some of these firms become stable, high profit businesses, limited in ultimate potential, but able to provide handsome livings and flexible life styles for their owners. Some of these firms generate what may be the highest returns in American industry, though ownership prerogatives like company-owned cars and liberal expense accounts may limit reported taxable income. The strategies of these firms have not been the subject of study, but many appear to focus on local or regional markets. They may include the local Chevrolet dealership, a McDonald's franchise, and a small manufacturer with a strong proprietary product line for limited markets. Because these firms are relatively stable in the stage of later growth, there is less need for outside capital or management from outside the family. Sometimes the owners develop strong management to handle day-to-day operations and devote themselves to civic affairs or hobbies. Almost every city council and every country club roster of low-handicap golfers includes some owners of stable, high profit businesses.

For high growth potential businesses the later growth stage can continue. Many family fortunes had their origin in this kind of business. Although the ultimate rewards are greatest in this kind of company, the growth can present great challenges to management. As the organization grows, the founder must inevitably lose contact with some aspects of operations. Typically, a hierarchical organization develops, with more definite areas of responsibility and less reliance on the personal skills of the founder. The founder must learn to delegate, to control through more formal methods, and to develop an organization (Buchele 1967).

High growth oriented companies usually require a succession of commitments that risk what has been achieved. They usually require external sources of funds, which may lead to loss of control. Management must be skilled in setting terms of sale, in negotiating with suppliers for trade credit, in working with bankers, and sometimes in raising additional equity capital.

These companies usually have strong management, with prior managerial experience and advanced education. As noted in earlier longitudinal studies, they often have multiple founders, whose skills in engineering, sales, or cost control govern the early competitive strength of the firms. To meet the challenges associated with growth, the managers of the firms must be willing to work hard and to take risks—to broaden product lines, to add facilities, to build their organizations. The extent to which founders are able and willing to make the changes associated with growth varies widely. Some give way to successors who, although they may not be able to found a firm, have the ability to make it grow.

Some recent research relates the use of formal management methods and company objectives to characteristics of the founders (Filley and Aldag 1979): "Craft" entrepreneurs derive satisfaction from handling technical production problems, are inclined to avoid risk, and concentrate on making a comfortable living. Their management methods are informal and the rate of change is low. "Promotion" entrepreneurs capitalize upon particular, possibly short-term, opportunities. Their policies are fluid and centrally controlled. "Administrative" entrepreneurs are oriented toward building organizations. They evolve hierarchical organizations and formal management methods. According to Filley and Aldag, it may be more accurate to say that formal methods permit growth than to say that growth causes management methods to change.

In earlier work, Smith concluded that "craftsman entrepreneurs" and "opportunistic entrepreneurs" had different personal goals, different ways of managing, and thus different patterns of evolution for their businesses (1967).

A similar study of technical entrepreneurs in Michigan concluded that some, called "caretakers," start firms primarily to do particular kinds of work, while others, called "managers," aim primarily for profitability. These different motivations were reflected in different growth rates for their firms (Braden 1977).

To summarize a considerable literature, the entrepreneur who moves from a general desire to a specific venture idea and then to an established firm encounters a succession of challenges. If the business is successful, its growth results in a series of additional challenges or crises. Whether growth occurs and whether the founder adjusts may depend upon his or her motivations and management style.

Opportunities for research

Research varies widely from topic to topic in this area. Cross-sectional studies have primarily compiled government data, without developing research questions with implications for entrepreneurs. Longitudinal studies have involved some ambitious research, some of which has produced findings which seem consistent from project to project. However, methods of analysis have often been inadequate, sometimes involving nothing more than frequency counts. Stages-of-development research has relied heavily upon case studies and wisdom-based literature, with some larger scale empirical research.

Overall, considerable progress has been made, but much remains to be done. Interesting research questions include the following:

1. What factors characterize the small firms that are extremely profitable?

2. What is the relationship between strategy and performance in small firms? How is the decision to offer particular products or services to particular markets made?

3. What is the relationship between the psychological characteristics of the entrepreneur and company performance? Do entrepreneurs with particular psychological characteristics or personal goals tend to choose particular strategies for their firms?

4. What factors influence potential entrepreneurs who decide not to go ahead?

5. In growing small firms, when should more formal methods of management be instituted?

6. What characteristics determine whether an entrepreneur can adjust to managing larger, more formal organizations?

The entrepreneurship–small business interface relates the founding process to the vitality and characteristics of the resulting firms. The opportunities for research and the potential benefits, in terms of more successful entrepreneurship, are great.

Commentary on the entrepreneurship–small business interface

Justin G. Longenecker

Professor Cooper's chapter on the entrepreneurship–small business interface presents an analysis of primary data and a survey of prior research in this area. Its principal limitation lies in the paucity and sketchiness of the research that has been conducted to date.

A general question to be considered is the connection between small business management and entrepreneurship. An operating small business is the end product or at least an intermediate stage of an entrepreneurial process. By looking at this product, we can infer something about the process, especially if we broaden our definition of entrepreneurship. The birth of a business includes both a prenatal and postnatal stage; this commentary examines the latter.

The cross-sectional studies in the chapter presented data on business failures. Unfortunately, most of the data is derived either directly or indirectly from only one source—Dun & Bradstreet. The way in which this data is compiled raises questions of validity and accuracy. There are also problems with the use and interpretation of failure data—for example, in the use of failure statistics to estimate total discontinuances.

Another part of the cross-sectional studies dealt with the profitability of small firms. The contrast in profitability was striking and might be even more so if all the facts were known. It must be recognized that profits for small firms are frequently understated or concealed in various ways. The spread between the two profit curves, therefore, might be even more dramatic if concealed profits could be considered.

With regard to the longitudinal studies, one must be concerned with their rather limited range. Only two of the six studies are dated later than 1964, and some are quite old. Four of the six were in manufacturing, including the only two recent studies. Moreover, the two recent studies were more specifically restricted to high-technology manufacturing in the two "hot spots" for this field—Palo Alto and Boston. The general question, therefore, is the extent to which these studies can be representative. A broader range would be helpful.

With regard to the need for additional research, efforts should be directed toward the nature or significance of failure. Is it as tragic as it sounds? Or is it part of a learning process? Do some entrepreneurs fail once or more only to come back and start successful firms? It is easy to find successful people who are willing to talk about their success. Those who fail, however, tend to disappear into the woodwork, making research more difficult.

Future research should also address the objectives of entrepreneurs. We may assume too much in thinking that growth is always desirable or that small firms always want to grow. We need to consider some of the non-growth objectives of small firms.

Finally, there is an urgent need for the development of a data base. A group effort must first develop a list of the pertinent data required. Information must then be collected from entrepreneurial ventures in all the various stages of the life cycle.

References

BAUMBACK, CLIFFORD, and MANCUSO, JOSEPH, *Entrepreneurship and Venture Management.* Englewood Cliffs, N.J.: Prentice-Hall, 1975.

BRADEN, PATRICIA, *Technical Entrepreneurship.* Ann Arbor: University of Michigan, 1977.

BUCHELE, ROBERT, *Business Policy in Growing Firms.* New York: Harper & Row, 1967.

CHURCHILL, B., "Age and Life Expectancy of Business Firms," *Survey of Current Business*, December 1955.

COLLINS, ORVIS, and MOORE, DAVID, *The Organization Makers: A Behavioral Study of Independent Entrepreneurs.* Englewood Cliffs, N.J.: Prentice-Hall, 1970.

COOPER, ARNOLD, and BRUNO, ALBERT, "Success among High Technology Firms," *Business Horizons* 20, No. 2 (April 1977).

DOUDS, CHARLES, and RUBENSTEIN, ALBERT, "Methodology for Behavioral Aspects of Innovation," in P. Kelly et al., *Technological Innovation: A Critical Review of Current Knowledge*, Vol. II. Washington, D.C.: U.S. Government Printing Office, 1975.

Enterprise Statistics 1972. Washington, D.C.: U.S. Government Printing Office, 1977.

FILLEY, ALAN, and ALDAG, RAMON, "Policy Implications for Small Business Growth and Survival" in *The Regional Environment for Small Business and Entrepreneurship*, eds. A. Cooper and W. Dunkelberg. Milwaukee: Center for Venture Management, 1979.

HOAD, W., and ROSKO, P., *Management Factors Contributing to the Success or Failure of New Small Manufacturers.* Ann Arbor: University of Michigan, 1964.

KINNARD, W., JR., and MALINOWSKI, Z., *The Turnover and Mortality of Manufactur-*

ing Firms in the Hartford, Connecticut Economic Area, 1953–1958. Hartford: University of Connecticut, 1960.

LAMONT, LAWRENCE, *Technology Transfer, Innovation and Marketing in Science Oriented Spinoff Firms* (Doctoral dissertation, University of Michigan, 1969).

MAYER, KURT, and GOLDSTEIN, SIDNEY, *The First Two Years: Problems of Small Firm Growth and Survival.* Washington, D.C.: U.S. Government Printing Office, 1961.

MILLER, HARRY, *The Way of Enterprise.* London: Deutsch, 1963.

PARKS, GEORGE, "How to Climb a Growth Curve," *Journal of Small Business Management* 15, No. 1 (January 1977) and No. 2 (April 1977).

Patterns for Success in Managing a Business. New York: Dun & Bradstreet, 1967.

ROBERTS, EDWARD, "Influences upon Performance of New Technical Enterprise," in *Technical Entrepreneurship: A Symposium,* eds. A. Cooper and J. Komives. Milwaukee: Center for Venture Management, 1972.

Statistical Abstract of the United States, 1979. Washington, D.C.: U.S. Government Printing Office, 1979.

Statistics of Income, 1967–68, Corporation Income Tax Returns. Washington, D.C.: U.S. Government Printing Office, 1977.

Statistics of Income, 1972, Corporation Income Tax Returns. Washington, D.C.: U.S. Government Printing Office, 1977.

VESPER, KARL, "Commentary" in *Strategic Management: A New View of Business Policy and Planning,* eds. D. Schendel and C. Hofer. Boston: Little, Brown, 1979.

WOODWORTH, ROBERT, et al., "The Entrepreneurial Process and the Role of Accountants, Bankers, and Lawyers (unpublished paper). Seattle: University of Washington, 1969.

chapter xi

Internal corporate entrepreneurship

Hans Schollhammer

Overview

This chapter focuses on entrepreneurship in existing, large business organizations. Internal entrepreneurship expresses itself in a variety of modes or strategies which firms adopt in their pursuit of technological and organizational innovation. We will examine the advantages and shortcomings of five internal entrepreneurship strategies: administrative, opportunistic, imitative, acquisitive, and incubative entrepreneurship. We will also explore the impact of the organizational climate on internal corporate entrepreneurship.

The basic concept of entrepreneurship is elusive and can only be approximately characterized by a broad range of personal qualities, activities, and outcomes. Entrepreneurship is most commonly associated with a heterogeneous range of personal traits: initiative, creativity, high achievement motivation, perseverance, enthusiasm, competitiveness, inventiveness, and willingness to assume risks (Redlich 1949). Entrepreneurial activities generally develop newly combined means of production, new products, new markets, new methods of manufacturing or distribution, new sources of material, or new forms of organization (Schumpeter 1934). The essential results of entrepreneurial activities are the various types of innovation (Zaltman 1973). In a corporate context, innovation enhances a firm's price discrimination power and its profit potential. Entrepreneurship is the key element for gaining competitive advantage and consequently greater financial rewards.

In light of these manifestations, it is evident that entrepreneurship is not confined to a particular business size (Scherer 1970) or a particular stage in an organization's life cycle, such as the start-up phase. In a competitive environment, entrepreneurship is an essential element in the long-range success of every business organization, small or large, new or long established.

The concept of entrepreneurship

Entrepreneurship has been described as "the purposeful activity (including an integrated sequence of decisions) of an individual or a group of associated individuals, undertaken to initiate, maintain, or aggrandize a profit-oriented business unit for the production or distribution of economic goods and services" (Cole 1959). Later the same author stated, "Entrepreneurship boils down in basic functions to innovation upon a solid operational base achieved through the medium of business decisions" (Cole 1965). Schumpeter, who pioneered the focus on the socioeconomic contributions of entrepreneurs, stressed that entrepreneurship is frequently a shared activity among several persons who work for the same business. The entrepreneurial function may thus be filled cooperatively; in large-scale operations, aptitudes that no single individual possesses can thus be built into a corporate personality (Schumpeter 1965). From the perspective of Cole, Schumpeter, and many others, entrepreneurship is not an absolute, an integral virtue, a person, or an organization that may or may not exist. Instead, the phenomenon is viewed as a combination of properties that characterize an individual or a group as part of an organization.

Collins and Moore differentiated between "administrative" and "independent" entrepreneurs. The latter create new organizations from scratch, while the former create new organizations within or adjunct to existing business structures (Collins and Moore 1970). This distinction has been used to suggest another between "internal entrepreneurship" and "independent entrepreneurship." The former involves "conducting entrepreneurial activities within existing (large) organizations, which sometimes allow or even encourage creation of new and relatively autonomous organizational subunits for pioneering new products or services" (Vesper 1980). Shils and Zucker use the term "internal entrepreneurship" in the same sense (1979), whereas Susbauer (1973) and others speak instead of "intra-corporate entrepreneurship." They refer to the establishment of relatively autonomous units within existing corporations, "which allow company members to act with the same kind of spirit, freedom, and commitment that typify the small, new enterprise." To identify internal or intra-corporate entrepreneurship in this way does not seem logical. Why should existing organizations be considered to exercise entrepreneurship only if they form "relatively autonomous organizational subunits" that emulate small, new enterprises? Entrepreneurship as characterized by the personal traits of individuals, their activities, and the results of these activities, is not confined to a particular organizational context.

The definition of internal corporate entrepreneurship

I suggest instead that internal (or intra-corporate) entrepreneurship be understood to refer to all formalized entrepreneurial activities within existing business organizations. Formalized internal entrepreneurial activities are those which receive explicit organizational sanction and resource commitments for the purpose of innovative corporate endeavors—new product developments, product improvements, new methods or procedures.

The purpose of this chapter is to delineate, characterize, and assess internal entrepreneurship strategies, the modes that existing enterprises adopt to achieve technological and organizational innovation.

Internal corporate entrepreneurship strategies

A strategy is generally perceived as a goal-oriented course of action that requires the deployment of resources. In a competitive environment, business enterprises require technological and organizational innovations to achieve their corporate objectives. An innovation is the successful introduction into an applied situation of means or ends that are new to that situation. An innovation brings something into new use, whereas an invention brings something new into being (Rogers 1962). The strategies firms use in the pursuit of innovation and the organizational constructs they adopt in its support vary considerably from firm to firm and within each firm over time. One can, however, shed some light on this diversity by focusing on certain key features: (a) the organization of the entrepreneurial effort itself; (b) the characteristic mode(s) by which the objective is to be attained; (c) the implementation or utilization of the results of entrepreneurial activity. Five broad types of internal entrepreneurship exist:

- Administrative
- Opportunistic
- Imitative
- Acquisitive
- Incubative (new venture management approach)

The magnitude of the innovative and entrepreneurial effort among business firms can be more accurately gauged by industrial research and development spending than by actual technological innovative achievements. Empirical evidence on this issue is not clear-cut, though some studies support the notion that innovative achievements rise with increased R & D spending (Mansfield 1964, Comanor 1965). Others support opposing views (Jewkes 1959, Nelson 1962). According to the National Science Foundation, total U.S. R & D expenditures in 1980 are expected to exceed $57 billion; more than $41 billion of this will be spent by private industry. Almost all of the corporate R & D spending—and the innovative, entrepreneurial activities which it supports—is subject to managerial and administrative planning, organizing, directing, and controlling. The entrepreneurial function directs subunits of the organization, such as corporate or divisional R & D units, in the development and commercialization of innovative ideas. Within the R & D units functional responsibilities are divided between scientific or technical personnel and managers or administrators, who select viable domains of activity, secure required resources, and create and maintain a conducive organizational environment. In this format innovation is perceived as a sequential, controllable process. Schon (1967) described it as a series of propose-dispose relationships across vertical and horizontal boundaries within the enterprise.

The large majority of established firms use such administrative entrepreneurship consistently and systematically in order to create and implement innovative ideas. This traditional R & D management approach offers advantages and opportunities, but it can also cause considerable problems. A major advantage of the specialization it entails is the optimal utilization of expertise. In addition, the bureaucratic stress on planning, scheduling, and budgeting enables an organization to monitor the progress of a project and to take rapid corrective action if problems or delays arise. An administrative entrepreneurship strategy also allows a massive concentration of physical and human resources which may shorten the time required for completion of an innovative project and may lead to economies-of-scale benefits. Scherer, in the most comprehensive analysis of industrial R & D activities, cites five advantages which accrue to large companies in their innovative efforts:

1. Large companies have greater resource availability, which facilitates a speedier innovation process.

2. Large companies can employ specialists from many disciplines to cross-fertilize one another and to lend temporary assistance when a team becomes bogged down by a technical problem outside its sphere of competence.

3. The lower capital costs of large firms make it easier for them to finance innovative undertakings.

4. Large companies have an advantage in the physical distribution and promotion of their output and thus have an advantage in gaining market acceptance of their innovations.

5. Large companies enjoy greater savings from process innovation. (Scherer 1970)

However, there are also considerable problems associated with an administrative approach to internal entrepreneurship: The entrepreneurial effort is embedded in a bureaucratic structure; the larger the organization, the more rigid tends to be the administrative mold. The firm may be slow to reach specific decisions and thus slow to react to environmental changes. There is also evidence that creative effort suffers under an administrative entrepreneurship. Mansfield (1964) observed that "increases in the size of the firm are associated with decreases in inventive input." However, there can be a long road from an invention to its actual commercialization. There is evidence that administrative entrepreneurship, although lacking in inventiveness, is strong in adopting inventions, a most significant phase of the innovation process (Mansfield 1963).

A distinct problem of the mode is the high conflict potential between researchers and R & D managers, due to their differences in attitude, value orientation, and authority. Another constraint on administrative entrepreneurship is that the implementation of innovative projects requires the support of various organizational units and may involve sharp discontinuities as the project moves from one sphere to another. Moving an innovative project toward implementation requires accommodation and compromise among various organizational subunits; this may easily fail.

By modifying structural and behavioral factors, a firm can reduce the impediments to effective administrative entrepreneurship. It can:

1. Place responsibility for initiation and implementation of innovative projects in boundary units of the organization, thus maximizing their contacts within and outside the firm.

2. Increase organizational flexibility by means of decentralization, a participative management style, and extensive horizontal and vertical communication.

The administrative mode is the most common entrepreneurial mode in existing business firms, regardless of their size or market position. The basic features of this approach tend to reduce its inventiveness but to make it very effective during implementation. Management can improve the overall effectiveness of the administrative approach by reducing formality and de-emphasizing the authority gap between technical experts and managers.

Opportunistic entrepreneurship

Accidental encounters with technical innovations which become the basis for corporate initiatives are not infrequent. In an extensive analysis of the origin of inventions, Schmookler (1966) came to the conclusion that engineers and operating personnel outside organized corporate research units are frequently the source of inventions. Corporate scanning and surveillance of internal and external environments for the purpose of detecting and adopting innovative developments may be characterized as opportunistic entrepreneurship. In this mode, the entrepreneurial effort is oriented toward the exploitation of relevant opportunities as they occur. The essential prerequisites for a successful use of this strategy are:

1. A willingness and ability to monitor innovative developments that directly affect the competitive position of the enterprise.
2. An ability to assess the value of an innovative achievement accurately and promptly.
3. Active support and promotion for the exploitation of a given opportunity.

Because it requires the involvement of a "product champion" or a new venture team, an opportunistic approach tends to encounter more intense resistance within an established firm than other entrepreneurship strategies (Schon 1963).

Examples of successful opportunistic entrepreneurship abound, as in the diversification of a manufacturer of semiconductor components into electronic consumer products pioneered by other firms. A firm's market entry strategy during the growth stage of a new product's life cycle generally expresses an opportunistic entrepreneurship strategy.

Imitative entrepreneurship

Since imitation implies a lack of innovation, "imitative entrepreneurship" seems to combine two contradictory concepts. However, entrepreneurship can only be judged from the perspective of an organization's existing programs or activities. Thus, if an organization initiates the development of new products, processes, or services, it shows an entrepreneurial spirit—even if the same developments already exist outside the organization. The internalization of such an external development is to be considered an innovative, entrepreneurial act. Levitt (1966) points out that "in spite of the extraordinary outpouring of totally and partially-new products and ways of doing things that we are witnessing today, by far the greatest flow of newness is not innovation at all. Rather it is imitation." Several studies (Grabowski 1968, 1973, Scherer 1965, and Kay 1979) conclude that technological competition forces firms to imitate each other's innovations as a conservative strategy for minimizing business risks. Some types of imitation are, in fact, innovative imitation—particularly if costs and uncertainties do not differ from those of the initial inventor or innovator. In addition, some forms of imitation may require technical modifications, refinements, or adjustments in scale which constitute innovations in themselves. In essence, organizations that are able to discern and internalize relevant external technical or organizational developments act in an entrepreneurial fashion.

The payoff of this approach can be very significant (Roberts 1973). A business policy case on the Crown Cork and Seal company shows how a shift in emphasis from technological leadership in the industry (necessitating extensive R & D programs) to technological imitation (requiring mere monitoring of innovative developments in the industry) was a major contributing factor to the company's subsequent financial success. A company executive characterized this strategy as "learning from the innovator's heartaches and prospering by refinement (of the innovation)" (Christensen, Andrews, Bower 1978).

Judging by the legal allegations of product- or technology-poaching (see *IBM* v. *Xerox, Kodak* v. *Polaroid, Caterpillar* v. *Goodyear*), imitative entrepreneurship seems to be an extensively used strategy. Yet the litigated cases of alleged imitation represent only a very small portion of imitative entrepreneurship.

An imitative approach does not necessarily deserve a derogatory assessment; the effective internalization of innovation is in many cases an innovative process. Sutherland (1959) stresses that "there are cases where uncertainty about the future of an industry may make the adoption of an apparently well-proved innovation almost as bold a step for the imitator as for the innovator."

The specific advantages of an imitative entrepreneurship strategy are a reduction in development costs and a reduction of uncertainty about the technical outcome or market acceptance. The more problematic aspects of an imitative approach are:

1. Uncertainty as to whether the internalization of an external development will actually be possible.

2. Uncertainty about the length of time a successful internalization may require.

3. High risks that the enterprise which is first on the market with a particular innovation may gain a reputation advantage and a dominant market position that increases entry costs for the competing firm.

4. Risks of retaliation, either in the form of litigation or increased competitive pressures which may erode the benefits on an imitative effort.

An imitative entrepreneurship strategy can generally be used effectively by a resource-rich enterprise enjoying a dominant market position. Such a firm may leave innovation to its smaller competitors and still benefit from prompt imitation. The imitative approach to entrepreneurship is generally more pronounced in technologically progressive industries (computers, electronic equipment, pharmaceuticals) than in technologically stable industries (textiles, fertilizer). The greater the innovating intensity in an industry, the greater is the pressure on each firm to imitate its competitors' innovative achievements (Scherer 1965). An imitative strategy can also be advantageous in a low-technology industry, especially when the product reaches maturity or the decline phase of its life cycle. In this case an imitative mode allows for reduction in internal R & D spending.

Acquisitive entrepreneurship

By acquiring other companies, a firm can achieve growth, diversification, and horizontal or vertical integration in less time and with greater cost efficiency than by internal innovative activities. Acquisitions and mergers play a very significant role in the transformation from a single business to multiple businesses (Rumelt 1974). In fact, acquisition has become an end in itself. Leontiades (1980) states, "there are some indications that the current (acquisition and merger) phase has passed from rational diversification to irrational imitation."

From an entrepreneurial perspective, the acquisitive mode can provide technological capabilities (Cooper and Bruno 1977) that will combine with other resources of the acquiring firm to provide a basis for accelerated growth, diversification, and improved financial performance. A firm may use the strategy to gain rapid access to new technological knowledge, to establish a bridgehead in a promising industry, and to improve or maintain a competitive position in an oligopolistic market.

Every acquisition involves a divestment. Under certain circumstances, divestment must also be viewed as an internal entrepreneurship strategy. It may concentrate resources for new entrepreneurial ventures or reduce a drain on resources by marginal activities.

Incubative entrepreneurship (new venture management approach)

Since the late 1960s, growing attention has been paid to the form of internal entrepreneurship now called "new venture management," "new venture development," or simply "venture management." Venture management refers to the creation of semi-autonomous units within existing organizations for the purpose of:

1. Sensing external and internal innovative developments.
2. Screening and assessing new venture opportunities.
3. Initiating and nurturing new venture developments.

The basic rationale for semi-autonomous venture management units is their more conducive climate for innovation and entrepreneurship. Several studies support the assumption of this greater conduciveness (Mansfield 1963, Cooper 1964, Johnson 1979). Venture management units within existing companies serve as incubators for innovative, high-risk business endeavors; they combine bureaucratic efficiency and the resource capabilities of the corporation as a whole with the free-wheeling informality of a small business. The separation of new venture units is expected to approximate the start-up environment of independent entrepreneurs. By internalizing the characteristics of small, innovative businesses, large corporations expect to attract and retain persons with entrepreneurial talent. The incubator units are designed to infuse innovative developments into the corporation, to explore and pursue novel business opportunities, and to develop them into viable, profitable entities. This approach is used by companies such as Xerox, General Electric, Exxon, 3M, IBM, and Texas Instruments.

In general, internal venture management develops innovative activities within the enterprise, and external venture management invests in outside endeavors initiated by independent entrepreneurs. In the latter capacity, a corporate venture management unit may act like any venture capital company that invests in an equity position of a company conceived and managed by an independent entrepreneur.

The essential responsibilities of venture management units are:

1. To create internal support for innovative, entrepreneurial endeavors.
2. To survey external and internal innovative developments on a continuing basis.
3. To screen and assess innovative opportunities.
4. To select promising entrepreneurial endeavors, marshal required resources, gain support for and initiate the new venture.
5. Nurture and commercialize the new venture.
6. Establish the venture as a separate division, fold it into an existing division or spin-off, or liquidate in case of failure.

Donald Slocum (1972) provides a detailed description of this process and concludes that "new venture methodology must be pragmatic. It should take advantage of internal expertise and developments. It requires commitment by all, especially upper management. While flexibility is necessary, unidirectionality and self-contained multi-disciplinary programs are critical to success."

Most of the existing literature on venture management is normative; it prescribes how venture management units should be structured, managed, and integrated for maximum benefit. The few empirical studies on venture management base their generalizations on data provided by a relatively small number of firms:

Jones and Wilemon (1972)—24 companies
Susbauer (1973)—145 companies
Vesper and Holmdahl (1980)—50 companies
Fast (1979)—18 companies
Erickson (1978)—6 companies
Nathusius (1979)—26 companies

Incubative entrepreneurship—some tentative conclusions

1. Assessment of usage and problems associated with incubator operations:
- Incubative internal entrepreneurship, the formation of semi-autonomous venture management units within large enterprises for the purpose of stimulating entrepreneurial activities, is not yet a widely adopted strategy (less than 20 percent of the Fortune 500 employ it).

- In most large companies, which potentially benefit the most from incubative entrepreneurship, these semi-autonomous units meet strong resistance in a number of forms: competition for scarce resources; concern over territorial infringement; personality conflict between entrepreneurs and managers; inadequate linkage to other entrepreneurial and developmental activities of the enterprise.
- New venture units are inherently unstable, with high turnover of personnel as well as of business activities.
- Since new venture activities tend to be very small in comparison with the other operations of an enterprise, it is easy to view them as marginal or inconsequential.
- There is no clear evidence that incubator units have actually helped firms retain or attract entrepreneurs. It has been argued that the "true entrepreneurs" are likely to leave large companies in order to establish their own firms despite the existence of "corporate playpens (i.e., venture management units) with wildly improvisational toys for scientific and creative people to play with" (Young 1972).

2. Preconditions for successful incubator operations:
   - The political posture of new venture units must mesh with the corporate strategic posture. (Fast 1979)
   - The corporate strategic posture should be oriented toward growth and diversification rather than consolidation. (Fast 1979)
   - Top management must provide strong support (Kierulff 1979, Erickson 1978, Susbauer 1973).
   - The corporate financial position must be strong; support for venture management projects will erode rapidly in the case of a declining financial position.
   - Effort must be concentrated on a small number of projects rather than a wide range of exploratory endeavors.
   - Managers of new venture units should have a more administrative orientation than do more "typical" entrepreneurs.

Entrepreneurship and environment

Innovative endeavors always take place in a particular context. It is customary to distinguish between the internal environment (the organizational specification of task roles and reporting relationships) and the external environment (economic, technological, social, regulatory, and other conditions that affect an organization). Both environments can have either a constraining or a conducive effect on entrepreneurship.

As far as the external environment was concerned, the large-scale public financing of the moon-landing program was highly conducive to entrepreneurial effort in certain industries. In contrast, regulatory measures frequently have adverse market effects (Peltzman 1974, Grabowski et al. 1976, Schwartzman 1976). In general, an individual firm has very little control over the external environment and must adapt to existing conditions. In contrast, the management of a firm has large control over the internal environment. In order to realize an organization's entrepreneurial potential, one must therefore address those internal characteristics that either constrain or enhance innovative efforts. Entrepreneurship in small, new venture firms is very frequently constrained by inadequate financial resources and inadequate stratification of personnel. Entrepreneurship in large organizations encounters very different constraints.

Internal constraints on entrepreneurship in mature organizations

Entrepreneurship is invariably associated with tough technological, marketing, financing, or managerial issues. Solution of these issues tends to be unpredictable and risky. It is the essence of entrepreneurship to deal with unpredictable outcomes, but the operational norms of large, mature organizations tend to minimize endeavors associated with risk and change. Entrepreneurship in mature organizations therefore encounters a variety of typical operations as obstacles.

The most common internal constraints are:

1. *The profitability-now syndrome.* The management of mature organizations is primarily concerned about current or short-term profits rather than future, long-range profits. Managers quite readily accept current profit levels as the main determinant of their success. As a consequence, corporate endeavors with uncertain, long-range payoffs are frequently sacrificed in favor of safer, short-term programs. The focus on profitability, combined with frequent budgeting and reporting cycles, undercuts entrepreneurial ventures that require a longer gestation period but may yield higher payoffs in the future.
2. *Executive incentive programs.* These are often based on accounting concepts of achievement (profit or cost targets) and accompanied by relatively brief executive tours of service. In this situation executives become reluctant to jeopardize their career potential by championing risky entrepreneurial projects.
3. *Excessive formalization in organization structure.* Extensive descriptions of functional responsibilities for managerial positions discourage personal initiative and creative departures from approved norms.
4. *Intra-organizational boundaries.* Separation of operations into semi-autonomous product divisions tends to hamper those entrepreneurial projects which require cooperation among various divisions.
5. *Resource allocation based on generation of revenue.* A concept initially propagated by the Boston Consulting Group specifies that the net cash flow from highly profitable operating divisions should be used to support new corporate ventures with a high growth potential. This concept, however, is not yet widely practiced. There are thus many mature firms in which the traditional resource allocation makes it difficult to secure funding for entrepreneurial endeavors.

In addition to these general internal constraints on entrepreneurship, other internal obstacles are specific to the various entrepreneurship strategies. The dominant internal constraints to administrative entrepreneurship stem from the separation of responsibilities between technical experts and managerial experts. Conflicts can seriously reduce the effectiveness of this entrepreneurship strategy.

A major internal constraint on opportunistic entrepreneurship is the difficulty of reaching consensus within the organization about the desirability of a specific opportunity. Lack of consensus often leads to internal bargaining, compromise, and inadequate support for a chosen entrepreneurial venture.

A typical internal constraint on imitative entrepreneurship is the tendency to ignore or to attribute an unrealistically low significance to relevant outside developments. The effective internalization of technological developments is a formidable problem, as witnessed by the large number of studies on the difficulties of technology transfer. Acquisition is subject to resource constraints and organizational obstacles to the effective integration of new acquisitions.

Incubative entrepreneurship confronts the problem of different operating norms and performance criteria for the incubator units and for other operating divisions. Differences in treatment, in size, and in resource availability make the new venture activities appear to be rather marginal (Fast 1979). In order to overcome this situation, top management must provide strong, sustained, and explicit support to incubator units.

Regardless of what specific strategy a mature organization may adopt, internal constraints will tend to limit the effectiveness of its entrepreneurial endeavors. Management must be aware of internal obstacles and contribute to the development of a conducive entrepreneurial environment.

Organizational climates conducive to internal entrepreneurship

The effects of various organizational structures and behaviors on innovation in existing firms have been analyzed in considerable detail (Burns and Stalker 1961, Lorsch 1965, Lawrence and Lorsch 1967, Hage and Aiken 1970, Zaltman 1973, Rogers 1976). Most of these studies address specific features of organizational structure (degrees of centralization, formalization, complexity, integration, and openness) and of interpersonal relationships and examine their effect on the initiation and implementation of innovative endeavors. As is so often the case with complex interrelationships, no clear-cut answers emerge. There is no single effective method of entrepreneurship in mature organizations; all that can be said is that specific organizational conditions may recommend a particular approach above another. There are, however, a few generally applicable guidelines for creating a climate conducive to entrepreneurial endeavors. The following features are important:

1. Psychological Security. Entrepreneurship is a creative, innovative effort, the results of which are often unpredictable. To stimulate entrepreneurship, an organization must separate the failure of innovative corporate projects from personal failure for its entrepreneurs and from losses in pay, status, and advancement potential. A General Electric executive formulated this concept in the title of an article: "If Managers Fear to Fail, Can Organization Succeed?" (Meyer 1969). A corporation that instills in its managers a fear of failure is not very likely to stimulate a high degree of entrepreneurial effort; it will probably be less successful than a firm that provides genuine incentives for entrepreneurship. The emphasis ought to be on the need for success, the desirability of innovation, support for innovative efforts, challenging standards, a friendly team spirit, and fair rewards for entrepreneurial success (Lehr 1979).

2. Continued stimulation. Internal entrepreneurship is a continuous process which requires ongoing stimulation: challenging goals for individual members of the organization, varied task assignments, easy access to information about new ideas or developments, or cross-fertilization through task groups. Many conceptual and empirical studies emphasize the importance of continuous incentives and provide explicit guidelines for the application of stimuli (Atkinson 1967, Atkinson and Feather 1966).

3. Diffusion of authority. In an organization that is conducive to entrepreneurship, authority is exercised in an unobtrusive manner; coercive power should be minimized.

4. A flexible time and resource framework. Ideally, innovative endeavors are not hampered by strict budgets or time schedules.

From these broadly-stated guidelines one can conclude that an organizational climate conducive to internal entrepreneurship combines a number of elements: individuals with high achievement motivation, corporate willingness, and resources for removing obstacles to innovation. In addition, administrative entrepreneurship requires sensitivity to the inherent conflict potential between R & D managers and innovators. Opportunistic, imitative, and acquisitive approaches call for well developed environmental scanning. The incubative approach requires a high degree of tolerance for different internal operating standards and a strong, sustained commitment from top management.

The various strategies for internal entrepreneurship can be equally effective if a company is able and willing to adapt those structural and behavioral measures that foster successful implementation.

A comparative analysis of internal entrepreneurship strategies

Existing firms can use a variety of entrepreneurship strategies to improve their competitive advantages, market standing, and profitability. Although a number of studies have examined the effectiveness of individual approaches to internal entrepreneurship, almost no comparative analyses exist. An exception is Hlavacek and Thompson 1973.

Based on the typology of internal entrepreneurship strategies as presented in this chapter, an empirical investigation of U.S. manufacturing firms is in progress. Data analysis is still incomplete, but Table 1 suggests the scope of the investigation and summarizes some of the findings.

Among large firms, the administrative approach to entrepreneurship appears to be, in strictly numerical terms, by far the most dominant form. A majority of the firms also use acquisitions for entrepreneurial purposes. The percentage of companies reporting opportunistic, imitative, or incubative entrepreneurship is relatively low. Those strategies most frequently used are also judged to be quite satisfactory. No clear pattern of cost efficiency emerges for the five strategies, but imitative entrepreneurship is generally considered to be the most cost efficient. Companies are generally well aware of the inherent limitations of the various approaches. There is strong evidence that companies using several internal entrepreneurship strategies are considerably more successful (in growth in sales, diversification, relative market dominance, and profitability) than are firms using only one or two of the strategies.

Summary and suggested directions for future research

In a competitive environment, internal entrepreneurship is an essential element in long-range corporate success. Internal entrepreneurship expresses itself in a variety of modes or strategies: Administrative (R & D management), Opportunistic (search and exploitation of entrepreneurial opportunities), Imitative, Acquisitive, or Incubative (formation of semi-autonomous units as breeding grounds for entrepreneurial strategies). Important internal constraints involve motivation, organizational structure and behavior, and resource capabilities.

The volume and diversity of research on the topic of internal entrepreneurship is already impressive. At the same time, many important issues are largely unexplored. We need longitudinal studies to analyze the effectiveness of various internal entrepreneurial strategies and to answer such questions as: How does internal entrepreneurship change with different operating conditions, the size of an enterprise, the type of business, and the firm's evolutionary phase? What is the impact of specific external environmental developments? Is there an optimum combination of approaches? How does the internal organizational context affect the various entrepreneurship strategies?

The long-range success of business firms depends to a large extent on their entrepreneurial and innovative endeavors. More systematic research on the conditions for effective internal entrepreneurship would obviously be of considerable benefit.

Table 1 *Comparative analysis of internal entrepreneurship strategies*

	Internal entrepreneurship strategies				
Assessment criteria	**Administrative**	**Opportunistic**	**Imitative**	**Acquisitive**	**Incubative**
Frequency of use	dominant	low frequency	depends on competitive pressure	high frequency	low frequency
Perceived effectiveness (in light of organizational objectives)	high	low	high/depends on circumstances	high	high/within narrow range of activities
Efficiency (relationship between input and results)	wide range high to low	mixed	high	mixed	generally low with exceptions
Inherent limitations and constraints	conflict potential	ad hoc unpredictable	litigation competition pressures retaliation	financing	limitations of scale
Potential scope for improvement	high	low	low	low	high
Predictability of results	high to low	low	high	high	high to low
Variability of results	wide range	wide range	relatively narrow range	wide range	wide range

commentary/elaboration

Commentary on internal corporate entrepreneurship

Edward Shils

While the Schollhammer chapter is a scholarly work, it spends too much time focusing on classifications and models of internal entrepreneurship in large business organizations. Does it matter if we call the entrepreneur an "internal corporate entrepreneur" or subdivide him into "intra-corporate" and "administrative" subclasses?

It is more important to investigate the corporate structure in which the entrepreneur must conduct his affairs. Can the large corporation be redesigned so as to contain a number of modules which approximate autonomous entrepreneurial businesses? Should the corporate board and the CEO stress standardization and uniformity, or counter the bureaucracy so often found in large corporations? Corporate objectives and policies will determine whether an executive can behave like an entrepreneur. If possible, he'll look to corporate headquarters as though it were a bank, rather than the pinnacle of the hierarchy.

Schollhammer says little about the important area of incentives. Why not establish earnings opportunities to encourage entrepreneurship? The right coupling of financial and psychological rewards could eliminate the need for excessive bureaucracy.

Schollhammer states that among the Fortune 500 corporations only 10 or 20 percent think in terms of internal entrepreneurship. This is true only if one considers venture management to be the major form of entrepreneurship. If internal corporate entrepreneurship is seen as an atmosphere that permeates the entire organization, more and more of the large corporations are becoming concerned about internal entrepreneurship in this total sense.

During the past two years, the Wharton Entrepreneurial Center at the University of Pennsylvania has actively surveyed companies in France and the United States in order to determine what is being done to develop internal corporate entrepreneurship. In France, a movement toward smaller modules within corporations was encouraging entrepreneurial decentralization. In both countries, decentralization receives a great deal of lip service. In France, the overconcentration of employment in urban areas suggests that employees be rerouted to villages or suburban areas in a type of geographic decentralization. This in itself, however, does not have any beneficial entrepreneurial aspect. It is only by stimulating entrepreneurial enterprise on the part of subsidiaries, which may or may not be located in other parts of the nation, that the true benefits of decentralization will be realized. It is possible to decentralize a corporation even if all subsidiaries are located in one city.

Schollhammer sees entrepreneurship as a manifestation of personal qualities: initiative, creativity, high achievement motivation, perseverance, enthusiasm, and so forth. Can we really distinguish those qualities from those which belong to good management? The entrepreneur may create by devising new combinations. Schollhammer's definition of administrative entrepreneurship includes the old management tasks of organizing, controlling, and delegating, those found in books on public and private administration for over 50 years.

The Wharton School studied eight U.S. corporations with volumes well in excess of $3 billion annually, in order to determine the methods used by these companies to stimulate internal entrepreneurship. The eight companies studied all agreed that such stimulation was desirable. Research on their strategies helped the French to take a new look at their own traditional formats.

The studies of Frederick Herzberg in the United States have indicated that the most successful organizations allow for internal entrepreneurship down to the operating level; each craftsman becomes an entrepreneur who is measured by his contributions and who is responsible for running his "business." Dedication and commitment must lead to financial rewards as well. Bic Pen, U.S.A., a subsidiary of a French corporation, has brought the concept of entrepreneurial responsibility down to the work level.

The corporate entrepreneur must have direct access to top corporate executives. The development of entrepreneurial modules can eliminate duplicative management levels and establish contact between corporate executives and operating entrepreneurs at the divisional level.

While some companies emphasize internal entrepreneurship, others emphasize external growth through acquisition. The large corporations were not sympathetic to the smaller companies they acquired in the 60s. Eleven major conglomerates in the United States were studied with regard to their multibillion dollar acquisition procedures. They were so inefficient in the management of acquisition that the programs actually favored the competition. Not only did they destroy over half of the small companies acquired because they didn't understand the goals and motivation of autonomous business leaders, but they even lost the market share they had had to begin with.

The mistakes of the 60s are being rectified by a more intelligent acquisition process today. The acquiring corporations employ senior executives who are venture capital–minded and who understand the mainsprings of the autonomous entrepreneur. They make certain that the acquired executives understand such factors as overhead charges. They refrain from over-managing the acquired company and give the former owners latitude and support for innovative behavior and accelerated growth. Formal structure is minimized, and former owners are kept as managers of the acquired firm when possible. In this environment, formerly independent companies have doubled and tripled their production and profit during the post-acquisition decade.

In summary, one finds creativity and an innovative spirit in both the independent entrepreneur and the aggressive internal corporate entrepreneur. Both individuals are venturesome and willing to put their personal careers on the line. A fear of failure stimulates the independent entrepreneur to put his business before family, leisure, and recreational opportunities. The internal entrepreneur faces less direct financial risks, but failure on a project may mean the termination of upward mobility, loss of prestige, routing to an unpromotable assignment, or even the loss of a position.

Both the independent owner and the internal corporate executive have a sense of independence that precludes the emulation of superiors. They show initiative and are not willing to take "no" for an answer. The independent entrepreneur will face the banker with persistence and, when confronted by a negative answer, will respond with "Why?" and "Why not?" The internal entrepreneur will go to headquarters to seek funding for ideas and will be equally persistent in obtaining an affirmative answer rather than accepting a negative. In contrast, most bureaucrats in large corporations are immediately brought to a halt by negative responses. With regard to personality, there is no great difference between the independent entrepreneur and the internal corporate entrepreneur.

Accumulating information about entrepreneurism in France and the United States, as well as in other nations, can be used by large corporations to generate a flourishing entrepreneurial attitude.

References

ATKINSON, JOHN W., "Motivational Determinants of Risk-Taking Behavior," *Psychological Review* 64, No. 6, Part 1 (November 1957).

ATKINSON, JOHN W., and FEATHER, NORMAN T., eds., *A Theory of Achievement Motivation.* New York: John Wiley, 1966.

BURNS, TOM, and STALKER, G. M., *The Management of Innovation.* London: Tavistock Publications, 1961.

CHRISTENSEN, R. C., ANDREWS, K. R., and BOWER, J. L., *Business Policy* (4th ed.). Homewood, Ill.: Richard D. Irwin, 1978.

COLE, ARTHUR H., "An Approach to the Study of Entrepreneurship," in *Explorations in Enterprise*, ed. Hugh G. J. Aiken. Cambridge: Harvard University, 1965.

COLE, ARTHUR H., *Business Enterprise in Its Social Setting.* Cambridge: Harvard University, 1959.

COLLINS, ORVIS, and MOORE, DAVID G., *The Organization Makers—A Behavioral Study of Independent Entrepreneurs.* Englewood Cliffs, N.J.: Prentice-Hall, 1970.

COMANOR, WILLIAM S., "Research and Technological Change in the Pharmaceutical Industry," *Review of Economics and Statistics* 47, No. 2 (May 1965).

COOPER, ARNOLD C., "Incubator Organizations and Other Influences on Entrepreneurship," *Entrepreneurship and Enterprise Development: A Worldwide Perspective.* Milwaukee: Center for Venture Management, 1975.

COOPER, ARNOLD C., "Incubator Organizations and Technical Entrepreneurship," in *Technical Entrepreneurship*, eds. Arnold C. Cooper and John L. Komives. Milwaukee: Center for Venture Management, 1972.

COOPER, ARNOLD C., "R & D Is More Efficient in Small Companies," *Harvard Business Review*, May-June 1964.

COOPER, ARNOLD C., and BRUNO, ALBERT, "Success among High-Technology Firms," *Business Horizons* 20, No. 2 (April 1977).

ERICKSON, GERALD A., *Another Look at the New Venture Approach* (M.B.A. thesis, University of Washington, 1978).

FAST, NORMAN D., "Key Managerial Factors in New Venture Departments," *Industrial Marketing Management* 8, No. 3 (June 1979).

GRABOWSKI, HENRY G., "The Determinants of Industrial Research and Development," *Journal of Political Economy* 76, No. 2 (March-April 1968).

GRABOWSKI, HENRY G., and BAXTER, NEVINS D., "Rivalry in Industrial Research and Development," *Journal of Industrial Economics* 21, No. 3 (July 1973).

GRABOWSKI, HENRY G., VERNON, JOHN M., and THOMAS, LACY G., "The Effects of Regulatory Policy on the Incentives to Innovate: An International Comparative Analysis," in *Impact of Public Policy on Drug Innovation and Pricing*, eds. Samuel A. Mitchell and Emery Link. Washington, D.C.: American University, 1976.

HAGE, JERALD, and AIKEN, MICHAEL, *Social Change in Complex Organizations.* New York: Random House, 1970.

HLAVACEK, JAMES D., and THOMPSON, VICTOR A., "Bureaucracy and New Product Innovation," *Academy of Management Journal* 16, No. 3 (September 1973).

JEWKES, J. D., SAWERS, DAVID, and STILLERMAN, R., *The Sources of Invention.* New York: St. Martin's Press, 1959.

JOHNSON, P. S., and CATHCART, D. G., "The Founders of New Manufacturing Firms: A Note on the Size of Their Incubator Plants," *The Journal of Industrial Economics* 28, No. 2 (December 1979).

JONES, KENNETH A., and WILEMON, DAVID L., "Emerging Patterns in New Venture Management," *Research Management* 15, No. 6 (November 1972).

KAY, NEIL M., *The Innovating Firm.* New York: St. Martin's Press, 1979.

KIERULFF, HERBERT E., "Finding—and Keeping—Corporate Entrepreneurs," *Business Horizons*, February 1979.

LAWRENCE, PAUL R., and LORSCH, JAY W., *Organization and Environment: Managing Differentiation and Integration.* Boston: Harvard University, 1967.

LEHR, LEWIS W., "Top Management Attitude and Its Role in Innovation." Presentation May 22, 1979. 3M Release.

LEONTIADES, MILTON, *Strategies for Diversification and Change.* Boston: Little, Brown, 1980.

LEVITT, THEODORE, "Innovative Imitation," *Harvard Business Review* 44 (September-October 1966).

LORSCH, JAY W., *Product Innovation and Organization.* New York: Macmillan, 1965.

MANSFIELD, EDWIN, *The Economics of Technological Change.* New York: W. W. Norton & Co., Inc. 1968.
MANSFIELD, EDWIN, "Industrial Research and Development Expenditures: Determinants, Prospect, and Relation to Size of Firm and Inventive Output," *Journal of Political Economy* 72, No. 4 (August 1964).
MANSFIELD, EDWIN, "The Speed of Response of Firms to New Techniques," *Quarterly Journal of Economics* 77, No. 2 (May 1963).
MEYER, HERBERT, "If Men Fear to Fail, Can Organizations Succeed?" *Innovation,* December 1969.
NATHUSIUS, KLAUS, *Venture Management.* Berlin: Ducker & Humbolt, 1979.
NELSON, RICHARD R., "Economics of Invention," *Journal of Business* 32, No. 2 (April 1959).
NELSON, RICHARD R., *The Rate and Direction of Inventive Activity: Economic and Social Factors.* Princeton: Princeton University, 1962.
PELTZMAN, SAM, *Regulation of Pharmaceutical Innovation.* Washington, D.C.: American Enterprise Institute for Public Policy Research, 1974.
PETERSON, RUSSELL W., "New Venture Management in a Large Company," *Harvard Business Review,* May-June 1967.
REDLICH, FRITZ, "A New Concept of Entrepreneurship," *Explorations in Entrepreneurial History* 1, 1949.
ROBERTS, EDWARD B., "Insights into Innovation," *Proceedings of the 27th National Conference on the Administration of Research,* September 1973. Denver: University of Denver, Denver Research Institute, 1974.
ROGERS, EVERETT M., *Diffusion of Innovation.* New York: Free Press, 1962.
ROGERS, EVERETT M., and AGARWALA-ROGERS, REKHA, *Communication in Organizations.* New York: Free Press, 1976.
RUMELT, RICHARD, *Strategy, Structure, and Economic Performance.* Boston: Harvard Graduate School of Business Administration, 1974.
SCHERER, F. M., "Firm Size, Market Structure, Opportunity and the Output of Patented Inventions," *American Economic Review* 55 (1965).
SCHERER, F. M., *Industrial Market Structure and Economic Performance.* Chicago: Rand McNally, 1970.
SCHERER, F. M., "Market Structure and Technological Innovation," *Industrial Market Structure and Economic Performance.* Chicago: Rand McNally, 1970.
SCHMOOKLER, JACOB, *Invention and Economic Growth.* Cambridge: Harvard University, 1966.
SCHON, DONALD, "Champions for Radical New Inventions," *Harvard Business Review,* March-April 1963.
SCHON, DONALD, *Technology and Change: The Impact of Invention and Innovation on American Social and Economic Development.* New York: Delta Publishing, 1967.
SCHUMPETER, JOSEPH A., "Economic Theory and Entrepreneurial History," in *Explorations in Enterprise,* ed. Hugh G. J. Aiken. Cambridge: Harvard University, 1965.
SCHUMPETER, JOSEPH A., *The Theory of Economic Development.* Cambridge: Harvard University, 1934.
SCHWARTZMAN, DAVID, *Innovation in the Pharmaceutical Industry.* Baltimore: Johns Hopkins University, 1976.

SHILS, EDWARD B., and ZUCKER, WILLIAM, "Developing a Model for Internal Corporate Entrepreneurship," *Social Science* 54, No. 4 (Autumn 1979).
SLOCUM, DONALD H., *New Venture Methodology.* New York: American Management Association, 1972.
SUSBAUER, JEFFREY C., *Intracorporate Entrepreneurship: Programs in American Industry.* Cleveland: Cleveland State University, 1973.
SUSBAUER, JEFFREY C., "U.S. Industrial Intracorporate Entrepreneurship Practices," *R & D Management* 3, No. 3 (June 1973).
SUTHERLAND, ALLISTER, "The Diffusion of Innovation in Cotton Spinning," *Journal of Industrial Economics* 7, No. 2 (March 1959).
VESPER, KARL H., *New Venture Strategies.* Englewood Cliffs, N.J.: Prentice-Hall, 1980.
WILEMON, DAVID L., and GEMMILL, GARY R., "The Venture Manager as a Corporate Innovator," *California Management Review* 16 (Fall 1973).
YOUNG, ROBERT, "No Room for the Searcher," *Managing Advancing Technology,* Vol. II. New York: American Management Association, 1972.
ZALTMAN, GERALD, DUNCAN, ROBERT, and HOLBEK, JONNY, *Innovations in Organizations.* New York: John Wiley, 1973.

Section Three

Entrepreneurship and Progress

The chapters in this section have a common theme: the process of entrepreneurship contributes to economic progress. It is the assumption that economic progress is something to be desired and encouraged. The entrepreneur is viewed as being the principal agent for bringing about this progress.

The first three chapters focus specifically on the role of the entrepreneur in economic development. Economic development is viewed not as an increase in the per capita production of goods and services but rather as a change in the total economic and social structure and in a population's standard of living.

Kent's chapter reviews the thoughts of economists on the role of entrepreneurship, as conditioned by both the supply and demand sides of the market. Over the years the focus of economics has changed. Early economists felt that total spending would always be sufficient to promote full employment and growth. The unanswered question was whether there would be a sufficient supply of entrepreneurial talent to create and act upon new investment opportunities. In the last 50 years the focus has switched: modern macroeconomics asserts that insufficient total spending is the inhibiting factor in the development process. The new school of thought assumes that if total demand is high enough, entrepreneurial innovation will be an automatic response.

Both lines of thought have obscured the essential role of the entrepreneur. It is the entrepreneur's foresight and ability which make investment possible and profitable as well. In recent years economists have replaced the profit motive with the planning process as the guide for economic action. It is the contention of Kent's chapter that without the profit motive, entrepreneurship will not exist in sufficient quantity to stimulate economic development.

Broehl's chapter advances the questions of entrepreneurship in the less developed world. The challenges faced by entrepreneurs in less developed countries are no less formidable but are significantly different than those faced by their western counterparts. Entrepreneurs in the underdeveloped world confront a host of cultural barriers which compound the problems of innovation and the introduction of new technology. Often entrepreneurs in the underdeveloped world perform their functions only imperfectly, because the conflict of values causes them to mix traditional ways with modern methodology. This complicates the process of technology transfer between the advanced and the underdeveloped world. Broehl postulates that the process of technology transfer will include more than mere imitation. He introduces the concept of the "meta-innovation," the total adaptation of an idea to a market characterized by imperfect information, limited capital, and primitive technology. The risk of such innovation is obviously high, since failure may be more devastating in the underdeveloped world than in the developed.

Kirzner demonstrates that traditional economic theory has been highly limited in explaining the role of the entrepreneur. It has been the assumption of economics that markets move continuously toward equilibrium. The preoccupation of economic theory is a search for those equilibrating conditions. By its very nature, entrepreneurship is a force which creates disequilibrium. By the process of innovation, the entrepreneur creates profit opportunities. If a market does not react to these newly-created opportunities, then it is inefficient. An allocation of resources to take advantage of opportunity improves the income not only of the entrepreneur but of all others affected. Kirzner contends that entrepreneurship is unlikely to come from the government or planned sector. While innovation may take place in such a setting, without the profit motive there is no way of knowing whether this innovation improves economic efficiency. Entrepreneurship will most thrive where rewards are paid to those with sufficient insight to exploit opportunity.

The next three chapters are concerned specifically with the role of entrepreneurship in innovation. In the first of these chapters, Krasner makes an important distinction between invention and innovation. While invention consists of developing a new idea, process, or technology, innovation is a more encompassing term which includes the successful commercial development and merchandising of an idea or process.

One of the more interesting questions investigated by Krasner is whether innovation is more likely to come from small or large organizations. Large organizations, according to the research, are more successful in developing "process innovations," concerned with the manufacture or marketing of products and with the upgrading and perfecting of existing techniques. The individual entrepreneur is more likely to be successful at "leap-frog innovation," which involves new methodology or technology, a significant change in the state of the art. The implication here is that large organizations are less interested in financing significant innovative change because of the high risk entailed. While the failure of a radical innovation may be disastrous to the innovator and immediate financers, its negative impact will not be widely felt. On the other hand, in a corporation with many shareholders, such a failure may have much more widespread ramifications.

Udell addresses the noncorporate industrial innovation process. The research problem here is compounded by the interdisciplinary nature of the inquiry and by the secretiveness of entrepreneurs. Those who are successful and those who fail both guard their experiences. Classroom simulation of the entrepreneurial process is impossible to achieve.

This is unfortunate, given the importance of noncorporate entrepreneurial innovation. Recent studies have demonstrated that the new technologies at the heart of growth and progress are being developed in this sector. Udell presents a basic model of nonindustrial innovation: from the generation of an idea through evaluation, research, development, and commercialization. He catalogues research needs in each of these areas.

One of the more interesting questions in the study of entrepreneurship is the degree to which environment contributes to the success of the entrepreneurial process. If there are conducive environments, public policy should promote them. In the chapters by Bruno and Tyebjee and by Pennings, this contention is investigated.

Bruno and Tyebjee analyze those factors identified as important to an entrepreneurial environment: available venture capital, experienced entrepreneurs, incubator organizations, technically skilled labor forces, accessible suppliers and consumers, new markets, restricted regulation and taxation, proximate universities, available land and facilities, accessible transportation, a positive reception by local populations, good general living conditions. The research highlighting these factors is found by the authors to be methodologically unsound and inconclusive. Almost all research to date has been wisdom-based and observational. Few have asked why these factors contribute or which of them are more important. Inadequate attention has been focused on entrepreneurial events occurring in environments which, by the criteria mentioned above, would be classified as inhospitable.

Pennings wishes to move the environment to the center of entrepreneurship analysis. He establishes two models to explain the entrepreneurial environment. The "resource exchange model" views organizations as continuously adapting to the forces in their environment; the entrepreneur attempts to control, change, or adapt the environment in which he operates. The "population ecology" model views entrepreneurship as a biological species which is doomed if it is incompatible with its environment. In the first model, the entrepreneur is seen as the master of his own fate, capable of minimizing threats and exploiting opportunities. In the second, the entrepreneur is seen as a victim of his environment. Pennings then turns to a discussion of entrepreneurship in urban areas and concludes that metropolitan areas are a more conducive environment for innovation than are small towns and rural settings. The clustering of entrepreneurs allows them to support each other and take advantage of agglomeration economics.

Bruno, Tyebjee, and Pennings share a common theme: In other countries, a great deal of public effort has been placed on improving the environment for entrepreneurship. Such attention should now be the object of public policy in this country as well.

chapter xii

Entrepreneurship in economic development

Calvin A. Kent

Overview

The theory of economic growth sees entrepreneurship as the key to investment in expanding productive capacity. Investment works on both the supply and demand sides of the growth equation. By creating new capital, the capacity for growth is expanded. By creating new spending, that capacity is utilized. Despite the importance of entrepreneurship, economic theory has yet to adequately explain either the process by which entrepreneurship springs forth or the results of entrepreneurial activity in stimulating growth. As a result, a consistent public policy to foster entrepreneurship has yet to be devised.

The theory of economics

Since the days of Schumpeter, economists have seen the entrepreneur as the key figure in the process of economic development. As Higgins so adequately stated,

He is the man who sees the opportunity for introducing the new commodity, technique, raw material, or machine, and brings together the necessary capital, management, labor, and materials to do it. He may not be, and historically has usually not been, a scientific inventor. His skills are less scientific than organizational. His skills are also different from those of a salaried manager, who takes over an enterprise after it has been launched. In any society, the rate of technological progress and so of economic development depends greatly on the number and the ability of entrepreneurs available to it. (Higgins 1968)

This chapter advances the hypothesis that, despite the importance ascribed to the entrepreneur in the literature of economic development, the entrepreneurial role has been too often ignored, imperfectly considered, or only partially included in the theory of economic development. Because of this neglect or inaccurate specification, the role of the entrepreneur has not been fully understood. As a result, public policies in developed and underdeveloped countries have not fostered the environment in which entrepreneurship thrives.

This discussion reviews contemporary growth theory to examine the role attributed to the entrepreneur and entrepreneurship. There is no attempt to be exhaustive. I have sought the major contributions, trends, and issues and have focused primarily on macroeconomic theory. Concerned with the operation of the total economic system, most macroeconomic theory is based on the work of J. M. Keynes (1936), which centered on developed areas. That emphasis continues in this chapter, since entrepreneurship in less developed lands is covered by the chapter which follows.

Economic growth and economic development

Economic development involves more than rising per capita output and income; it constitutes change in the structure of production and society (Hagen 1980). It is impossible to have development without growth. Significant structural changes are implemented or allowed because output has risen and there is more to be divided among claimants. For example, the recent debate (Heilbroner 1980, Mishan 1973, Meadows et al. 1972, Thurow 1977) in the developed world between growth and no-growth advocates has been made possible by rising affluence. In a poor nation, the question of diverting a significant percentage of national income toward an "improved quality of life" is, at best, of only academic interest. The difference between growth and development is indicated by the question, "Is more better?"

Economic theory has tended to emphasize the expansion of output while at the same time recognizing that the social changes which result from growth will set parameters within which future growth occurs (Kindleberger 1965). The common denominator of economic theory is supply and demand. Economic growth is a process whereby factors on the supply side allow expanding output, while those on the demand side determine how far growth will proceed.

On the supply side of the market there are four ingredients, sometimes known as the implemental factors:

1. Quantity and quality of natural resources
2. Quantity and quality of human resources
3. Stock of capital goods
4. State of technological art

While these supply side factors are necessary, they are not sufficient by themselves to bring about growth. On the demand side of the market, there must be a sufficient level of total spending. Without it, factors will be underutilized and growth will be unrealized. Aggregate demand is the implemental factor which causes growth when the supply side allows it. In the economist's geometry, change in the implemental factors causes the production possibilities, or transformation curve, to shift outward and to the right. It is the level of aggregate demand which determines whether the economy will operate on the curve or inside it. The factors of growth are not isolated events. If an economy fails to utilize its resources fully in any given year (operates inside its production possibilities curve), potential capital formation is reduced and growth will be restricted in the following year below what it could have been.

The entrepreneur plays roles on both the supply and demand sides of the growth equation.

Supply side considerations

From 1776, when Adam Smith penned the first book in economics, *The Wealth of Nations*, to the time J. M. Keynes' *General Theory* (1936) emerged during the Great Depression, supply side considerations have dominated economic thought on the subject of development. It was implicitly assumed in these early writings that aggregate demand would be sufficient to cause maximum growth. Insufficient aggregate demand was thought to be temporary unless rigidities like monopolies, labor unions, and banking structures prevented prices from adjusting markets to a new, full employment equilibrium.

Adam Smith's is a handbook on economic development. He saw economic growth as the product of expanded factors of production; he saw increased efficiency as the product of specialization, division of labor, and improved methods of exchange. Such increases in efficiency would lead to growth in the same manner that physical increases in the supply would.

As David Ricardo (1921) saw, so long as population and land could increase together in the same proportion, then economic growth could continue and accelerate as superior organization increased efficiency. Thomas Malthus (1970) pointed to the fatal flaw in Smith's ever-expanding economy. As fertile virgin land disappears, new laborers crowd onto cultivated soils and are forced to till less productive plots. This not only creates the necessity for private property and the concomitant institution of land rent, but also calls forth the law of diminishing returns. As the labor-to-land ratio increases, and the output-to-land ratio decreases, then wages will fall, ultimately to the subsistence level.

As every student who has successfully completed Principles of Economics knows, the world did not fall into the Malthusian trap and succumb to the Ricardian iron law of wages. Changes in technology introduced by entrepreneurs (Schumpeter 1936) and external economics of scale which allowed costs to fall as the volume of output expanded (Marshall 1946) altered the economic forecast. While technology and mass production did not repeal the law of diminishing returns, they are generally viewed as offsetting it, at least in the developed world.

The role of the entrepreneur on the supply side of the economic development equation then comes to the forefront. The entrepreneur is the one who brings about the technological change necessary to forestall the fate which caused Carlyle (1923) to label economics as the dismal science. It is also the entrepreneur who lowers costs by adopting mass production techniques, thus obtaining a competitive advantage over his rivals.

Theory of profit

In this scenario, it is economic profit (a return in excess of explicit or opportunity costs) which spurs the entrepreneur into action. While the theory of profits has occupied the minds of many great economists, there has not yet been a satisfactory explanation of why profit arises. The most common definition was most eloquently advanced by Knight: "Profits are a reward that owners of business receive for bearing risks" (1921). It is the nature of economic life that the future is not known with certainty; people working for wages avoid risks through contractual guarantees. Some security is even offered against the default of banks and to corporate bondholders. It is the owners of a business who will bear the risk of loss if the enterprise fails. In return, they keep the profits if revenues are sufficient to pay off contractual obligations. While most people are risk-avoiders, entrepreneurs are not. For the economy as a whole, the excess of profits over losses is a reward earned by people who bear the business risks. Other factor-owners are willing to accept less than the whole value of the product of the firm because they are shielded from these risks.

The somewhat limited view of the entrepreneur as risk-taker would not be wholly acceptable to Schumpeter (1936), whose explanation of profit is based on the role of innovation. The entrepreneur, as an innovator, is one who creates profit opportunities by devising a new product, a new production process, or new marketing strategy. If successful, the entrepreneur is able to achieve a position of temporary monopoly, which permits pure economic profit to be earned until rivals catch up or leap ahead with innovations of their own. The Schumpeterian dynamic is that one innovation opens the door to others. Growth is sparked by "a thundering herd" of entrepreneurs, each creating his own temporary advantage.

Kirzner (1973) advances a third explanation for profit. He equates profits with the result of arbitrage, where the entrepreneur takes advantage of spontaneously occurring opportunities to buy low and sell high. This concept of profit is not to be thought of in the narrow terms of commodity trading on known price differentials between markets. Profit is not the result of acting on known imperfections in the market, but of correctly anticipating where the next imperfections and imbalances will be. The entrepreneur receives this profit because he acts on an opportunity before, not after, it occurs.

Even if one grants that profit is the necessary force to bring forth entrepreneurial activity, an important supply side question remains: What brings forth entrepreneurship in various amounts, in various places, and at various times? As we try to answer this question, we will join Kilby (1971) in "hunting the 'Heffalump.' " Having reviewed the literature on entrepreneurial supply, Kilby comments:

The economist who operates in the mainstream of his discipline assumes that the supply of entrepreneurial services is highly elastic, and the failures in entrepreneurships are attributable to maladjustments in the external environment. (1971)

Many of the sociological and psychological explanations of entrepreneurial supply are analyzed in depth in other chapters of this volume. Brief mention is made here to allow a complete development of the conceptual strand.

McClelland (1961) relates the supply of entrepreneurship to the need for achievement stemming from ideological values and family socialization. His theory is an improvement on the concepts of Weber (1930), who described the transition from ideological values to entrepreneurial behavior without first recognizing the role of the family and the need for achievement as necessary intermediary steps. While somewhat consistent with McClelland's observations, Hagen's (1962) view of economic development pays little attention to markets and perceived profits as factors inducing entrepreneurial supply. As seen by Hagen, the entrepreneur brings about technological change because of a duty to achieve rather than a desire for profit. Cochran (1964) stresses cultural values, role expectations, and social sanctions. In his system, entrepreneurs represent society's model personality. Entrepreneurship is a result of cultural values, which award status to that type of activity.

None of these explanations have gone unchallenged. None of them directly face the question, "Why are those with entrepreneurial personalities directed into business pursuits?" Both Hagen and McClelland suggest that the need for achievement and social status can best be met through business activity. If status is not awarded to those who achieve material success, then entrepreneurship will not be practiced.

One cannot leave the supply side of the analysis without noting that considerable literature has assigned the entrepreneur an insignificant or passive role in the process of economic development. Either explicitly or by omission, certain economists have downplayed the role of the entrepreneur. North (1961) omits the entrepreneur from his discussions of U.S. economic development on the ground that the entrepreneurial response is autonomous and virtually automatic when demand is sufficient and markets are functioning properly. In his more recent writings, North and his collaborators (Davis, North, and Smorodin 1971; North and Thomas 1973) have seen development principally as a result of institutional changes. Innovation is viewed, not as a technological phenomenon, but as the creation of new institutions (often governmental) "which can permit the capture of potential increases in income arising from externalities, economies of scale, risks and transaction costs" (Davis et al. 1971).

Baumol (1968) and his predecessors (Aubrey 1955, Rosenberg 1960) have seen the desire for profit as a universal force transcending time and society. To them, the supply of entrepreneurship is highly elastic in response to anticipated profit. The level of entrepreneurship at any place or time is then determined principally by the demand for final outputs, availability of inputs, and environmental variables such as inflation, taxation, regulation, and political stability. Current research (U.S. Congress, Joint Economic Committee 1979, Weidenbaum 1977, MacAvoy 1979), which blames the decline in innovation, investment, and productivity in the United States on perverse taxation and regulation, implicitly embraces this model.

Forces in economic growth

Recently, the works of Denison (1962, 1974, 1979) have attempted to explain the forces influencing U.S. economic growth in the twentieth century and causing different growth rates among nations (Denison and Poullier 1967, and Denison and Chung 1976). These papers have focused on supply side characteristics, and their conclusions are summarized in Table 1. Nowhere does Denison's work explicitly attribute economic development to entrepreneurship. This omission may be due to the difficulties of quantifying entrepreneurship as a productive input. The improvements in technology may be viewed as a proxy for the entrepreneurial element which is embodied in new technology. It is also entirely possible that much of what Denison qualifies as "improved education and training" is also due to entrepreneurship.

Table 1 *Sources of U.S. economic growth, 1909–1976*

Source	Percentage of total growth 1909–1929	1929–1969	1969–1976
Total growth in national real income	100	100	100[c]
Increase in labor force[a]	35	24	23
Improved education and training	13	15	31
Increased stock of capital goods	23	15	31
Improved technology	19	35	18
Economies of scale[b]	10	11	15

Source: Edward Denison, *The Sources of Economic Growth in the United States* (Committee for Economic Development 1962); *Accounting for U.S. Economic Growth, 1929–1969* (Brookings Institution 1974); and *Accounting for Slower Economic Growth: The United States in the 1970s* (Brookings Institution 1979). Figures before and after 1929 are not strictly comparable; see sources for details.

[a]Adjusted for decreasing number of working hours per year.

[b]Economies of large-scale production with growing total size of the market.

[c]Negative 14% for costs of pollution abatement, worker safety measures, etc., not shown separately.

While Denison's allocations may be questioned (Griliches 1973, Hudson and Jorgenson 1978), the factors he identifies are widely accepted as being the appropriate ones for study. It would be useful for future scholars to isolate entrepreneurship as a factor or to identify its contribution to those factors included in Denison's model. In essence, the Denison studies bring us back to Schumpeter, who saw technology as saving us from the Malthusian trap. The technological advance so important to Denison's conclusions is what happens when entrepreneurs ply their trade.

Technical progress is not the only reason that growth in the factors of production cannot entirely account for economic growth in general. Education and investment in human capital (Becker 1962), improved managerial skills and the growth of markets (Harbison 1956, Chenery and Syrquin 1975), and government policy (Gerschenkras 1962) have also contributed to a more favorable growth environment.

Demand side considerations

For over 150 years, economic analysis neglected the demand side of the growth situation. During this period, economists were occupied with problems other than growth, partially because it had proceeded almost without sustained interruption in Western Europe and North America. Since economic growth had not halted in the developed world, the debate over whether decline would be caused by insufficient supply or demand seemed irrelevant. Most economists followed Adam Smith, who saw supply as the constraint and stressed the desirability of additional capital accumulation. (Smith's principal concession to demand considerations was his statement that the degree of specialization would be limited by the size of the market.)

For nearly four decades following the Great Depression and the publication of Keynes' *General Theory*, economists have been preoccupied with macroeconomic considerations (Stiglitz and Uzawa 1969). Aggregate demand is the essence of macroeconomic analysis and forms the demand side of the economic growth model. The simplest model says that aggregate demand is the result of consumption spending by households, investment spending by business, spending by political entities, and the net spending (either positive or negative) accomplished in the foreign sector. Each of these components is then subjected to separate analysis, and the determinants of each are delineated. The great contribution of Keynesian economics was the revelation that aggregate demand might be insufficient to produce full employment of resources. In the Keynesian model, there was no reason to expect automatic forces which would insure that a deficiency in aggregate demand would be self-correcting.

In the modern macroeconomic theory of growth, investment is the most important variable. Investment is a double-edged sword serving not only as a determinant of aggregate spending on the demand side, but also creating productive capacity and allowing growth on the supply side. Investment is both a permissive and implemental factor in the process of growth.

The Harrod-Domar models

The synthesis is summarized in the Harrod-Domar models (Harrod 1939, Domar 1946), only the bare bones of which are sketched below. In these models, the problem of economic growth is one of keeping aggregate demand expanding as quickly as productive capacity. The economy's productive capacity (its full employment income) will increase throughout time because of increases in the quantity and quality of resources, as well as improvements in efficiency due to technological advance; in Harrod's terminology, this is the warranted growth rate. For example, if the quantity of productive factors grows by 2 percent a year, and productivity increases by 2 percent, then the full employment level of income will rise by 4 percent in the next period.

Harrod noted that the full employment level of income this year would not be sufficient next year because of the additional capacity created by this year's investment in new plants and technology. The necessary amount of additional aggregate demand is determined by the capital/output ratio. A capital/output ratio of 4:1 means that four dollars net investment in this time period would raise the full employment capacity of the economy next year by one dollar.

In the simple Harrod model, savings and investment must be equal at equilibrium income since the level of investment is a function of the resources society frees from consumption (savings) in a given year. Harrod views the growth rate as the saving ratio divided by the capital/output ratio. Real growth per capita is the absolute growth rate minus the rate of expansion in the population. Thus, given a savings ratio of 8 percent, a capital/output ratio of 2:1, and a population growth rate of 2 percent, the per capita growth rate is 2 percent. If the savings ratio rises (allowing more investment) or the capital/output ratio declines (signifying a greater increase in productive capacity out of each new dollar invested), then the growth rate will rise.

Of more relevance to this discussion is the dynamics of the model. An increase in savings will cause investment to grow, which generates additional income and further expands savings. A contraction in savings leads to a chain reaction in the opposite direction. A growth problem occurs when the actual rate of growth differs from the growth path warranted by the increasing capacity of the economy. Harrod recognized, as did Keynes, that even though savings and investments are equal at equilibrium, it is changes in income which cause investment to change. In turn, these investment changes produce further income changes in the same direction: an accelerator effect. Domar's contribution to this analysis was to indicate the potential for a business cycle. There can be booms and busts. If the actual growth rate exceeds the warranted one, an inflationary boom results; recession results from an actual growth rate lower than the one warranted by expanding productive capacity.

The Harrod-Domar model is rejected by the neoclassical school as too inflexible (Tobin 1955). The theory assumes a rigid relationship between labor and capital; if either grows faster than the other, it will not be fully employed. As Solow has noted (1956, 1962), the model fails empirically, since examples can be cited where economic growth has proceeded at a faster rate than can be explained by the expansion of capital.

The theory also fails to explain the role of the entrepreneur and the impact of technological advance. In the Harrod-Domar scheme, the entrepreneur invests because of changes in income. A given level of investment is maintained so long as income is sufficient to purchase the products generated by new investment. If the capacity created by new investment grows faster than the income induced, investment in the next time period collapses. No role is assigned to entrepreneurial innovation and technological change.

Induced and autonomous investment

Hansen (1947, 1964) provides a useful distinction between two types of investment: autonomous and induced. Unlike the Harrod-Domar model, where all investment is induced by changes in the level of income, Hansen sees a certain amount of investment arising independent of changes in income. Autonomous investments are basically innovations which, consistent with the thoughts of Schumpeter, provide new and additional investment.

The principal concern of growth theory should be this autonomous investment, which is the result of entrepreneurial activity. If innovation can constantly expand and open new profit opportunities, investment may induce a sufficiently high level of aggregate demand to insure full employment and continued economic growth.

Hansen (1941) thought this unlikely, in that many "capital saving" innovations reduce the rate of return to capital. In addition, the nature of technological progress has weakened the response of investment to technological change. Agreeing with Schumpeter, Hansen thought few of the twentieth-century innovations would bring forth "great new industries" to call out large "clusters of followers." Twentieth-century innovations have largely been in the form of improved production techniques or for new and improved consumer durables. These innovations do not generate the same volume of secondary investment that the great new industries of the nineteenth and early twentieth century did. Put another way, innovation today does not make the capital accumulated in the past obsolete. Therefore, the higher rates of return necessary to create additional investment are not present.

Domar has suggested that the growth of monopoly and the institutionalization of research may also have contributed to the problem which Hansen identified (Domar 1948). Obsolescence is a major threat to the profitability of established enterprise. The monopolists and oligopolists tend to delay the introduction of new techniques in order to earn additional returns on past investment. Isolated from competitive forces, the introduction of new technology can be postponed. Hansen's writings also suggest that attitudes have changed: What he referred to as the "frontier spirit" has tended to diminish; risk-taking has given way to security-seeking as a principal motive for entrepreneurial action.

To summarize the Hansen position, which is often referred to as secular stagnation, the really dynamic factor is autonomous investment, a function of population growth, the discovery of new resources, and technological progress. The growth of potential output (the supply side) depends on the size of the labor force, the stock of known resources, available capital, and technological art. But autonomous investment will fail for reasons noted above, requiring increased public investment, reduced taxes, and income redistribution.

The neoclassical contribution

The neoclassical school has improved on the Harrod-Domar and Hansen models by allowing for variance of the capital-to-labor ratio and the substitution of one factor for the other (Arrow et al. 1961, Solow 1957, Johansen 1959). This work indicates that imbalances in factor prices will lead to entrepreneurial opportunity. Meade (1961) advanced the neoclassical model an additional step by adding to labor and capital a third factor, technological improvement. Meade's theory is dependent on constant improvements in technology over time. If this occurs, then capital-to-labor ratios may alter without a decline in growth.

Kaldor (1960) and Robinson (1956) questioned the degree to which capital could be substituted for labor, because of the embodied technology of machines which require relatively fixed proportions of the two variables. They also rejected the idea that changes in technology were necessarily a function of time. In their schemes, investment is a race between technology and growth of capital. If technology improves, the profitability of capital increases, so long as the rate of improvement exceeds the rate at which capital stock expands. If the growth of capital exceeds the rise in its marginal efficiency due to improved technology, profitability declines and investment is retarded. The result of the first scenario is growth; of the second, stagnation.

Stage theories

The theories discussed above have all focused on the process of economic growth as an expansion of per capita output. There is a long tradition of writers who have seen economic growth as part of a fundamental structural change in the fabric of society as a whole (Marx 1936; Weber 1930; Tawney 1954). Economic growth is caused and determined by the development process.

Explanations of this kind are known as stage or historical theories. The most popular and controversial is that of Rostow (1956, 1960, 1964), who divides development into five stages. In the first or traditional stage, the economy goes nowhere, trapped in static equilibrium. Modern technology has not encroached on traditional means of production. There is little social mobility due to hierarchical structures. Low productivity ties most of the population to near subsistence agriculture.

For some reason this system is disturbed, and the society moves into the precondition stage where social mobility becomes possible, transport is cheaper, and new technology is adopted first in agriculture, later in industry. Central to the precondition stage is the emergence of the entrepreneur. If investment in new methods is to take place, someone must take the risks of introducing and financing it. New ideas must be commercialized. Rostow's model is no different than Schumpeter's, except that entrepreneurship must also be accompanied by a change in the political fabric which encourages structural change.

During the precondition phase, a leading sector becomes the growth nexus. Often, by exploiting a natural resource or a technological advantage, this sector may develop the Schumpeterian "clustering of followers." Rostow notes that the process must be cumulative and the takeoff process repeated if it is not to fail.

The third, or takeoff stage, occurs when self-sustaining growth is achieved. Investment and savings rise dramatically as the economy rises from subsistence and generates a margin that can be plowed back. The takeoff is discontinuous when change spreads so rapidly that old structures disappear. Political, social, and institutional frameworks quickly emerge to exploit the possibilities provided during this phase.

After takeoff, there is the drive to maturity. In a poorly specified sequence, new leading sectors replace the old. The acceptance and encouragement of growth become widespread and ingrained. Growth in output clearly outdistances population. The culminating stage is that of high mass consumption, when expansion is centered in consumer durables, industries, and services. Somewhere in here Rostow loses sight of the entrepreneur, who must still be exploiting opportunities for personal advantage and the common good.

Rostow spends much of his effort dating and explaining the takeoff stages of various nations. Considerable criticism has been levied against this historical approach. Kuznets (1962, 1964) has presented historical data to demonstrate that no clearly defined "takeoff" stage exists in British economic history, Rostow's prime example. Nor does such a period appear for other industrialized nations. The predictive capacity of the theory and its usefulness in designing public policy to promote growth has seemed dubious to many economists (Solow 1964). While interesting, the historical approach has yet to add to the understanding of the entrepreneurial process.

Government as entrepreneur

Economic growth requires some form of governmental policy, from complete central planning to leaving the market alone. No existing economic system represents either of these two extremes, but economic growth has taken place in countries which approach either end of this continuum. In the post–World War II decades, economists have been fascinated with economic planning and the use of input-output analysis (Chakravarty and Lefeber 1965, Echaus and Parekh 1967, Millikan 1967, Blitzer et al. 1975). Generally, they ignore the entrepreneurial function or view it as a dependent variable which will respond in a predictable fashion to some planned stimulus.

The economic roles assigned to government can be encapsulated as follows:

1. Maintenance of internal stability and enforcement of legal rights.

2. Defense of the nation from external aggression.

3. Provision of public goods which are consumed jointly by all users (police and fire protection, flood control, roads, parks, etc.).

4. Expansion of the consumption of goods with high external benefits (education, public health, etc.).

5. Prevention of external costs by taxation, prohibition, or regulation (pollution, depletion of natural resources, establishment of standards, etc.).
6. Elimination of wasteful competition by the franchising and regulation of natural monopoly.

In all these cases, the government is responding to conditions of market failure. Additional responsibilities assumed by government have included counter-cyclical fiscal and monetary policies, as well as the redistribution of income.

Government as innovation of choice

Davis, North, and Smorodin (1971) have postulated that government action may be "the innovation of choice" when there is a well developed governmental structure and poorly developed private one. The inherent superiority of the government is its power to coerce. If the government is not able to exercise political control, as is often the case in the underdeveloped world, private action is the superior agent of change.

The second reason to prefer government innovation occurs when existing patterns of private ownership bestow significant advantages to certain individuals or groups. These advantages reduce economic mobility so there is little hope that voluntary action will capture external gains which call for the reduction of longstanding property rights.

The final reason for governmental action is the desire to redistribute income. Innovators may profit not only from funding new or better inputs but also from redistribution. In this situation, innovative activity does not lead to growth, but rather to a different division of a constant output. Since someone will be made worse off by this type of innovation, coercive powers must be employed. While in certain instances, voluntary arrangements like trade associations or guilds may perform the redistributive function, they are likely to be short-lived without government sanction.

Kindleberger (1965) and others (Gerschenkras 1962, Aitken 1959) have suggested three additional reasons why a governmental arrangement may be preferred to a private one for performing the entrepreneurial function. First, the inherent risk in innovation can be spread over the whole economy. This may be an advantage if capital markets are poorly developed, but the use of public funding reduces the likelihood of entrepreneurship, since the important profit motive is lacking. Without the threat of personal loss, risks may be underestimated or even ignored by public officials. Second, the government may possess superior information and, third, it has a greater ability to recruit. This last factor is paramount in societies where great status is given to civil servants, as is the case in many underdeveloped lands, for example, while government service is socially downgraded in most advanced societies.

There are problems with reliance on the government for entrepreneurial leadership. Planners may be overconcerned with monumental or showcase projects. Government, whether in developed or underdeveloped lands, has a proclivity to buy votes by underpricing governmental goods and services. This leads to serious market misallocations (Harbison and Myers 1959). The planning process can be confused with implementation: Hanson (1959) testifies that implementation is more likely to occur if left in private hands, rather than subjected to governmental contrivance.

Even if one accepts the idea that governmental entrepreneurship arises to fill the vacuum created by a lack of private initiative, there is no reason to assume that public entrepreneurship can adequately replace its private counterpart. If there is an insufficient supply of private entrepreneurs, civil servants are unlikely to remedy the deficiency. Efficient government organization will very likely be lacking in just those instances when effective entrepreneurship is lacking.

Bellush and Hausknecht (1962) say that public officials in developed economies can perform the three functions that characterize entrepreneurship:

1. The capitalist function of supplying money.
2. The managerial function of organizing the enterprise.
3. The creative function of bringing about new organizations and technologies.

While stressing the managerial function, they acknowledge that not all managers are entrepreneurs and vice versa. But,

> *American political structure places the three functions in the elected executive. . . . He is supposed to administer the machinery of government. The office he occupies, the endorsement of the electorate . . . give him a fund of "political capital" power that can be invested. Finally . . . [he] is expected to be a "leader" in achieving the ends of the community.*

Kirzner offers the obvious reply to this when he says that only the last of these functions is potentially entrepreneurial.

What is missing is motive. Civil servants will not be able to capture the "fortune available to the winner," which is Kirzner's economic profit. Modern bureaucracies, working as they do, may make successful innovation financially unrewarding, unless illegal transactions are involved. If the supply of entrepreneurs is sensitive to profit opportunity, as economists assert, then few entrepreneurs will be found in public service. In addition, while there are few rewards to the bureaucrat for success, there may be direct costs for failure which will discourage risk-taking. It should be noted that Kirzner sees the same type of problem developing within corporations unless managers can "reap private benefits for themselves."

While offering nothing but anecdotal evidence, Hagen says,

The conception . . . that an individual will function efficiently in economic endeavors only if he is working in a private enterprise to further his individual interest has been proven false by history. (1980)

This view is consistent with sociological interpretations of the entrepreneurial supply function, since it assumes that success in innovation is associated with status improvement or role fulfillment. To this, Schumpeter takes exception. Schumpeter's entrepreneurs are social deviants, at least until their success is established. In fact, successful entrepreneurship may reduce the status of the entrepreneur:

The very success of the business class in developing the productive powers of its country, and the very fact that this success has created a new standard of life for all classes, has paradoxically undermined the social and political position of the same business class whose economic function, though not obsolete, tends to become obsolescent and amenable to bureaucratization. . . . (Schumpeter 1950)

While it may be possible to substitute government action for private entrepreneurship, the evidence suggests that this is unlikely.

Hughes feels that entrepreneurship has undergone significant change due to the new constraints created by government. To him, the history of American entrepreneurship in the first half of this century cannot be repeated in the years to come. While entrepreneurs of the past were exploiters of technology, the new group:

must be adept in exploitation of federal, state, and local regulations at a time when the preponderance of power is on the side of the regulators, who mold the entrepreneurial function to a large extent. The government sector is now a "market" to be exploited. . . . The modern symbiotic relationship between the regulated and the regulators, as well as between government entrepreneurs and their clients, differs from the rough-and-ready graft and corruption of the classical period . . . because it is a continuing everyday relationship. . . . The entrepreneur in any important economic sector must admit permanent regulation and government interest as part of his decision-making process. . . . The private entrepreneur's decision-making horizons are at once more complex and more limited because of the constraint. (Hughes 1980)

Noting the growing dominance of government in the money market and the resultant "crowding out" of private investors, he concludes that governmental entrepreneurship is destined to expand relative to the private.

One thing is certain: Government is important in allowing the supply of entrepreneurs to come forth. In the underdeveloped world, and increasingly in the developed world, governmental activity is growing inimical to entrepreneurship.

Directions for future research

This chapter has summarized the current thinking of economists on the role of entrepreneurship in economic growth and development. In his critique of the economist's work, Kilby sets forth a tentative agenda for future researchers:

A major problem with the economist's model is its excessively narrow definition of the entrepreneurial function. This definition is based upon implicit assumptions about the nature of a well-functioning underdeveloped economy. These assumptions are that factors of production possess a relatively high degree of mobility; that inputs and outputs are homogeneous; that producers, consumers, and resource owners have knowledge of all the possibilities open to them; and that there are no significant indivisibilities. These assumptions conveniently produce a situation where risk and uncertainty are minimal, where change is continuous and incremental, and where the influence of social institutions is neutral. When the assumptions are relaxed, and ignorance, heterogeneity (segmented markets), impeded factor mobility, lumpiness, pervasive administrative controls, and input nonavailabilities are brought into the model, then the extraordinary qualities required of the entrepreneur—and the possibility of their limited supply—become apparent. (Kilby 1971)

Two recent writers (Hirschman 1958, 1963, Leibenstein 1954, 1968) have advanced theories that attempt to account for economic growth under less than the ideal conditions of a competitive market which have characterized past economic models. In these works, a low income economy is caught in the Malthusian trap until some powerful force rapidly increases growth. This "powerful force" may be the response of entrepreneurs to disequilibrium conditions which have created profit opportunities. These disequilibrium conditions cannot be accounted for by the competitive market model of the economist. What is lacking in these works is an explanation of entrepreneurial supply. It is assumed that entrepreneurs will respond to disequilibrium, but the strength of the "powerful force" depends on the elasticity of entrepreneurial supply.

The research agenda includes further exploration of the linkages that create growth in economies where less than perfect competition prevails. For economists who have not yet untied the knot of fixed factor proportions in the production function, this will be no easy task.

The second item on the agenda is further inquiry into the entrepreneurial response to market disequilibrium. The case studies cited in the chapter after this provide insights but no answers. The usefulness of economics lies in its capacity to produce policy recommendations. This requires the construction of sufficiently general models for reliable prediction. Generalization from case studies is risky, but it may be the only alternative available.

Considering the spectacular growth of public sectors at the expense of the private, in developed as well as underdeveloped lands, further inquiry into the potential for public entrepreneurship must be conducted. The basic view of this chapter is that public entrepreneurship is not likely to break the vicious cycle in the underdeveloped world or to sustain the momentum of growth in matured economies. The public sector lacks sufficient rewards incentive systems. Political considerations aside, public entrepreneurship and the incentive structure which brought it about must be identified and categorized.

Closely related to this must be an investigation of the free enterprise segments of command economies. Reports of flourishing, small-scale free enterprise activities in the Soviet Union, Communist China, and the Eastern Bloc nations should be explored to discover the compatibilities of planning and entrepreneurship. It may be that these activities are the result of failures in plan design or execution rather than opportunities consciously created by the planners.

Economic planning has fallen in public regard in the developed world, yet governmental structure is securely entrenched. Making the public sector a positive force in the field of entrepreneurship is a worthy goal for future research.

References

AITKEN, H. A. J., ed., *The State and Economic Growth.* New York: Social Science Research Council, 1959.

ARROW, KENNETH J., CHENERY, H. B., MINHAUS, B. S., and SOLOW, R. M., "Capital-Labor Substitution and Economic Efficiency," *Review of Economics and Statistics* XLIII (1961).

AUBREY, H. G., "Industrial Investment Revisions: A Comparative Analysis," *Journal of Economic History*, December 1955.

BAUMOL, W. J., "Entrepreneurship in Economic Theory," *American Economic Review* supplement, May 1968.

BECKER, G. S., "Investment in Human Capital: A Theoretical Analysis," *Journal of Political Economy* LXX (October 1962).

BELLUSH, JEWEL, and HAUSKNECHT, MURRAY, "Entrepreneurs and Urban Renewal: The New Men of Power," *Journal of the American Institute of Planners* XXXII, No. 2 (September 1962).

BLITZER, CHARLES R., CLARK, PETER B., and TAYLOR, LANCE, eds., *Economy-Wide Models and Development Planning.* London: Oxford University, 1975.

CARLYLE, THOMAS, *Letters of Thomas Carlyle to John Stuart Mill*, ed. Alexander Carlyle. New York: Fredrick Stocker, 1923.

CHAKRAVARTY, S., and LEFEBER, LOUIS, "An Optimizing Planning Model," *Economic Weekly* 17 (February 1965).

CHENERY, HOLLIS B., and SYRQUIN, MOISES, *Patterns of Development, 1950–1970.* London: Oxford University, 1975.

Cochran, Thomas C., "The Entrepreneur in Economic Change," *Behavioral Science* IX, No. 2 (April 1964).

Davis, Lance E., North, Douglass, and Smorodin, Calla, *Institutional Change and American Economic Growth.* Cambridge: Cambridge University, 1971.

Denison, Edward F., *Accounting for Slower Economic Growth: The United States in the 1970's.* Washington, D.C.: Brookings Institution, 1979.

Denison, Edward F., *Accounting for United States Economic Growth 1929–1969.* Washington, D.C.: Brookings Institution, 1974.

Denison, Edward F., *The Sources of Economic Growth in the U.S. and the Alternatives before Us.* New York: Committee for Economic Development, 1962.

Denison, Edward F., and Chung, William K., *How Japan's Economy Grew So Fast.* Washington, D.C.: Brookings Institution, 1976.

Denison, Edward F., and Poullier, J. P., *Why Growth Rates Differ: Postwar Experience in Nine Western Countries.* Washington, D.C.: Brookings Institution, 1967.

Domar, Evsey D., "Capital Expansion, Rate of Growth, and Employment." *Econometrica* 14 (April 1946).

Domar, Evsey D., "Investment Losses and Monopolies," *Income Employment and Public Policy: Essays in Honor of Alvin Hansen.* New York: McGraw-Hill, 1948.

Eckaus, Richard, and Parekh, Kirit, *Planning for Growth.* Cambridge: MIT, 1967.

Gerschenkras, Alexander, *Economic Backwardness in Historical Perspective.* Cambridge: Harvard University, 1962.

Griliches, Zvi, "Research Expenditures and Growth Accounting" in *Science and Technology in Economic Growth*, ed. B. R. Williams. New York: Halstad Press, 1973.

Hagen, Everett E., *The Economics of Development* (3rd ed.). Homewood, Ill.: Richard D. Irwin, 1980.

Hagen, Everett E., *On the Theory of Social Change: How Economic Growth Begins.* Homewood, Ill.: Dorsey Press, 1962.

Hansen, Alvin H., *Business Cycles and National Income* (ex. ed.). New York: W. W. Norton & Co., Inc., 1964.

Hansen, Alvin H., *Economic Policy and Full Employment.* New York: McGraw-Hill, 1947.

Hansen, Alvin H. *Fiscal Policy and Business Cycles.* New York: McGraw-Hill, 1941.

Hansen, Alvin H., *Public Enterprise and Economic Development.* London: Routledge & Kegan Paul, 1959.

Harbison, Frederick, "Entrepreneurial Organization As a Factor in Economic Development," *Quarterly Journal of Economics*, August 1956.

Harbison, Frederick, and Myers, Charles A., *Management in an Industrial World.* New York: McGraw-Hill, 1959.

Harrod, R. F., "An Essay in Dynamic Theory," *The Economic Journal* XLIX (March 1939), and errata (June 1939).

Heilbroner, Robert L., *An Inquiry into the Human Prospect* (rev. ed.). New York: W. W. Norton & Co., Inc., 1980.

Higgins, Benjamin, *Economic Development* (rev. ed.). New York: W. W. Norton & Co., Inc., 1968.

Hirschman, A. O., *Journeys through Progress: Studies of Economic Policy-Making in Latin America.* New York: Twentieth Century Fund, 1963.

HIRSCHMAN, A. O., *The Strategy of Economic Development.* New Haven: Yale University, 1958.

HUDSON, E. A, and JORGENSON, D. W., "Energy Prices and the U.S. Economy," *Data Resources Review*, September 1978.

HUGHES, JONATHAN R. T., "Entrepreneurship," in *Encyclopedia of American Economic History*, ed. Glenn Porter. New York: Scribner's, 1980.

JOHANSEN, LEIF, "Substitution vs. Fixed Production Coefficients in the Theory of Economic Growth: A Synthesis," *Econometrica* XXVII (April 1959).

KALDOR, NICHOLAS A., *Essays on Value and Distribution: On Economic Stability* and *Growth: On Economic Policy.* London: Duckworth, 1960.

KEYNES, J. M., *General Theory of Employment, Interest and Money.* New York: Harcourt Brace Jovanovich, Inc., 1936.

KILBY, PETER, ed., *Entrepreneurship and Economic Development.* New York: Free Press, 1971.

KINDLEBERGER, CHARLES P., *Economic Development* (2nd ed.). New York: McGraw-Hill, 1965.

KIRZNER, ISRAEL M., *Competition and Entrepreneurship.* Chicago: University of Chicago, 1973.

KNIGHT, FRANK, *Risk, Uncertainty and Profit.* New York: Harper & Row, 1921.

KUZNETS, S. S., "Notes on the Take-Off," in *The Economics of Take-Off into Sustained Growth*, ed. W. W. Rostow. London: Macmillan, 1964.

KUZNETS, S. S., "Quantitative Aspects of the Economic Growth of Nations," *Economic Development and Cultural Change* X, No. 2 (January 1962).

LEIBENSTEIN, HARVEY, "Entrepreneurship and Development," *American Economic Review*, May 1968.

LEIBENSTEIN, HARVEY, *The Theory of Economic-Demographic Development.* Princeton: Princeton University, 1954.

MACAVOY, PAUL W., *The Regulated Industries and the Economy.* New York: W. W. Norton & Co., Inc., 1979.

MCCLELLAND, DAVID, *The Achieving Society.* Princeton: D. Van Nostrand, 1961.

MALTHUS, THOMAS ROBERT, *Essay on the Principle of Population*, ed. Anthony Flew. New York: Penguin, 1970.

MARSHALL, ALFRED, *Principles of Economics* (8th ed.). London: Macmillan, 1946.

MARX, KARL, *Capital: A Critique of Political Economy*, ed. Friedrich Engels. Chicago: Henry Regency, 1936.

MEADE, J. E., *A Neo-Classical Theory of Economic Growth.* London: Allen and Unwin, 1961.

MEADOWS, D. H., et al., *The Limits to Growth: A Report on the Club of Romes Project on the Predicament of Mankind.* New York: Universe Books, 1972.

Midyear Review of the Economy: The Outlook for 1979. Washington, D.C.: U.S. Congress, Joint Economic Committee, 1979.

MILLIKAN, M. F., *National Economic Planning.* New York: Columbia University, 1967.

MISHAN, E. J. "Growth and Antigrowth: What Are the Issues?" *Challenge*, May-June 1973.

NORTH, DOUGLASS C., *The Economic Growth of the United States 1790–1860.* Englewood Cliffs, N.J.: Prentice-Hall, 1961.

NORTH, DOUGLASS C., and THOMAS, ROBERT P., *The Rise of the Western World: A New Economic History.* London: Cambridge University, 1973.

RICARDO, DAVID, *Principles of Political Economy and Taxation.* London: Macmillan, 1921.

ROBINSON, JOAN, *Accumulation of Capital.* London: Macmillan, 1956.

ROSENBERG, NATHAN, "Capital Formation in Underdeveloped Countries," *American Economic Review,* September 1960.

ROSTOW, W. W., *The Economics of Take-Off into Sustained Growth.* London: Macmillan, 1964.

ROSTOW, W. W., *The Stages of Economic Growth.* Cambridge: Cambridge University, 1960.

ROSTOW, W. W., "The Take-off into Sustained Growth," *Economic Journal* LXVI (March 1956).

SCHUMPETER, JOSEPH, "The March into Socialism," *American Economic Review: Papers and Proceedings* XL (May 1950).

SCHUMPETER, JOSEPH A., *Theory of Economic Development.* Cambridge: Harvard University, 1936.

SMITH, ADAM, *The Wealth of Nations,* ed. Edwin Cannon. London: J. M. Dent & Son. New York: E. P. Dutton & Co., 1933–1934.

SOLOW, ROBERT M., "A Contribution to the Theory of Economic Growth," *The Quarterly Journal of Economics* LXX (February 1956).

SOLOW, ROBERT M., "Substitution and Fixed Proportions in the Theory of Capital," *Review of Economic Studies* XXIV (June 1962).

SOLOW, ROBERT M., "Summary Record of the Debate" in W. W. Rostow, *The Economics of Take-Off into Sustained Growth.* London: Macmillan, 1964.

SOLOW, ROBERT M., "Technical Change and the Aggregate Production Function," *Review of Economics and Statistics* XXXIX (1957).

STIGLITZ, JOSEPH E., and UZAWA, HIROFUMI, *Readings in the Modern Theory of Economic Growth.* Cambridge: MIT, 1969.

TAWNEY, R. H., *Religion and the Rise of Capitalism.* New York: NAL, 1954.

THUROW, LESTER C., "The Implications of Zero Economic Growth," *Challenge,* March–April 1977.

TOBIN, JAMES, "A Dynamic Aggregative Model," *The Journal of Political Economy* LXIII, No. 2 (April 1955).

The U.S. Economy in the 1980's. Washington, D.C.: U.S. Congress, Joint Economic Committee, 1979.

WEBER, MAX, *The Protestant Ethic and the Spirit of Capitalism.* New York: Scribner's, 1930.

WEIDENBAUM, MURRAY L., *Business, Government and the Public.* Englewood Cliffs, N.J.: Prentice-Hall, 1977.

chapter xiii

Entrepreneurship in the less developed world

Wayne G. Broehl, Jr.

Overview

This chapter focuses on the process of entrepreneurship in the less developed countries. The model constructed here calls attention to the differences between entrepreneurial environments in the industrialized and in the third world. Entrepreneurs in low-income, predominantly rural areas face not only the problems of entrepreneurs in advanced countries but problems created by a highly traditional cultural background. The entrepreneurial process is impeded by the conflicts of old and new. Technology transfer is the chief concern of entrepreneurs in less developed countries and is seen as more than mere imitation of the industrialized West. Such adaptation, viewed as meta-innovation, takes place under conditions best described by theories of X-efficiency, where imperfect knowledge and markets are the rule.

An entrepreneurial system model

Entrepreneurs are important agents of change in every society, yet they are among the most enigmatic characters in the drama of economic development, particularly in the less developed world. Although it is their purposive activity that bridges the gap between plan and reality, the precise functioning of entrepreneurs is often unclear.

A better understanding of entrepreneurship in the less developed countries could have a particularly high return for mankind. Entrepreneurship is clearly not a uniformly distributed quality, yet the appearance of the entrepreneur is considered by most analysts to be nonrandom. If scholars could identify the origins of entrepreneurship, policy-makers might be able to develop educational methods for upgrading entrepreneurial skills.

It will be helpful in this analysis of entrepreneurship to view both its nature and its locus. Our first concern will be the psychological attributes of successful entrepreneurs: Why is it that particular individuals are achievement-oriented or prepared to take risks? We will then turn to the organization and management of operating economic units, where entrepreneurship is framed in a dynamic system of interdependencies and scattered over a wide range of business functions.

Entrepreneurs mediate between the larger society and the single operating unit, and their actions produce system-wide effects. These features pose special problems in less developed countries, where it is often difficult to distinguish the functions of the economy from those of other social institutions. A complex pattern of integration between rural entrepreneurs and their counterparts in the metropolitan, industrial economy is generally the rule. Foreign capital usually plays a significant part. Corporate structures form a heterogeneous pattern of widely varying levels of sophistication, in which decision-making and implementation are often so fragmented that it is impossible to identify an individual entrepreneur. Although the family is often dominant in entrepreneurial activities, the state may play a major entrepreneurial role. Researchers should attempt to map these complex entrepreneurial functions.

Broehl's explanatory model (1978) provides guidelines for further investigation. The model, presented schematically in Figure 1, is built on the seminal work of earlier writers (Schreier and Komives 1973, 1975), but includes additional relevant variables. By analyzing the entrepreneur's actions in a particular context, we can focus on his observable behavior rather than on some mysterious charisma or the perception of opportunity. Of primary interest is the entrepreneurial breakthrough, conceived in both operational and sequential terms. This system approach, in short, emphasizes an interdisciplinary view.

Influences on the entrepreneur

Entrepreneurial individuals and groups are equally significant in less developed countries. At any given moment the entrepreneur is playing many different roles, a part of a family, a religious sect, a political party, a kinship group, a caste, and so on. These all represent particular value determinants and constraints.

We must not assume, incidentally, that the world of entrepreneurs will be

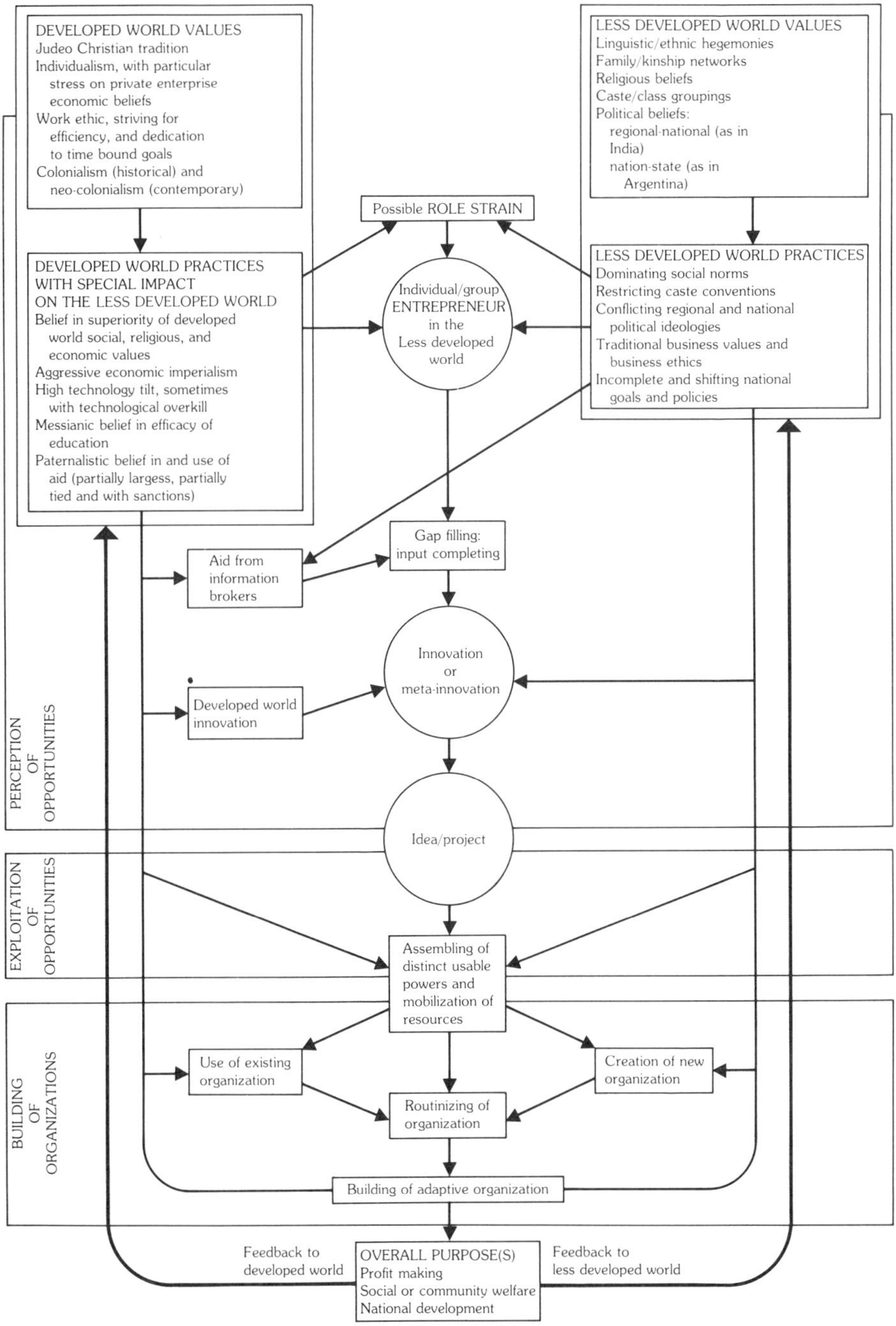

Figure 1 *A model of entrepreneurship in the less developed world*

synonymous with the nation-states in which they live. More likely they will see their world in much more complex terms—some values will come from the government itself, some from political segments within it, others from the social and religious roles. Some less developed countries are strongly nationalistic; the Italian corporatist legacy adopted in Argentina over the past three decades is a good example. Conversely, a large number of these countries are characterized by complex political grouping, derived from linguistic, ethnic or geographic bonds. In such a structure there tend to be conflicting regional and national ideologies that produce incomplete and shifting national policies. Business values and business ethics tend to be tradition bound rather than subject to the maximization concepts of Western microeconomics. The entrepreneur must move back and forth from one value orientation to another, constantly attempting to accommodate role effectiveness to the pressures of divergent values.

The special dimensions of rural entrepreneurship

Most underdeveloped countries have two sharply differentiated sectors: one limited mainly to peasant agriculture, small industry, and their various trading activities; the other composed of plantations, transport and major trade, manufacturing, petroleum and mining endeavors. In other words, the country is divided along the lines of development, typically along rural-urban lines. The Western market economy, with its focus on price, market exchange, and optimization, is not likely to coincide with this rural economy, which tends to be characterized by inflexible or sluggish prices, inelastic supply, and inelastic demand. Barter in kind is common; gift trading is complex, based on status, kinship, superstition, etiquette, and a host of other subtle non-market relationships.

For example, only part of the labor time of rural cultivators is actually spent in agricultural efforts; a significant amount is expended to satisfy needs for clothing, shelter, entertainment, and ceremony. The patterns of exchange are often established by longstanding beliefs. Complicated adjustments between non-cash and cash markets lead the peasant economy still further from the classic of model profit-maximization (Malinowski 1922, Polanyi 1944, Polanyi, Arensberg, and Pearson 1957, Dalton 1968, Rottenberg 1958, Hymer and Resnick 1967).

The panoply of barter and exchange within this system makes most villagers no less materialistic than any Western Adam Smith. The exchange of services among cultivators and artisans has evolved over the centuries into an intricate set of relationships carried on every day in the village and at weekly fairs, markets, and religious festivals.

Peasants in these rural societies tend to share what George Foster (1967) has called the "principle of the limited good." They behave as though all the desired things of life—land, wealth, health, friendship, love, manliness, honor, respect, status, power, security, and safety—existed in finite quantities and were always in short supply. If these limited goods cannot be expanded, then it appears to the peasant that the system is closed. An individual or family can improve its position only at the expense of others.

This has two consequences. First, the solidarity of the extended family subordinates individual needs and desires to determinations of "the elders." Typically this group is defined by consanguinity, but sometimes it is cast more broadly on a clan or a tribal basis (Broehl 1964).

Second, external dealings are envisioned as a zero-sum game, an unrelenting struggle with others for possession or control of scarce resources. Mistrust and skepticism begin to dominate.

Typically, the role of the "business person" is denigrated. Loss minimization becomes the dominant concern, rather than profit maximization. People are wary of risk-taking and are content to provide for their subsistence needs. Business people may make high profits, but frequently these will be based on scarcity and a black market. Neither buyer nor seller has a developed notion of a fair or a good price; both hope for a windfall. Business people wait in anticipation of scarcity. The gyrations of the market itself may generate this scarcity, or the government may bring it about through inept price regulation or other manipulation of the market. Often business people can accentuate this scarcity by hoarding. Thus all of their acumen is directed toward gaining the confidence of buyers by "reasonable" transactions in order to take advantage of the same buyers at a later point through black market tactics.

The peasant, keenly aware of oppression or deprivation, constructs his own adaptive mechanisms and designs for living (Hagen 1960–1961, 1962, Fromm 1970, Lewis 1951, 1958, 1963, 1966). Traditional society has three tiers: the peasantry, the elite, and the trader-financiers. These three groups operate in a well-defined and authoritarian set of relationships. The society as a whole exhibits impotence and rage in the face of uncontrollable forces (weather, disease, macroeconomic vicissitudes) and relies heavily on religion or magic.

The peasantry depends strongly on the elite, and the elite find protection in their own economic dominance and ability to levy on the peasant. In these two groups there is a latent desire to dominate, to take aggression out on others. The peasantry thus always leans toward authoritarianism. There is a basic lack of creativity, a mistrust of outsiders, a dislike of strange or new ways. The elite often dislike manual labor and emphasize property: land, cattle, jewelry.

Unrational beliefs often exert profound influences on daily life in the villages. There are auspicious times for various activities and ritualistic ways of carrying them out. The practice of consulting one's horoscope before business dealings is widespread, even among sophisticated urban people. The fatalistic nature of these decision-making tools inevitably leads to a gambling mentality. The notion of a probability-based discounted risk would be sharply at variance with such thinking. Villagers may have a keen sense of risk-taking in their various agricultural and business dealings, yet many of their decisions are infiltrated by superstition and guessing; villagers tend to swing widely between gambling and risk aversion. The result is often pervasive mistrust, fatalism, and rage at the implacability of fate. Hatred and suspicion readily arise among participants in a business arrangement.

Often an elaborate pattern of economic interdependence reduces or eliminates the divisive effects of competition. In the jajmani system in India, for example, each household is economically dependent on other households from specialist jatis (castes) and ritually dependent on households from each of the major jatis in the area. "In effect," says Allen Beals, "the myth that makes multi-jati villages possible is the myth that the survival and proper functioning of any one jati is dependent on the survival and proper functioning of every other" (1974).

Given these traditional patterns, what are the potentials for entrepreneurship in rural areas? To begin with, there is often a supply problem. Rural people with the strongest intellects either obtain what education is available at home and then migrate to the cities, or go to the cities for the education itself. In either case it is difficult to get many of them back, and the human capital of the rural areas dwindles. Often the more modern, innovating attitudes are correlated with better education, and the progressiveness of the rural areas is channeled off with these same people.

For those who do remain in the rural areas, there are perennial and often worsening problems of underemployment and unemployment. Birth rates tend to be high and exacerbate problems of land tenure and other ownership patterns. Very large numbers of agricultural and village industry laborers have no ownership stake in the enterprises in which they work. Problems of infrastructure complicate the situation. Ineffectual transportation systems are common: poor roads, inefficient rail service, and serious shortages of transport equipment abound. Agricultural services, irrigation, or field and processing equipment are often too unreliable to warrant input. Finance, especially credit, is less available than in the cities.

Still, the people who remain have valuable strengths—balanced practical skills and traditional knowledge—that make the rural population potentially more capable of change than many have assumed. There is often greater social unity among villagers than among city people. Agriculturists see the literal fruits of their labors; workers in village industries see at least the first stages of vertical integration—their products are processed within the village from nearby raw materials before they are sent away to the city. It seems legitimate to hypothesize that there is an identifiably different pattern of rural entrepreneurship, and that entrepreneurs are indeed present.

Neither the rural nor the urban sectors of these less developed countries can operate in a vacuum; inevitably, strong influences flow in from the developed world. Potent beliefs in the efficacy of individualism, in the virtues of the private enterprise system, in the value of work and efficiency, all are exported to these countries in one form or another. Colonialism performed this function straightforwardly in the past, more subtly in the present. The social, religious, and economic values of the developed world impinge on the traditional. The result is often an aggressive economic imperialism, a high-technology tilt, and nearly Messianic belief in the efficacy of education. As many countries of the developed world face up to their privileged positions, extensive aid arrives in the less developed countries, generally under a paternalistic rubric sometimes linked to economic, political, or social sanctions.

Little wonder, then, that this cacophony of value determinants can easily produce "role strains" for entrepreneurs. As the certainty and constraints of the traditional world give way to a complex pattern of indigenous and imported modernity, the environment for entrepreneurship can quickly become personally threatening. The international business world is a fast paced one, with change and adaptation a necessary way of life.

Whether or not the village entrepreneurs actually participate directly in international trade, they are influenced by this stepped-up pace, which is contrary to the traditional way of life. Faced with conflicting "solutions" to problems, they may allow their cultural background to dominate business decisions, often with less than effective results. Alternatively, they may become indecisive, mixing traditional and modern in a way they can little understand or articulate. They may break completely away from tradition and adopt new values in their entirety. This is often unsatisfactory too, for it allows little ground for later rapprochement with their own culture.

Schumpeter's innovator

We should now be more precise with the term "innovation." Today many analysts seem to confuse true entrepreneurship with other closely related endeavors. We can gain some perspective by returning to one of the seminal thinkers in this field, Joseph Schumpeter, whose concepts have renewed relevance for the study of comparative entrepreneurship.

Schumpeter (1934, 1939) starts with that necessary abstraction, "equilibrium." Into this pure model an entrepreneur intrudes. Central to this intrusion is a "new production function," the Schumpeterian way of describing an innovation. This term is not used in its narrow sense, but includes one or more of the following:

1. A new product with which consumers are not yet familiar, or a new quality of product.

2. A new method of production, one not yet tested by experience. This can be a new discovery or "a new way of handling a commodity commercially."

3. A new market, new to a given country, regardless of whether it has existed before in other locations.

4. A new source for raw materials or intermediate manufactured goods. Again, this may have existed previously in another location.
5. The new organization of an industry, like the creation or the breaking up of a monopoly position.

These new production functions are brought about by the purposeful action of entrepreneurs. These entrepreneurs belong to a distinct class: They possess more than ordinary ability to visualize possibilities in unproved commodities, organizations, methods, and markets. The first entrepreneur in a given field must overcome all sorts of obstacles and smooths the way for others, producing a wave of business activity that finally exhausts the opportunities for gain.

It is hard to distinguish entrepreneurs, not because of lack of precision about their special contribution, but because the persons who actually engage in entrepreneurial activity are difficult to find. No one is an entrepreneur all the time, and no one is only an entrepreneur. It follows from the nature of the function that it must always be combined with and lead to other activities.

Entrepreneurship is not the process of invention. Although a highly creative function, it does not rest solely on originality. An invention may not lead to innovation. Economically and sociologically, the two are completely different conceptual functions.

Entrepreneurs may, but need not, furnish the capital. Financial risk-bearing is not a necessary part of the entrepreneurial function. Capitalists bear risks, and entrepreneurs bring about the changed production function. There is probably no more confusing distinction today than between entrepreneurship and risk-taking. The entrepreneur clearly takes great personal risk in introducing new and often traumatic production functions. He may also put his own money into the new project and thereby become a financial risk-taker. The first type of risk-taking is directly involved in entrepreneurship; the second may or may not be present.

In sum, the Schumpeterian entrepreneur is a special kind of creative person, one who brings about growth through changes in production functions. It is this special quality of change, innovation, that sets the entrepreneur apart.

Meta-innovation

Sometimes an innovation in the less developed world becomes an innovation in worldwide terms. The wheat and rice miracle seeds may legitimately be placed in this category. Although the two research institutes responsible for the appearance of these seeds were largely financed and staffed by the developed world, the new varieties were actually evolved in Mexico (wheat) and the Philippines (rice). One is hard pressed to think of equally significant innovations in industrial management. Industrial innovators have come from the less developed world, it is true, but their innovations have occurred in the developed world.

In rural areas of the less developed countries, there appears at first to be little or no true innovation; indeed, there seem to be no entrepreneurs. However, a closer look reveals a special form of innovation: the adaptation of a concept from the developed world to the special constraints and opportunities of the less developed world.

This process can be known as "meta-innovation." The prefix, according to Webster, can denote "more highly organized or specialized." I suggest that both attributes are characteristic of entrepreneurship in less developed countries. Not many analysts share this view. James J. Berna (1960), in a study of entrepreneurship in South India, called his respondents "humbler entrepreneurs," as distinguished from the "Schumpeterian innovators" of the developed world. This interpretation seems to overlook the crucial fact that innovation on a small scale is not necessarily a "humbler" process or an easier one than the same application in the developed world.

The literature makes some useful distinctions among original innovation, transferred innovation, and adaptive innovation (Kristensen 1974, Spencer and Woroniak 1967, Baranson 1969, Driscoll and Wallender 1974). Common to these definitions is the notion that an original or true innovation involves the shifting of a production function. This innovation can be transferred in basic outline to other situations, can be modified, changed, and adapted to differing environments.

Such adaptation, called "technology transfer," has been widely researched (Bhattasali 1972, 1973, Balsaubramanyam 1973, and Behari 1974). The dominant pattern is one of transferred innovation within the developed world itself. But there is also great interest in the process of technology transfer to the less developed world. Methods and materials vary, yet the process remains in essence a mirroring of the original innovation. Some analysts use the term "imitation" here, examine the circumstances under which imitation is more attractive than innovation, and define which firms are the leaders and which the followers (Kaimen and Schwartz 1972, 1975, Baldwin and Childs 1969). In some developed countries, there is irritation about the "mimicry" syndrome and a resulting dependency relationship between the original high-technology innovators and their followers.

Adaptation is intrinsically different from both original innovation, and its transferred variants. It is not a lower-technology, less complex variation on the original innovation, but itself a meta-innovation. The sheer process of adaptation in environments markedly different from the original is itself an innovative act. Given the gaps in understanding and information and the weaknesses in infrastructure, the path of "simple" adaptation is often highly discontinuous. It is this "innovation boundary" (Slevin 1971) that changes the act from a simple modification or adaptation to innovation, perhaps more complex than the original innovation. What is "market filling" in the developed world may be "market creating" in the less developed world (Dahmen 1970, Gerschenkron 1968). Schumpeter often used the term "imitators" for those who spread a new innovation through the economy in a secondary wave, but the secondary wave may well be primary when it hits the shores of a less developed country.

Risk-taking that moves from the developed world to the less developed world therefore has a special quality. What is old hat in the developed world may well be startlingly new in the other. If we think of a time continuum for risk-taking, we can posit that the first innovators in the developed world encounter the highest incidence of risk. Those who adapt an innovation further down the line encounter less. When the innovation is carried to a less developed country, there is a discontinuity in the time line. Within the confines of a new and less certain situation, the incidence of risk rises to a level that may be even higher than the original. A primitive society on the edge of starvation risks life itself when it seeks to employ new methods.

Information needs and how they are met

If there is any single dominant feature of meta-innovations in the less developed countries, it is that they are initially ill defined. Certain information must precede the act of innovation, yet some data are simply not yet available in particular economies. Often the information needs are subtly political in nature rather than straightforwardly economic; business advantage is often sought (and realized) through political institutions no less than in market interactions. Gaining requisite information may be difficult; less developed countries, in the words of economist Harvey Leibenstein, are "obstructed, incomplete and 'relatively dark' economic systems" (1968).

Leibenstein suggests that maximization is always a less than perfect process, that there is an "X-efficiency" short of optimization that is almost always the norm (1966, 1969, 1972, 1973, 1976, Jameson 1972). This is particularly so, he suggests, in the less developed world. The production function turns out to be a range of possible efficiencies, rather than a point of optimum allocative efficiency:

> *One can visualize a production function as a set of "recipes." Each recipe indicates most of the essential elements that enter into the production of the output, but like a real recipe, or a real blueprint, it does not truly indicate all of them. A given recipe may be carried out slowly or quickly or with careful or sloppy workmanship. . . . After all, different cooks will turn out meals of different quality on the basis of the same recipe. (1973)*

In searching for new information and techniques, individuals and firms generally do not work as hard or as efficiently as they might, nor is their effort maintained at a constant level. This slackness implies an entrepreneurial opportunity, an occasion for gap filling and input completion. Leibenstein suggests that we should distinguish "routine" entrepreneurship—administering a well-established, growing concern with well-known production functions and clearly defined markets — from "new-type" entrepreneurship. In the latter, the entrepreneur must in some way compensate for great gaps in the knowledge of the production function. A crucial gap in information may prevent a particular project from getting off the drawing board.

In the less developed world, says Leibenstein, the special entrepreneur is the one who performs most or all of these functions:

1. Searches for and discovers new economic information.
2. Translates this new information into new markets, techniques, and goods.
3. Seeks and discovers economic opportunity.
4. Evaluates economic opportunities.
5. Marshals the financial resources necessary for the enterprise.
6. Makes time-binding arrangements.
7. Takes ultimate responsibility for management.
8. Provides for and is responsible for the motivational system within the firm.
9. Provides leadership for the work group.
10. Is the ultimate risk-bearer.

The truly scarce talents are those for assembling information in less developed countries. A few entrepreneurs can connect different markets, make up for market deficiencies, create or expand business organizations. These special entrepreneurs are the key individuals in the less developed world.

Israel M. Kirzner (1973) has noted that it is the alertness to information, rather than its possession alone, that is the essential entrepreneurial talent.

Ultimately, then, the kind of "knowledge" required for entrepreneurship is knowing where to look for knowledge, rather than knowledge of substantive market information. . . . Entrepreneurial knowledge may be described as the "highest order of knowledge," the ultimate knowledge needed to harness available information already possessed (capable of becoming discovered).

A certain critical mass of data is necessary to the most astute entrepreneur in order that innovation may be initially discerned. Leibenstein (1957) develops at length his thesis that a "critical minimum effort" must occur to bring about sustained development in the less developed countries. Part of this critical minimum effort must inevitably be a critical minimum of information.

Beyond this there is a further dimension, linked to Kirzner's concept of alertness. Many years ago sociologist Vilfredo Pareto (1935) noted man's basic "instinct for combination." It is the ability to link together individual pieces of information — to actively combine — that distinguishes the new type of entrepreneur.

In a society where family linkages and kinship affiliations play an important part in the founding of a business enterprise, and where there is a dearth of technical know-how, the entrepreneur may develop a network of "information brokers" who supply necessary information and who may even help to formulate the innovative idea or project. Such a situation helps explain why large, extended family connections often give the vested oligarchy so much power. Sometimes the information brokers may formalize their activity by becoming professional suppliers of ideas or projects (on a regular fee basis) for future entrepreneurs.

Information brokerage may also come from outside the country, supplied on a formal or informal basis by individuals and firms from the developed world. A straightforward consulting contract, varying patterns of ownership, licensing, and other tie-in arrangements may be used to determine the fee. This advice from outside the country is, incidentally, not always appropriate. The unperceived subtleties and complexities of traditional society often lead the armchair analyst to make serious errors; indigenous solutions may then be wiser.

Interaction between the entrepreneur and the various information brokers is important, and the astute use of brokers can markedly increase the information reach of an entrepreneur. But as Kirzner (1973) points out, "Information costs are the costs of transportation from ignorance to omniscience, and seldom can a trader afford to take the entire trip." Inevitably some gaps will remain and some inputs be incompletely integrated.

How the entrepreneur operates

Within this frame of diversity, entrepreneurs in the less developed world perceive certain innovational opportunities. Their hope is that these opportunities will come to fruition, yet only when the innovation can be framed in a realistic manner does it become a project. Entrepreneurs must start thinking at once about alternative strategies for action and must choose the most feasible and satisfying course. Judgment, intuition, and flexibility are essential to future breakthroughs.

Once projects are formulated, entrepreneurs must combine a finite number of usable powers. Discrimination is important for overall strategy. Only a limited number of coalitions are possible, given the particulars of a project. This success of a project is of course dependent on the availability of economic opportunities within a given society, but its realization depends on a politically feasible set of coalitions. It is the artistry involved in assembling such distinct powers that explains why some entrepreneurs succeed and others do not.

An organization, newly created or adapted, must soon be routinized, or established within a dynamic equilibrium to fulfill its objectives and interact with its environment through relevant adaptations. Casualties can occur for any of a number of reasons. For each stage of the process we can posit a different leadership style. Brilliant entrepreneurs who make first breakthroughs may become so frozen in their initial modes of functioning that they are unable to handle the emergent problems of a routinized or adaptive organization. A developing economy is particularly volatile, and entrepreneurs must be especially responsive to the changing milieu. This crucial adaptive behavior is itself generally innovative, for it succeeds in maintaining the initial thrust, preserving a tenuous equilibrium, and absorbing new technology. Thus, entrepreneurs are inevitably agents of change.

An interactive system

Our linear model indicates the entrepreneur's rugged path to achievement. The model clarifies the issue of differential response—why certain people fail where others succeed, even though the economic opportunities are the same for all. To repeat, entrepreneurship does not stop with accomplishment of the initial breakthrough. Long-term success relies on an organization, without which purposeful activity cannot be sustained for any length of time. We are interested in the entire ongoing process of entrepreneurship, for the internal dynamism of an organization is as important as the initial manipulation of the environment.

The feedback process, as indicated in Figure 1, is an essential part of the model. The move from a newly created organization to a routinized or adaptive one precipitates new environmental problems, which in turn lead to a fresh perception and exploitation of opportunities and require the assembling of different powers to achieve fresh breakthroughs. If feedback is absent or inadequate, new challenges are met with old responses only.

This chapter has come full circle: the entrepreneur affects the social system as well as being affected by it. Equally demanding of attention is the environmental change provoked by the adaptive response of the organization. The interactive system necessarily comprehends both.

References

BALDWIN, W. L., and CHILDS, G. L., "The Fast Second and Rivalry in Research and Development," *Southern Economic Journal* 36 (July 1969).

BALSAUBRAMANYAM, V. N., *International Transfer of Technology to India.* New York: Holt, Rinehart & Winston, 1973.

BARANSON, JACK, *Industrial Technologies for Developing Economics.* New York: Holt, Rinehart & Winston, 1969.

BEALS, ALLEN, *Village Life in South India.* Chicago: Aldine, 1974.

BEHARI, BEPIN, *Economic Growth and Technological Change in India.* New Delhi: Vikas Publishing House, 1974.

BERNA, JAMES J., *Industrial Entrepreneurship in Madras State.* Bombay: Asia Publishing House, 1960.

BHATTASALI, B. N., *Transfer of Technology among the Developing Countries.* Tokyo: Asian Productivity Organization, 1972.

BHATTASALI, B. N., *UN Industrial Development Organization, Guidelines for the Acquisition of Foreign Technology in Developing Countries.* New York: United Nations, 1973.

BROEHL, WAYNE G., *The Molly Maguires.* Cambridge: Harvard University, 1964.

BROEHL, WAYNE G., *The Village Entrepreneur.* Cambridge: Harvard University, 1978.

DAHMEN, ERIK, *Entrepreneurial Activity and the Development of Swedish Industry, 1919–1939,* trans. Axel Leijonhufvud. Homewood, Ill.: Richard D. Irwin, 1970.

DALTON, GEORGE, *Primitive, Archaic and Modern Economics: Essays of Karl Polanyi.* Garden City, N.Y.: Anchor Books, 1968.

DRISCOLL, ROBERT E. and WALLENDER, HARVEY W., *Technology Transfer and Development: An Historical and Geographic Perspective.* New York: Fund for Multinational Management Education, Council of the Americas, 1974.

FEDER, ERNEST, "Six Plausible Theses about the Peasant's Perspectives in the Developing World," *Development and Change* 5 (1973).

FEDER, ERNEST, "Vendetta against Indigenous Technology," *Economic and Political Weekly* (Bombay), April 5, 1975.

FOSTER, GEORGE, "Introduction: Peasant Character and Personality," in *Peasant Society: A Reader*, ed. Jack M. Potter. Boston: Little, Brown, 1967.

FROMM, ERICH, *Social Character in a Mexican Village: A Sociopsychoanalytic Study.* Englewood Cliffs, N.J.: Prentice-Hall, 1970.

GERSCHENKRON, ALEXANDER, "A Schumpeterian Analysis of Economic Development," *Continuity and Other Essays in History.* Cambridge: Harvard University, 1968.

HAGEN, EVERETT E., "The Entrepreneur as Rebel against Traditional Society," *Human Organization*, 1960–1961.

HAGEN, EVERETT E., *On the Theory of Social Change: How Economic Growth Begins.* Homewood, Ill.: Dorsey Press, 1962.

HYMER, STEVEN, and RESNICK, STEVEN, "Responsiveness of Agrarian Economics and the Importance of Z Goods" (Center Discussion Paper No. 25 (rev.), Economic Growth Center, Yale University, 1967).

JAMESON, KEN, "Comment on the Theory and Measurement of Dynamic X-efficiency." *Quarterly Journal of Economics* 86 (1972).

KAIMEN, MORTON I., and SCHWARTZ, NANCY L., "Market Structure and Innovation: A Survey," *Journey of Economic Literature* 13 (1975).

KAIMEN, MORTON I., and SCHWARTZ, NANCY L., "Timing of Innovations under Rivalry," *Econometrica* 40 (1972).

KIRZNER, ISRAEL M., *Competition and Entrepreneurship.* Chicago: University of Chicago, 1973.

KRISTENSEN, THORKIL, *Development in Rich and Poor Countries: A General Theory with Statistical Analyses.* New York: Holt, Rinehart & Winston, 1974.

LEIBENSTEIN, HARVEY, "Allocative Efficiency versus 'X-efficiency,' " *American Economic Review* 56 (1966).

LEIBENSTEIN, HARVEY, *Beyond Economic Man: A New Foundation for Microeconomics.* Cambridge: Harvard University, 1976.

LEIBENSTEIN, HARVEY, "Comment on the Nature of X-efficiency," *Quarterly Journal of Economics* 86 (May 1972).

LEIBENSTEIN, HARVEY, "Competition and X-efficiency: Reply," *Journal of Political Economy* 81 (May-June 1973).

LEIBENSTEIN, HARVEY, *Economic Backwardness and Economic Growth.* New York: John Wiley, 1957.

LEIBENSTEIN, HARVEY, "Entrepreneurship and Development," *American Economic Review Papers and Proceedings* 58 (May 1968).

LEIBENSTEIN, HARVEY, "Notes on X-efficiency and Technical Progress," in *Micro Aspects of Development*, ed. Eliezer B. Ayal. New York: Holt, Rinehart & Winston, 1973.

LEIBENSTEIN, HARVEY, "Organizational or Frictional Equilibria, X-efficiency, and the Rate of Innovation," *Quarterly Journal of Economics* 83 (November 1969).

LEWIS, OSCAR, *The Children of Sanchez.* New York: Random House, 1963.

LEWIS, OSCAR, *Life in a Mexican Village: Tepoztlan Restudied.* Urbana: University of Illinois, 1951.

LEWIS, OSCAR, *Pedro Martinez.* New York: Random House, 1966.

LEWIS, OSCAR, *Village Life in Northern India.* Urbana: University of Illinois, 1958.

MALINOWSKI, BRONISLAW, *Argonauts of the Western Pacific.* London: Routledge & Kegan Paul, 1922.

PARETO, VILFREDO, in *Sociological Writings,* ed. S. E. Finer. New York: Holt, Rinehart & Winston, 1966.

PARETO, VILFREDO, *The Mind and Society.* New York: Harcourt Brace Jovanovich, Inc., 1935.

POLANYI, KARL, *The Great Transformation.* New York: Holt, Rinehart & Winston, 1944.

POLANYI, KARL, ARENSBERG, CONRAD W., and PEARSON, H. W., *Trade and Market in the Early Empires.* New York: Free Press, 1957.

ROTTENBERG, SIMON, "Trade and Market in the Early Empires," *American Economic Review* 48 (1958).

SCHREIER, JAMES W., and KOMIVES, JOHN L., *The Entrepreneur and New Enteprise Formation.* Milwaukee: Center for Venture Management, 1973.

SCHREIER, JAMES W., and KOMIVES, JOHN L., "Provisional Annotated Bibliography on Entrepreneurship and Small Enterprise Development," and Supplement No. 1 (Technology and Development Institute, East-West Center, Honolulu, 1975).

SCHUMPETER, JOSEPH A., *Business Cycles.* New York: McGraw-Hill, 1939.

SCHUMPETER, JOSEPH A., *The Theory of Economic Development: An Inquiry into Profits, Capital, Credit, Interest, and the Business Cycle*, trans. Redvers Opie. Cambridge: Harvard University, 1934.

SLEVIN, DENNIS P., "The Innovation Boundary: A Specific Model and Empirical Results," *Administrative Science Quarterly* 16 (1971).

SPENCER, DANIEL L., and WORONIAK, ALEXANDER, *The Transfer of Technology to Developing Countries.* New York: Holt, Rinehart & Winston, 1967.

STIGLER, GEORGE J., "Imperfections in the Capital Market," *Journal of Political Economy* 75 (June 1967).

chapter xiv

The theory of entrepreneurship in economic growth

Israel M. Kirzner

Overview

The previous two chapters have examined the curious inability of economists, and particularly econometricians, to recognize the existence and role of the entrepreneur. It is this author's opinion that such descriptions stem from an incomplete understanding of the economist's perspective. If entrepreneurship is one area in which multidisciplinary work is to flourish, then there has to be sympathetic understanding among practitioners of each discipline. It is imperative that economists consider entrepreneurship in the development of their models, and that other professionals consider the economists' special definition of entrepreneurship.

The value of entrepreneurship

Why is entrepreneurship good for the economy? It is in answering this question that economics has its contribution to make. Economics explains that where there are unexploited profit opportunities, resources have been misallocated and resulted in some kind of social "waste." If a resource unit can be used to produce $15 worth of output and is currently being used to produce $10 worth of output, the current use of the resource is a wasteful one and offers an opportunity for pure profit, i.e., for entrepreneurship. A profit opportunity implies a preexisting waste. Entrepreneurship corrects waste.

Imperfect knowledge may be responsible for unexploited profit opportunities and for misallocated resources. But knowledge can be bought. If knowledge is cheaply available, how can there ever be an unexploited opportunity? The kind of ignorance responsible for profit opportunities may be an ignorance that people do not recognize. If I don't know someone's telephone number, I can expend resources to obtain the information. If, however, I don't know that this information exists, I won't be seeking information. Likewise, if I don't know that profit opportunities exist, these opportunities will remain unexploited. Entrepreneurial profit opportunities exist where people do not know what it is that they do not know, and do not know that they do not know it. The entrepreneurial function is to notice what people have overlooked.

Entrepreneurship and equilibrium

In a state of economic equilibrium and perfect knowledge no misallocation would have occurred. It has been the economists' achievement to show that there are powerful forces which point towards equilibrium. Unfortunately, economists have often fallen into the trap of taking the equilibrating forces for granted and assuming that no entrepreneurial work remains to be done. On the one hand, economists are right to draw attention to these forces. On the other hand, they are wrong to assume that the forces are so powerful and so rapid as to make the entrepreneurial process unimportant.

This can be clarified by an analogue: In any post office or bank, the lines of waiting people are of approximately equal length. The obvious explanation for this not-so-remarkable phenomenon is that whenever these lines happen to be of different length, it becomes "profitable" for someone to change from a long line to a shorter line. Were I to say that at all times lines in post offices and banks are of equal length, I would be wrong. In fact, it is precisely as a result of this imperfection that the analogue holds.

A century ago, William Stanley Jevons (1911) developed the Law of Indifference. This law declares that a commodity will not sell for two prices in the same market. The basis for the law is obvious. If the same commodity is selling for two prices, why would anybody pay the higher price? Also, why would anybody sell for the lower price? Yet it is known that the same commodity can indeed sell for two prices in the same market. It is here that entrepreneurship is involved: The successful entrepreneur buys low and sells high. This equilibrating process is set into motion precisely when the equilibrium law does not hold.

It is crucial to recognize, as economists have emphasized, the entrepreneurial role in a continuing equilibrium situation. The world is a disequilibrium world. Continuous and continual changes constantly generate new opportunities. But the stationary state of equilibrium, so important in economic analysis, is one in which the entrepreneur has no function.

Schumpeter argued that the entrepreneurial role not only exists in disequilibrium, but is in fact disequilibrating. Schumpeter's entrepreneur disrupts the existing equilibrium. Entrepreneurs may also be viewed as impinging upon a situation where equilibrium has not been achieved. When the entrepreneur makes a profit where resources have been misallocated, this tends to bring the process toward equilibrium. Markets are continually being pushed away from equilibrium by changes in the environment and brought back by entrepreneurial pressures. The entrepreneur keeps things more or less on course.

Many non-economists have ignored the insight that entrepreneurship is fundamentally a disequilibrium phenomenon. They have stressed aspects of entrepreneurial behavior which would exist in a hypothetical state of equilibrium. They have, for example, emphasized autonomy, control, and the combining of resources. Even risk-bearing, as distinct from uncertainty, which can be insured against, could exist in equilibrium. If the economist talks about entrepreneurship, he is talking about that analytical facet of behavior that cannot coexist with equilibrium. This means that, to a certain extent, economists and non-economists understand different things by the term "entrepreneur." It is important to recognize this fact if much sterile misunderstanding is to be avoided.

Entrepreneurship in macroeconomics

Kent points out that, due to insufficient aggregate demand, equilibrium may exist in the form of unemployed resources and that entrepreneurship can correct a situation of this kind. The notion of equilibrium with unemployed resources is a fundamental denial of the scope of entrepreneurship. This is a weakness of Keynesian macroeconomics. Equilibrium with unemployed resources is, from the entrepreneurial point of view, a contradiction in terms. Unemployed resources could be used to satisfy people's wants. If these wants are not being satisfied, there is scope for entrepreneurship.

An opportunity for profit-making exists when someone needs something and is willing to pay for it, and at the same time a relevant resource is available. If something can be bought at a low price and used to produce something of higher value, there is scope for profit. As long as profit-motivated entrepreneurs are waiting in the wings, a situation with scope for pure profit can hardly be in equilibrium.

Entrepreneurs both identify and stimulate demand through advertising. This is often not properly understood by economists. One might argue that if consumers do not know they need something, they simply do not need it. But imagine consumers who, were they to know of the existence of some object, would want it. If their attention is drawn to the existence of this object, this might be described as an act of persuasion or "stimulating" demand. It could also be described as an exercise of entrepreneurship on behalf of the consumers. If the consumers were entrepreneurs on their own behalf, they would notice the opportunity and would realize that it is good for them. Not being entrepreneurs, they may notice neither the item nor its usefulness. Admittedly, there is a fine line between this entrepreneurial activity and persuasion or demand manipulation. Nonetheless, entrepreneurship through advertising may enable consumers to realize what it is that is available to them and what they would like to take advantage of.

Government and entrepreneurship

What role can the government play as an entrepreneur? Can the government encourage innovation in a country, such as the Soviet Union, where entrepreneurship is not permitted? In a recent definitive study, J. S. Berliner (1976) concluded that there is a considerable amount of innovation in the Soviet Union, if less than in capitalist countries. However, to extol innovation in an economic system without market prices and without profit criteria comes perilously close to glorifying innovation for its own sake.

How are we to know whether, and to what extent, the innovations are socially worthwhile? It is possible to manipulate bonuses or incentives so that people will do new things, but innovation is not necessarily desirable. The entrepreneurial incentive provided by the capitalistic market serves to identify precisely those new venture activities that are useful for society. Society is willing to pay a greater price for the output than it exacts for the inputs, indicating that resource allocation has been faulty. Without the market guide of profit and prices, the whole question of innovation must be very seriously reconsidered. New methods of production may not necessarily raise efficiency; new products may be ones that no one wants.

Is entrepreneurship more useful in the wealthier countries or in developing economies? From the economists' perspective, this depends on where greater disequilibrium exists. One might assume that entrepreneurship is more important to those countries where growth in the standard of living is most urgently needed. Given the specific values, the resources, and the relevant constraints, it is conceivable that the economic system in the less developed country is already close to equilibrium. Innovative change which would move the economy out of equilibrium may not be a good thing, at least from the perspective of current social attitudes. In fact, imposing entrepreneurship and change on such an economy may be doing it a disservice. It is not likely that perfect equilibrium will exist in any economy, but to conclude that a low standard of living means scope for entrepreneurship is in error. Economists could only demonstrate scope for entrepreneurship if they knew in advance what needed to be done, if they were themselves prepared to act as entrepreneurs.

Are the hypotheses testable as proposed? If researchers are dealing with scope for entrepreneurship, they are dealing with disequilibrium, which occurs when people do not know what needs to be done. Scholars are dealing with an area of essential ignorance. If people know that a gap needs to be filled, and that it is worthwhile to fill it, the task is no longer entrepreneurial; it can be handled by competent managers through routine production methods. In such circumstances, the market will have already valued the resources necessary to produce the final product. Profit arises because the market does not know what needs to be done.

Entrepreneurship and economic freedom

The government can stimulate entrepreneurship by stimulating an environment of economic freedom. An eminent economist, Fritz Machlup, describes this action as the "fertility of freedom": In a free environment, there is a propensity for discovering profitable opportunities. People may know what needs to be done and can be given freedom to do it. But the primary economic question is: How do we discover what needs to be done, when this has not yet been perceived?

Hosts of opportunities are waiting to be discovered. How do they enter in the consciousness of decision-makers? It is here that the fertility of freedom becomes relevant. A free society permits profit-seeking business people to discover unexploited opportunities. The opportunities are socially important but will not be discovered unless private individuals are stimulated to notice them through the lure of entrepreneurial profit.

References

BERLINER, J. S., *The Innovation Decision in Soviet Industry.* Cambridge: MIT, 1976.

JEVONS, WILLIAM STANLEY, *The Theory of Political Economy* (4th ed.). London: Macmillan, 1911. (Originally published in 1871.)

chapter xv

The role of entrepreneurs in innovation

O. J. Krasner

Overview

This chapter defines innovation and outlines a proposed typology. Large organizations are typically more successful in process, as opposed to product, innovation and in the improvement of existing products. Entrepreneurs are more successful in "long-leap" product innovations. Research has yielded clues for improving the innovation yield of the entrepreneurial process. These clues apply both to the internals of the entrepreneurship as well as to the environment.

This chapter is less a comprehensive review of relevant research than a sharing of perspectives. It seeks to identify appropriate action and to increase the availability and application of research to date.

Essentially, this chapter will address the following questions:

- What working definition of innovation will best illuminate the process in general and the role of entrepreneurship in particular? What typology will best distinguish innovation from such related concepts as invention, adaptation, and diffusion?
- Which institutions, including the institution of entrepreneurship, are most appropriate for which types of innovation?

- How can the innovation yield be improved?
- What actions should be taken in research, in education, in advising and assisting entrepreneurs, in establishing interfaces with community and government?

Innovation: definition and types

The most consistently useful definition of innovation is a very recently stated one:

The overall innovation process encompasses a spectrum of activities from basic research to commercial application and marketing. For the innovation process to be productive, the generation of new knowledge and the translation of that knowledge into commercial products and services must be linked. (Prager and Omenn 1980)

On the entity that undergoes the process, the above definition is implicit. More explicit is the definition offered by Mansfield (1977). He says the innovation process takes technology (either of a new product or a new process) from the state of invention to the state of first commercial application. Viewed this way, innovation is bounded on the upstream side by invention and on the downstream side by adaptation or diffusion, the widespread propagation that occurs after initial commercial success.

Research and development, or invention and innovation are not mutually exclusive stages. Some inventions are generated in the development cycle, and some research during the innovation process.

Of particular significance is the difference between risks of invention and risks of innovation. If risk is the probability of an unfavorable outcome, the differences are as follows:

Invention	***Innovation***
The product (process) will not perform its intended function	The product (process) cannot be priced, placed, or serviced in a manner acceptable to its potential users

In the past 15 years, research in allied fields of management has made substantial gains by moving toward typologies (Lawrence and Lorsch 1967, Hoffer 1975). A comparable move seems warranted in the study of innovation.

Innovation and institutions

Research on successful technological entrepreneurs can be used to compile the types of innovation that appear to dominate particular types of organization (Cooper and Komives 1972, Cooper 1971, Shapero 1969, Lamont 1969). On the other hand, research into the actual allocation of resources for research and development may yield clues about appropriate matching of innovation to organizations (*National Patterns of R & D Resources 1953–1977* 1978, Prager and Omenn 1980, Hamberg 1966). A third source of potentially relevant data is the study of patents and potential usage (Schmookler 1957).

Large organizations are notably more successful than entrepreneurship in:

- Process innovations, and
- Product innovations that are essentially improvements.

Large organizations are characteristically more capital-intensive. Their internal structures develop persons who, while expanding their own technical expertise, invent or are attracted to new process technology. Successful innovation here may reduce costs with little perceived product risk. At the same time, large organizations have more discretionary resources available to support these process innovations.

Regarding their product expertise, it is likely to be strongest in the technology of current products; a large, successful M.O.S. semiconductor firm is not likely to have "bubble-memory" experts dominating its technostructure. The firm is most likely to invent or attend to improvements in that technology—doubling the storage capacity of an M.O.S. chip, in our example. Technicians will have an easier time gaining a commitment of resources to such relatively low risk increments. Indeed, such commitment will be viewed as a most responsible utilization of existing facilities and human capabilities.

Of equal importance, such incremental innovations risk little in the established markets of the large firm. An exciting stream of industrial buyer research has great potential relevance here (Sheth 1973). In industrial products, where most innovation occurs, the interface of buyer and seller calls for high stability and minimum discontinuity. "Leap-frog" product innovation is perceived as too great a discontinuity for the buyer, so incremental innovation is much more likely to be supported to a successful conclusion.

The appropriateness of the entrepreneurial process for the "leap-frog" innovation appears equally explainable. First, it is the latent entrepreneur's frustration with the large organization's inertia that triggers the "displacing event" (Shapero 1969). Three other factors identified by Shapero will lead entrepreneurs outside large organizations:

- Their high need for autonomy as measured by locus-of-control instruments.
- The existence of credible models; the evidence that "it can be done."
- The availability of starting resources, which almost never came from formal financial institutions.

It should be noted that these factors have little to do with the magnitude of the technical leap. The essential judge of innovative feasibility is the launching entrepreneur and not the decision-makers in a large organization. The initial resource providers are not formal financial organizations but usually friends, associates, and relatives. Therefore, the typical risk minimization evaluations applied to an analysis leap need not be made. Even with a significant failure rate, large-leap innovations are more likely to be achieved by the entrepreneurial process. The research record confirms this.

One other significant point made by many researchers is that a significant process innovation in a large organization may have positive consequences for one group (such as investors), but have adverse consequences for another (such as employees displaced by automation). In a large organization a failed attempt at process innovation tends to have minimal effect on those involved. A failed attempt at large-leap product innovation may be disastrous to the entrepreneur and a relatively small number of persons.

Clues to improving entrepreneurial innovation yield

Most of the research here is in the early stages, but significant clues do exist: (a) those internal to entrepreneurship, and (b) those concerning the environment in which the entrepreneur functions.

The successful technological entrepreneurs are not those who never worry. Rather, they are those who worry about the right things. The right worry profile may well be a contingency phenomenon. For example, the more exotic the technology of the innovation, and the greater the attempted leap, the greater ought to be the product development. On the other hand, the more the innovation is dependent upon post-delivery product support, the more worry there should be about personnel development. The appropriate worry profile will promise increased innovation success.

Entrepreneurs ought also to be sensitive to their own propensities. For example, if they know where they are along the craftsman-opportunist spectrum (Smith 1967), they will better understand how to deal with financial and personnel worries in the innovation process.

In the environment, at least three changes will potentially improve the innovation yield:

- Changes in the acquisition of financial resources at launching. New linkages can be developed to funding sources, including university-stimulated assistance to large-leap entrepreneurship (Prager and Omenn 1980). Community industrial development programs can offset the effects of plant relocation by a few large companies with smaller packages of assistance to innovative entrepreneurs. (Shapero 1969)
- Changes in "de facto" patent protection and in associated protection from litigation and regulatory harassment during crucial phases of the innovation process. The

literature is replete with anecdotes describing the trials and tribulations of entrepreneurs when facing large government, large business, and large union interests.

- Changes in vendor support and cooperation. Innovation entrepreneurs are characteristically dependent financially, technically, and contractually on vendors. Anecdotal descriptions of entrepreneurial innovation very often include the supportive vendor as a key figure in success.

A plan of action

Based on these clues is an outline for a plan of action:

- In the process of education an effort must be made to replace simplistic stereotypes. Neither entrepreneurship nor the large organization equals innovation. Students should know that innovation takes place in both settings and should select the one for which they are best suited.
- It must be recognized that the present understanding of the management process comes heavily from large organizational settings. This is understandable, but it argues for special candor about the state of research.
- As advisors to or performers of the entrepreneurial process, educators must apply research to the internals of the enterprise and to the external environment. Internally, educators must help assess the propriety and timeliness of an entrepreneurial attempt. They must relate the "worry profiles" to the key variables in the situation and learn to confront, not minimize, the large risks that characterize innovation through entrepreneurship. Externally, educators must help the enterprise develop new resource sources. Litigation and regulative harassment ought to be minimized. Vendors and customers ought to be facilitated in their interactions.
- As researchers, educators must continue the thrust for active interchange among members of the research community. Consider how the quality of research has already been enhanced by the input of different disciplines and perspectives.
- There should be a strong effort to establish and maintain a National Data Base on Entrepreneurial Research, structured to locate, integrate, and retrieve through multiple search logics and information networks.
- Finally, as agents-for-change in the institutional structure, educators must more actively support productive innovation and entrepreneurship at the community level through political and commercial institutions. They may encourage the use of research-based predictors of success, rather than non-entrepreneurial criteria, for such decisions as approving loans, granting community amenities, and assisting new forms of vendor and customer cooperation.

A very significant portion of all innovation in our society can best be achieved through the entrepreneurial process. Research to date has begun to identify this process and what makes for its success. Also needed are means to help society realize the benefits of entrepreneurship.

commentary/elaboration

Elaboration on entrepreneurs and innovation

Gerald Udell

Overview

This comment will address the noncorporate industrial innovation process.

The noncorporate industrial innovation process may be defined as the series of events involved in moving a new product, process, or service from invention to development to production to commercialization in an entrepreneurial or small business setting. In other words, it is the product of a marriage between the entrepreneur and industrial innovation processes.

Research on this process is the examination of that marriage, not of the individual partners. The objective of such research is to increase the fertility of the marriage. The central concern is industrial innovation in an entrepreneurial setting.

The difficulty of noncorporate industrial innovation research

Entrepreneurship and industrial innovation are both emerging areas of research in academia. The amount of research done on either topic by business or technical faculty is quite small when compared with other recently developed areas. Two possible explanations for this phenomenon are the interdisciplinary nature of both processes and the difficulty of doing research in both areas. The study of entrepreneurship, for example, can involve an understanding of law, finance, psychology, regulation, and production marketing. Innovation crosses similar academic boundaries, and the nature of both beasts frequently requires that they be studied in total, thereby requiring of the researcher a breadth not typically found in this era of academic specialization.

The more serious problem, however, may be the difficulty of research. Entrepreneurs are elusive creatures, difficult to define, much less study. Industrial innovation is a secretive animal. Those who know how guard their secrets with a vigor exceeded only by those who don't and who label their failures "Top Secret." Neither area is easily carved up into bite-sized research pieces. Both must be studied in situ. Classroom or laboratory replication is difficult to achieve. The numbers which fuel most academics are often exceedingly difficult to come by and more difficult to validate.

The importance of noncorporate industrial innovation

As studies show, entrepreneurial innovation is of significant national importance. First, noncorporate industrial innovation is still a major source of the new products, processes, and services which fuel the nation's economy, increasing productivity, providing jobs, and raising standards of living. In a 1977 study, the Office of Management and Budget concluded that "firms with less than 1000 employees accounted for almost half of the major U.S. innovations during 1953–1973." This conclusion was reached, as noted in the OMB Report (1977), after an extensive literature search and may be based on an NSF study which concluded that firms with less than 1000 employees were responsible for half of the "most significant new industrial products and processes." Firms with 100 or fewer employees accounted for 24 percent of such innovations. In addition, these small firms produced 24 times as many major innovations per R & D dollar expended as did their larger counterparts with over 10,000 employees and about four times as many as medium-sized firms with 1000–10,000 employees (Zerbe 1976).

Second, noncorporate industrial innovation appears to be in very serious decline. There are no precise indices for measuring the rate of innovation. However, general indicators support this conclusion:

The number of U.S. patents granted per year to U.S. inventors has declined steadily since 1971, whereas U.S. patents granted to foreign residents has increased. ("Science Indicators 1976")

As a percent of net sales, R & D of U.S. manufacturing industries declined from over 9 percent in 1961 to slightly less than 6 percent in 1974. ("Science Indicators 1976")

The number of scientists and engineers per 1000 employees in U.S. manufacturing industries also declined from 1961 to 1974. ("Science Indicators 1976")

The number of new equity issues declined from 1298 in 1969 to 25 in (midyear) 1977. The value of these issues in 1977 was $230 million compared to $3.3 billion in 1969. (Landu 1978)

The number of new publicly financed small technical companies declined from 104 in 1969 to four in 1974. Funding for these firms declined from $349 million in 1969 to $6 million in 1974. ("The Role of New Technical Enterprises" 1976)

The impact of this decline can be seen in the declining rate of U.S. productivity. According to a report prepared for the President's Domestic Policy Review on Innovation by the small business members of the Industrial Innovation Advisory Committee,

From the close of World War II until the mid-1960s the average annual productivity increase for each manufacturing worker was approximately 4.1 percent. From the late 1960s through the mid-1970s, it averaged 1.6 percent per year. In 1978 it was 1.0 percent, and some economists are predicting a rate of 0.4 percent for 1979. (Small Business and Innovation, 1979)

Less obvious but equally significant may be the impact on economic growth, for innovative and young high-technology firms add more jobs to the economy and pay more taxes as a percentage of sales than do mature companies (*Small Business and Innovation* 1979).

Idea generation stage

Ideas are the offspring of creativity. Creativity can be developed, nurtured, stimulated, and studied, but probably not structured. While a substantial body of literature deals with creativity, most of it is not specific to noncorporate industrial innovation. This body of literature needs to be winnowed and in some cases recast into entrepreneurial settings.

In addition, new ways of stimulating or turning creative talent toward industrial innovation must be developed. Necessity is still the mother of invention. However, psychological and economic rewards must be offered to the solution finder. Patent laws and public policies, government rights to inventions made under federal sponsorship, tax laws, and programs for financial, management, and technical assistance must be studied and subjected to experimentation.

Idea evaluation stage

Idea evaluation is too often ignored. Inventors and innovators alike frequently charge into the latter stages of the innovation process only to fail for reasons apparent from the beginning. Given the high cost of industrial innovation, proper screening is essential. A noncorporate preliminary evaluation system has been developed by the author under the National Science

Foundation's Innovation Center. It is efficient (cost effective) and effective as it is capable, at least, of identifying nonfeasible ideas and inventions (Udell 1980).

Research and development stages

There is a large body of literature dealing with research and development (Clarke 1975). However, the bulk of this literature is corporate-oriented and needs to be recast in an entrepreneurial setting to be relevant to the noncorporate innovator.

Commercialization stages

It is a sobering fact of life that many, if not most, new products, processes, and services fail during the commercialization stages. The overwhelming share of these fail for nontechnical reasons. Inadequate financial planning accounts for most new product and new venture failures.

A growing body of literature deals with the commercialization stages. Unfortunately, as revealed by a recently published survey of such literature, it is corporate-oriented (Udell and O'Neill 1975). Many of the theories, tools, and techniques are relevant to entrepreneurial commercialization efforts. However, there are basic differences between corporate and noncorporate innovation (Charpie 1967), and much of this research needs to be recast in entrepreneurial terms.

Conclusion

The noncorporate sector, small business innovators and entrepreneurs, contributes half and perhaps more of the major technological innovations produced in the United States. Unfortunately, this sector has not received its fair share of attention from the nation's academic researchers and from policy-makers.

One of the reasons for this is the difficulty of doing research in a noncorporate setting. Another less documented, but equally important factor, is the commonly held but erroneous notion of corporate superiority. While much of the literature about innovation in a corporate setting has at least partial relevance to entrepreneurial innovation, there are basic differences between the two environments.Thus, research and experimentation which focuses on noncorporate industrial innovation is urgently needed.

References

CHARPIE, ROBERT A., *Technological Innovation: Its Environment and Management.* Washington, D.C.: U.S. Department of Commerce, Panel on Invention and Innovation, 1967.

CLARKE, THOMAS E., *R & D Management Bibliography.* Ottawa: The Innovation Management Institute of Canada, 1975.

COOPER, A. C., *The Founding of Technologically Based Firms.* Milwaukee: Center for Venture Management, 1971.

COOPER, A. C., and KOMIVES, J. L., eds. *Technical Entrepreneurship.* Milwaukee: Center for Venture Management, 1972.

HAMBERG, D., *R & D: Essays in the Economics of Research and Development.* New York: Random House, 1966.

HOFFER, C. W., "Toward a Contingency Theory of Business Strategy," *Academy of Management Journal,* December 1975.

LAMONT, LAWRENCE M., *Technology Transfer, Innovation and Marketing in Science Oriented Spin-off Firms* (Doctoral dissertation, University of Michigan, 1969).

LANDU, RALPH, "Entrepreneurship in the Chemical Industry and in the United States," *Innovators and Entrepreneurs: An Endangered Species.* Washington, D.C.: National Academy of Engineering, 1978.

LAWRENCE, P., and LORSCH, J., *Organization and Environment: Managing Differentiation and Integration.* Boston: Harvard Graduate School of Business, 1967.

MANSFIELD, EDWARD, et al., *The Production and Application of New Industrial Technology.* New York: W. W. Norton & Co., Inc., 1977.

National Patterns of R & D Resources, 1953–1977. Washington, D.C.: National Science Foundation, 1978.

PRAGER, D. J., and OMENN, D. S., "Research, Innovation, and University-Industry Linkages," *Science* 207 (January 1980).

The Role of New Technical Enterprises in the U.S. Economy: A Report of the Commerce Technical Advisory Board to the Secretary of Commerce, Washington, D.C.: U.S. Department of Commerce, January 1976.

SCHMOOKLER, J., "Inventions Past and Present," *Review of Economics and Statistics* 39 (1957).

"Science Indicators 1976." Washington, D.C.: National Science Foundation, 1977.

SHAPERO, ALBERT, *The Role of the Financial Community in the Formation, Growth, and Effectiveness of Technical Companies.* Austin: Multi-disciplinary Research, 1969.

SHETH, J. N., "A Model of Industrial Buying Behavior," *Journal of Marketing,* October 1973.

Small Business and Innovation. Washington D.C.: U.S. House of Representatives, Committee on Small Business, 1979.

Small Firms and Federal Research and Development (A Report to the Office of Federal Procurement Policy). Washington, D.C.: Office of Management and Budget, 1977.

SMITH, NORMAN R., *The Entrepreneur and His Firm: The Relationship between*

Type of Man and Type of Company. East Lansing: Graduate School of Business, Michigan State University, 1967.

UDELL, GERALD G., ed., *Guideline for Establishing the Preliminary Innovation Evaluation System.* (Volume II of the Final Report on the Oregon Innovation Center Experiment 1973-1980). Washington, D.C.: National Science Foundation, 1980.

UDELL, GERALD G., and O'NEILL, MICHAEL F., *The New Product Decision Making Process: A Selected Annotated Bibliography of the Current Literature.* Washington, D.C.: National Science Foundation, 1975.

ZERBE, RICHARD O., "Research and Development by Smaller Firms," *Journal of Contemporary Business,* Spring 1976.

chapter xvi

The environment for entrepreneurship

Albert V. Bruno

Tyzoon T. Tyebjee

Overview

The intense concentration of entrepreneurial activity in areas such as the San Francisco peninsula and Route 128 around Boston is believed to be a result of environmental factors that stimulate entrepreneurship. Among the most influential factors are venture capital availability, the presence of experienced entrepreneurs and incubator organizations, a technically-skilled labor force, accessibility of suppliers, customers, or new markets, favorable government policies, proximity of universities, availability of land or facilities, accessibility of transportation, a receptive population, availability of supporting services, and good living conditions. Since most of this research is wisdom-based, the absence of a theoretical framework severely limits the results. In this chapter a theoretical perspective is suggested, methodological issues are raised, and areas for future research are identified. The environmental factors identified by various authors are first discussed.

Environmental factors in entrepreneurship

A number of authors have approached this topic by identifying a set of factors which constitute the environment for entrepreneurship. These factors, summarized in Table 1, are briefly discussed below. Naumes argues that the "sources of external support for financing, technology, management, and productive capacity" are largely responsible for the success of many new ventures in the major entrepreneurial areas (1978). Draheim (1972) identifies similar factors in the entrepreneurial environment of Minneapolis-St. Paul, including a pool of labor and available venture capital and operating facilities.

Vesper and Albaum (1979) provide the following list:

1. Presence of local market contacts;

2. Presence of incubator industries;

3. Technical manpower resources;

4. Universities with doctoral programs, funded research in engineering and physical sciences, and affiliated research laboratories;

5. Research laboratories of major companies and government;

6. Sources of venture capital (SBICs, commercial banks, local securities regulation, and local stock underwriting firms);

7. Favorable state government policies (tax incentives, government research contracts, industrial parks, and incubator facilities).

Shapero distinguishes "first" company formation from later start-ups and states that the former is dependent upon

the ability of the founders to get financial support, to obtain technically skilled workers, to provide services not available in the area (usually at an increased cost to operations), and to bring the market to the company. (1972)

Later start-ups are the result of spin-offs from existing companies and therefore utilize the same technology. As a result of an increase in the number of technologically related companies, the demand for special material and services arises and attracts technical professions. Shapero also measures social, economic, and demographic factors to determine their correlation with the number of technical companies in an area. His findings show that in a community with a population of less than 100,000, the number of service establishments, total local expenditures on education, and population were the factors most highly correlated with the number of technical companies. In contrast, where the population was greater than 100,000, manufacturing had the highest correlation. It was also found that high tourist attraction (Florida, California, Colorado, Arizona) was a prevalent environmental characteristic in areas with the highest rates of company formation.

Cooper (1973) lists the following environmental factors as important in the entrepreneurial decision: examples of entrepreneurial action, knowledge about entrepreneurship, societal attitudes toward entrepreneurship, salary and taxation levels, availability of venture capital, availability of personnel and supporting services, accessibility of customers, accessibility to universities, opportunities for interim consulting, and general economic conditions. In another paper he defines a conducive entrepreneurial environment as "a situation in which prospective founders of new firms have a high awareness of

Table 1 *Environmental factors stressed in entrepreneurial research*

	Cooper (6 articles)	Danilov	Draheim	Hoffman	Hollingsworth & Hand	Mahar & Coddington	Naumes	Schöllhammer & Kuriloff	Shapero	Siropolis	Susbauer	Vesper & Albaum	TOTAL
Venture capital availability	A	B	A	A	A	A	A		A	A		A	10
Presence of experienced entrepreneurs	A	C	A			A	A				A	A	7
Accessibility of customers (markets)	A	A						A	C			A	5
Technically skilled labor force	A	A	A			A	C		A	A		A	8
Proximity to universities	A	A				A	A		A		A	A	7
Favorable tax and licensing policies	C	B			A	A				A		A	6
Availability of raw materials		B					C			A			3
Availability of land (facilities)	A	B	A			A	C			A			6
Accessibility of supplies	A							A	A				3
Accessibility of transportation	C	B			A	A			A	A			6
Favorable loan and financial policies	C		C	A	A				A				5
Receptive population	A				A	A							3

Availability of supporting services	A			A		A	A						4
Cultural and living conditions	A	B				A			A				4
Community size									A	A			2
Pollution										A			1
Environmental regulations	A							A					2
Economic conditions	A		A										2
Interim consulting	A												1
Pushes and pulls			A								A		2
Structure of R&D function			A									A	2
Government financial assistance and contracts			A			A			A			A	4
Capital intensiveness			A										1
Degree of change in state-of-the-technology			A										1
Proximity to corporate headquarters		A											1
Competition					A								1

A = stated as of major importance
B = stated as of minor importance
C = implied, not stated

past entrepreneurial action, of sources of venture capital, and of individuals and institutions that might provide help and advice" (Cooper 1970). The existence of small, new incubator firms, a pool of experienced entrepreneurs, the presence of specialized sources of venture capital, universities, a complex of related firms, attractive living conditions, and established incubator organizations are major influences that vary from region to region (Cooper 1971).

Taking a slightly different view of environmental effects, Danilov (1972) discusses research parks and regional development as major contributors. The following factors are identified as most important in the selection of a science site: proximity to universities, availability of technical manpower, proximity to corporate headquarters, cost of living, proximity to new markets, and availability of skilled labor. When respondents (1200 research scientists and engineers, 200 R & D directors, 100 company presidents, and 70 organizations located in research parks) were asked what factors should be considered, environmental factors were ranked as follows: availability of above-average schools, availability of technical manpower, proximity to universities, availability of adequate land, availability of air transportation, availability of skilled labor, cost of taxes, proximity to other research activities, proximity to recreational opportunities, cost of living, and availability of a technical library.

Mahar and Coddington (1965) adopt the perspective of a community that wishes to attract entrepreneurs through creation of a scientific complex. These authors stress three elements that characterize successful scientific complexes in the U.S.:

1. Science-based industry composed of (a) industrial research and development laboratories that may or may not be part of production facilities; (b) technically oriented manufacturing plants; and (c) supporting suppliers and services.

2. One or more major universities which emphasize (a) a wide range of graduate studies in science, engineering, and mathematics; (b) basic and applied research in science and engineering; (c) graduate studies in business management.

3. Federal government research facilities administered either (a) directly by the government, or (b) by private industry or universities.

Mahar and Coddington also stress the importance of spin-offs to the formation of a scientific complex. Such complexes encourage others to develop new firms and thus attract new research-based industry. The authors cite several conditions as necessary to successful spin-offs: key persons who can attract a large amount of research money; research in new growth areas of technology; adequate financing; low-cost facilities.

In addition to the above factors, attraction requirements must be met by the community. Mahar and Coddington (1965) list five: (1) high quality industrial space; (2) reasonable operating costs and supporting circumstances (labor relations and productivity, taxes, local government policies, air transportation, etc.); (3) living conditions better than those found in the average U.S. metropolitan areas (climate, secondary schools, taxes, recreational opportunities); (4) a nearby university offering advanced courses in science and engineering (for employees' benefit and for increased labor supply), and (5) a well developed, vigorous professional environment, and a thriving cultural environment.

"Pushes and pulls" are environmental factors that personally affect an entrepreneur. Among those identified by Draheim (1972) are: perceived threats to employees of existing companies, such as absentee management or remote control of budgets; actual threats to employees, such as layoffs caused by economic conditions, mergers, or relocation; the availability of government contracts and government financial assistance programs; and the credibility of forming a new company. Susbauer (1972) identifies the following pushes and pulls: threat of relocation, business decline that leads to layoffs, decreased job enjoyment (due to internal management fights, being passed over for a promotion, etc.), rejection of the entrepreneur's ideas or product by existing companies, and existence of a guaranteed first customer. The desire to amass wealth or the opportunity to bring all of the right people together at the same time are also potential pushes and pulls. These factors are not major environmental factors, but they can stimulate or hinder entrepreneurial activity.

As previously enumerated, the environmental factors overlap considerably. The most frequently cited "essential" factors are:

Venture capital availability
Presence of experienced entrepreneurs
Technically skilled labor force
Accessibility of suppliers
Accessibility of customers or new markets
Favorable governmental policies
Proximity of universities
Availability of land or facilities
Accessibility to transportation
Receptive population
Availability of supporting services
Attractive living conditions

Each of the factors will now be reviewed.

Venture capital availability

Venture funding of some form is usually essential if a new company is to be started. In an environment where entrepreneurial activity is well established, one source of venture capital is the already successful entrepreneurs in the area. They will often be sympathetic to other new ventures as managerial and financial outlets.

In the Palo Alto area, there have been continuous venture capital sources for a number of years; many people who provide venture capital developed their capital base as entrepreneurs. According to Cooper (1970) an important source of initial capital for many firms is stock held by the founders in the firms for which they previously worked. In the U.S. electronics industry, stock options which were intended to bind the executives to firms sometimes make it financially feasible for them to leave the firm and become entrepreneurs.

In Austin, an atypical situation meant that venture capital was not a critical environmental factor. Most companies were formed with internal sources of capital, because most were not highly capital-intensive. The initial capital needed was only in the tens of thousands of dollars (Susbauer 1972).

As Hoffman (1972) observes, if local banks or other local sources will not provide loan money because they lack experience in financing technical companies, then entrepreneurs will go elsewhere. This lack of experience arises from regional economic history and strongly affects loan policies and practices.

Cooper (1970) points out that, in the Palo Alto area, most new firms were financed locally because:

1. The founders did not know potential investors in other areas.
2. Investors in the San Francisco Bay area were more likely to understand and be sympathetic to technologically-oriented businesses.
3. Potential local investors could easily check into the background of the aspiring entrepreneur. Often, they knew the individual personally.
4. Investors could keep in close touch with the new firm.
5. Presentations and proposals to local investors did not need to be elaborate.

Experienced entrepreneurs and incubator organizations

The notion that entrepreneurial activity precipitates more activity is the thesis of several authors. Cooper argues that "technical entrepreneurship in a particular area appears to be related closely to the incubator organizations (established firms) already there. Unless such incubator organizations exist in a region, it is unlikely that there will be any new, technologically-based firms born there" (1970). If the first technical companies are successful, they begin to change the environment and attract other entrepreneurs. Naumes states that "the mere fact that there are other entrepreneurs in the vicinity who have succeeded at new venture initiation draws entrepreneurs to the area and encourages potential entrepreneurs already in the area" (1978). Particularly, successful entrepreneurs can draw upon the experience and knowledge derived from previous successes and failures. If they study their predecessors, they can understand the formula for success.

Spin-off companies are able to draw on an existing talent pool. That talent is more likely to leave secure positions in the area if the risks associated with the new enterprise are controlled and easily assessed. A source of debate is whether small companies or larger companies are the better incubators for new start-ups. On the one hand, it can be argued that employment in a small company exposes the potential entrepreneur to the full range of problems and decisions the entrepreneur can expect to encounter in his own start-up. On the other hand, it can be argued that the experience of working for some large companies seems to precipitate entrepreneurial yearnings in the employee.

The incubator organization is important to the potential entrepreneur. He is able to acquire managerial insights to supplement his technical expertise, and he is able to gain familiarity with customers and suppliers while on someone else's payroll. The networks he develops are bound to the environment of the incubator organization, so that when he starts up a venture it tends to be in the same area.

Technically skilled labor force

A technically skilled labor force is another important environmental factor conducive to entrepreneurial activity. In the Twin Cities, the hearing aid industry provided a technical base; many technicians and engineers were employed in the area (Draheim 1972). Labor skilled in the particular area of the new venture facilitates the formation of new companies. An SRI study of small businesses in the electronics industry concluded that the "availability of the type of labor required in the industry is one of the most important considerations in determining the location of electronics companies" (Stanford Research Institute 1962). Since a new firm is viewed as a high-risk place of employment, skilled labor is not willing to relocate. The new firm must locate where the labor pool already exists.

Accessibility of suppliers

Although several authors (Cooper 1970, Shapero 1972, Schollhammer and Kuriloff 1979) have noted the importance of supplier access to entrepreneurship, no published research has been found to support this proposition. In some situations, it is likely that good access to suppliers has had a positive impact on the decision to start a company. One suspects, however, that this is the exception rather than the norm, and that accessibility to suppliers is seldom a deciding factor. The consideration is likely to be highly specific to particular industries, depending upon the bulkiness of raw materials and the degree of personal service desired from suppliers.

Accessibility of customers or new markets

Again, little published research is available. An SRI (1962) study concludes that since the government is often a principal customer, the problem of locating near the market is minimized. In general, this factor appears to be more significant when the entrepreneurial activity has local rather than national or international scope, or when customers are geographically concentrated. It should also depend on the amount and frequency of personal interaction required by customers.

Favorable governmental policies

Taxation rates, licensing policies, and other government activities can have a positive or negative impact on entrepreneurship. Of course, these influences occur at local, state, and federal levels. Several researchers address the governmental influence factor: Hollingsworth and Hand (1979) observe that state and local legislation on taxation and licensing can make one location more attractive than another. Cooper (1973) maintains that this legislation affects the ability to collect "seed" capital with which to start new ventures. Mahar and Coddington (1965) observe that taxes on business must bear some relationship to the services provided, but assert that if tax costs were the only consideration, Boston, Palo Alto, and Los Angeles would never have developed as centers of entrepreneurial activity, since California and Massachusetts have high taxes. Vesper and Albaum (1979) point to the lack of encouragement given by state governments in the Pacific Northwest to industrial innovation. They also point to the area's unfavorable business tax structures as deterrents to new start-ups. Galvin (1978) notes that taxation laws often defer rather than forward the decision to start a new business: government will not allow a current deduction of the sums spent by a taxpayer in investigating a new business. Although a recent ruling has allowed deduction of expenses incurred in an unsuccessful attempt to acquire a specific business, general investigatory expenses are still not deductible.

Proximity of universities

It is a popular belief that universities are the source of technical spin-off companies, but this is actually the exception, not the rule. If it does occur, it is due to the positive encouragement by the administration or its passive acceptance of entrepreneurial activity on the part of the faculty, and the presence of contract research, contract research centers, or laboratories (Shapero 1972).

Cooper maintains that

universities have undoubtedly played a role in attracting able young men and women to particular regions, and sometimes in giving the firms located there competitive advantages in recruiting and retaining these people. They also provide sources of consulting assistance and opportunities for continuing education for professional employees. However, the degree to which universities play a central or essential role in technical entrepreneurship appears to vary widely. (1973)

Mapes (1967) observes that "many other professors and laboratory researchers at big universities throughout the country are going into business for themselves. Mostly they take theories that they develop while doing university research work and put them to practical use in highly specialized new products." There is also some evidence that university spin-offs are more likely to succeed than the average new business venture. One advantage is their connection with university research labs and the government agencies that finance them. Mapes quotes F. Terman of Stanford University as saying "more universities now believe a spin-off is in their enlightened self interest. It builds the community as a more attractive place for faculty and students, and it keeps scientists in touch with the engineering problems that exist in the practical world" (1967).

Allison (1965) concedes that schools with strong engineering and science capabilities and policies that encourage entrepreneurship stimulate new enterprises. The presence of academic institutions, however, may be merely a facilitating factor and not a necessary one. Dallas did not have a "natural attractiveness" in terms of climate or academic institutions but was able to develop an industrial community by creating a connection between its research centers and the rest of the community. Pennings' (1979) empirical investigation of organizational births found the presence of a university to be insignificant.

Availability of land or facilities

Mahar and Coddington emphasize the importance of low-cost facilities for newly-formed companies, since they have little capital with which to operate. They recommend the construction of shell-type buildings with easily movable partitions if incubator space is not available in older buildings. High quality industrial space is also essential, since firms usually do not want to worry about the "availability of water, power, sewage, roads, or zoning" (1965).

Recent developments in California suggest the negative impact that land availability and related factors can have. Quirt (1978) points out that California-based high-technology companies are not building their new plants in California because of rising labor costs, environmental regulations, high business taxes, and generous unemployment compensation rates. The uncertainty over energy supplies, the absence of industrial revenue bonds, and soaring housing costs also influence decisions to locate plants elsewhere. California society is also believed to be hostile toward economic growth; less land is therefore rezoned for industrial use.

Accessibility to transportation

Accessibility to transportation and transportation costs are cited as important environmental factors by a number of authors. "Although transportation costs may not be very important with many high-technology products, the ability to work closely with customers is sometimes essential" (Cooper 1973). Mahar and Coddington (1965) emphasize the importance of airline transportation. Schary (1979) says that industry type, competition, general and specific location, firm size, product, markets, energy, and regulation affect the importance of transportation to businesses in the Pacific Northwest.

Receptive population

Cooper (1970) notes that public reception of new issues of stock can substantially affect the availability of venture capital, an important factor for success. Societal attitudes toward business and entrepreneurship undoubtedly influence individual decisions, but there has been a minimum of research in this area.

Mahar and Coddington conclude that it is difficult for a firm to operate successfully in an unsupportive environment. They define an encouraging environment as "an attitude which recognizes that small firms are making important contributions to the economic development of the area" (1965).

Availability of supporting services

This factor usually affects a company after the initial formation stage. These services are provided by accountants, tax experts, lawyers, and consultants specializing in new ventures and small businesses.

These advisors understand the typical problems present in starting a new enterprise. They help entrepreneurs overcome many of the initial stumbling blocks to successful new venture initiation. One area in particular in which expert advice could be of great help is in the preparation of a prospectus for financing purposes. . . . Another area providing a source of trouble to successful new venture initiation is knowing how much capital to seek at the outset. (Naumes 1978)

The existence of supporting services further assures that new ventures will be more successful in the future.

Attractive living conditions

The cultural, climatological, and recreational amenities were given the greatest importance by the companies Shapero surveyed.

A community must become an exciting and attractive place if it is to attract and retain the technical professional work force that is the chief production factor in high-

technology industries. This highly trained body of workers is relatively young, highly mobile, in great demand, and has a choice of places to work and live. It will not stay in a community that does not have within it a selection of amenities that are available elsewhere. (1972)

In contrast, Cooper (1970) maintains that technical entrepreneurs tend to start firms where they already live and work because it is easier to secure labor and facilities. Few founders were attracted from other areas of the country at the time their companies were formed. In another article, Cooper contends that "although attractive living conditions may attract technical people to an area as employees, they rarely attract people who are in the act of founding companies" (1973).

Mahar and Coddington (1965) note that primary and secondary schools are very important because most scientists and engineers, well-educated themselves, want good educational facilities for their children.

Directions for future research

The paragraphs which follow deal with: possible schemes for the classification of environmental factors and entrepreneurial activity; theoretical perspectives and methodological concerns for future research; and research topics of possible interest.

Classification and stratification of environmental factors and entrepreneurial activity

At this point, the reader might give some consideration to the problems and implications of classifying the environmental factors already discussed. For example, factors might be classified as enhancing or inhibiting. Enhancing factors would be those that stimulate entrepreneurship, inhibiting factors, those that stifle it. Another means of classification might be maturity of environment. In this case, certain environmental factors will alter with the growth of entrepreneurial activity in a particular environment.

These schemes may merge. Some enhancing environmental factors, such as readily available land and facilities, will become inhibiting factors as the entrepreneurial environment matures and costs of land and facilities escalate. Other factors, such as the availability of venture capital, actually become more positive in mature environments.

Another perspective is that of cause and effect. Obviously some factors, such as the proximity of universities, influence entrepreneurial activity and do not result from it. Other factors are not so easily classified. For example, one might assume that a liberalization of the traditional capital gains tax structure might positively influence entrepreneurship. At the same time, it can be argued that the recent change in the capital gains law is the effect of previous successful entrepreneurial activity. The ordinary corporate taxes paid on successful entrepreneurial ventures sufficiently offsets the loss to the government from liberalization of the capital gains laws (*Capital Formation Survey* 1977).

One of the problems of classifying entrepreneurial activity is that entrepreneurship seems to hold a different meaning for various researchers. At the simplest level entrepreneurs can be defined as those in business for themselves. This broad a definition, however, fails to recognize the stages in the life cycle of business. A key issue is whether the firm can be regarded as entrepreneurial throughout its life cycle. It is tempting to limit the scope of the field by focusing attention on the early stages of the venture only. However, this equates entrepreneurship with start-up and excludes the entrepreneurial activity manifested by expansion into new markets or the development of new products. A more fruitful approach is to introduce the venture stage as a stratifying variable: Prestart-up, start-up, profitability, growth, and disposition are five possible stages.

A second important stratifying variable is the innovative nature of the product or service undertaken by the entrepreneur. The sources of risk are likely to differ between an innovation and an initiative entry. Innovations may be classified into three categories, depending on how radically new they are to the market:

1. Continuous, those that have the least disrupting influence on the market.

2. Dynamically continuous, those that have some disrupting influence but do not generally disrupt customer buying and use patterns or competitor strategy.

3. Discontinuous, those that involve the introduction of an entirely new product and cause significant changes in customer or competitor behavior.

A third stratifying variable, related to the second, is the technological content of new undertakings. The term high-technology has traditionally been taken to be synonymous with electronics, aerospace, and chemical industries. This type of categorical partitioning must be revised to allow a more operationally valid definition of technology content. R & D intensity for the product class is one possible indicator. It would be naive to expect that environmental influence will remain the same for all combinations of these variables.

If the effect of environmental variables on entrepreneurial activity is to be empirically determined, we must develop measures for these concepts. Entrepreneurial activity can be measured in terms of three types of outcome: start-up outcome, performance outcome, and residual outcome.

Start-up outcomes include the number of start-ups, equity and legal structure of start-ups, and scale of start-ups. They record the impact of the environment on emerging entrepreneurs. Performing outcomes, on the other hand, record how entrepreneurs fare in various environments. Indicators include profitability measures such as ROI, ROA, return on sales, growth and market share, ability to attract new customers, establishment of a market position. Failure of the firm, of course, is also a negative performance outcome.

Residual outcomes occur in the latter stages of the firm's life cycle. Changes in the capital structure, particularly the exit of venture funds from the equity base, are residual outcomes. The issue of shares "going public" on the market is another. Merger and acquisition activity is a third. Finally, new start-ups by the firm's principal, and the development of new products, markets, or technologies are evidence of residual entrepreneurial activity.

These groups of variables measure different aspects of entrepreneurial activity and hence need to be separately delineated. To date most research on entrepreneurship has focused on narrow ranges of outcome.

In Figure 1 environmental influences have been partitioned into two groups and linked to the three outcome levels. The first group includes resources necessary to start a firm. The second group includes factors that influence the cost of doing business. Resource availability will affect start-up outcomes and residual outcomes. The projected cost of doing business will influence start-up outcomes, particularly the decision to start a venture, and the realized cost of doing business will influence performance outcomes.

Classification and stratification schemes can provide a more useful re-

Figure 1 *The impact of the environment on entrepreneurial activity and its outcomes*

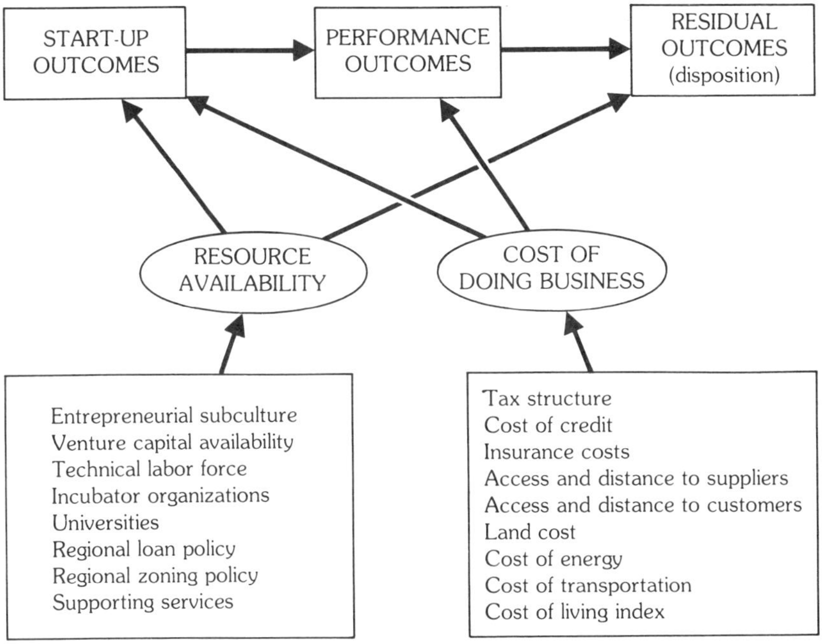

search perspective than the mere examination of gross relationships between environmental factors and entrepreneurial activity. More meaningful research may result from attempts of this type.

Theoretical perspectives

As the review of the literature clearly indicates, much of the current knowledge about environmental influence on entrepreneurial activity is based on anecdotal evidence, case histories, and folklore. There is a notable absence of theoretical frameworks. Correspondingly, there is a dearth of empirical verification. The lack of a theoretical paradigm has three consequences: a lack of constructs by which to conceptualize the environment; a lack of theoretically-based hypotheses regarding the functional relationship between the environment and entrepreneurship; a lack of impetus for collecting suitable data, measuring, and testing. In the discussion that follows, several theoretical perspectives will be offered, and resulting methodological issues will be examined.

Behavioral research has found that actors and participants in a particular event tend to attribute the outcomes to environmental factors, whereas observers tend to attribute outcomes to the drive and abilities of the actors. This phenomenon may partly explain the extent to which researchers have focused on the entrepreneur as opposed to the environment. Moreover, the causal attribution bias can lead to different conclusions depending on the research methodology used. Clinical interviews with key individuals in an entrepreneurial firm are likely to find environmental factors to be the dominant influence on the firm's fortunes. On the other hand, a more detached observation is likely to focus on intra-organizational factors such as leadership, motivation, and structure.

Research methodologies that compare entrepreneurial firms to mature ones undoubtedly find the intra-organizational characteristics of the two very different. For example, the different selection processes are likely to result in administrative structures with radically different patterns of authority, communication, and managerial profiles. To attribute entrepreneurship to a particular type of administrative structure begs the issue of cause and effect. It seems far more persuasive to argue that a firm's administrative structure is its attempt to adapt to its peculiar environment. An entrepreneurial firm typically faces a more uncertain environment and has poorer access to environmental resources. Its administrative structure must be sufficiently flexible to react to these uncertainties and sufficiently skilled to improve access to resources.

One theoretical perspective views organizations as resource-dependent on their external environment (Pfeffer and Salancik 1978). The environment is characterized in terms of six constructs. Three are structural characteristics: concentration—the extent to which power and authority in the environment are widely dispersed; munificence — the availability or scarcity of critical resources; and interconnectedness — the number and pattern of linkages among organizations. Two other constructs characterize the relationship among different organizations in the environment: conflict — disagreement about the goals of the social system — and interdependence — the degree to which one organization influences the others. Finally, a global construct called environmental uncertainty — the degree to which the future can be accurately predicted — results from the other five aspects by the mechanism shown in Figure 2. Though Pfeffer and Salancik are not directly concerned with applying their model of the environment to entrepreneurship, many of their conclusions as to how firms seek to increase their control of the environment are relevant.

It can be argued that the more munificent an environment, the greater the access a new firm will have to its resources. However, existing competitors in the same environment may make the market difficult to enter. The informal structure and small size of an entrepreneurial firm give it the necessary flexibility to cope with a high degree of environmental uncertainty. Hence, uncertain environments may see many new start-ups that seek to capitalize upon this differential advantage. These effects are shown in Figure 3.

Performance outcomes such as increased size and profitability are viewed by Pfeffer and Salancik as mechanisms which reduce uncertainty. Organizational size provides stability and increases the firm's survival potential. Munificence and interdependence continue to have the same effect they did on start-up outcomes. Although in the long run the growth of new entrants could alter the concentration dimension of the environment, it is unlikely that this impact will be noticeable in the short term. These hypotheses are summarized in Figure 4.

Pfeffer and Salancik conceptualize what we have termed residual outcomes as different types of growth vectors, which decrease the firm's dependence or increase its control of the environment. Vertical integration is a means of controlling the firm's supply and distribution environment; horizontal expansions, such as mergers or entry into new products or markets, are a means of in-

Figure 2 *A resource dependence perspective on organizational environments*

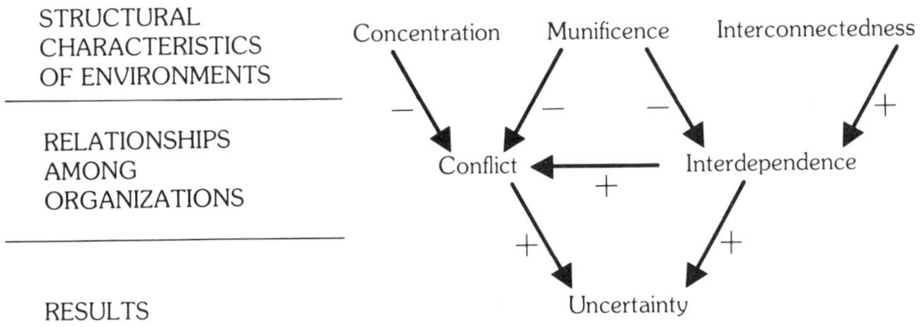

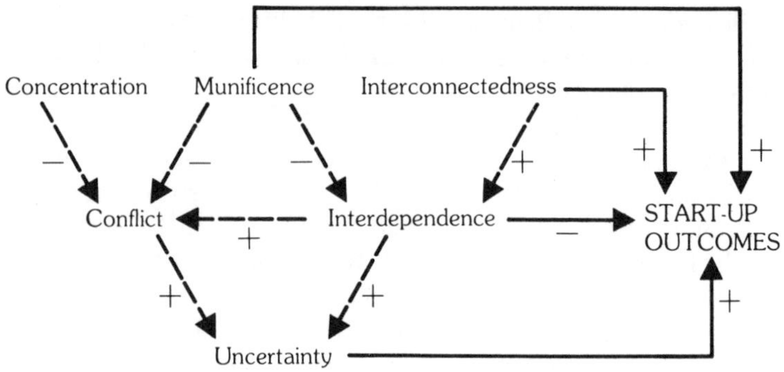

Figure 3 *The impact of the environment on start-up outcomes*

creasing power in its exchange relationship with the environment; and diversification is an attempt to spread its dependence over more aspects of the environment. Other growth vectors influence different relationships with the environment. For example, vertical integration will reduce munificence as one firm gains more control of resources; diversification will reduce interdependence. For the sake of brevity, we will not hypothesize complete relationships between these other growth vectors and the environment, particularly since these residual outcomes are not peculiar to organizations. Figures 3 and 4 are intended to be provocative rather than definitive. Alternative conceptual relationships must be considered and tested.

Pennings' (1979) theoretical approach is also derived from an ecological framework. He identifies various characteristics of urban areas as predictors of organizational birthrates. Centrality or connection with other areas, urban size, and the rate of socioeconomic change are believed to have a positive impact on entrepreneurship. The differentiation of population subgroups has an inverted U-shaped relation to organizational birthrates: The size of the organizational population reflects the available pool of potential entrepreneurs and is expected to have a positive impact on organizational birthrates; the concentration of organizations, however, constitutes a barrier to entry and has a negative impact. Finally, the availability and favorable pricing of various resources also have a positive impact on start-ups.

The theoretical perspectives discussed above are of the type we believe is necessary if research in this area is to reach its appropriate stature. Obviously, much work needs to be done. We are heartened by the opportunities, the importance of the problem, and the level of interest shared by interested parties.

Methodological concerns

There have been some significant barriers to empirical research in this area. Perhaps the most significant problem is the lack of available data.

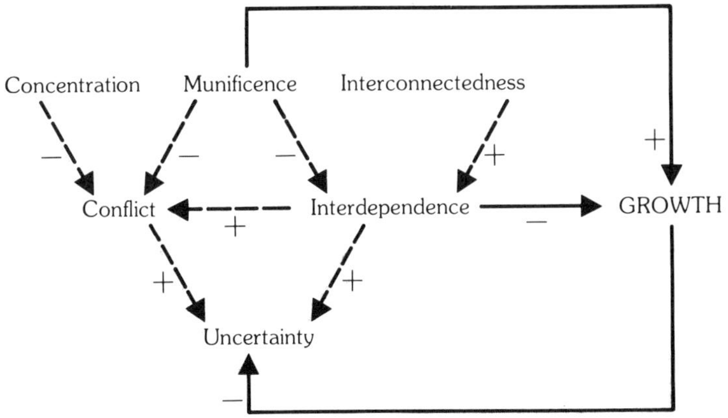

Figure 4 *The impact of the environment on growth*

To the best of our knowledge, there is no ongoing record of start-ups and failures according to geographic area and industry. The researcher is left with the formidable task of tracing the appearance and disappearance of corporate entities in annual directories such as the Dun & Bradstreet publications. This data must be adjusted for changes in name, legal status, and location. Even then the error factor is likely to be high. Pennings (1979) found 50 percent of the 1967–1975 start-ups in four-digit SIC industries to be in error when cross-referenced between Dun & Bradstreet, trade directories, and telephone directories.

A related problem is the lack of reliable data on environments. Not only is the data generally incomplete but it is often measured in ways which make different areas incomparable. Pennings intended to use 70 SMSAs as his sample, but was forced to delete over half of them because of incomplete data.

A third problem is the lack of consensus on significant environmental variables. The economist, the sociologist, the demographer, the geographer, the student of government policy, all bring a legitimate viewpoint to examination of the environment. A model with too many variables is incompatible with small data bases. A myopic viewpoint, though technically feasible, cannot control for a host of competing variables in the environment.

A final problem is distribution in time and space. Organizational births in particular industries are infrequent events and a data base may have to cover large time periods. But the larger the time period, the less satisfactory it is to measure the environment in static terms alone. Each environmental variable will change over the period of interest. This, in turn, further aggravates the problem of underspecification. Organizational births are also heavily concentrated in certain urban areas. The distribution of key environmental variables, on the other hand, is less concentrated. This raises the problem of predicting events whose distribution is quite different from those of the explanatory variables.

Methods of counteracting these problems include:

1. A more directed, comprehensive effort on the part of federal, state, and local governments at recordkeeping and distribution of statistics on entrepreneurial activity.

2. Data reduction techniques, such as factor analysis, for developing composite characterizations of an environment that has been measured in terms of a large number of variables reflecting several disciplinary perspectives. Factor analysis identifies variable subsets which are highly correlated internally. Each subset is an inferred dimension of the environment, and a composite index can be computed for the dimension based upon the variables in the subset. This results in a smaller set of predictors and reduces the problem of duplication in subsequent explanatory analyses.

3. Multivariate rather than bivariate explanatory analyses. Most studies which have used inferential statistics have been limited to bivariate statistics such as crosstabulations. On the rare occasions when a multivariate method has been used, it has been regression. Due to the concentrated distribution of the dependent variables, discriminant analysis may be more appropriate than regression. Also, the linear and loglinear regression approach must be evaluated against the threshold models where certain variables cease or start to have an influence only beyond a certain threshold level.

4. The construction of hypothetical environments. Entrepreneurs can be asked to state intentions or preferences towards various entrepreneurial activities in such environments.

5. Characterizing environments in terms of the perceptual judgments of entrepreneurs, rather than in terms of objective secondary data. It can be argued that it is not the objective aspects of the environment but rather the subjective interpretation of entrepreneurs which guides their behavior.

Suggested research topics

Examples of research topics appear below. Space limitations prohibit a more extensive treatment at this time.

1. Constructs and measurement procedures. As was noted above, the critical first step is to develop and test constructs for multiple traits and through multiple methods. Obviously, extensive theoretical development must precede this effort.

2. Subjective versus objective characteristics of environments. Research methodologies that link objective environmental characteristics to organizational start-ups ignore the crucial role of the entrepreneur's subjective interpretation. Research must address the terms in which entrepreneurs assess an environment, the relative weight they give to its different aspects, and the information they use for evaluation.

3. Impact of federal and state regulations on new start-ups. The cost of complying with state and federal regulations is an increasing component of the overall costs of start-up. How much additional cost does compliance represent? Are there circumstances where the costs or difficulties of compliance stifle the rate of innovation? The answers to these and related questions could have significant implications for policy-makers and regulatory agencies.

4. *Characteristics of incubator firms.* Incubator organizations are believed to be important breeding grounds for prospective entrepreneurs, yet little is known about the characteristics of such firms. Are large firms or small firms better incubators?

5. *Venture capital.* Venture capital research studies abound. However, little interest has been directed toward those proposals that are denied funding by venture capitalists. Do they receive support from other sources? What are their characteristics as compared to those of funded ventures? This research could be of importance to government agencies that contemplate possible interventions on behalf of viable but unfunded proposals.

6. *Inter-industry comparisons.* Research results must be assessed for different industries. Do certain factors apply to entrepreneurship in some industries but not in others?

Conclusions

In this review of the published research, a number of environmental factors that affect entrepreneurial activity have been identified and reviewed. Most of the literature is wisdom-based and observational. This tendency reflects a lack of theoretical perspective and a host of methodological difficulties associated with research in this area. Future research must be guided by more sophisticated theory and by a greatly expanded data base.

commentary/elaboration

Elaboration on the entrepreneur and his environment

Johannes M. Pennings

Overview

Environments vary a great deal in the incidence of new business start-ups. One has only to refer to well-known examples such as Palo Alto, Austin, and Boston to illustrate this point. The conduciveness of certain environments to entrepreneurship seems to hinge on the socioeconomic infrastructure as well as on the availability of resources. It is mandatory to identify these factors. However, apart from treating environment as a set of antecedents for entrepreneurship, it is also important to examine its role after a venture has materialized. The very commitment to a socioeconomic area will constrain the new venture during various phases of its life cycle. The viability of the enterprise might well be a function of location.

Part of this research was generously supported by a stipend from the Samuel Bronfman Chair of Democratic Business Enterprise at Columbia University, in the City of New York.

The entrepreneurial framework

Research on the environments for entrepreneurship has been comparatively limited. As the previous chapter demonstrates, most studies do not deal with environment in its own right but treat it instead as one of many factors to be considered in the study of entrepreneurs. Indeed, most studies of entrepreneurship have a strong individual bias, attending primarily to the resources, traits, motivation, and background of the organization makers.

This bias is most visibly illustrated in the psychological studies of entrepreneurs (McClelland 1965). Comparisons have been made between entrepreneurs and other managers (Howell 1972, Litzinger 1965). In the economic literature there is a similar emphasis on the individual as a productive factor, as the agent who disrupts the economic equilibrium by successfully introducing innovations (Schumpeter 1934). Although current statements on the theory of the firm (Cyert and March 1963) entail an organization without entrepreneurs, economists still stress that many decisions are made by individual entrepreneurs (Deeks 1976). The treatment of entrepreneurs in the literature lends further credence to the belief that entrepreneurship is essentially an individual phenomenon. Sociologists have sometimes focused on race and ethnicity which act as barriers for upward mobility and which instigate achievement-oriented individuals toward alternative avenues of social mobility (Deeks 1976).

The bulk of this entrepreneurship literature depicts the creation of organizations as a matter of individual goals, skills, motivations, and background factors. Environmental factors may impede or enhance entrepreneurial vigor, but rarely are they analyzed in a central way. One can move away, however, from the entrepreneur, his origin, and role to focus on the environment in its own right. This examination requires a well-defined notion of environment and a delineation of those attributes that render it conducive to entrepreneurship.

Our current concept of environment is rich and complex compared with the early notions of Dill (1958) and Burns and Stalker (1961), who viewed the environment as the external conditions to which a firm had to adapt. More recent authors have tried to arrive at a more specific definition. In the contemporary literature two dominant frameworks prevail, which for brevity's sake we label "resource exchange" and "population ecology" frameworks. Entrepreneurship receives rather different treatment within each of these two frameworks.

The resource exchange model

The resource exchange model is the older of the two, associated with such writers as Hirsch (1975), Pfeffer and Salanick (1978), Child (1974), Evan (1976) and Starbuck (1976). It views the organizations as entering into a transactional relationship with environmental factors because it cannot generate all necessary resources internally. Because of this dependence, the organizations actively attempt to secure control over external contingencies, to obtain a predictable, uninterrupted supply of critical resources. Interdependent organizations will coordinate with one another. They will maneuver themselves to minimize outside interference and will adjust their posture whenever environmental conditions change.

The population-ecology model

This resource exchange framework contrasts rather sharply with population ecology approaches (Aldrich 1979, Hannan and Freeman 1977, Meyer, 1978). The term "population" denotes a categorical demarcation of the environment analogous to biological "species." Firms are members of organizational populations. The key word for describing organization-environment relationships is not adaptation but selection: Organizations survive if they are isomorphic with their environment; they are doomed unless they meet the environmental test of fitness. This Darwinistic view has been slightly softened by postulating that organizations mutate at a much faster rate than their biological counterparts. Also, they can sometimes manipulate the environment for better congruence. Generally, however, this framework ascribes a fairly passive posture to organizations.

Table 1 lists some key differences between the two frameworks. While it may be difficult to draw a sharp distinction, Table 1 accentuates the relative emphasis on the impact of environmental factors.

It is obvious that Bruno and Tyebjee have adapted the first framework and treat the environment as a pool of resources upon which the entrepreneur can draw. While their array of relevant resources provides a nice checklist, it does not provide for an integral treatment of the environment. It seems also to be more appropriate for existing organizations than for new ventures. When we ask what makes some environments more prone to entrepreneurial vigor than others, the population-ecology framework is more useful.

Table 1 *Two frameworks for entrepreneurial environments*

Resource-exchange	Population-ecology
Acts of the entrepreneur are primarily volitional.	Acts of the entrepreneur are predominantly deterministic.
The entrepreneur makes strategic choices to secure the best transactions with the environment.	The entrepreneur's choices are predicated and molded by the industry.
The environment is a pool of resources which the entrepreneur selects and acquires to establish his venture.	The environment is a set of influences which selectively permit some ventures to survive.
The entrepreneur masters fate and makes strategic choices to minimize threats and exploit opportunities.	The entrepreneur is an exponent of environment and an instrument of economic development.

Urban area analysis

Within the population-ecology tradition we can empirically delineate the environment in terms of the metropolitan area. Within the urban setting we can detect an array of organizational populations with a distinct collective structure. Urbanization has resulted in a high concentration of people and organizations which enhances the creation of new organizations. According to Hawley's (1950) classic *Human Ecology*, urban areas accommodate a community of organizational populations whose growth and decline can be traced to environmental richness and the characteristics of collective structure. A territorial and functional division of labor exists within such areas. In support of urban areas as environments for entrepreneurs is the empirical observation that most new firms are created by native entrepreneurs, i.e., by individuals who were born in the city where they began their new ventures (Boswell 1973).

Naturally there are difficulties in segregating the city from its larger economy and in controlling for internal variations. For example, the impact of taxation and regulation may often exceed civic or geographical boundaries. On the other hand, the urban area might be defined too broadly, as in the case of the Standard Metropolitan Statistical Area (SMSA): Are outlying counties relevant for entrepreneurial decisions? Ironically, such areas include the city's hinterland and exclude the regional infrastructure. Elsewhere we have provided a range of solutions to these definitional problems (Pennings 1980).

Within the urban area, one might distinguish the first members of a new class of organization from those that join an existing population. When the new organization has no precedent one might refer to niche theory: Such entrepreneurs enter an ecological vacuum that others have failed to detect, thus acquiring an initial advantage over imitators. Hearing aid ventures in Minneapolis and electronics firms in the Silicon Valley of California illustrate the second type of entrepreneurship: new ventures that join an existing class of organizations. Clearly, entrepreneurship can be analyzed at the level of the single organization, or at a higher, industry level. In the latter case, entrepreneurship is merely an aspect of an industry's growth.

It is also crucial to distinguish smallness from newness. Many populations typically consist of small firms, which often enjoy a comparative advantage over large firms. Optimum efficiency (bakeries, repair shops), a specialized market segment (subcontracting, engineering services), or specialized components (car rear view mirrors) may dictate smaller size.

Populations of small firms offer low entry barriers and less serious liabilities attaching to newness. These considerations suggest that one should also consider the structure and interdependencies of industries when attempting to define the environments of entrepreneurs.

Ecological structure and entrepreneurship

The review of entrepreneurial environments revolves around ecological structure on the one hand and the accessibility of resources on the other. Resources determine the "carrying capacity" of the human ecology. The creation of new organizations can be investigated by analyzing the effects of the overall ecological structure and of industry characteristics.

Relevant aspects of the ecological structure include urban size, differentiation, and change. Thompson (1965) specifies several reasons why larger cities have a higher level of entrepreneurial activity: They have more power to influence governmental decision-making, an economy oriented toward customers rather than sources of supply, and the sheer size to ensure a steady supply of invention. Larger cities also show a greater diversity of industries, occupations, ethnic groups, and immigrants. Diversity engenders innovation and unconventionality. The proximity of multiple industries and professional groups facilitates exposure to alternative modes of behavior and permits experimental combinations of value systems.

Entrepreneurs are often viewed as recombining established ways of thinking into some novel pattern. In our research we found that industrial and occupational differentiation are strong predictors for entrepreneurial activity levels. Others have shown that ethnic groups and immigrants are important sources of entrepreneurs (Bonacich 1973). Socioeconomic change erodes social control and allows individuals to try out unconventional ideas. Peterson (1981) summarizes the mutual influence of entrepreneurship and change rather well when he writes, "Each act of equilibrating entrepreneurship has disequilibrating consequences as well."

Agglomeration economics

As mentioned before, the treatment of an entrepreneur's environment should also include aspects of that industry his venture is joining. Relevant aspects include industry size and size distribution. Carlton (1978) found that the creation of new firms is highly dependent on what he calls "agglomeration economics," defined by the number of production man hours in two- or four-digit industries. Indeed the industry can be viewed as a pool of potential entrepreneurs or a combined set of incubator firms. Shapero (1975) assumes that the founders of new firms are primarily recruited from the pertinent industry. It follows that the greater the population, the bigger the pool of entrepreneurs and the higher the organizational birthrate. Variations in start-up frequencies can thus be explained by either agglomeration economics or the favorableness of the urban environment.

Relevant characteristics

There are social and psychological reasons for expecting higher birthrates in industries with low concentration ratios. Industries and metropolitan areas with many small firms provide role models for potential entrepreneurs (Shapero 1975). They provide concrete examples of entrepreneurial feasibility and encourage a higher birthrate. Their visibility might also increase the detachment of employees from large organizations that frustrate their need for innovation and creativity (Peterson 1981).

The impact of ecological structure has to be supplemented by a review of available resources. The list in the previous chapter is very complete and can help to specify the carrying capacity of a given urban area.

The importance of resources might vary depending on the nature of the industry. For example, proximity of universities will be more important to an industry with a high population of scientists and engineers, the electronics industry for example, than to an industry with a low population of such specialists, like the primary metals or chemical industries. It is therefore not surprising that in our research, proximity of universities was an important predictor for start-ups in the electronics industries (Pennings 1980). One would also expect that industries with high transportation costs would be more sensitive to local availability of resources. Our study also showed that urban diversity might be more critical for some industries than for others. Economists have pointed to the importance of "external economics" (James and Struyk 1975), the complementarity of new firms to existing firms. Some urban areas might provide new ventures with a more favorable external economic situation.

The preceding chapter indicated that availability of venture capital might be a critical factor. Some economists believe the capital market to be efficient and national or regional in scope. However, suppliers of venture capital might discriminate against entrepreneurs outside their immediate geographic area, due to lack of familiarity. Availability of venture capital would then depend on the presence of wealthy individuals and venture capital sources. One would also expect that the concentration of the banking industry in an urban area and the consequent elimination of many small banks would increase the difficulty of obtaining venture capital. Our research supports this hypothesis: The greater the proportion of savings capital deposited in a region's four largest banks, the lower the level of entrepreneurial activity (Pennings 1980).

While the above considerations are highly speculative, some of them have found support in research that is currently in progress. This suggests that it is possible to examine the socioeconomic make-up of an urban environment in its entirety. The population-ecology framework also makes it possible to focus on the environmental antecedents of entrepreneurship without recourse to the individual motivations of founders. Entrepreneurial activity can be accounted for by assessing and evaluating a large array of socioeconomic variables.

Conclusions

In conclusion, this approach might also be defended on practical grounds. The field of public policy shows an increasing desire to foster entrepreneurial activity. In Europe, in particular, there has been a great deal of effort to improve local conditions (Bolton 1972). It is crucial to know which conditions are important to specific types of new ventures. At present there is relatively little information on these matters. Clearly, by better understanding the environment of entrepreneurs, we can begin to foster the conditions that stimulate new business start-ups.

References

ALDRICH, HOWARD E., *Organizations and Environment.* Englewood Cliffs, N.J.: Prentice-Hall, 1979.

ALLISON, DAVID, "The University and Regional Prosperity," *International Science and Technology*, April 1965.

BOLTON, J. E., *Small Firms: Report of the Committee of Inquiry on Small Firms*, (The Bolton Report). London: HMSO, 1971.

BONACICH, EDNA, "A Theory of Middleman Minorities," *American Sociological Review* 30, No. 5 (October 1973).

BOSWELL, J., *The Rise and Fall of Small Firms.* London: Allen and Unwin, 1973.

BURNS, T., and STALKER, G. M., *The Management of Innovation.* London: Tavistock, 1961.

"Capital Formation Survey of High Technology Companies" (Unpublished). American Electronics Association, 1977.

CARLTON, DENNIS W., "Models of New Business Location" (Working paper, Department of Economics, University of Chicago, 1978).

CHILD, JOHN, ed., *Management and Organization.* New York: Halstead Press, 1974.

Cooper, Arnold C., "The Entrepreneurial Environment," *Industrial Research*, September 1970.

Cooper, Arnold C., *The Founding of Technologically-Based Firms*. Milwaukee: Center for Venture Management, 1971.

Cooper, Arnold C., "Incubator Organizations and Technical Entrepreneurship," in *Technical Entrepreneurship: A Symposium*, eds. Arnold C. Cooper and John L. Komives. Milwaukee: Center for Venture Management, 1972.

Cooper, Arnold C., "The Palo Alto Experience," *Industrial Research*, May 1970.

Cooper, Arnold C., "Strategic Management: New Ventures and Small Business (Working paper, Krannert Graduate School of Management, Purdue University, 1978).

Cooper, Arnold C., "Technical Entrepreneurship: What Do We Know?" *R & D Management* 3, No. 2 (February 1973).

Danilov, Victor J., "Research Parks and Regional Development," in *Technical Entrepreneurship: A Symposium*, eds. Arnold C. Cooper and John L. Komives. Milwaukee: Center for Venture Management, 1972.

Deeks, John, *The Small Firm Owner–Manager: Entrepreneurial Behavior and Entrepreneurship: A Symposium*. Milwaukee: Center for Venture Management, 1976.

Dill, W. R., "Environment as an Influence on Managerial Autonomy," *Administrative Science Quarterly* 2 (March 1958).

Draheim, Kirk P., "Factors Influencing the Rate of Formation of Technical Companies," in *Technical Entrepreneurship: A Symposium*, eds. Arnold C. Cooper and John L. Komives. Milwaukee: Center for Venture Management, 1972.

Evan, W. M., *Organizational Theory: Structures, Systems, and Environments*. New York: John Wiley, 1976.

Galvin, Paul F., "Investigation and Start-up Costs: Tax Consequences and Considerations for New Businesses," *Taxes* 56 (July 1978).

Hannan, Michael T., and Freeman, John H., "The Population Ecology of Organizations," *American Journal of Sociology* 82, No. 5 (March 1977).

Hawley, Amos, *Human Ecology*. New York: Ronald Press, 1950.

Hirsch, P. M., "Organizational Effectiveness and the Institutional Environment," *Administrative Science Quarterly* 20 (1975).

Hoffman, Cary, "The Role of the Financial Community in the Formation, Growth, and Effectiveness of Technical Companies: The Attitude of Commercial Loan Officers," in *Technical Entrepreneurship: A Symposium*, eds. Arnold C. Cooper and John L. Komives. Milwaukee: Center for Venture Management, 1972.

Hollingsworth, A. Thomas, and Hand, Herbert H., *A Guide to Small Business Management: Text and Cases*. Philadelphia: Saunders, 1979.

Howell, R. P., "Comparative Profiles—Entrepreneurs versus the Hired Executive: San Francisco Peninsula Semi-Conductor Industry," *Technical Entrepreneurship: A Symposium*, eds., Arnold C. Cooper and John L. Komives. Milwaukee: Center for Venture Management, 1972.

James, F., and Struyk, R., *Intrametropolitan Industrial Location: The Pattern and Process of Change*. Lexington, Ky.: Lexington Books, 1975.

Litzinger, W. D., "The Motel Entrepreneurs and the Motel Manager," *Academy of Management Journal* 8, No. 4 (December 1965).

McClelland, David S., "Need Achievement and Entrepreneurship: A Longitudinal Study," *Journal of Personality and Social Psychology* 1 (1965).

MAHAR, JAMES F., and CODDINGTON, DEAN C., "The Scientific Complex: Proceed With Caution," *Harvard Business Review*, January-February 1965.

MAPES, GLYNN, "Profs and Profits: More Professors Put Campus Lab Theories to Work in Own Firms," *Wall Street Journal*, March 13, 1967.

MEYER, JOHN W., "Strategies for Further Research: Varieties of Environmental Variation," in *Environments and Organizations*, ed. Marshall W. Meyer. San Francisco: Jossey-Bass, 1978.

NAUMES, WILLIAM, *The Entrepreneurial Manager in the Small Business*, Reading, Mass.: Addison-Wesley, 1978.

PENNINGS, JOHANNES M., "An Ecological Perspective on the Creation of Organizations," in *The Organization Life Cycle*, eds. John R. Kimberly and Robert H. Miles. San Francisco: Jossey-Bass, 1980.

PENNINGS, JOHANNES M., "Organizational Birth Frequencies: An Empirical Investigation" (Working paper, Columbia University, 1979).

PETERSON, REIN, *Small Business: Building a Balanced Economy*. Erin, Ontario: Porcepic, 1977.

PFEFFER, JEFFREY, and SALANCIK, GERALD R., *The External Control of Organizations: A Resource Dependence Perspective*. New York: Harper & Row, Pub., 1978.

QUIRT, J., "Why the Future No Longer Looks So Golden in California," *Fortune*, March 27, 1978.

SCHARY, PHILIP B., "Transportation Problems of Small Business in the Pacific Northwest" (Working paper, Oregon State University, 1979).

SCHOLLHAMMER, HANS, and KURILOFF, ARTHUR H., *Entrepreneurship and Small Business Management*. New York: John Wiley, 1979.

SCHUMPETER, JOSEPH A., *The Theory of Economic Development*. Cambridge: Harvard University, 1934.

SHAPERO, A. R., "The Displaced, Uncomfortable Entrepreneur," *Psychology Today*, November 1975.

SHAPERO, ALBERT, "The Process of Technical Company Formation in a Local Area," in *Technical Entrepreneurship: A Symposium*, eds. Arnold C. Cooper and John L. Komives. Milwaukee: Center for Venture Management, 1972.

SIROPOLIS, NICHOLAS C., *Small Business Management: A Guide to Entrepreneurship*. Boston: Houghton Mifflin, 1977.

A Study of Small Business in the Electronics Industry. Washington, D.C.: Small Business Administration, 1962.

STARBUCK, W. H., "Organizations and Their Environments," in *Handbook of Industrial and Organization Psychology*, ed. M. D. Dunnette. Chicago: Rand McNally, 1976.

SUSBAUER, JEFFREY C., "The Technical Entrepreneurship Process in Austin, Texas," in *Technical Entrepreneurship: A Symposium*, eds. Arnold Cooper and John L. Komives. Milwaukee: Center for Venture Management, 1972.

THOMPSON, WILBUR, *A Preface to Urban Economics*. Baltimore: Johns Hopkins University, 1965.

VESPER, KARL H., and ALBAUM, GERALD, "The Role of Small Business in Research, Development, Technological Change and Innovation in Region 10" (Working paper, University of Washington, 1979).

Section Four

Entrepreneurship and Academia

In recent years entrepreneurship has become a boom industry on American campuses. The subject is viewed, not only as a practice to be taught, but as a promising field for academic inquiry. The chapters in this section investigate both aspects of this swelling academic interest.

Vesper provides a comprehensive review of the growth and development of entrepreneurship education programs. The growth of courses in entrepreneurship, as well as the establishment of graduate and undergraduate degree programs, testifies to rising enthusiasm. It is not surprising to find that the overwhelming majority of the course and degree offerings are found in four-year business schools. To a lesser degree, schools of engineering are also integrating entrepreneurial courses into their curriculum. It is difficult to determine if this is due to increased student demand, a growing recognition by school administrators of the need for these programs, or the lure of federal money for research, small business institutes (SBIs), and innovation centers.

While all these courses have a common base, in that they emphasize skills the entrepreneur needs to successfully identify, launch, and continue a venture, course methodologies and evaluations differ greatly. Many of the programs directly involve the students in venture initiation projects: They discover an idea and develop a business plan to meet the need they have identified. Often the student actually works with an entrepreneur, providing assistance which can be directly applied to the business situation. In a few instances, when students plan their own venture, the school helps them implement their venture design.

There is an unresolved debate on whether entrepreneurship can be taught. There seems to be little question that skills needed by the entrepreneur can be effectively communicated. But what about the motivation and the desire to leave the security of corporate or government employ and strike off on one's own? The limited experimentation in this area is inconclusive and of little value. Pioneering efforts are still needed in the evaluation and design of entrepreneurial education programs.

While entrepreneurship education has concentrated in business and engineering schools, some increasing attention to the subject has occurred at the junior college level. These programs are usually lower-level clones of those at the four-year institutions. It is unfortunate that entrepreneurship is virtually excluded from elementary and secondary school curricula. Despite the growth of the free enterprise and economic education movements across this nation, entrepreneurship has rarely been included as part of such programs. Materials are scarce, and research nonexistent. Entrepreneurial research and education offer fertile fields at all levels.

It may be that nontraditional approaches are the most effective; entrepreneurial education may become less of a classroom and more of a service activity. The typical practicing entrepreneur is unlikely to suppress his motivations long enough to graduate from a structured college program. Nontraditional delivery modes may prove to be the most effective.

In his comment on Vesper's chapter, Brown details the activities of Utah's innovation program. Loucks draws a clear distinction between management and entrepreneurship and indicates why education designed for the former is inappropriate for the latter.

The final chapter by Paulin, Coffey, and Spaulding deals with the methods and directions of entrepreneurship research. This chapter surveys past research and develops a framework for classifying the techniques used. Most earlier work reviewed in this chapter employs haphazard, contemplative, or anecdotal methods. In recent years, entrepreneurial research has become more systematic and empirical. Researchers attempt to verify theory by applying appropriate quantitative techniques.

In theoretical research, a hypothesis is established and then tested through observation or the employment of quantitative techniques. To date there has been little theory building in the area of entrepreneurship. What theory there is has been only casually evaluated.

Much of the entrepreneurial research has been done on the basis of sample surveys, in which practicing entrepreneurs have been questioned about their personalities or the processes by which they have carried on their ventures. What is being sought are the constant elements that characterize entrepreneurs and entrepreneurial events. There is always the danger in this type of research of a sample which is too small or biased.

Little use has been made of more sophisticated research techniques, such as field studies and field experimentation, although some work has been done in the former. Laboratory experiments seem to be peculiarly unsuited for entrepreneurial research, as is the case with most businesses and social sciences. Computer simulations, which have come to dominate economic research in other areas, are in their infancy as a research tool for the field of entrepreneurship. In terms of research strategy, the field of entrepreneurship lags significantly behind other disciplines.

Of particular value in this chapter is a discussion of the applicability of various research designs: the nonmethodological, the logical, the case study, the correlational and comparative, and the quasi-experimental. An understanding and use of these approaches would upgrade the level of entrepreneurial research considerably.

Data collection techniques in the field are not as underdeveloped as are strategies and designs. While much of the research is still of the armchair variety, increasing reliance is being placed upon questionnaires, tests, and interviews as a means of more precisely verifying conclusions.

Research in entrepreneurship has focused in four areas. The first of these is evaluation of individual entrepreneurs and their characteristics. The second, inquiry into the process of venture initiation, deals with how businesses get started and what determines success or failure. The third area of entrepreneurial research has been the role of the entrepreneur in society, particularly in economic development; research in this area needs to be expanded. The fourth field has been called "entrepreneurship supporting topics." Included here are discussions of entrepreneurial education, research on entrepreneurship, the relationship between entrepreneurs and consultants, and the effect of government policy on the entrepreneurial process. Peterson, Horvath and Perryman point to the dangers of narrowing research to only those questions that can be handled by sophisticated research tools. To do so would lead to an unbalanced research effort and would leave many of the most relevant questions unanswered.

What the chapters in this section present is an emerging new discipline for both research and instruction. To date, developments on both fronts have been extremely uneven. While quality is improving, there remains considerable room for advancement. Particularly crucial is the evaluation of educational programs to determine what techniques are effective and should be expanded. Without such information, entrepreneurial education is likely to be of limited value; potential and practicing entrepreneurs will continue to do without the assistance that user-based systems could offer.

The upgrading of research in entrepreneurship will allow better educational designs to be developed. It will also permit scholars to reach more definite conclusions about what causes entrepreneurship and how it can be enhanced through both public and private activities. The universal standard must be usefulness to those in the field. Entrepreneurship must be a user-based discipline or it has little justification for being a part of American academia.

chapter xvii

Research on education for entrepreneurship

Karl H. Vesper

Overview

Courses in entrepreneurship have increased greatly in number over the past decade, but relatively little academic publication has examined their effects. This chapter describes the variety of courses, in four-year schools of business and engineering, in two-year colleges, in high school and commercial programs, and in experimental government programs. Independent and dependent variables which could form the basis for more systematic study are set forth, and some particularly inviting areas for examination are suggested. Not only courses, but the entrepreneurship programs which are beginning to emerge at a few schools, require evaluation. To evaluate more effectively, researchers should track and query alumni for some years following graduation.

Growth of programs

A few schools have long offered courses on how to enter independent business. Over the past decade the number of such schools has increased by an order of magnitude, from around a dozen to over 130, as

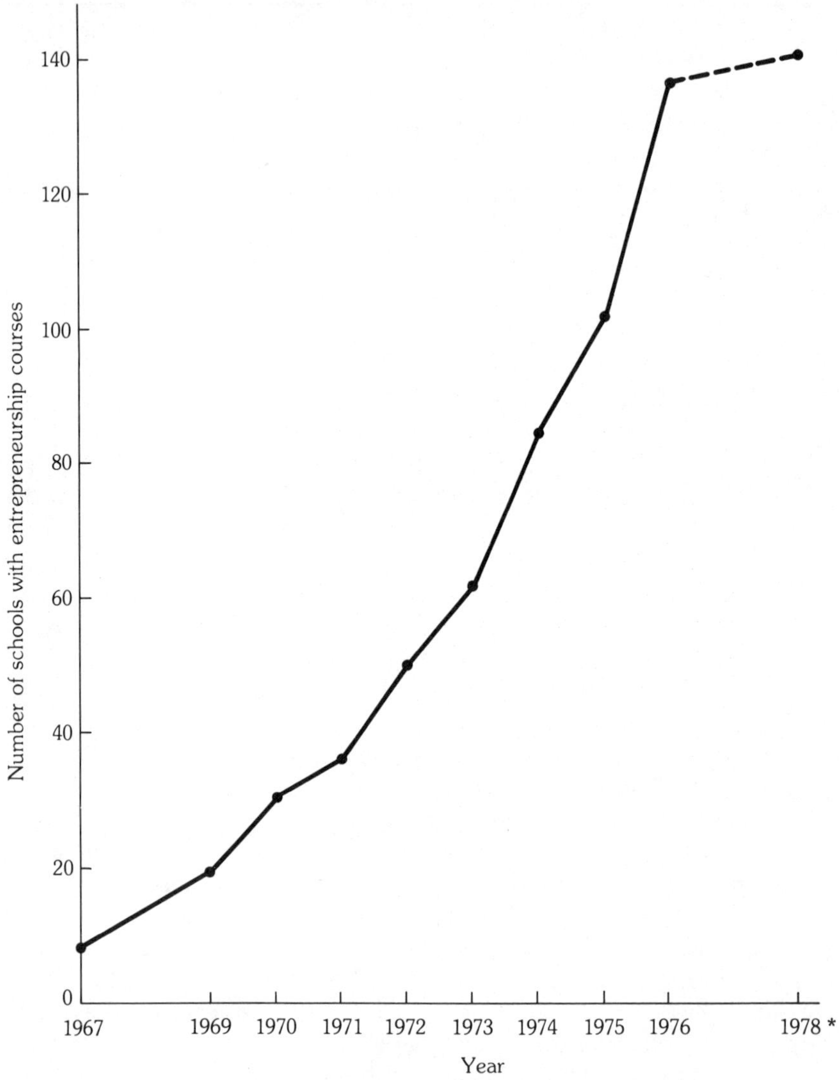

Figure 1 *Growth in number of schools with entrepreneurship courses. (1978 data may be incomplete because no complete survey was done for that year. Some additions and deletions were included in the 141 figure.)*

illustrated by the graph in Figure 1. Most of this increase has been in four-year schools of business administration, but some schools of engineering, some two-year colleges, and some commercial courses have also begun to teach about entrepreneurship. During the last ten years, some government-sponsored training programs have been designed to increase entrepreneurial activities both in the United States and abroad. There has been much commonality among these courses, but also a substantial number of variations. In aggregate these new teaching activities represent a sizable educational experiment.

It has not been a scientifically controlled experiment, and few of the results have been published. This chapter will briefly review the modest amount of publication and will then describe the great variety of educational approaches. Drawing mainly upon reports that have appeared in *Entrepreneurship Education* (Vesper 1979), I will offer comments about which teaching strategies and mechanics seem to work best, which seem to be less effective, and what directions remain to be explored.

Review of the literature

The most fully documented experiments in entrepreneurial training began with the achievement motivation work of David McClelland. Having coined the term and identified the need for achievement as an entrepreneurial characteristic, McClelland (1971) correlated this property with the proclivity to start or expand a business enterprise. The next logical step appeared to be to inculcate that property through deliberate training and to create more effective entrepreneurs by achievement motivation conditioning.

There followed a series of educational experiments, in India, in Ireland, in Washington, D.C., and in Appalachia, seeking to produce this effect. Results were somewhat mixed, but generally support the notion that achievement motivation training has a positive effect on entrepreneurial performance. Attempts were made to couple business training with achievement motivation training, and again the results were mixed. The most recent article (Miron and McClelland 1979) summarizing the work in this area indicates that the effects of achievement motivation training are stronger than those of the business training, although coupling the two enhances the benefits of both.

Two characteristics of participants in these training programs should be particularly noted. First, for the most part they were entrepreneurs already in business. The purpose of the training was to make them more effective, more hardworking, more conscientious, and more capable of better business practices. Some of the trainees were aspiring entrepreneurs; some turned out to be both "runners" and "starters" who already had their own firms but went on to start additional businesses. Miron notes that achievement motivation training appeared to enhance both ongoing and starting performance.

Second, most of the participants were from economically disadvantaged groups. They were people of limited education, mature years, and meager resources. Their businesses, with low technology, small investment, and thin margins, were concentrated largely in retail and service trades where high profits are rare and failure rates are high. Some participants in the Appalachian group had had more substantial prior business success, including manufacturing enterprises that grew to considerable size. But for the most part the experiments focused on "down and out" types of enterprise where survival, not high profit, constituted success. This choice of participants was probably based on the availability of government support, rather than greatest generalizability. Application to other types of subjects and enterprises awaits trial.

Although large numbers of college students have been receiving entrepreneurship instruction recently, on the order of 3000 to 4000 a year, publications analyzing this instruction are exceedingly scarce. Kramer (1971) said that entrepreneurship should be conveyed through marketing courses. Kierulff (1974) and Roscoe (1973) have raised questions about whether entrepreneurship can be taught at all. None of these articles contain corroborating data for the authors' claims. Lacho and Newman (1974) report on an experimental comparison of marketing classes with different degrees of entrepreneurial orientation, but they do not state which was more effective. The main source of information about university entrepreneurship courses is the compendium, *Entrepreneurship Education* (1979), in which some five dozen professors have reported over the past few years on their teaching activities in this field.

Four-year schools

With one exception (South Florida) the only four-year schools in the United States that offer courses in entrepreneurship are schools of business administration and schools of engineering. At last report 118 business schools and 28 engineering schools offered such courses. In business schools the courses are often seen as "integrative," since entrepreneurship, here defined as the start-up or take-over of a business by one or a small group of individuals, tends to involve all business functions: marketing, operations, control, strategic planning, etc. Since the course is thus a natural parallel to courses in business policy, it is most often found in business policy or management departments. Less often, the course crops up in marketing or finance departments, where some professors who teach entrepreneurship report that it is a lonely existence. Faculty of those departments typically take less interest in the subject than do members of business policy and management departments.

In engineering schools the course represents more of a departure from the established pattern. One of the more natural linkages is with industrial engineering, where students normally receive training in accounting, economic analysis, and a survey of other business subjects. There, the entrepreneurship course can serve as a convenient overview of the business firm. As can be seen in Table 1, about one-third of the engineering entrepreneurship courses are currently in industrial engineering.

Table 1 *Entrepreneurship in engineering schools*

Engineering schools	Engineering departments			Business schools
	Industrial	Mechanical	Other	
Bradley	X			
BYU		X		
Bridgeport	X			
Carnegie		X		X
Cornell			X	X
Dartmouth			X	X
George Washington			X	
Georgia Tech	X			
Iowa State	X			
Long Beach State		X		
Massachusetts		X		
MIT			X	X
NJIT	X			
Oklahoma		X		X
Rutgers		X		
San Jose State	X			X
Stanford	X			X
Texas, Austin		X		X
Texas A & M			X	
Texas Tech			X	X
Toledo	X			
Utah		X		X
Virginia			X	X
Waterloo			X	X
W. New England	X			
Totals	9	8	8	12

Creative design, another likely linkage for entrepreneurship, most frequently turns up in mechanical engineering and less frequently in chemical and aeronautical engineering.[1] To be complete, a design analysis must go beyond purely technical factors to consider economic costs, attractiveness to the user, practicality, servicing, and other "business" aspects.

It is remarkable in a way that these new courses have been able to penetrate the resistive curricula of established schools. The past few years have been fraught with many difficulties for colleges: leveling or declining enroll-

[1]Design courses in engineering schools bear striking parallels with policy courses in business schools. Both lack established esoteric methodologies and bodies of knowledge, both lack "right" answers and demonstrable "rigor," and both require divergent or creative thinking. Both tend to be disdained by more mathematically inclined faculty, who alternately charge that nobody knows anything about those subjects or that everybody knows all about them. Both tend to be difficult tracks for obtaining tenure, because publication channels and competition defy clear definition. Both are periodically reconsidered for retention in the curriculum, and it is invariably concluded not only that they are too important to be left out, but that they should be required of all students.

ments, tightened budgets, inflation, and aging faculties. Engineering schools have the added difficulty imposed by mathematical discipline of having to require long series of courses, each prerequisite to the next. It is not surprising that entrepreneurship courses have made less headway there than in business schools.

Several forces appear to have propelled these courses in spite of the resistance. Students have always liked entrepreneurship as a subject, and at leading schools like Harvard and Stanford, where the students are aggressive customers, such courses have been around for many years. In the '60s, students wanted the subject more than ever. Many schools were capitulating to all sorts of student whims, ungraded classes, black studies programs, free universities, credit for "life experience," and even new courses in entrepreneurship. To be sure, both business and engineering schools tended to have students who were politically more docile than those on other parts of campus. But faculty and administrative compliance were the trend, and these schools were not untouched by the breeze.

More important to the future of the field, however, were the impelling forces that came later. Beyond the '60s, the courses could not be dropped easily, even though the militant storm was over. Every school, it seemed, had at least a few faculty members who were sympathizers with the subject of entrepreneurship. Many schools were launching such courses, including some of the most highly regarded schools, and that gave the field a new kind of credibility.

The federal government greatly added to the momentum by putting money behind it. First, the National Science Foundation gave million-dollar grants to each of three new innovation centers, at MIT and Carnegie-Mellon engineering schools and at Oregon's business school. Each of these centers found that entrepreneurship was central to innovation. Although their overall strategies were otherwise distinct, all three introduced courses in entrepreneurship. The fourth center, started later at Utah, has continued this pattern.

Finally, the Small Business Administration introduced its "SBI" (Small Business Institute) program, which offered schools money for having their students perform consulting jobs on small local companies. Business schools were startled by the prospect of federal money with so few strings attached. Because the SBI did not pay for cases until they were completed with satisfactory results, it did not specify what schools were to do with the money. As a result of this new funding, numerous schools which before had shunned small business and entrepreneurship suddenly saw new importance and academic respectability in these subjects. (The subjects are related because most companies start small and most entrepreneurial acquisitions involve small companies.) Small business courses were promptly inaugurated all over the country, and entrepreneurship courses found a wave of new sympathy.

The SBI program has continued and been expanded. The innovation centers, although in somewhat uncertain straits, appear destined to increase in numbers but to alter somewhat in form. Entrepreneurship courses are popular, some students are starting to major in the fields, some doctoral students are writing theses on it, and professors are pursuing it as a field for research.

Course evaluation criteria

Performance criteria for the achievement motivation courses mentioned earlier were explicit: Was a new company started? Did a company survive? How much did sales, profits, and employment go up? Some dimensions were more difficult to assess: How did the behaviors of the manager change? Was the manager's need for achievement heightened?

In contrast, the performance criteria for college entrepreneurship courses have so far been much more vaguely defined. In two surveys by the author, one in 1972 (20 respondents) and another in 1974 (46 respondents), professors were asked how they thought their courses should be judged. Almost all replied that several criteria were appropriate, and no single criterion stood out as the measure of most importance. In fact, no single criterion was even selected by all respondents. The largest number in the first survey (84.2 percent) thought alumni comments should be a measure; the average among those respondents said it should be weighted as 30.0 percent of the overall rating. The largest number in the second survey (67.4 percent) thought informal comments of students should be the main criterion, and gave it an average weighting of 17.7 percent. In order of importance, these two criteria were roughly reversed in the two surveys, as can be seen in Table 2.

Other criteria that drew strong emphasis included enrollment demand, formal course ratings by students, and number of companies started by students, in roughly that order, as can also be seen from Table 2. Somewhat less emphasized as a criterion was the judgment passed on the course by visitors from industry. Examination results received least emphasis of all. In 1972, only 26.3 percent of the courses used examinations in grading.

Thus, the collective judgment of the faculty teaching entrepreneurship was that no single measure could indicate course effectiveness; that alumni comments, student comments, enrollment demand, formal student ratings, and number of start-ups should all be considered; and that examinations were not a valid yardstick.

Teaching objectives in the basic course

Most schools begin entrepreneurship instruction with a "basic" course, which typically consists of three components: (1) readings, which may include both articles and cases; (2) lectures, typically by both the instructor and outside industrial visitors; and (3) student field projects to develop written

Table 2 *Criteria by which courses should be judged*

	Survey 1 (1972)			Survey 2 (1974)		
Course evaluation criteria	**Number* indicating**	**Percent** indicating**	**Average percent**	**Number* indicating**	**Percent** indicating**	**Average† percent**
Alumni comments years later	16	84.2	30.0	26	56.5	21.6
Informal feedback from students	12	63.2	22.5	31	67.4	17.7
Enrollment demand	13	68.4	19.2	25	54.3	10.9
Formal course ratings	9	47.3	32.8	19	41.3	11.1
Number student companies started	11	57.9	30.6	19	31.3	10.1
Comments from industry observers	5	26.3	15.0	15	32.6	6.6
Examination results	1	5.2	N.A.	14	30.4	9.7
Can't be evaluated	1	5.2	N.A.	3	6.5	N.A.
Other††	2	10.5	N.A.	12	26.0	11.0

*The number of people who indicated that particular criterion had some importance.

**The fraction of respondents who indicated that criterion had some importance. The total adds up to more than 100% because most respondents checked more than one item.

†The average number of points out of 100 that respondents indicated should be allocated to that item or given that item in evaluating the course.

††Other objectives included number of students who come to recognize they should not start companies; student observed performance on projects, venture plans, and other activities; "feel" of the instructor; the comment that it was difficult to say.

venture plans. This course usually covers information about venture capital, acquisition as a mode of entry, legal forms of enterprise, how to protect ideas, tax angles, and historical examples of venturing.

In the two surveys mentioned above, teachers were asked how students were supposed to change as a result of this educational experience. It was not surprising to find a wide range of answers to the question. In 1972, general personal qualities such as dedication, courage, confidence, awareness, motivation, perspective, self-reliance, and eagerness were frequently mentioned. The question asked left it unclear whether these qualities were to be added by the entrepreneurship course or simply reinforced. Presumably, qualities like wisdom, open-mindedness, and drive would be accepted aims of education in general.

Some answers linked goals more closely to the specific subject of entrepreneurship. There was some emphasis upon conveying information about the nature of the entrepreneurial process, about the kinds of problems involved, and about the kinds of solutions that sometimes work. Some professors wanted to give students a "feel for the game, how it is played, and what the players are like," and to convince them that entrepreneurship is a credible career option.

Some professors wanted students to assess their own career options; some wanted them to analyze potential venture deals realistically. With a couple of exceptions, the respondents did not say that their students should necessarily become entrepreneurs, despite the earlier reference to start-ups as a criterion for judging courses. Rather, those who mentioned the issue wished only that students be able to evaluate their own careers with added intelligence.

In an attempt to derive more specific components from these rather general objectives, the 1977 survey asked respondents to sort them into five categories: knowledge, tendencies, habits, skills, and attitudes. Again, not surprisingly, a spectrum of answers emerged. "Knowledge" to be conveyed by the course included a number of "how to" topics: tapping information sources, performing market analysis, analyzing cash flow, preparing business plans, assessing deals, locating and working with professionals, and the more general "how to turn ideas into businesses." General technical areas in which venture-relevant knowledge should be given included: regulations, taxes, financing alternatives, market research, accounting systems, and other quantitative methods for analyzing prospective businesses. History of entrepreneurship and role demands of entrepreneurship were also mentioned. Thus, respondents did seem to feel that there was a fairly specific body of knowledge that could be taught. The low emphasis placed on examinations, however, may indicate that verification of this teaching has been a relatively low priority thus far.

Skills to be developed in the entrepreneurship course were typically those of general management. Some respondents said these should be particular to new ventures, but did not specify how this should be accomplished. The skills category was listed fourth, and was not strongly distinguished from earlier categories.

Learning objectives for the other three categories, tendencies, habits, and attitudes, overlapped among the categories and also with those of the 1972 survey. In 1977, professors were interested in reducing orientations toward a big business, reducing start-up mistakes, and suiting ventures psychologically to the entrepreneur. Both surveys emphasized similar habits and attitudes, as well as such attributes as creativity in spotting venture opportunities.

The consensus as to whether entrepreneurship can be taught was somewhat closer: 93 percent of the respondents in 1977 disagreed with the notion that it is "an art that cannot be taught." Comments on this issue were often qualified: "Certain aspects of entrepreneurship can be taught, e.g., how to investigate the feasibility of an enterprise, what pitfalls to avoid. Others can be developed, e.g., certain behavior patterns" (UCLA). Those who said it could not be taught also qualified responses, such as "It cannot be taught. It can be learned. It is a combination of personality, skill, opportunity, and perseverance" (SMU). "It [cannot be taught] now, since we don't have a theoretical base; operations research didn't have a theoretical base in 1950 either" (Michigan).

Confounding the problem of defining specific teaching objectives is the fact that they must fit individual students, and students differ in their reasons for studying entrepreneurship. Some have already decided that entrepreneurship is their career goal; others come to browse and see whether the subject will interest them; a few are simply in it for the credits and a course time compatible with their schedules. Regardless of preconceived reasons, students may shift learning objectives as the course proceeds. More perhaps than any other single course, entrepreneurship tends to be career decision–oriented; therein lies the diversity of learning objectives.

Still, it may be possible to stratify the student population and define more specific and more operational objectives for each stratum. This is a task, however, that appears to have received little systematic attention and no publication to date. Such a refinement of objectives may lead as well to a redetermination of course evaluation criteria, and to greater weight on examinations.

Independent variables and experimentation

If teaching objectives and their attainment constitute the dependent variables in entrepreneurship courses, then those aspects of the course that the school and instructor control may be regarded as the independent variables. Characteristics like location of the school and makeup of the student body may be regarded more as fixed parameters.

The main independent variables, things the school can control, may be grouped for convenience into six categories: students, teachers, readings, exercises, projects, and course support. These are listed in Table 3. Beyond these, but also controllable, are such issues as advanced course sequences, concentrations, majors, and programs in entrepreneurship. These will be taken up later.

The pattern in most entrepreneurship courses has been to admit all students who qualify by virtue of enrollment and completion of prerequisite courses. Student demand has been healthy over the past decade: Of the five dozen or so schools reporting on their programs, only one has encountered problems recruiting for the course. At a number of schools (Michigan, Nebraska, and New Hampshire, for instance), enrollment has been limited and students selected by grade averages or other outstanding qualities (Vesper 1979).

Calgary, Stanford, and Utah have all combined business and engineering students in entrepreneurship classes with no ill effects. At Calgary, the engineers performed as well as the business students despite their lack of prior business training, which perhaps raises questions about need for prerequisites. (It may be noted, at this point, that most entrepreneurs also went ahead without formal business training.) In Canada, St. Mary's and Waterloo have combined undergraduate and graduate students in the same entrepreneurship

Table 3 *Main dimensions of the teaching situation*

A. Main fixed parameters
   1. Geographical location (big city, small town, rural)
   2. Student body characteristics
   3. Weeks per term
   4. Administrative support, encouragement, initiative
   5. Presence of engineering school
   6. Availability of resources and support
   7. Weight of teaching load

B. Main dependent variables (from Table 1)
   1. Alumni comments years later
   2. Informal feedback from students
   3. Enrollment demand
   4. Formal course ratings
   5. Number of companies students start
   6. Comments from industry
   7. Examination results

C. Main independent variables
   1. Students, type and class size
   2. Instructors
   3. Readings
   4. Exercises and class format
   5. Projects, support
   6. Elective courses
   7. Programs

courses without difficulty. Perhaps most interesting, however, has been the combination of regular students and extension students, as reported at Southern Methodist. This would seem to be an ideal combination in some ways: The extension students bring professional know-how and market contacts while regular students presumably have the benefit of more business training plus greater time and career flexibility. Regrettably, there appears to have been no published study of this experiment, how it was handled, and how it has worked out.

The number of students per class ranges widely among schools, from around a dozen to over 150. Clearly, this substantially affects the cost per student of running the course. It also affects the way the course can be taught: The very large class is probably more committed to cases and lectures, while smaller ones may include more student presentations and individual interaction with the instructor. How learning and student venture output may be affected is not known. If no differences are observed, then larger classes would seem to make more sense than smaller ones. Other factors that determine class size, such as student demand, variable selectivity, school policies, and methods of determining faculty workload, also have to be recognized.

Instructors of entrepreneurship courses typically find it easy to conclude that they are doing a good job. Students usually indicate that they like the course and turn out in sufficient numbers to give it a healthy enrollment. These encouraging symptoms can obscure the need for improvement and analysis of teaching styles.

The 1977 questionnaire asked whether previous experience as an entrepreneur is essential to the teaching role. Of the respondents, 9.3 percent said it was essential, 76.7 percent said it was not, and the remaining 14.0 percent said it was a matter of degree (e.g., "it helps"). Those who said it was essential or helpful were among the 55.3 percent of respondents who said they personally participated in ventures outside school. Those who did not think it essential typically argued along the lines of one respondent, who said, "It doesn't take a hen to identify a good (or a rotten) egg." As regards the other personal dimensions of instructors, there has been no evidence to date about effect upon teaching success.

As of the 1977 survey, it appeared that only a small minority of faculty conducted research on entrepreneurship. Many appeared to do their research in other fields, while lecturers from industry, for instance, were not doing any academic research at all. The majority of entrepreneurship teachers are relatively senior faculty or established industrial people brought in as lecturers. Some courses have also been taught by beginning faculty, but none by graduate teaching assistants. Whether some of these younger faculty members decide to pursue research in entrepreneurship will be important for the future of the field. Its impact, if any, upon student learning should also be of interest.

Regardless of who is the principal instructor, most of the courses (89 percent in the 1972 survey, 87 percent in 1977) include lectures by visiting entrepreneurs and assorted professionals, such as lawyers, bankers, and accountants. The average amount of class time given over to such visitors was 24 percent in 1972 and 40 percent in 1977. Whether this substantial allocation is temporary and due to the newness of the field, or whether the outsiders are a permanent, essential ingredient would seem to have important implications, especially for schools in non-metropolitan areas where vastly fewer such people are available. Experience with outsiders has not been uniform: Some work out well while others "bomb." If a choice of visitors is therefore essential, then non-metropolitan schools may face a permanent and serious handicap.

There may be remedies for the inconsistent success of visitors. Speakers can be briefed more fully in advance. Students can write out questions in advance, so they will draw out more helpful information. Other members of the faculty, with venture experience or at least with different perspectives on the subject, can be brought in as well, though there are limitations on their time.

More promising, perhaps, especially for non-metropolitan schools, is the prospect of bringing in videotapes or movies of outsiders. Several schools, notably Babson, Cleveland State, Harvard, Indiana, South Carolina, and Western Ontario, have been collecting such performances. Although no sharing has yet been done on an appreciable scale, this would seem to be most worthy of trial in the future. One or more schools could work out an experimental course design and a strategy for selecting, utilizing, and evaluating "canned" performances. This would perform a most valuable service for other schools, particularly those with a shortage of nearby entrepreneurs. Purdue presented a recorded speech by a venture capitalist and stopped it at preselected points for class discussion. Response was reported as "minimal," but it took place during the last class meeting before vacation.

Books like those of Baty (1974), Baumbach and Mancuso (1975), Dible (1971), and Weaver (1973), selected periodical readings, and booklets from the SBA and Bank of America were used by roughly half of those responding to the 1977 survey. Since the incentive of prospective royalties for improved text materials can be expected to grow with the field, it seems likely that better readings will automatically emerge, embodying new information from research.

The most widely used casebook at present (Liles 1974) is virtually the only one to deal exclusively with entrepreneurship, as opposed to small firm management. Although it is well regarded, this six-year-old book is due for revision or replacement. Shorter cases and cases dealing more fully with the problems of entrepreneurship might also be well received. The Liles book contains only 15 cases. A larger number might better represent the stages, the variety, and the problems of venture development. Shorter cases might permit more of them to be used in a term and thereby broaden students' exposure to the field.

Tulane puts the reports of prior students on reserve in its library. This is particularly helpful for students working on projects. By replacing these examples with stronger ones selected over time, the quality can be progressively enhanced.

Exercises in the entrepreneurship courses have taken a variety of different forms. The University of Pennsylvania, for instance, assigned five written analyses of cases selected to illustrate main areas of learning; the University of Rochester required written assignments on all cases. The University of Virginia required students to prepare written abstracts, as well as oral presentations, on other course readings. Students may also write summaries of the main lessons learned from the course; Harvard, Miami (Ohio), and St. John's have all used variations of this approach. Written final examinations are often used. At the University of Washington a typical two-hour final includes one case to be analyzed plus one essay question based upon the readings, lectures, and other parts of the course. Students seem to put more effort into the course if told they will have to take a final. A drawback to all these written exercises is the substantial faculty time required to read them. It therefore seems unlikely that these will increase in volume over time.

Not more work for the instructor, however, is a venture search exercise used at the University of Washington in which each student comes each week with at least one new venture idea. These can be recorded on a ditto master passed around at the start of class and copies can be run off for all students. Repeating this week after week may help students develop the habit of looking for business opportunities; exchanging the ideas can expose them to a variety of thoughts. The lists can serve as a basis for class discussion about sequences for putting ideas into action and for brainstorming in search of still more ideas.

Role playing can be used in many ways. At Purdue, the instructor plays the role of venture capitalist and students take the roles of entrepreneurs trying to work out financial support. At Harvard several students are given different information and different roles in a buyout: One is the owner, another a relative, another a buyer, and so forth.

Other types of simulation have included "in-basket" exercises (Purdue), computer modeling of new ventures (Long Island), and "live cases" (USC) where a real entrepreneur submits his problem and attends the class to have students advise him as consultants. Going one step further, some schools send students out into the field to work with entrepreneurs and other participants in new ventures. At Wisconsin the class has used field trips, has sent students to meetings where company founders compare notes, and has had students make loan proposal presentations to bankers. Several schools allow students to work with entrepreneurs on SBI projects. Still other schools require students to present new venture designs to venture capitalists.

Venture design projects

Venture design projects are a major component of entrepreneurship courses across the country, but the setting in which projects take place, the kinds of assignments given, the way projects are run, and the way they are wrapped up at the end of the term vary substantially. A few schools, notably those with NSF Innovation Center financing, provide substantial support for students on their projects. MIT has an Invention Laboratory where resources are available for making and testing prototypes. Carnegie-Mellon and Utah offer similar support. Oregon has drawn ideas from independent inventors for products that students might analyze and seek ways to exploit. Out of thousands of ideas over the past six years, very little real promise was found, however; this appears to have been an experiment that did not succeed. The other Centers may be faring somewhat better, but evaluation is not yet complete. Utah's Center is just beginning. MIT's is concentrating more upon selected industries to the exclusion of others. Oregon's Center appears destined for termination in the near future. It differed from the other Centers in concentrating upon ideas from independent inventors. Unfortunately, the proportion of chaff was high. The other centers, focusing upon ideas from within the university, from industry, and from independent entrepreneurs, have found a much higher percentage of "winners."

Entrepreneurship courses at other schools are aimed to a lesser extent at direct industrial results than are the innovation centers. The aim of their projects is primarily educational, and an actual industrial success is regarded as a happy surprise.

The projects begin with various options from which the students choose. Washington offers three: (1) design of a new venture, (2) writing the detailed history of an actual ambitious start-up, and (3) helping an entrepreneur outside school get started. Under the new venture design the student may work alone or with a team, may design a very humble enterprise and actually do some business, or may design a more ambitious venture, write a prospectus, and present it to a venture capitalist off-campus. Waterloo uses three projects per term. At Babson and Mount Mary, the whole class works together on one actual enterprise, somewhat like Junior Achievement.

Most schools require students to search out their own ideas for projects. A few students enter classes with ideas already in mind. Utah and Bridgeport assign ideas to the students; MIT offers students a list of needs; Berkeley brings in ideas from the Young Presidents' Organization. Any approach seems to have drawbacks. Few ideas have real merit, and few of those people who happen to discover or possess them are willing to give them away. Faculty lack time and occasion to find them on their own; most are not in working contact with the markets where they might become aware of promising needs. Students typically have even less likelihood of encountering and recognizing market holes. If they spend the term searching, they have little time left for the project. Students may perform their idea searches in advance of the project course, as will be discussed later. But the problem seems likely to remain a major one.

Once the project is underway, the learning experience and level of performance can be monitored and guided in several alternative ways. At Northwestern students were required to prepare a PERT chart for development of the venture design by the end of the first week of school. Intermediate review has been accomplished through submission of intermediate written reports (St. Louis), a series of oral "show and tell" sessions (Oklahoma), and scheduled conferences with the instructor (New Orleans). At least two schools have experimented with videotaped presentations of projects (Bridgeport and Humboldt State). Another has made extensive use of alumni, assigning one to each student project team as off-campus coach (USC).

Final presentations of student projects are sometimes made in class, other times at the offices of venture capitalists (Texas, Washington) or other businessmen and entrepreneurs (Fairleigh Dickinson, USC). A dress rehearsal may be required (Long Island), an advance report in the form of a mini-proposal (New Orleans), or a summary (Oklahoma State). Panels are sometimes brought in to read these advance reports and hear an oral presentation (Bradley, Long Island, New Orleans). Typically, an effort is made to salt the panel with industrialists who are familiar with the particular lines of business involved (Northwestern). Visitors may also be asked to help grade the projects (Texas Tech, Worcester). One school (Carnegie-Mellon) has given prizes to the best team projects.

Follow-up has thus far not been attempted at most schools, because no resources for doing so have been available. An exception are the Innovation Centers funded by NSF, which have pursued patents, licenses, and actual start-ups for some of the student projects. Other schools have considered setting up venture capital funds that might be used to finance some of the student enterprises (Babson, Baylor). An alumnus at Purdue offered to back a group of students for one year to get a business going. At last report the students still had a going concern. They also started a company that did not continue. A hurdle for this approach may be motivating faculty to midwife the start-ups. Working with students to help them learn may be different than working to help them make money. The lack of tangible profit possibilities for the teacher may be a disincentive. A tangible profit motive may represent a conflict of interest and may inspire a negative reaction from colleagues and "the system." The possible gain for students, faculty, and school (Grinnell College more than doubled its endowment by investing a modest amount in an alumnus' venture, Intel Corp.) would seem to justify some effort at solving this problem.

Series of courses

Several schools have moved beyond the basic entrepreneurship course described above to a series of courses in the area. These may be divided into two types: Some are "general" courses because they deal with total enterprises; others are "specialized" because they concentrate on selected functions or activities in entrepreneurship. We will consider five general courses in entrepreneurship.

First is the course described above which combines readings, cases, lectures, and projects. Second is one that concentrates on content and eliminates the project. Such a course is now being explored at Babson. Here students will learn what entrepreneurship is all about, size it up as a potential career, practice analytic skills particularly applicable to new ventures, and absorb information on legal aspects, taxes, venture capital, strategy options, etc. It could also provide opportunity and encouragement for seeking out a venture idea that can be pursued after the course as a project. Thus the student would not be crowding the idea search and venture design into the same term. A third type of course, devoted exclusively to project development, might follow this.

A fourth type of general course might not be regarded as an entrepreneurship course proper, because it treats the management of ongoing small businesses, rather than start-up or acquisition. Because most new enterprises begin small, however, management of a small ongoing business is central to virtually every entrepreneur. By studying existing small businesses, the entrepreneurial student may develop clearer scenarios for "projecting" (to use the term of Collins and More 1970) an enterprise. We might, in fact, explore whether students find it more beneficial to study small business management first and then entrepreneurship or to follow instead the actual chronology of enterprises and examine entrepreneurship before small business management.

Small business management itself may be split up into many areas: by functional areas (marketing, finance, and so forth) and by type of business (real estate, retailing, manufacturing, and so forth). Adjunct to the management courses may be consulting courses. These are usually Small Business Institute (SBI) activities, paid for by the SBA directly or through a local Small Business Development Center.

A fifth type of general course combines entrepreneurship and small business management. Some of the best selling texts (Broom and Longenecker 1979, Baumback and Lawyer 1979) have used this approach, which is especially prominent in two-year colleges. As the subject of entrepreneurship expands, however, it does not seem probable that these combination courses will lead the way.

Specialized courses would seem more likely to be in the forefront. Some examples which have been tried so far include the following:

1. Ideation and Invention
Dartmouth (engineering), MIT (engineering), Oregon.

2. Concept Evaluation (Feasibility Analysis)
Georgia Tech (engineering), Oregon.

3. Concept Development and Trial
MIT (engineering), Oregon, Utah (engineering), York.

4. Innovation Management
Oregon, Texas A & M.

5. Internal Entrepreneurship
UCLA, Wharton.

6. Venture Finance
Baylor (planned), Long Island, Montana, Oregon.

7. New Venture Marketing Strategies
Baylor (planned).

8. Venture Accounting and Taxation
Baylor (planned).

9. Economics of Entrepreneurship
Hawaii.

10. Tycoon History
Wisconsin.

These courses can be grouped into three types: The first three are associated with product invention and development and have been taught primarily in engineering rather than in business schools. This is not surprising, but it raises an important question for entrepreneurship education. If product development is an important part of entrepreneurship, should business schools ignore the teaching of that subject? Engineering, where the subject is normally treated, could in a sense be treated as a functional area of business, like accounting and marketing, but it contains such a large body of esoteric knowledge that business schools have found it easier to leave alone. It might be worth thinking about how this tradition could be altered. For their part, some engineering schools have undertaken to teach courses in entrepreneurship.

Categories 4 and 5 on the list are in fact concerned with managing companies in such a way as to encourage product development. These courses are somewhat off the track of entrepreneurship, since they deal with the management of ongoing companies, typically large ones at that. Internal and independent entrepreneurship share a certain orientation toward innovation, so they can be mutually supportive in a program. More importantly, perhaps, many students are likely to be interested in both. How much entrepreneurial "technology" may be transferred between the two is a question research may seek to answer.

Courses 6 through 10 on the list, normally taught in different departments, emphasize functional specialties with an emphasis on entrepreneurship perspectives. They suggest that a whole curriculum could be built around entrepreneurship. After all, it was the business success of law students taught by the case method that inspired Harvard to teach business in a similar fashion. If students can learn to be effective business professionals by studying law materials, perhaps they could also reach that goal by studying entrepreneurship materials.

Programs in entrepreneurship at four-year schools

A few schools have now begun to offer concentrations or majors in entrepreneurship, some at the undergraduate and some at the graduate level. Possible course combinations and some of the programs already announced appear in Table 4. This display may do injustice to the programs of some schools, but illustrates nevertheless the major options. Some schools with concentrations in small business or innovation, where entrepreneurship is only a part of the program, have had to be left out. The table lists only those courses already in existence and does not attempt to anticipate courses which may be created in the future.

No two schools at present use the same combinations to form their program. Also, some courses offered at schools without programs have yet to be incorporated into the schools with programs, so no school has a "complete set" of existing courses at this time. The efficacy of various combinations will provide interesting future study.

Entrepreneurial instruction may also be introduced in other established courses of the curriculum. At present this does not appear to be happening. In addition to cutting existing material, the faculty for those courses might have to reorient their thinking, and in a direction that has been lowly regarded by most schools. (In the 1972 survey over 75 percent responded that entrepreneurship was not regarded by colleagues as academically respectable. In 1977 the fraction was 65 percent.) This too could change in the future.

Research activities could make a large difference. More research will introduce more competition for places on programs, for grants, for intellectual excellence. This in turn should bring greater respectability, as well as clearer ideas of education goals and methodology. School performance in this competition will depend upon a number of factors. Interested faculty members

Table 4 *Formal multi-course programs in entrepreneurship*

Course types	Babson	Baylor	North-eastern	Oregon State	SMU	USC	Wharton
Level of major or concentration	U	U	B	U	B	B	B
General courses							
1. Basic entrepreneurship	B	B	B	U	B	B	B
2. Content only course	U				B	B	G
3. Design project course	U		B		B	U	
4. Small business management			B		B		
5. S.B.I. project course		U				B	G
6. Combination course		U					
Specialized courses							
1. Ideation and invention							
2. Concept evaluation (feasibility)					B		
3. Concept development and trial							
4. Innovation management							B
5. Internal entrepreneurship							B
6. Venture finance	U	U	B		B		
7. New venture marketing		U				G	
8. Venture accounting and taxes		U					
9. Economics of entrepreneurship							
10. Tycoon history							
11. Other							U
Totals	5	6	8	3	6	8	9

Key:
U = undergraduate
G = graduate
B = both undergraduate and graduate

and supportive administrators will be crucial. Location in a highly active industrial area, especially high-technology areas like Los Angeles, Boston, and San Francisco, will be an advantage. Lighter teaching loads will allow more time for conducting research and experimenting with new types of courses. Student interest and capabilities may also prove to be an important variable. Schools with part-time students who hold industrial jobs may have an advantage, at least in spawning ventures. The presence of engineering schools may be an advantage. Administrative attitudes toward faculty participation in start-ups should be examined for their effect on productive scholarship.

Courses in two-year schools

Data on programs outside four-year schools is much more sketchy. Courses that combine start-up and small business management topics have long been widespread among two-year colleges, but courses focused entirely on business entry or entrepreneurship have not. Recently, Diablo Valley College (Pleasant Hill, California), Sinclair Community College (Dayton, Ohio), Southwestern Oregon Community College (Coos Bay), and Westchester Community College (Valhalla, New York), have expressed interest in entrepreneurship courses, but have published no reports of how their programs have fared.

If an appreciable number of two-year schools entered seriously into entrepreneurship instruction, it could be a major event for the field, because such schools are so numerous. They also typically serve a different student population than do four-year schools, one that tends to achieve less academically but one that has close ties to industry, since many community college students hold jobs off-campus and attend school only part time. Entrepreneurship instruction might produce different results in these schools than in four-year schools, and researchers might profitably track their results.

Courses in high schools

Still less is known of entrepreneurship activities in high schools, with two exceptions. One is the Junior Achievement program in which students start and operate small ventures of the handicraft type under industrial sponsorship. The second includes programs that aim to indoctrinate students in support of capitalism. No published studies document the extent to which these programs enhance entrepreneurship. If academic course work in entrepreneurship per se is also offered in secondary schools, it is not reported.

Nonacademic educational programs

Outside formal academic programs, many organizations have to varying degrees become involved in entrepreneurship education. The SBA sponsors publications and courses; *Entrepreneur Magazine* and Entrepreneur Press (Donald Dible) provide short programs on how to start firms; chambers of commerce overlap to some degree the function of schools. The Canadian Centre for Entrepreneurial Studies in Toronto, the Center for Entrepreneurial Management (now part of the American Management Association) in Worcester, Massachusetts, and the Entrepreneurship Institute in Columbus, Ohio, all non-profit, offer educational programs as well as publishing and organizing conferences. Another proposed center, the Enterprise Institute of Washington, D.C., would be a "university for entrepreneurs." The Institute for Innovation and Development of Schenectady, New York, has proposed a series of seminars on "how to start your own high potential venture." None of these has as yet published reports on the methodology used or results achieved.

At least two non-degree residential schools have specialized in entrepreneurial training. Burklyn, a business school in Vermont, was characterized by one of its students as a part of "the new entrepreneur hand-holding and cheerleading industry." Offering one-day seminars, one-weekend programs, and a six-week course ($5000), the program used case studies, lectures, and exercises in a combined program of business training and "human potential" activities. At last report, the school was in financial difficulty, not because of operation costs, but because of losses on commodity speculation by its managers. It was scheduled for relocation to more modest quarters in San Francisco as soon as its Vermont estate could be sold.

The School for Entrepreneurs operated by the Tarrytown House Executive Conference Center in New York has offered both a two-weekend program ($475) and a correspondence course ($175). The advertising literature suggests that the course focuses on self-assessment and business planning. As described in a magazine article, the program includes encounter sessions, personality tests, psychological games, role playing, and venture designing and evaluation. For the Tarrytown School as for Burklyn, the only published information about results is anecdotal.

Other programs

In the United States and in other countries, the government has supported a further variety of training programs for entrepreneurs. The East-West Center in Hawaii has conducted classes for aspiring entrepreneurs, particularly in Southeast Asia. Sweden and India have sponsored entrepreneurship programs. Again, published results appear to be nonexistent.

Future potential

This discussion has primarily been confined to what has been done so far in the field of entrepreneurship education and to programs that might be tried. It is to be expected that teachers will push beyond prior experiments to devise fresh ideas, some of which will represent significant departures from what has been tried so far.

Training experiments should be part of the future territory for exploration, but only part. Some mental processes can certainly be aided by education, but most entrepreneurship in the real world takes place without any such training: Key entrepreneurial ingredients combine to form an opportunity, and not as the result of any deliberate seeking or training.

Future entrepreneurial education might go beyond simply mental programming to find ways of bringing other key ingredients into combination as well. These include resources (some entrepreneurship programs are recruiting venture capital), contacts (some are exploring ways to arrange "networking"), technical know-how (school programs have trouble with this and suggest industrial experience following graduation), customer orders (these a would-be entrepreneur can deliberately pursue), time to devote to the venture project (probably least available to entrepreneurs who have most of the other ingredients) and, most important, a viable business idea (some programs require likely venture concepts as a prerequisite for admission). The NSF-sponsored Innovation Centers have tried some approaches, with mixed results. But the effort applied in this combinatory field has been small, and it seems reasonable to hope that significant breakthroughs lie ahead. If they are, it should not require statistical tests to measure the effects. They should be dramatic.

Substantial departures from traditional school patterns may be needed. For instance, students and faculty might intermingle more closely with industrialists who have market contacts and technical know-how. Faculty incentives and school policies will have to be reconsidered if the faculty are to work on such projects.

The objectives of entrepreneurship programs will need continual review. Are the courses and related activities to be aimed at short- or long-term results, or both? What should be the incentives for the school itself? How far from conventional ways of teaching and operating should a school go? Not all schools will find the same answers; private schools and public schools may reach different conclusions. Credit and non-credit programs may differ.

Since alumni assessments were consistently advocated as the main criterion by which courses should be judged, it would seem logical that such assessments should be systematically assembled and employed to improve the courses. More dramatic results might be associated with entrepreneurship programs than with single courses, since the latter represent such a small fraction of college study. But the feedback might also suggest which course formats and teaching techniques were more effective, even in single courses. One way to obtain this feedback might be to work through alumni offices, possibly on a statistical sampling basis. Alternatively, faculty members teaching such courses might form a collaborative consortium, gathering data on their respective courses and co-publishing comparative results. Clubs formed by alumni of the courses themselves might also assist such a project. Harvard now has a club of this sort in operation; Babson and USC are working in that direction. Particularly successful alumni may even see fit to finance the effort. Results like that would be the most positive feedback of all.

commentary/elaboration

Elaboration on education in entrepreneurship

Kenneth E. Loucks

Research on education for entrepreneurship is at a stage that may be compared to home remedy medicine or alchemy. The effort is still to develop meaningful concepts.

Given the current research base, the best that can be achieved by educators is a change in perception: Students can be made aware of what entrepreneurship entails; what characteristics and role demands attach to the entrepreneur; what impact social, economic, and political environments have on the new venture. The vast majority of entrepreneurship courses are taught to full-time students at colleges and universities. Practicing entrepreneurs, without the benefit of these courses, must learn by doing and learn by mistakes. Some schools are attempting to reach the practicing entrepreneur through continuing education, professional development, and business outreach programs, but much more needs to be done in this area.

One possible difficulty in reaching practicing entrepreneurs is that they are usually not ready to seek information until a problem arises. Even then there is a tendency to seek only a specific solution and not the general concepts or techniques that could have prevented the problem from occurring. Perhaps trade associations, chambers of commerce, and industrial development commissions could be more effective in this area.

Regardless of venue, we must better understand the educational needs of entrepreneurs and the most effective means of disseminating the required information. Once a better understanding has been achieved, objectives for entrepreneurship courses can be more clearly defined. Many of the existing courses accord with the needs and objectives of the university or the individual professor, not those of the student.

The stated objectives for an enterprise often differ dramatically from the objectives of the enterprise creator. Course objectives are more often stated for the benefit of deans, senates, boards of trustees, and academic councils than to clarify the intentions of the academic offering the course. Thus, stated goals may feature regional, national, or international economic development considerations ("to increase the supply of entrepreneurs"). They may echo the university's traditional pursuit of truth ("to understand the origins, environment, motives, and behavior of those who create economic enterprises"). They may feature social and economic benefits ("to minimize the incidence and social and economic consequences of new business failures"). Or they may be stated in terms of program objectives ("to convey skills and knowledge relevant to the creation of new enterprises").

If the objectives of the teachers were examined, one might find them attempting to advance particular values ("small is beautiful," or "entrepreneurship is a good way of life"). They may be attempting to legitimize their own career paths ("to convey an understanding and appreciation of the role and function of the entrepreneur"). They may reveal personal motivation ("to escape the demands of a discipline group," or "to make a mark, to create something new," or "to legitimize extracurricular activities"). In short, the personal objectives of the instructor may be quite different from the published objectives of the course.

Many of the professors who are starting entrepreneurship courses in universities are those who were "born over the store" or who have themselves been entrepreneurs. They have something to profess. At the same time their commitment to inquiry, research, and validation may not match that of newer colleagues who come straight through the educational system with strong orientations toward research and publishing. If the field is to advance, a successful merger of these orientations will be required, not unlike the management succession process faced in all new enterprises. Founders usually have different skills and orientations than those who manage the enterprise later on. However, if successors lack the entrepreneurial spirit, the venture ultimately stumbles.

Among the literature used in entrepreneurship courses, there appears to be a heavy dominance of opinion-based, small-sample generalizations. It is very difficult to say that a body of knowledge exists in the field. Not only is there lack of agreement on its boundaries and definition, but there is also a lack of consistency in the components. Consequently, what is taught varies from the simplistic to the abstract, and from general concepts to specific techniques.

Entrepreneurship is fundamentally different from, but not independent of, management. Professors teaching in this area are attempting to use techniques derived from management curricula, techniques developed to optimize the use of time, money, and people. Entrepreneurs face the same constraints but in quite different ways. They attempt to optimize the personal use of time, which is finite and defined by a life span. Professional corporate managers are more concerned with the time value of money and are less constrained by the life span of owners since it does not coincide with the life span of corporations. Entrepreneurs are constrained by personal resources and frequently attempt to minimize the amount of capital necessary to establish a profitable venture, whereas managers attempt to maximize the amount of capital gainfully employed. The people constraints are also quite different. Entrepreneurs are individuals (occasionally small groups) who must make decisions without the aid of internal specialists. As generalists, entrepreneurs must avoid overspecialization. Professional corporate managers are either functional specialists themselves or specialists in the use of specialists.

However inadequately these differences may have been expressed above, the fact remains that, for the entrepreneur, the business is more a person than an economic activity. Innovation and management are fundamentally different activities and require fundamentally different tools and techniques. Entrepreneurship cannot continue to be bought with the tools and techniques of professional management.

commentary/elaboration

Commentary on entrepreneurship education

Wayne S. Brown

Overview

This comment addresses technical innovation and the utilization of universities.

Importance of technical innovation

This presentation is based on two assumptions: (1) The high-technology business is an asset to our country, and (2) the ability of inventors-entrepreneurs to establish and develop technology-based firms is a critical component of technological innovation and, indeed, of the free enterprise system. The American inventor-entrepreneur has been almost unique in his ability to create successful technology-based enterprises. The Joint Senate and House Hearings on Small Business and Innovation reported in 1978: "Simply stated, an individual who has made a discovery wants to reap as many of the benefits of commercialization as possible, and the vehicle for maximizing these benefits is a new business" (*Small Business and Innovation* 1978). The report cites an important American Electronics Association study:

The results of the study of this technology industry likewise reflect a similar pattern: the new and small enterprises with new innovative products demonstrated higher rates of growth, job creation and other contributions to the U.S. economy in terms of overall growth, taxes paid and export sales. (Small Business and Innovation *1978*)

The Charpie Report of the Senate Small Business Joint Hearings Report makes the following statements:

In our overall deliberations, we came to some general conclusions about the kind of total environment that seems to encourage the creation of new technological enterprises. Included in this environment are . . . technologically oriented universities, located in an area with a business climate that encourages staff, faculty, and students to study and themselves generate technological ventures. (Senate Small Business Joint Hearing Record 1978)

Role of universities

Universities played a significant role in the establishment of the high-technology business centers along Route 128 near Boston and in Santa Clara County in California. The universities in these areas provided an innovative research atmosphere and trained engineers, scientists, and managers capable of building new companies around emerging technologies. Indeed, many of the technical concepts that made the businesses possible originated in the research laboratories of the universities. Frederick Terman, who served successively as Chairman of Electrical Engineering, Dean of Engineering, and Provost of Stanford University, deserves much of the credit for establishing an environment conducive to technical innovation and entrepreneurship around Stanford. By providing encouragement and limited assistance to such firms as Hewlett-Packard and Varian Associates, he helped establish the nucleus for what was to become Silicon Valley. As investors achieved success in such businesses, financing became available for other new ventures. Capable people were attracted to the area, and today its climate for high-technology business is unequaled anywhere else in the world.

The National Science Foundation has sponsored four Innovation Centers across the country, at Carnegie-Mellon, Massachusetts Institute of Technology, the University of Oregon, and the University of Utah. The Oregon Center has been closed and its activities transferred to Baylor University. The University of Wisconsin Extension will begin a similar program.

Case study of the Utah Innovation Center

The newest of the four NSF-sponsored Innovation Centers, at the University of Utah, emphasizes new business start-ups. Prior to the establishment of the Center, the College of Engineering produced several successful spin-offs that employed significant numbers of people in the Salt Lake City area. Some of these spin-offs include:

Kenway, Inc., founded in 1964 as a contract engineering firm. The firm now dominates the market for high-rise automated warehouse systems, employs 800 people, and has annual sales in excess of $100 million. It was recently purchased by the Eaton Corporation.

Terra Tek, Inc., which grew out of a rock mechanics research program at the University. The company specializes in performing tests for the oil and gas industry, the geothermal industry, and government agencies. It determines the properties of rock samples under high pressure like those encountered deep in the earth.

The Drilling Research Laboratory, a wholly-owned subsidiary of Terra Tek. The Laboratory operates a unique facility in which a full-scale oil well drilling rig performs drilling tests within a large pressure vessel. The apparatus can simulate the field conditions encountered in an oil well 20,000 feet deep. Terra Tek has annual sales of $8 million and employs 160 people.

Native Plants, Inc., a partially-owned subsidiary of Terra Tek. This biology-based company is concerned with reforestation and reclamation of lands damaged by natural or man-made events, such as mining, that have resulted in erosion or other deterioration of the original plant life.

Evans and Sutherland Computer Company, originated in 1968. The company is a leading producer of computer graphics and simulation systems. It is located adjacent to the campus in University Research Park and has effective ties with the University. This company employs 350 people and has sales in excess of $20 million per year.

Ceramateck, Inc., founded in 1976 to commercialize a ceramic element developed for use in a high performance sodium-sulfur battery.

Motion Control, Inc., a biomedical engineering firm. The company is developing sophisticated products which are largely a fall-out from sponsored research projects on the campus. These include an advanced artificial arm controlled by the patient's natural nerve impulses and an iontophoresis device that permits a physician to introduce drugs into the body without breaking the skin.

The Utah Innovation Center has been established to further enhance the formation of new high-technology business start-ups. Its characteristic features are:

1. Joint conduct of the program under the auspices of the Colleges of Engineering and Business.

2. Program objectives modeled after the new venture requirements of the professional venture capital industry.

3. A program focused exclusively on ventures with a reasonably high level of technology.

4. Emphasis on utilization of university-developed technology, with target technologies identified to parallel the specific strengths of the University's research program.

5. Strong encouragement of start-up ventures in preference to licensing or other alternatives.

The Center's activities are organized into the following program areas: (a) education program, (b) innovation projects, (c) new enterprise development projects, (d) research on the innovation process, and (e) public affairs.

Education program

The objectives of the education program are to equip students with the background, skills, and experience to generate innovative ideas, develop them into useful products, and establish and operate successful businesses. A two-quarter course sequence, offered jointly through Engineering and Business, is entitled "Innovation and Entrepreneurship." Student teams are assigned the task of developing business plans to manufacture and market products selected by the faculty from concepts presented to the Center. Lecture sessions are devoted to engineering and business principles pertinent to the products. A number of guest lectures are given by successful technical entrepreneurs.

Innovation projects

Innovation projects are defined as projects which are sufficiently promising to justify significant attention and a moderate amount of funding (less than $5000) for services, but not mature enough to warrant a new venture. Technical services to refine the innovation are provided through existing resources of the College of Engineering. Such services include technical consulting by members of the faculty, analytical or test services, and prototype fabrication. Through the College of Business, faculty members provide consulting services, and MBA students perform planning surveys and in-depth feasibility assessments under the supervision of senior faculty from management, finance, marketing, and accounting.

New enterprise development

New enterprise development projects are sufficiently mature and promising to justify further commitment of the Center's resources. The goal is to advance the project from the point of technical and business feasibility through the pre–venture capital stage to operational business organization. These projects are Utah's primary means of identifying, recruiting, and training managers. The end goal of the new enterprise development project is the formation of a new company. The Center staff will provide further assistance to those projects that appear to have real potential for success, by helping to locate venture capital and recruiting additional talent for the management team.

The Center's primary resource is the wealth of talent and facilities at the University. Any major university contains a formidable array of specialized talent that could be marshalled to further technical innovation.

The Center is attempting to establish a small equity or royalty position with the companies it assists in order to provide operating income for the Center in future years. However, the time required for a new company to reach maturity and pay dividends is long. For eight or ten years, until equity positions yield sufficient income to make the Center self-sustaining, it will have to rely on continued government funding, industrial contracts, or gifts for interim financing. Prospects for success are good.

The reasoning of the Charpie Report is as valid now as it was when written. The report states,

It goes without saying that the United States could not depend solely on the innovative contributions of the small firms. The large firms are indispensible to economic and technological progress. From a number of points of view, however, we are persuaded that a unique cost-benefit opportunity exists in the provision of incentives aimed at encouraging independent inventors, inventor-entrepreneurs and small technologically-based businesses. The cost of special incentives to them is likely to be low. The benefits are likely to be high. (Small Business and Innovation *1978*)

References

BATY, GORDON B., *Entrepreneurship: Playing to Win.* Englewood Cliffs, N.J.: Prentice-Hall, 1974.

BAUMBACH, CLIFFORD, and LAWYER, KENNETH, *How to Organize and Operate a Small Business* (6th ed.). Englewood Cliffs, N.J.: Prentice-Hall, 1979.

BAUMBACH, CLIFFORD M., and MANCUSO, JOSEPH R., *Entrepreneurship and Venture Management.* Englewood Cliffs, N.J.: Prentice-Hall, 1975.

BERLEW, D. E., and LECLERE, W. E., "Social Intervention in Chicago: A Case Study," *Journal of Applied Behavioral Sciences* 10, No. 1 (1974).

BROOM, H. N., and LONGENECKER, JUSTIN, *Small Business Management* (5th ed.). Cincinnati: Southwestern Publishing Co., 1979.

"Colleges are Replacing School of Hard Knocks for Some Businessmen," *Wall Street Journal,* December 9, 1977.

COLLINS, ORIS, and MOORE, DAVID G., *The Organization Makers: A Behavioral Study of Independent Entrepreneurs.* Englewood Cliffs, N.J.: Prentice-Hall, 1970.

CYERT, RICHARD M., and MARCH, JAMES, *Behavioral Theory of the Firm.* Englewood Cliffs, N.J.: Prentice-Hall, 1963.

DIBLE, DONALD M., *Up Your Own Organization.* Santa Clara, Ca.: Entrepreneur Press, 1971.

DURAND, D. E., "Effects of Achievement Motivation and Skill Training on the Entrepreneurial Behavior of Black Businessmen," *Organizational Behavior and Human Performance* 14 (1975).

GUSTAFSON, ROBERT, "An Entrepreneurial Spirit," *Mechanical Engineering News* 5, No. 4 (November 1968).

"How the Classroom Turns Out Entrepreneurs," *Business Week*, June 18, 1979.

KIERULFF, HERBERT E., JR., "Education for Entrepreneurship," *A.A.C.S.B. Bulletin,* April 1974.
KRAMER, HUGH E., "New Entrepreneurial Dimensions of Business Education," *Collegiate News and Views* XXV, No. 1 (Fall 1971).
KURILOFF, ARTHUR H., SCHMIDT, W., and MENKIN, D., "An Educational Venture in Entrepreneurship" (Working paper, UCLA Graduate School of Management, 1972).
LACHO, K. J., and NEWMAN, A.A., "The Use of New Venture Projects as a Teaching Device at the Undergraduate Level" (Presented to the Southwest Division, Academy of Management, March 1974).
LILES, PATRICK R., *New Business Ventures and the Entrepreneur.* Homewood, Ill.: Richard D. Irwin, 1974.
MCCLELLAND, D. C., and WINTER, D. G., *Motivating Economic Achievement.* New York: Free Press, 1971.
MIRON, DAVID, and MCCLELLAND, D. C., "The Impact of Achievement Motivation Training on Small Businesses," *California Management Review* XXI, No. 4 (Summer 1979).
ROSCOE, JAMES P., "Can Entrepreneurship Be Taught?" *MBA Magazine*, June 1973.
SCHOCH, SUSAN, "How Business Schools Handle Entrepreneurs," *Venture Magazine* 1, No. 8 (September 1979).
SCHREIER, J. W., ed., "Training and Education for Entrepreneurship," *Proceedings of Project ISEED.* Milwaukee: Center for Venture Management, 1975.
SCHULMAN, JEFFREY, and HORNADAY, JOHN, "Experimental Learning in an Entrepreneurial Course" (Paper presented at the Annual Meeting of the Academy of Management, August 12, 1975).
Small Business and Innovation. Washington, D.C.: U.S. Senate Select Committee on Small Business, 1978.
Small Business Joint Hearings Record. Washington, D.C.: U.S. Senate, 1978.
TIMMONS, J. A., "Black Is Beautiful, Is It Bountiful?" *Harvard Business Review,* November-December 1971.
TIMMONS, J. A., "Motivating Economic Achievement: A Five Year Appraisal," *Proceedings of the Fifth Annual Meeting, American Institute for Decision Sciences,* 1973.
VESPER, K. H., *Entrepreneurship Education.* Milwaukee: Center for Venture Management, 1979.
VESPER, K. H., "Two Approaches to University Stimulation of Entrepreneurship," in *Technical Entrepreneurship.* Milwaukee: Center for Venture Management, 1972.
VESPER, K. H., "Venture Initiation Courses in U.S. Business Schools," *Academy of Management Journal,* December 1971.
VESPER, K. H., and SCHLENDORF, J., "Views on U.S. College Courses in Entrepreneurship," *Academy of Management Journal*, September 1973.
WAGNER, G. R., and BRIGHT, J. R., "Technical Entrepreneurship for Engineering Seniors" (Working paper, University of Texas, 1973).
WEAVER, PETER, *You, Inc.* Garden City, N.Y.: Doubleday, 1973.

chapter xviii

Entrepreneurship research: methods and directions

William L. Paulin

Robert E. Coffey

Mark E. Spaulding

Overview

For this survey of research methods used in the field of entrepreneurship, 81 studies were reviewed and classified according to a five-part scheme: (1) research purpose, (2) research strategy, (3) research design, (4) data collection technique, and (5) data analysis technique. The 81 studies were also classified into one of four major streams of entrepreneurship research: (1) the entrepreneur as an individual, (2) the processes or mechanics of entrepreneurship, (3) the functions of entrepreneurship in society, and (4) entrepreneurship supporting topics. The article concludes with suggestions of possible methodological directions for the field.

Objectives

The objectives of this study were: (1) to survey the research methods literature and develop a framework for classifying the techniques utilized in past studies of entrepreneurship; (2) to sample the entrepreneurship literature, identify the major streams of research in the area, and classify the research methods used in each stream; and (3) to suggest how various methods might be used in future research.

The study employed a non-random sampling of a large number of entrepreneurship research studies.[1] It was not our intent to delve deeply into the topical content and controversies of any particular research stream. Rather, we tried to achieve a broad perspective on the methods and topics of the field.

The a priori position is that the important questions should be the researcher's prime study (Schendel and Hofer 1979). The fact that the present authors were preoccupied with method does not mean method should take precedence over substance. Research methods are a means to the better understanding of important phenomena.

Specifically, research aims to make predictions or to explain phenomena (Kerlinger 1964). Research processes include the following steps: (1) definition of areas, topics, or questions to be studied; (2) description of phenomena, discovery of facts, definition of concepts, and identification of variables in the area of study; (3) development of theories and hypotheses about relationships and behaviors of key variables; and (4) testing, refinement, and verification of hypotheses and theories.

Research can take many forms: At one end of the spectrum are nonsystematic descriptions of events or opinions, while at the opposite end are formal, complex, and methodical investigations. The appropriate form should depend upon the topic to be studied. McGrath (1964) discusses the tensions and trade-offs between those who wish to study great questions simply and those who want to study narrowly defined topics with formal rigor. His key point is that both approaches have their place in the development of a field.

This chapter takes the position that research should be as carefully and systematically designed as possible, given the topic and practical circumstances. Better methods, if feasible, will improve the validity of research findings.

Survey of research methods: a five-dimensional classification

Our review of the research methods literature resulted in a five-part classification. This scheme is outlined in Table 1 and summarized briefly in this section.

[1]Sources for this sample included: ABI/INFORM and Management Contents computer data bases, Long Beach State and University of Southern California libraries, and a mailing to participants in the Conference on Research and Education in Entrepreneurship. The search was keyed on variations of the words "entrepreneur" and "research methods."

Table 1 *Research methods classification*

I. *Research Purpose*		
A. Exploratory (theory building)		
B. Explanatory (theory testing)		
II. *Research Strategy or Approach*		
A. Theory		
1. Anecdotal		
2. Formal		
B. Sample survey		
1. Questionnaire		
2. Ex post facto field study		
C. Judgment task		
D. Field study		
E. Field experiment		
F. Lab experiment		
G. Experimental simulation		
H. Computer simulation		
III. *The Research Design*		
A. Non-methodical		Non-empirical
B. Logical		
C. Descriptive and case study		Empirical research
D. Correlational and ex post facto	Hypothesis testing	
E. Experimental and quasi-experimental		
IV. *Data Collection Techniques*		
A. Contemplation		
B. Questionnaires and tests		
C. Interviews	Empirical research	
1. Structured		
2. Unstructured		
D. Observation		
1. Direct		
2. Archival (indirect)		
V. *Data Recording and Analysis Techniques*		
A. Qualitative		
B. Quantitative		

Research purpose

Duncan (1979) and Smith (1975) describe two fundamentally different types of research which we have termed (1) exploratory and (2) explanatory.[2] While both types may add to empirical knowledge and develop theory, each has a more specific purpose.

Exploratory research is essentially inductive and descriptive. It is intended to discover the nature of the phenomenon in question. Typically, researchers choose the explanatory mode because a lack of previously developed knowledge, theory, or method makes it difficult to construct specific hypotheses or to anticipate subject responses prior to data gathering. Data for exploratory

[2]Duncan uses the terms "qualitative" and "quantitative" for these categories. The other labels are used here because quantitative numerical data may be used in either mode of research.

research is therefore usually unstructured and qualitative in nature. According to Kerlinger (1964), this complex type of research data must be "content analyzed" according to some sort of logical rules and procedures. Exploratory research tends to be more suitable for initial theory building because it focuses on discovering *what* real phenomena occur and *how*. Eighty percent of the studies reviewed for this chapter were classified as exploratory research.

Explanatory research, on the other hand, is essentially deductive, intended to ascertain or verify causes and relationships between phenomena. It tends to be better suited to explaining relationships and refining theory because it focuses on cause and effect, on *why* known phenomena occur. According to Duncan, data for this type of research is usually structured and quantitative. Well established knowledge, theory, or methods help researchers develop measurement scales and apply them without serious enactment problems.[3] Because of this structure, more formally controlled research strategies and statistical analysis techniques can be used to improve study reliability and conclusion validity.

One of Duncan's major points is that the research purpose and methods must be based on the research topic and on the research and theorizing that has gone before. Exploratory research studies are necessary when development in the field won't allow the use of more systematic research techniques. Researchers must determine *what* occurs before they test *why* it occurs.[4] In emerging fields like entrepreneurship, exploratory research often makes fundamental contributions.

The research strategy or approach

Runkel and McGrath (1972) have developed the eight-part research strategy classification scheme that serves as our second dimension. It is reproduced in Figure 1. These strategies define the researcher's choice of settings, subjects, behaviors, and measurements to be taken.

Theory, it could be argued, is not research. We agree with Runkel and McGrath, however, who classify both theory and computer simulation as research because "they use prior empirical knowledge in their construction [and] rearrange existing information into new forms to make it more useful." Theory building is a nonempirical strategy in that it does not result in any new

[3]What Duncan calls enactment problems (interactive or reactive effects, according to Campbell and Stanley 1973) occur when the actual measurement or data gathering changes the behavior in question, and thus the data. Without prior research and experience, it is difficult to tell whether pre-structured data recording techniques will work.

[4]We do not intend to imply that the actual process of exploration, theory formulation, and testing develops in a simple linear manner. Rather, we see the process as circular, evolutionary, and iterative, better described by McGrath's programmatic research concept. See Figure 2 for a more complete formulation.

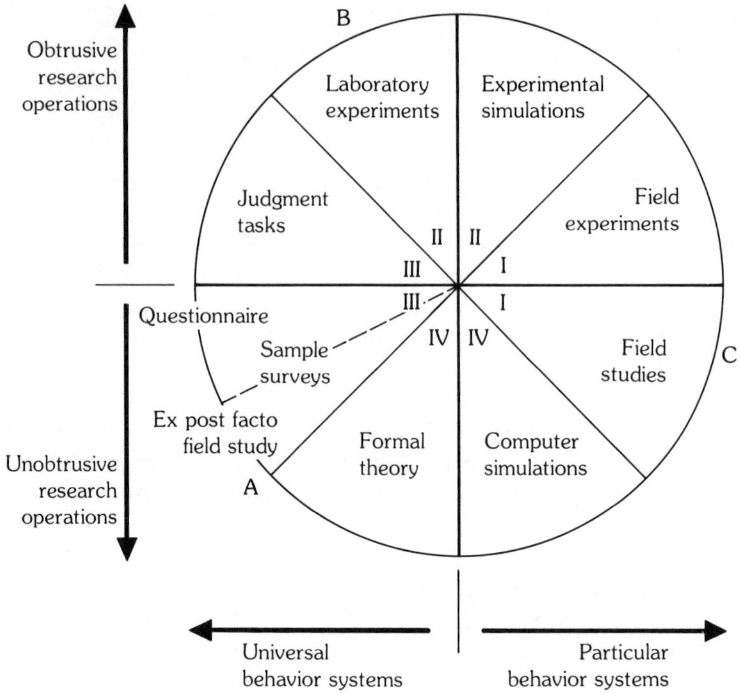

I. Settings in natural systems
II. Contrived and created settings
III. Behavior not setting dependent
IV. No observation of behavior required

A. Point of maximum concern with generality over actors
B. Point of maximum concern with precision of measurement of behavior
C. Point of maximum concern with system character of context

Figure 1 *Research strategy of approach (from Runkel and McGrath 1972, page 85)*

information, but it does use empirical data to hypothesize relationships. Theory is developed through contemplation and logical analysis. Kerlinger defines formal theory as a "set of interrelated constructs (concepts), definitions, and propositions that present a systematic view of phenomena by specifying relations among variables, with the purpose of explaining and predicting the phenomena." Formal theory is testable. It serves as the basis for empirical research strategies and provides a link between exploratory and explanatory types of research.

The entrepreneurship literature contains quite a bit of informal, anecdotal theory developed from non-methodical research designs. About a quarter of the studies on the entrepreneurship process were so classified.[5] This type of work is valuable but can be difficult to evaluate or test empirically. Sometimes it can also be wrong! Most researchers can cite instances where common sense did not work and contrary wisdom did. This type of theory, however, often suggests fruitful areas for future research. We conclude that the trend toward more explicit statement of issues; more empirically-based, testable theories; and more testing of informal prescriptions is crucial for entrepreneurship research and ought to be continued.

Sample survey is independent of setting because data collection does not take place where the phenomena in question naturally occur. Respondents are asked to give their opinions about the phenomena, usually at their own temporal and locational convenience. Sample surveys offer the advantage of random sampling to control unwanted or unobserved variation. A disadvantage is that the researcher is separated from the setting and phenomena in question. Sample survey was by far the most common entrepreneurship research strategy, employed in 64 percent of the sampled studies.

As a result of our sampling, we offer a tentative modification to Runkle and McGrath's classification scheme. While many of the sample surveys we reviewed sought opinions through interviews or questionnaires, many did not. Researchers frequently asked subjects to describe historic events rather than to answer specific questions with personal opinion (Cohen and Smith 1976). The difference between this strategy and actual field study is that researchers "observe" the phenomena in question through the memory of the subject rather than directly, hopefully avoiding undesired respondent interpretation or evaluation.

Judgment task is also a setting-independent strategy. Subjects are brought together to perform tasks or make judgments in circumstances that are designed to minimize enactment problems. For example, market researchers use focus groups to determine consumer reactions to new products or product prices, because survey questions like "Would you pay this price for it?" typically draw unreliable responses. Projective measure judgment tasks were frequently used in research on individual entrepreneurs. Studies by Collins, Moore, and Unwalla and by McClelland used the judgment task technique.[6]

Field study involves direct observation of phenomena as they occur in the natural setting. Observation must be as unobtrusive as possible to avoid enactment problems. Field studies are typically longitudinal in nature. Only a few examples of this approach were found in the literature, but these appeared to have great impact (see Mayer and Goldstein, Hoad and Rosko).[7]

[5]We have subdivided the entrepreneurship area into four historic streams of research. The process, or mechanics, area is one of these four. See the next section for discussion. See also Appendix A, Part II for examples of the anecdotal nature of many works in this area.

[6]See Appendix A, Part I for complete references.

[7]See Appendix A, Part II for complete references.

Field experiment, like field study, is a longitudinal strategy conducted in a natural setting. Field experiment, however, includes active researcher manipulation of some aspect of the phenomena in question. In this respect, field experiments are similar to laboratory experiments. Typically, however, they cannot be as rigorously controlled as experiments performed in the lab. Studies by Loucks, Schumann and Timmons are examples of field experiments.[8]

Laboratory experiment must emphasize reliability of observation (repeatability of behavior and measurement) and internal validity of conclusions (ruling out alternative explanations). This means that all major variables should be either controlled, manipulated, or measured. They should not be ignored. Typical methods of control are randomized selection of subject or control group and randomized treatment. Natural settings are not deemed important. No laboratory experiments were found in our sampling of the entrepreneurship literature.

Experimental simulation is also performed under controlled laboratory conditions. At least some features of the natural setting or of naturally occurring behavior are recreated, however. No experimental simulations were found in the sampling.

Computer simulation is another nonempirical strategy. Theories are described mathematically to allow independent, nonexperimental manipulation of relevant variables. Simulations normally tend to reproduce the dynamic (time dependent) behavior of real systems. No computer simulations were reported in the literature.

McGrath's (1964) programmatic research concept (Figure 2) supports the notion that all types of research, exploratory and explanatory, are necessary to the development of a field of knowledge. The process of understanding a particular phenomenon, according to McGrath, progresses from exploratory studies in the field, through formal theory development, to testing in the lab, and finally back to the field for verification. It appears that different streams of entrepreneurial research are at somewhat different stages along this path.[9]

The research design

The research design dimension, developed from Campbell and Stanley (1972), is essentially complementary to the strategy classification, but focuses more on the degree and formality of research methods, structure, and control.

Non-methodical designs are not research in the strictest, formal sense. Rather, they tend to be shaped by rules or advice from experienced entrepreneurs or observers. This type of work, however, may supply the initial

[8]See Appendix A, Part IV for complete references.

[9]Many studies of the entrepreneur as an individual, for example, appear to be well on the way to stages 3, 4, or 5, while research on the process of entrepreneurship appears to be more commonly at stage 1 or 2. See the next section for a more complete discussion.

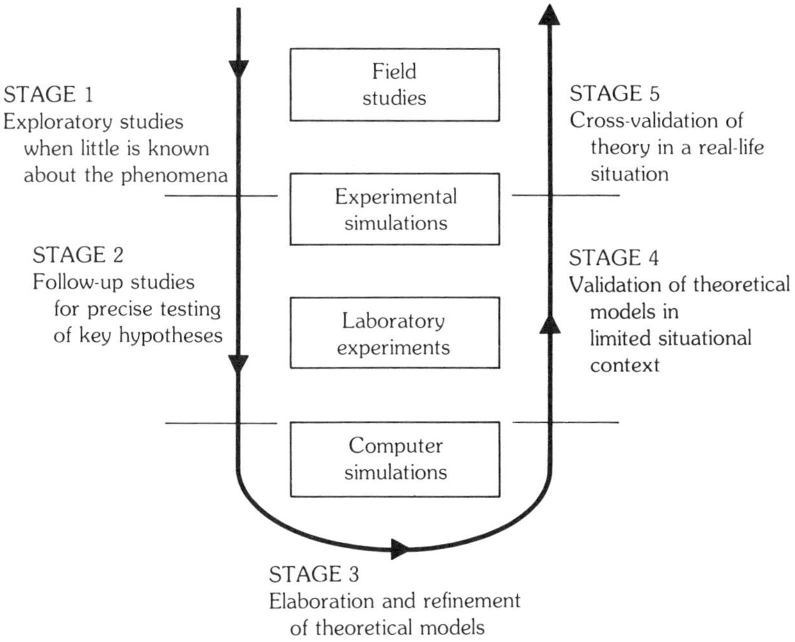

Figure 2 *Five-stage path for programmatic research (from McGrath 1964)*

"spark" for exploratory research. About 15 percent of the entrepreneurship studies reviewed for this article, and many of the entrepreneurship and small business textbooks, fall into this category.

Logical designs are also nonempirical, but explicitly present issues, definitions, assumptions, relationships, derivative logic, and supporting data. This type of theoretical research provides integration for the entire programmatic research process. Currently there is a trend toward more of this type of work in entrepreneurship. Vesper's book (1980) is an example.[10]

Descriptive or case study designs can have either a pedagogical or a theory building orientation. Typically, they employ nonexperimental and non-quantitative methods. In McGrath's terms, these designs usually have the greatest scope and capacity for external validity but the least control and precision for internal validity and reliability. We found that this type of design was seldom used to test hypotheses, but did help to form theories by sampling what happened in the "real world." Usually exploratory in nature, case study designs appeared to provide the methodological roots for each of the four major streams of entrepreneurship research. They were used in 52 percent of the sampled studies.

Correlational and ex post facto designs can be used for both exploratory

[10]See Appendix A, Part II for a complete reference.

and explanatory studies. The key to these design types is predictability. Cause and effect relationships are examined by correlating dependent and independent variables, or distinguishing characteristics are studied by comparing subjects and control groups. The research is more than descriptive, but experimental manipulations or comprehensive control techniques are commonly missing. Our review indicates these designs are being used with increasing frequency. Research by Brockhaus, Hornaday, and Timmons employs correlational designs.[11]

Experimental and quasi-experimental designs require that all variables relevant to the phenomena in question be either controlled (usually through fixing or randomization), manipulated, or at least observed and measured. They can't be ignored, or the research findings will be confounded. Hypotheses about causation or the relationships between variables are tested. In McGrath's terms, these studies have the least scope and external validity but the greatest precision and internal validity. Few attempts at experimentation appear in the entrepreneurship literature, probably because of the difficulty, time, and expense associated with this type of design. Yet the field experiments we did review appeared to have a significant impact. The studies by Schumann, Loucks, or Timmons are examples of quasi-experiments.

While professionals believe that true research requires experimentation, we would side with McGrath's programmatic research concept and regard all of the methodological designs discussed in this section as research. Nevertheless, the current trend toward more correlational and comparative designs may well benefit entrepreneurship study because of the gain in predictive ability.

Data collection techniques

According to Bouchard (1976), there are three primary methods of data measurement or collection: (1) observation, (2) questionnaire, and (3) interview. To this list can be added a fourth: contemplation.

Contemplation involves the subconscious or unspecified "analysis" of internally stored data and its rearrangement into new patterns. While contemplation is the primary technique of nonempirical theorizing research, the discovery of new relationships through contemplation is an important part of any research study.

Questionnaires and tests provide subjects with specific directions and either pre-structured or unstructured response alternatives. Typically, researchers do not observe the phenomena in question; in the case of mail surveys, they may not even speak to respondents. Questionnaires offer the opportunity for larger samples but tend to remove researchers from observation of their subjects.

[11]See Appendix A, Part I for complete references.

Interviews require personal interaction between researchers and subjects. Researchers may or may not observe the phenomena, but they do ask the research questions. Responses may be recorded by either researchers or subjects in structured or open-ended formats. Interviews have the advantage of researcher involvement and provide a "feel" for the meaning of responses, but they are time consuming and more prone to researcher bias.

Observation involves either prerecorded archival data or the actual phenomena in question. In either case researchers record the data, and subjects may or may not be aware of the observation. It is also possible to have subject-observers. Both quantitative and qualitative data may be recorded, usually in some pre-planned format. Direct observation can provide researchers with valuable insights not otherwise available, yet it was used in only 5 percent of the studies sampled for this article (see Hoad and Rosko, Mayer and Goldstein).

Entrepreneurship research has made use of all of these techniques, but questionnaires and interviews have tended to dominate the field. Thirty-five percent of the sampled studies used questionnaires and 48 percent used interviews.

Data recording and analysis techniques

This dimension completes the research methods classification scheme developed for this study. There are two primary methods of recording and analyzing research data: qualitative and quantitative.

Qualitative techniques are used to draw conclusions from non-quantitative types of data, from data recorded in words and pictures. This unstructured, nominal, or ordinal data must be "content analyzed" according to some sort of formal and reproducible procedure if the analysis is to be repeatable and reliable.

Quantitative and statistical techniques involve recording data on some sort of numerical scale that is subject to statistical analysis. This generally means that interval, cardinal, or ration scales must be developed prior to data gathering, although post hoc classification schemes are possible. Various statistical techniques, such as regression or factor analysis, may be applied to add insight and support to analytic conclusions. The internal validity of these conclusions may also be estimated through significance and reliability tests.

Both qualitative and quantitative techniques have been used frequently in all types of entrepreneurship research.

Summary of research methods classification

We found more formal research on entrepreneurship than we had anticipated. Much of the earlier work tended to use non-methodical, contemplative, or anecdotal methods. But a definite trend to more systematic, empirical methods has begun in recent years. Although more explanatory and correlational designs are being employed, exploratory sample survey approaches, descriptive or case study designs, questionnaires and interviews are still the predominant methodologies in the field.

It appears to us that the development of these methods has reflected the development of entrepreneurship research as a whole. As the field continues to evolve, we expect to see a broader range of research methods, partaking of the newest developments and suited to the needs of particular research topics.

Streams of entrepreneur research: four topic areas

We also examined the correlation of research methods and topics under study. We identified four general topic areas: (1) the entrepreneur as an individual; (2) the processes or mechanics of entrepreneurship; (3) the functions of entrepreneurship in society; and (4) supporting topics. These research streams are outlined and cross-referenced to three other classification schemes in Table 2 (pp.364–65).

The entrepreneur

Research studies on the entrepreneur as an individual include both psychological and sociological approaches to the study of entrepreneurial characteristics, personality, and behavior. Prominent examples in this area are the studies of McClelland and Collins, Moore, and Unwalla.[12]

This subject appears to be more extensively developed than the others discussed here. With its roots in exploratory biographies and case histories, the area has evolved to complex, correlational studies that test theoretical propositions about entrepreneurs. The most common current research methodologies observed in this stream were explanatory sample survey or judgment task correlational designs that used questionnaires or interviews to assemble both quantitative and qualitative data. Current work appears to be moving toward contingency approaches to the study of entrepreneurs.

Entrepreneurship processes or mechanics

Focusing on entrepreneurship processes at the level of the firm, research in this stream is aimed at the problems and mechanics of venturing. The effort is to describe and explain entrepreneurial action. Some examples

[12]See references to these and other authors in Appendix A, Part I for studies on the entrepreneur as an individual.

of work in this area include that of Mayer and Goldstein, Hoad and Rosko, and Bunn and Terflinger.[13] The topic began to emerge clearly only in the 1960s and 1970s.

While this stream seems to have a more anecdotal and exploratory focus than other streams of entrepreneurship research, Vesper (1980) marks a milestone in the development of formally researchable topics in this area. Several tentative classification schemes for these topics are listed in Table 2.

Two types of research methods have distinguished this stream. Less prevalent but of increasing prominence are methodical, exploratory studies using sample survey critical incident methods, and even a few full-fledged field studies and field experiments. These studies employ both descriptive and correlational designs, questionnaires and interviews, and qualitative and quantitative recording techniques.

Historically, however, the entrepreneurship process stream has been represented primarily by normative or "how to" publications. While this type of work can be valuable, "the basis for advice from experienced entrepreneurs is usually anecdotal . . . and may be less than universally applicable. Typically, the basis for such remarks will be based on a sample of experience which [is] . . . confined to small numbers of people and ventures" (Vesper 1980). Such work is often unconvincing to critical analysts and is sometimes difficult to test or prove.

The subject appears to be emerging from this incubator stage to one where research questions are being stated more clearly and research designs are becoming more methodical. While it is difficult to spot an academic trend as it is occurring, we believe that this stream holds much promise for the near future.

Entrepreneurship and society

Focusing on the role of entrepreneurs and entrepreneurship in society, this stream consists of three sub-areas: (1) the economic role of the entrepreneur, (2) cultural and crosscultural case histories, and (3) "what it's like to be an entrepreneur."

All of these sub-areas focus on the social, political, economic, or legal environment of the entrepreneur. The research methods employed follow either the case history approach or the non-empirical, theoretical approach often used in economics. For examples of this substream see Schumpeter and Baumol.[14] While this subject goes back a long way, it appears to have been rather inactive in recent years (Baumol 1968). It could provide relatively untapped and fertile opportunities for empirical research.

[13]See references to these authors and others in Appendix A, Part II, for recent work in the entrepreneurship process area.

[14]See the references to these authors and others in Appendix A, Part III for works in the area of entrepreneurship and society.

Table 2 *Four streams of entrepreneurship research*

The Paulin, Coffey, and Spaulding classification of three entrepreneur research traditions	**Entrepreneurship conference topic list (Vesper 1980)**	**Schendel & Hofer's four schemes (Schendel & Hofer 1979)**	***The entrepreneur and new enterprise formation resource guide list* (Schreier & Komives 1973)**
I. *The entrepreneur* (Studies of individuals and what makes them tick) A. Case histories B. Psychological approaches C. Sociological approaches	*Academic sub-fields* • Tycoon history • Literature on living entrepreneurs • Psychology of entrepreneurship • Sociology of entrepreneurship	*Academic sub-fields* • Tycoon history • Psychology of entrepreneurship • Sociology of entrepreneurship	*Academic sub-fields* • The entrepreneur • Female entrepreneur • Minority entrepreneur • Biography • Psychology • Sociology
II. *Entrepreneurship and the firm* (Micro entrepreneurship—studies of its functions and processes) A. Case histories B. Business industry studies C. Functional studies D. Normative, "how to do it" studies, anecdotal wisdom E. Entrepreneurial strategies F. Venture stages or life cycles	*Academic sub-fields* • Non-academic literature on entrepreneurship • Innovation • Venture finance • Internal entrepreneurship	*Academic sub-fields* • Start-up methodology • Venture finance *Venture strategies* • Mom 'n pop • Unintentional underachieving • Conscious underachieving • High payoff, small, stable • Intercorporate *Entrepreneurial strategies* • Self-employment • Building work force • Product innovation • Exploitation of underutilized resources • Economies of scale • Pattern multiplication • Takeover • Capital aggregation • Speculation	*Academic sub-fields* • Finance • Venture capital • Innovation • Management concepts

	Venture stages • Business entry • Stages in venture development	*Venture stages* • Pre-start-up • Start-up • Profitability • Later growth • Disposition	*Venture stages* • Start-ups • Small business management • Terminations
III. *Entrepreneurship and society* (Macro entrepreneurship—studies of the entrepreneur's role in society and society's impact on the entrepreneur) A. Economic theory B. Cross cultural case studies C. Entrepreneurial environment	*Academic sub-fields* • Environment and entepreneurship • Economic development from entrepreneurship	*Academic sub-fields* • Economics of entrepreneurship	*Academic sub-fields* • The entrepreneur in other cultures • Historical entrepreneurship • Small business environment and economics • Economic development
IV. *Related topics* A. Education and entrepreneurship B. Research and entrepreneurship C. Consulting and entrepreneurship D. Government and entrepreneurship	*Academic sub-fields* • Education for entrepreneurship • Research methodology		*Academic sub-fields* • Education • Counseling the small business • SBA

Supporting topics

These include such related topics as consulting for entrepreneurs, government programs for entrepreneurs, entrepreneurial education, and entrepreneurial research. Interestingly, this stream evinced a higher percentage of experimental designs than did the other streams. Works by Loucks and Schumann,[15] as well as this article, exemplify this area.

Summary of entrepreneurship research streams

Two of these four streams, the entrepreneur as an individual and entrepreneurship and society, appear to be well developed. Each has a theoretical tradition and is built on a broad base of studies utilizing methodical research techniques. Currently, the first topic seems to be a field for active research, while the second appears to be somewhat inactive.

The processes or mechanics of entrepreneurship stream appear to be a somewhat less mature subject. Until recently this stream appeared to lack a clear theoretical base. It is currently, however, evolving a core of better defined theory and a more scientific concern for method. We believe that the entrepreneurship process area has great promise.

The 81 studies we reviewed for this chapter are classified according to this four-part topic scheme in Appendix A. Appendix B classifies the publications in which these studies were found.

Future directions for entrepreneurship research: some suggestions and speculations

We find that both the quantity and quality of ideas are increasing steadily. Accompanying the broader range of research topics will be an increasing need for more diverse and more systematic research methods. The following are some suggestions for the development of improved research methods.

Develop more theories and define more precise research questions

Important propositions can be more precisely stated in a form amenable to testing. Observations and generalizations can be used to develop explicit hypotheses that are empirically testable. More normative checklists will do less to advance our knowledge than will explicit, formal, and methodi-

[15]See the reference to these and other authors in Appendix A, Part IV for examples of work on other entrepreneurship topics.

cal studies. In addition, the body of existing knowledge in the entrepreneurship area is growing, and new research can often build on what has been done.

One outcome of the growing body of methodical work is the awareness that conventional wisdom sometimes does not hold up under the light of careful scrutiny. For example, in a recent study of student SBI consultants, Paulin (1980) found that most people assume, quite plausibly, that graduate students make better small business consultants than undergraduates. However, a large sample of graduate and undergraduate consulting teams from several universities had exactly the same average performance ratings.

Much of the knowledge in the field comprises propositions supported mainly by untested or narrowly based anecdotal wisdom. Explicitly stating and testing these propositions should provide many good research opportunities.

Increase the proportion of methodical research studies

Exploratory research is needed in most fields of study. This is especially true in an emerging area like entrepreneurship. Exploratory studies can, however, be followed up with more structured research. Increased efforts to develop and test specific hypotheses derived from previous exploratory studies should be highly rewarded.

We think the field can be advanced by supplementing sample survey and descriptive research methods with critical incident techniques, field studies, and even field experiments. When more longitudinal studies are completed, allowing more explicit attention to be paid to phenomena under study, the research is likely to produce more accurate and valid results. Also, a variety of methods reduces the chance of drawing method-bound conclusions.

More face-to-face interviews and direct observation should be used. While this is not possible or appropriate to some research questions, personal involvement can frequently produce more reliable and insightful results. For example, in the study cited above, Paulin (1980) found that clients reported significantly higher student consulting success rates in a mail questionnaire than they did in a personal, in-depth interview. The interview results corresponded much more closely to the results of other methodical studies.

Finally, whenever possible, more comparative and correlative research should be undertaken. Comparative designs help clarify distinctive characteristics, and correlational designs help identify causal relationships. In a comparative study, Brockhaus (1980) found that attitudes toward risk did not distinguish entrepreneurs from the general population. In a correlation study, Paulin (1980) found that many factors identified with successful consultants in descriptive studies did not distinguish between successful and failed consultants.

Conclusions about future directions

Entrepreneurship has generated increasing research and theory development during the last ten to fifteen years. Based on the trends observed in this study, the field will continue to develop and grow as a viable part of academic research and education.

The area would benefit from the continuation of two methodological trends observed in this study: (1) increased emphasis on clear specification and testing of important topics, theories, and propositions; and (2) increased reliance on methodical, longitudinal, direct, comparative, and correlational study designs.

Of course, these are only broad directional suggestions; the specific choice of a research design must also depend upon the topic choice and the state of prior research and theory. The ideal components of good research methods are not the only factors researchers must consider when designing their studies.

Appendix A Studies reviewed

Each of the research studies reviewed for this article is classified here according to the topic areas discussed in Section 2. The letters in parentheses refer to the classification of research methods used in the study. The key to classification appears in Table 1.

I. The entrepreneur

BROCKHAUS, ROBERT H., "Psychological and Environmental Factors Which Distinguish the Successful from the Unsuccessful Entrepreneur: A Longitudinal Study," *Academy of Management Proceedings*, 1980 (B, B1, D, B, B).

BROCKHAUS, ROBERT H., and NOLD, WALTER R. "An Exploration of Factors Affecting the Entrepreneurial Decision: Personal Characteristics vs. Environmental Calculation," *Academy of Management Proceedings*, 1979 (B, B2, D, B, B).

CARROLL, JOHN J., *The Filipino Manufacturing Entrepreneur: Agent and Product of Change.* New York: Cornell University, 1965 (A, B1, C, C2 & D2, A).

COCHRAN, THOMAS C., and REINA, RUBEN E., *Capitalism in Argentine Culture.* Philadelphia: University of Pennsylvania, 1962 (A, B2, C, C2 & D2, A).

COLLINS, ORVIS F., MOORE, DAVID G., and UNWALLA, DARAB, "The Enterprising

Man," *MSU Business Studies*, 1964 (A, A1 & B1 & B2 & C, B & C & D, A & B & C1, A & B).

DECARLO, JAMES F., and LYONS, PAUL R. "A Comparison of Selected Personal Characteristics of Minority and Non-Minority Female Entrepreneurs," *Academy of Management Proceedings*, 1979 (A, B2, D, B, B).

DOUGLASS, MERRILL E., and ERICKSEN, ERIC W. "Limits to Growth: Entrepreneurial Characteristics of Small Business Owners," *Academy of Management Proceedings*, 1980 (A, B1, C, B1, B).

DURAUD, DOUGLAS, "Training and Development of Entrepreneurs," *Journal of Small Business Management* 12, No. 4 (October 1974) (B, E, E, C1 & C2, A & B).

HARTMAN, HEINZ, "The Enterprising Woman," *Columbia Journal of World Business* 5, No. 2 (March-April 1970) (A, B2, C, C2, A).

HORNADAY, JOHN A., and ABOUD, JOHN, "Characteristics of Successful Entrepreneurs," *Personnel Psychology* 24 (1971) (B, B1 & C, C & D1, B & C1, A & B).

HORNADAY, JOHN A., and BUNKER, CHARLES S., "The Nature of the Entrepreneur," *Personnel Psychology* 23 (1970) (B, B1 & C, C, B & C1, A & B).

JAVILLONAR, GLORIA V., and PETERS, GEORGE R., "Sociological and Social Psychological Aspects of Indian Entrepreneurship," *The British Journal of Sociology* 24, No. 3 (1973) (B, B1 & C, D, B & C1, A & B).

JESSUP, CLAUDIA, and CHIPPS, GENIE, *Super Girls*. New York: Harper & Row, Pub., 1972 (A, B2, C, C2, A).

JOHNSON, CURTIS S., *The Indomitable R. H. May*. New York: Vantage Press, 1964 (A, B2, C, C2 & A2, A).

KETS DEVRIES, M. F. R., "The Entrepreneurial Personality: A Person at the Crossroads," *Journal of Management Studies* 14, No. 1 (1977) (A, A2, C, D2, A).

LITZINGER, WILLIAM D., "The Motel Entrepreneur and the Motel Manager," *Academy of Management Journal* 8, No. 4 (December 1965) (A, B1, C, B, A & B).

LYNN, RICHARD, *The Entrepreneur: Eight Case Studies*. London: George Allen & Unwin, 1973 (A, B2, C, C2 & D2, A).

MANCUSO, J. R., *Fun 'n' Guts, the Entrepreneur's Philosophy*. Reading, Mass.: Addison-Wesley 1977 (A, A1, A, A, A).

MCCLELLAND, DAVID C., *The Achieving Society*. New York: John Wiley, 1961. (B, A2, B, A & D2, A).

PALMER, MICHAEL, "The Application of Psychological Testing to Entrepreneurial Potential," *California Management Review* 13, No. 3 (1970-71) (B, A2, B, A & D2, A).

PANDEY, JANAK, and TEWARY, N. B., "Locus of Control and Achievement of Entrepreneurs," *Journal of Occupational Psychology* 52, No. 2 (June 1979) (B, B1 & C, D, B & C2, A & B).

ROBERTS, E. B., "Entrepreneurship and Technology," *Research Management*, July 1968 (A, B1, C, D2, B).

SCHRAGE, HARRY, "The R & D Entrepreneur Profile of Success," *Harvard Business Review*, November-December 1965 (A, B1 & C, C & D, B & C1, A & B).

SEXTON, DONALD L., "Characteristics and Role Demands of Successful Entrepreneurs," *Academy of Management Proceedings*, 1980 (B, B1, C, B & C, C).

TIMMONS, JEFFREY A., "Black Is Beautiful—Is It Bountiful?" *Harvard Business Review*, November-December 1971 (B, E, E, C1, A).

VICARS, WILLIAM M., JAUCH, L. R., and WILSON, H. K., "A Scale to Measure General Entrepreneurial Tendency (GET)," *Academy of Management Proceedings*, 1980 (A, B1, B, A & B1, B).

WAINER, HERBERT A., and RUBIN, IRWIN M., "Motivation of Research and Development Entrepreneurs: Determinants of Company Success," *Journal of Applied Psychology* 53, No. 3 (1969) (B, B1 & C, D, B & C1, A & B).

WATSON, JOHN G., and SIMPSON, LEO R., "A Comparative Study of Owner-Manager Personal Values in Black and White Small Business," *Academy of Management Journal* 21, No. 2 (1978) (A, B1, C, B, A).

II. Entrepreneurship in the firm

BOOMS, BERNARD H., and WARD, JAMES E., JR., "The Cons of Black Capitalism," *Business Horizons* 12, No. 5 (October 1969) (A, A2, C, D2, A).

BUNN, VERNE A., and TERFLINGER, CURTIS D., *Buying and Selling a Small Business.* Wichita, Kans.: Wichita State University, 1963 (A, B2, C, B & C2, A & B).

Business Manuals. Santa Monica, Ca.: International Entrepreneurs Association, 1979 (A, B2, C, C2, A).

COPULSKY, WILLIAM and MCNULTY, HERBERT W., *Entrepreneurship and the Corporation.* New York: Amacom, 1974 (A, A2, C, C & D2, A).

DEEKS, JOHN, *The Small Firm Owner Manager: Entrepreneurial Behavior and Management Practice.* New York: Holt, Rinehart & Winston, 1976 (A, B1, C, B & C2, A).

GASSE, YVON, "The Processing of Information in Small Business and the Entrepreneur as Information Processor," *Academy of Management Proceedings*, 1980 (A, B1, D, B & C2, B).

GLUECK, WILLIAM F., and MESCON, TIMOTHY S., "Entrepreneurship: A Literature Analysis of Concepts," *Academy of Management Proceedings*, 1980 (A, A2, B, A & D2, A).

HANAN, MACK, *Venture Management: A Game Plan for Corporate Growth and Diversification.* New York: McGraw-Hill, 1976 (A & B, A1, A, A, A).

HOAD, WILLIAM M., and ROSKO, PETER, "Management Factors Contributing to the Success and Failure of New Small Manufacturers," Ann Arbor: Bureau of Business Research, University of Michigan, 1969 (A, B2 & D, D, B & C2 & D1, A & B).

JUSTIS, ROBERT T., and KREIGSMAN, BARBARA, "The Feasibility Study as a Tool for Venture Analysis," *Journal of Small Business Management* 17, No. 1 (January 1979) (A, A1, A, A, & A).

MAYER, KURT B., and GOLDSTEIN, SIDNEY, *The First Two Years: Problems of Small Firm Growth and Survival.* Washington, D.C.: Small Business Administration, 1961 (A, B2 & D, D, B & C2 & D1, A & B).

PARK, WILLIAM R., *How to Succeed in Your Own Small Business.* New York: John Wiley, 1978 (A, A1, A, A, A).

PAULIN, WILLIAM L., "Improving Small Business Student Consulting: An Empirical Study," *Academy of Management Proceedings*, 1980 (A, B2, D, C1 & C2, B).

ROBINSON, RICHARD B., JR., and GLUECK, WILLIAM F., "The Role of 'Outsiders' in Small Firm Strategic Planning: An Empirical Study," *Academy of Management Proceedings*, 1980 (A, B1, D, D2, B).

ROCKWELL, WILLARD F., "How to Acquire a Company," *Harvard Business Review*, September-October 1968 (A, A1, A, A, A).
Small Business Bibliographies. Washington, D.C.: Small Business Administration, 1979 (A, B1 & B2, C, B & C1, A).
Small Business Reporter. San Francisco, Ca.: Bank of America, 1979 (A, B1 & B2, C, B & C1, A).
STANFORD, MELVIN J., *New Enterprise Management.* Provo, Utah: Brigham Young University, 1975 (A, B2, C, C2, D2, A).
STEINER, GEORGE A., "Approaches to Long-Range Planning for Small Businesses," *California Management Review* 10, No. 1 (Fall 1967) (A, A1, A, A, A).
SULLIVAN, JACK, "Entrepreneurship and Small Business Management: What Is Known and What Needs to Be Known" (Unpublished Paper, Pennsylvania State University, 1979) (A, A2, B, A & D2, A).
VESPER, KARL H., "New Venture Ideas: Do Not Over Look Experience Factor," *Harvard Business Review* 57, No. 4 (1979) (A, B2, C, C2, & D2, A).
VESPER, KARL, *New Venture Strategies.* Englewood Cliffs, N.J.: Prentice-Hall, 1980.
VESPER, KARL H., and VORHIES, KENNETH A. "Entrepreneurship in Foreign Trade," *Journal of Small Business Management* 17, No. 2 (April 1979) (A, B2, C, C2, A).
VOZIKIS, GEORGE, and GLUECK, WILLIAM F., "Small Business Problems and Stages," *Academy of Management Proceedings*, 1980 (A, B1, D, B, B).
"Where Do You Get the Money?" *American Machinist*, August 10, 1970 (A, B1, C, C2, A).

III. Entrepreneurship in the society

BAUMOL, WILLIAM J., "Entrepreneurship in Economic Theory," *The American Economic Review* 58, No. 2 (May 1968) (B, A2, B, A & D2, A).
BROEHL, WAYNE G., JR., "A Less Developed Entrepreneur," *Columbia Journal of World Business* 5, No. 2 (March-April 1970) (B, A2, B, A & D2, A).
DAHMEN, ERIK, *Entrepreneurial Activity and the Development of Swedish Industry, 1919-1939*, trans. Axel Leijonhufvud. American Economic Association. Homewood, Ill.: Irwin, 1970 (A, B2, C, C2 & D2, A).
GOUGH, J. W., *The Rise of the Entrepreneur.* New York: Schocken Books, 1969 (A, B2, C, D2, A).
JOHNS, B. L., DUNLOP, W. C., and SHEEHAN, W. J., *Small Business in Australia: Problems and Prospects.* Sydney: George Allen & Unwin, 1978 (A, B2, C, B & C2 & D2, A).
LEIBENSTEIN, HARVEY, "Entrepreneurship and Development," *The American Economic Review* 58, No. 2 (May 1968) (A, A2, A, A, A).
MARRIS, PETER, and SUMMERSET, ANTHONY, *African Businessmen: A Study of Entrepreneurship and Development in Kenya.* London: Routledge & Kegan Paul, 1971 (A, B2, C, C2, A).
MILLER, WILLIAM, *Men in Business: Essays on the Historical Role of the Entrepreneur.* New York: Harper & Row, Pub., 1952 (A, B2, C, C2 & D2, A).
SCHLOSS, HENRY H., *Contribution of Private Investors to Development in a Mixed Economy.* Los Angeles: Research Institute for Business and Economics, University of Southern California, 1971 (A, A1, A, A, A).

SCHUMPETER, JOSEPH A., *The Theory of Economic Development.* Cambridge: Harvard University, 1934 (A, A1, A, A, A).

SHETTY, M. C., "Entrepreneurship in Small Industry," *International Development Review* VI, No. 2 (June 1964) (A, A2, B, A, A).

TOWNSEND, HARRY, and EDWARDS, ROLAND S., *Business Enterprise: Its Growth and Organization.* London: Macmillan, 1961 (A, A2 & B2, B & C, C2 & D2, A).

WALTON, SCOTT D., *Business in American History.* Columbus: Grid Inc., 1971 (A, B2, C, D2, A).

IV. Others

COMEGYS, CHARLES, "Research Needs of Prospective Entrepreneurs," *Atlantic Economic Review* 28, No. 3 (1978) (A, A1, A, A, A).

DOCTORS, SAMUEL I., "The Impact of State and Local Governments on Small Business," *Academy of Management Proceedings*, 1980 (A, A1, C, C2, A).

KLEIN, RICHARD H., "Financial Results of the Small Business Administration Minority Business Loan Portfolio," *University of Michigan Business Review* 30, No. 1 (January 1978) (A, B1, C, C2 & D2, A).

LOUCKS, KENNETH E., "An Experiment in Combining Financial and Management Assistance for New and Small Business, *Proceedings of the Fourth International Symposium on Small Business* (Seoul, Korea) 1977 (B, E, E, C2, D1, A).

LOUCKS, KENNETH E., "Survey of Small Business Management and Entrepreneurship Educational Activities in Canada," *Small Business Secretariat.* Ottawa: 1979 (A, B1, C, B & C1, A).

PEARCE, JOHN A., II, "Underwriting Small Business Community Growth through Tourism Development," *Academy of Management Proceedings*, 1980 (A, B1, C, B, B).

SAWYER, JOHN E., "Entrepreneurial Studies: Perspectives and Directions 1948–1958," *The Business History Review* 32, No. 4 (1958) (A, A2, B, D2, A).

SCHUMANN, JEFFREY C., and HORNADAY, JOHN C., "Experimental Learning in an Entrepreneurship Course," *Academy of Management Proceedings*, 1975 (A, E, E, D1, A).

SHAGORY, GEORGE, and SHUMANN, JEFFREY, "Entrepreneurship by Experience," *Journal of General Management* 3, No. 3 (Spring 1979) (A, A1, A, A, A).

SNIZCK, WILLIAM E., "The Use of Research Entrepreneurship as a Potential Role Conflict Reduction Mechanism," *Pacific Sociological Review* 19, No. 3 (1976) (A, B1, C, B, A).

SOLOMON, GEORGE T., "National Woman's Prebusiness Workshop Evaluation," *Academy of Management Proceedings*, 1980 (A, B1, C, B1, B).

SOLTOW, JAMES H., "The Entrepreneur in Economic History," *The American Economic Review* 58, No. 2 (May 1968) (A, B2, C, D2, A).

TIMMONS, JEFFRY A., BROEHL, WAYNE G., and FRYE, JOSEPH M. "Developing Appalachian Entrepreneurs," *Academy of Management Proceedings*, 1980 (A, D, B & C2, B).

Appendix B
Journals that have published articles concerning entrepreneurship*

	I	II	III	IV	Total	%
Academy of Management Journal	3				3	4
Academy of Management Proceedings	2	6		5	13	18
American Economic Review	1		2	1	4	5
American Institute of Planners Journal			1		1	1
American Machinist		1			1	1
Atlantic Economic Review				1	1	1
Behavioral Science			1		1	1
British Journal of Sociology	1				1	1
Business History Review	1				1	1
Business Horizons		1			1	1
The Business Quarterly	4		1		5	7
Business Sciences	1				1	1
California Management Research				1	1	1
California Management Review	1				1	1
Columbia Jounal of World Business	1		1		2	3
Generation		1			1	1
Harvard Business Review	2	3			5	7
Human Organization	1				1	1
IEEE Transactions on Engineering Management	1				1	1
Indiana Academic of Social Sciences Proceedings			1		1	1
International Development Review			1		1	1
Journal of Applied Psychology	1				1	1
Journal of Business	1				1	1
Journal of General Management				1	1	1
Journal of Management Studies	1				1	1
Journal of Occupational Psychology	1				1	4
Journal of Personality and Social Psychology	1				1	1
Journal of Small Business Management	2	2			4	5
Journal of Social Issues	1				1	1
Michigan Business Review		1			1	1
MSU Business Topics	2				2	3
Pacific Sociological Review				1	1	1
Personnel Psychology	2				2	3
Research Management	1				1	1
Small Business Secretariat				1	1	1
Dissertations	4	2			6	8
Totals	36	17	8	11	72	100%**

*This sample is not random.
**Does not total to 100% due to rounding.

commentary/elaboration

Commentary on research in the field of entrepreneurship

Rein Peterson

Deszo Horvath

Overview

This book contains an apologetic undertone about the state of research in the field. As an academic discipline, entrepreneurship is still in its infancy. It is also a very complex phenomenon. A large number of variables, most of them difficult to measure experimentally, are intertwined. Theory and research findings have been slow in developing. This should not be surprising. Entrepreneurship research is in an early stage of development simply because it is new.

The tendency to be apologetic about research done in the past comes about because there are few purists in the field. Those who have contributed to this volume are mostly "refugees" from other disciplines; the Horvaths, the Petersons, the Knights, and the Shaperos were at one time management scientists. These are people who identify with entrepreneurship emotionally, since they are academic entrepreneurs themselves. They are launching a new field of study; they feel a missionary zeal to impart what knowledge there is to their students, to battle bureaucrats who block any departure from academic orthodoxy, to raise research funds for programs in this underdeveloped field. What should be said is that students of entrepreneurship are like the alchemists, trying to explain complex phenomena with four blunt variables: fire, water, earth, and air. One need not be apologetic, nor is it appropriate *only* to exhort young researchers to develop more rigorous methods.

In the young field of entrepreneurship research, there has been more concern with asking the right questions about complex, relevant problems than with research rigor per se. In a paper delivered at a conference held under the auspices of the Business Planning and Policy Division of the Academy of Management, Robert B. Duncan writes: "Policy questions in their relevant scope have tended to be ignored by organizational theorists who have been more concerned about rigor. Organizational theorists seem to learn more and more about less and less" (1979). In our opinion, research on entrepreneurship is in danger of falling into the same trap.

In any particular academic field, the state of the art must be appraised before one can focus on an appropriate methodology for research. One must identify the significant research thrusts, the major conclusions emerging, and the major unanswered questions.

The previous chapter attempts to evaluate research on entrepreneurship. But the research methodology followed by the authors in their study is unclear. How was the sample of 81 papers selected?

Very few research papers from outside the United States are reviewed. Since entrepreneurship is strongly value-laden, it is almost mandatory that crosscultural studies be undertaken. Researchers in countries all over the world are examining entrepreneurship. Extensive studies have been conducted on Nova Scotia and on the Swedish "socialist economy." If the authors' sample of 81 papers represents no specific segment of the field, it is unclear to us what they have accomplished.

In their own research methodology, the authors illustrate the problematic nature of the empirical research they appear to prefer. The classification scheme they propose consists of 25 categories, for the most part suggested by Runkel and McGrath in 1972. The small and probably unrepresentative sample of 81 papers is a relatively weak test of a 25-category scheme. But more importantly, why is such a classification scheme of *methodologies* needed?

The authors "identify" only broad topics in entrepreneurship research: the individual, the processes at the firm level, societal functions, and other. But they do not tell us what burning unanswered issues were uncovered in their research. What were some of the most important *methodological* difficulties faced by earlier researchers? How can these difficulties be avoided? What specific gaps did they uncover in each of the streams?

In speculating about future research methods the authors seem to favor empirical methodologies. They also imply that there exists something that can be called "the best method" for doing research in a particular area. The real issue is seldom which and how many methods to use; the real issue is to define the research question precisely and meaningfully. A well-defined research question usually suggests what kind of methodology is appropriate given the available data, the prevailing state of theory in that particular area, and the personal skills of the researchers. It is not wise to overemphasize rigor at the expense of relevance; methodological rigor requires that one deal with simpler, less realistic forms of the total problem. The field of entrepreneurship and policy demands that researchers deal with a totality. No one would argue with the proposition that a well formulated question should be investigated with the best method available, but it is unlikely that a useful methodology is unique to any stream.

Consider the confusion that seems to exist around the term "entrepreneur." Some researchers say that an entrepreneur can be any one of the four: inventor, new venture initiator, owner/manager, or employee/manager (Peterson 1977). This author has no quarrel with those who say that the boundary lines between these conceptual differences tend to get blurred, but strongly disagrees with those who do not think this burning issue needs to be defined more precisely before research in this area can continue. If the concept of entrepreneurship is all-inclusive, it becomes useless from a research standpoint.

Research indicates that it is very difficult for an inventor to make the transition into launching an economic enterprise. At the same time research indicates that venture initiators tend to get bored once their venture is successfully underway; day-to-day management does not interest them. Furthermore, managers who own their own companies seem to display different risk-taking capacities than do employee/managers who play with the money of other people. Admittedly, the research on the dividing lines between the four concepts is rather sparse. But this identifies a gap in entrepreneurship research.

Shapero's entrepreneurial event model doesn't focus on the individual but rather identifies a number of variables that influence the creation of a new venture. While his paradigm is very useful, there is still a need for better understanding about the different concepts of inventor, entrepreneur, owner/manager, and employee/manager.

Those who administer funding to encourage economic development through entrepreneurship must determine to whom support should be given. This describes Shapero's entrepreneurial climate. But how such a climate is generated is less clear. In the end the issue comes down to individuals. Methodological finesse does not provide adequate help for policy-makers who need to know more about individual entrepreneurs.

commentary/elaboration

Commentary on research methodology in entrepreneurship

M. Ray Perryman

Overview

Professors Paulin, Coffey, and Spaulding provide an excellent survey of contemporary research methods in the field of entrepreneurship. Their thorough exposition carefully delineates various strains of development within the discipline, and will undoubtedly be of great value to investigators. In one sense, however, the prescriptions advanced in the analysis may be too limited in scope and may tend to inhibit progress in this research area.

The state of entrepreneurial research

My background is that of an academic economist and, hence, my a priori knowledge of entrepreneurship involves its role in economic theory, as part of the biological processes of Alfred Marshall (1890), a systematic element of the capital and cycle theories of Frank Knight (1921, 1957) and Joseph Schumpeter (1939), a catalyst in the innovation process of John Maynard Keynes (1936), and the subject of analytical exploration by William Baumol (1968). This literature, however, is generally highly formalistic and, as such, does not address the problems of the entrepreneurial process in a meaningful fashion. In fact, one of the greatest shortcomings of modern economic modeling, both theoretical and empirical, is its failure to adequately integrate the risk-taking and innovative functions in simulation exercises.

Even my minimal exposure, however, when coupled with the information obtained from the Paulin, Coffey, and Spaulding chapter, permits two conclusions. Initially, it is apparent that entrepreneurship, like economics, is emerging as a distinct discipline of study in response to evolving societal structures. Economics evolved from moral philosophy as the simple mechanisms of tradition and command were replaced by the dynamics of a market system functioning within an increasingly complex external environment. Similarly, entrepreneurship is developing as an outgrowth of management, finance, and economics as the pragmatic difficulties confronting innovative activity have become sufficiently distinct to demand separate analytical treatment. This situation has resulted largely from the evolution of an institutional and legal framework that poses significant barriers to entrepreneurial achievement.

The second obvious factor regarding this area of inquiry lies in its present state of progress. Specifically, it is entirely correct to say that entrepreneurial research is in its formative stages and, hence, corresponds to the "pre-science" phase of the Kuhnian scientific structure (Kuhn 1970). It is presently characterized by the absence of both a definitive set of precepts and a universally accepted methodological process. The latter omission is, of course, more relevant to the present topic. It is apparent that, like virtually any embryonic field, this area is currently producing studies based on a broad spectrum of analytical devices, ranging from formal theoretical models to the anecdotal evidence of experienced practitioners. In view of this disparity, Paulin, Coffey, and Spaulding advocate an immediate and significant move toward precise theory and verification, a strategy from which I must dissent.

The future of entrepreneurial research

If any discipline is to be propelled from its origins to a more advanced state, the initial myriad of seemingly incoherent theories, assumptions, notions, rules of thumb, and wives' tales must be organized into a unifying framework for investigation. This dictum applies whether the ultimate source of progress is a definitive Kuhnian scientific revolution or, as will more probably be the case for entrepreneurship, a simple Hegelian synthesis (Hegel 1837). The predominance of theory and verification, while a distinctly positive sign, must occur as a natural part of the evolutionary process, not as a dictated maxim. To effectively bring order to the chaos, it is first essential for the chaos to be apparent.

Given the current state of entrepreneurial research, the commonality of results is not sufficient to expect a synthesis in the immediate future. Thus, the chaos must be allowed to continue. Economics must explicitly account for risk-taking and innovative functions in models, finance and management must address the unique aspects of entrepreneurial enterprise, and practitioners must share their experience, both systematically and anecdotally. Sherlock Holmes, a noted investigator in another area and of another generation, once noted that "It is a capital mistake to theorize before you have all the evidence. It biases the judgment" (Conan Doyle 1887). With respect to the development of a research discipline, the "data" (all forms of existing investigation) must be accumulated before the "judgment" (an initial synthesis) can be meaningfully rendered.

References

BAUMOL, WILLIAM J., "Entrepreneurship in Economic Theory," *The American Economic Review* 58, No. 2 (May 1968).

BOUCHARD, T., "Field Research Methods: Interviewing, Questionnaires, Participant

Observations, Systematic Observations, Unobtrusive Measure," in *Handbook of Industrial and Organizational Psychology*, ed. Marvin D. Dunnette. Chicago: Rand McNally, 1976.

BROCKHAUS, ROBERT H., "Psychological and Environmental Factors Which Distinguish the Successful from the Unsuccessful Entrepreneur: A Longitudinal Study," *Academy of Management Proceedings*, 1980.

CAMPBELL, DONALD T., and STANLEY, JULIAN C., *Experimental and Quasi-Experimental Design for Research.* New York: Rand McNally, 1973.

COHEN, A. M., and SMITH, D. R., *The Critical Incident in Growth Groups.* La Jolla, Ca.: University Associates, 1976.

CONAN DOYLE, SIR ARTHUR, "A Study in Scarlet," *The Complete Original Illustrated Sherlock Holmes.* Secaucus, N.J.: Castle, 1887.

DUNCAN, R. B., "Qualitative Research Methods in Strategic Management," in *Strategic Management: A New View of Business Policy and Planning*, eds. D. E. Schendel and C. W. Hofer. Boston: Little, Brown, 1979.

HEGEL, GEORG W. F., *The Philosophy of History.* New York: Dover, 1956 (Originally published in 1837).

KERLINGER, N., *Foundations of Behavioral Research.* New York: Holt, Rinehart & Winston, 1964.

KEYNES, JOHN MAYNARD, *The General Theory of Employment, Interest, and Money.* London: Macmillan, 1936.

KNIGHT, FRANK H., *Risk, Uncertainty and Profit.* New York: Kelly, 1957 (Originally published in 1921).

KUHN, THOMAS, *The Structure of Scientific Revolutions.* Chicago: University of Chicago, 1970.

MCGRATH, J. E., "Toward a Theory of Method for Research in Organizations," in *New Perspectives in Organizational Research*, eds. W. W. Cooper, H. J. Leavitt, and M. W. Shelly. New York: John Wiley, 1964.

MARSHALL, ALFRED, *Principles of Economics.* London: Macmillan, 1890.

PAULIN, W. L. *Consulting of Small Business by Students: Experience at Three Universities* (Doctoral dissertation, University of Washington, 1980).

PETERSON, REIN, *Small Business: Building a Balanced Economy.* Toronto: Press Porcepic, 1977, Chapter 2 (Currently distributed by Macmillan of Canada).

RUNKEL, P. J., and MCGRATH, J. E., *Research on Human Behavior.* New York: Holt, Rinehart & Winston, 1972.

SCHENDEL, D. E., and HOFER, C. W., *Stategic Management.* Englewood Cliffs, N.J.: Prentice-Hall, 1979.

SCHREIER, J. W., and KOMIVES, J. L., *The Entrepreneur and New Enterprise Formation: A Resource Guide.* Milwaukee: Center for Venture Management, 1973.

SCHUMPETER, JOSEPH A., *Business Cycles: A Theoretical, Historical, and Statistical Analysis of the Capitalist Process.* New York: McGraw-Hill, 1939.

SMITH, C. B., "Measurement Fundamentals in Entrepreneurship," in *Entrepreneurship and Enterprise Development: A Worldwide Perspective*, eds. J. W. Schreier et al. Milwaukee: Center for Venture Management, 1975.

VESPER, K. H., "Research on Education for Entrepreneurship" (Paper presented at the Conference on Research and Education in Entrepreneurship, Baylor University, March, 1980).

VESPER, K. H., *New Venture Strategies.* Englewood Cliffs, N.J.: Prentice-Hall, 1980.

Section Five

Areas for Future Research

chapter xix

Research needs and issues in entrepreneurship

chapter xix

Research needs and issues in entrepreneurship

Donald L. Sexton

Overview

As evidenced by the preceding chapters, the field of entrepreneurship has expanded considerably over the past few years. However, the field is still in its infancy, perhaps at about the same position business policy was, as a functional area, a decade ago. Research is for the most part still in the exploratory stage and quite fragmented. Efforts must be directed toward developing a total framework for future research. Such is the goal of this book: to review the research that is reported in the literature, to examine current research, and to identify those areas in which additional research is needed.

In this chapter, a discussion of broad research issues will be followed by more specific research topics derived from the four earlier sections of the book. No specific hypotheses or research methods will be suggested for a given topical area. The areas in which additional research would make a significant contribution to the body of knowledge in the field are identified both as a summary of the book and as a guide for future work.

Entrepreneurship means many things to different people, as evidenced by the variety of current research. Some researchers regard almost anyone who starts a venture as an entrepreneur. Others prefer a much narrower definition, which includes risk and an innovative product or service. To some, risk is exclusively financial risk. To others, the risk of losing a position in a large firm satisfies this component. Some feel that innovation is a necessary element in entrepreneurship; others do not.

Clearly there is a need for a definition that is acceptable to all, a definition that lends itself to measurement, comparison, and performance results. Until such time as a usable definition is developed, researchers should clearly state the definition used in their particular research effort.

The field may not yet be sophisticated enough to produce complex or complete models. However, the development of models will illuminate the interrelationships of the various components. Reductive models unfortunately ignore real problems in order to fit in neat packages. Models in this field must move toward full descriptions of all the relevant relationships. Through such efforts researchers will be able to view the field of entrepreneurship as a whole rather than looking at fragments or subsystems.

There is still considerable discussion as to whether entrepreneurial tendencies are hereditary or environmental and therefore subject to learning and application. There seems to be general agreement among researchers that although certain characteristics may be inborn or acquired early in life, one can be taught techniques and methodologies that significantly enhance the probability of initiating and successfully completing a new venture. Further studies in the area are needed to resolve the issue so that serious researchers need not expend effort justifying their research.

While there will be overlap, issues and topics for further research will be delineated according to the four areas covered in this book. The purpose is not to identify specific research topics or to be exhaustive but to provoke ideas that can be translated into research.

Research on the entrepreneur

This area forms the basis upon which the other areas of inquiry are constructed. Research in this area is still highly fragmented. Much is being learned about specific topics, but there is no framework to unite the research into an overall description or definition of the entrepreneur.

Much has been learned from the efforts of the few who write entrepreneurial history. As more is learned from living entrepreneurs, the base is broadening. Researchers are finding that gathering data while the subject is still living is much easier than reconstructing history. The problem is that we still do not know what questions to ask.

Although entrepreneurial psychology has received a great deal of attention, there is a considerable need to broaden, clarify, and test the published results.

The three major questions in this area are:

1. Are there psychological characteristics that distinguish the successful entrepreneur from other persons?
2. If so, were these characteristics present prior to the entrepreneurial experience, or were they produced by the entrepreneurial experience itself?
3. If there are distinguishing characteristics and if they were present prior to the entrepreneurial activity, how can these factors be reliably measured in advance of initiating a new enterprise?

Much of the past research in this area has focused on successful entrepreneurs, so much so, in fact, that the word "entrepreneur" has almost become synonymous with "successful entrepreneur." Since these studies were conducted after ventures had been initiated, they do not address the question of whether the entrepreneurial characteristics had a prior existence. Once additional studies have been performed on both unsuccessful entrepreneurs and successful business executives, comparisons can be made among all three types. With this type of effort, researchers can move from descriptive to predictive research.

Further, most studies have concentrated on male entrepreneurs. The increasing number of female entrepreneurs provides another area of potential comparative characteristics research.

The test instruments used in most entrepreneurial characteristics research were developed for other uses. A prime area for additional research is in the development and validation of additional measuring instruments which provide the desired information and at the same time offer easier or more efficient administration.

Additional comprehensive longitudinal studies of a comparative nature are needed. Ideally, data collection would begin before the entrepreneurial decision is made. This represents a considerable effort but lends itself well to a team approach of researchers in the field. If more than psychological characteristics were examined and a large random sample of entrepreneurs across the country were involved, the data could be categorized in many ways for comparison and still provide subsets of sufficient size for statistical interpretation. It is only by such means that we can more accurately interpret the impact of psychological characteristics on the entrepreneurial decision and frequency of success.

One paradigm suggests that entrepreneurial formations result from the interaction of social and cultural forces rather than psychological characteristics.

Most researchers agree that individuals are conditioned by their social and cultural inheritance and experience. However, these factors and their impact on the entrepreneurial decision are still being identified. Once this has been completed, a model could be developed to combine psychological and sociological factors, as they influence not only the decision but the outcome of the business venture. Studies of this type combined with longitudinal studies could lead to predictive research in future efforts.

Research in entrepreneurial technology

This area includes such topics as new venture creation, risk and venture capital, and the relationships between entrepreneurship and firm size. In the nonacademic literature, researchers discuss their findings on innovation, economic development, and business terminations in layman's terms.

The last ten years have spawned a remarkable burst of interest and activity in entrepreneurship and venture creation. New models have appeared, several new academic books have emerged, and many articles and papers have been published. Yet the research needs in new venture creation are overwhelming. In the areas of models and methodologies, several specific topics have been delineated by Professor Timmons. Broader areas for research include such issues as the economic and social contributions made by new and growing firms, the effects of public policy and resource allocation on new ventures, and the relative effectiveness of various forms of training and assistance to venture creation.

In the area of risk capital or venture capital research, some very good models and methodologies have been developed. Unfortunately, most of the research has been theoretical in nature, and empirical tests of theoretical propositions have revealed a bias toward large firms. There is an absence of reliable data for systematic, longitudinal studies of smaller firms, and the link between small firms and organized financial markets is not as well established or as easily observed as the link between large firms and financial markets.

Financial theory can be applied in many ways to the problems of new venture and small firm finance and to the modeling of microeconomic processes. The contributions of risk capital and entrepreneurship to job creation, technological innovation, productivity, tax generation, and price performance must also be more broadly and more precisely quantified. Research on the efficiency of risk capital markets and the information circuits between entrepreneurs and investors could yield public policies designed to improve the performance of these markets.

In the area of entrepreneurship and small business, there are four major topics for additional research: First, what factors account for the wide variations in profitability among small firms? Second, what is the relationship between new venture strategy and small firm performance? Third, what characteristics enable entrepreneurs to adjust their management styles to the more formal organization of a growing firm? Last, what is the nature or significance of small business or new venture failures? Is failure as bad as it may first appear, or is it part of the learning process? The difficulty of analyzing failing firms clearly establishes the need for additional research.

Research needs: entrepreneurship and progress

In this section, the roles of entrepreneurship in economic development and innovation are considered. Most economists, and particularly the econometricians, seem unable to recognize the existence and role of the entrepreneur. When they do, they assign an excessively narrow definition to the entrepreneurial function. Economists tend to ignore, or hold constant, the disequilibrium conditions that create profit opportunities for entrepreneurs. Research must consider the imperfect competition and knowledge that prevails in most economic situations. The usefulness of economics lies in the capacity of the discipline to produce policy recommendations. This requires the construction of sufficiently general models to allow the outcome of policy alternatives to be predicted with some degree of certainty.

Further, researchers must investigate the free enterprise segments in controlled economies to discover the compatibility of planning and entrepreneurship. The benefits of government planning have been severely questioned as a result of academic investigation. Making the public sector a positive force in entrepreneurship is a worthy goal for future research.

Academic inquiry can substantially help the private sector to supply the new products, processes, and services needed by society. Much of the literature on entrepreneurial innovation is corporation oriented and must be recast in a setting that is relevant to the non-corporate innovator. Many, if not most, new inventions never reach commercial fruition. Research can improve the innovation yield.

On a more theoretical plane, researchers still need a working definition of innovation to illuminate the process in general and the role of entrepreneurship in particular. Research must identify which institutions, including the institution of entrepreneurship, appear to be most appropriate for the various types of innovation.

There is a notable absence of theoretical frameworks regarding the impact of environmental factors upon entrepreneurship. Research has not empirically verified the relative importance of different environmental components. A number of factors have impeded research developments: the lack of available data, the incompatible formats of available data, and the lack of consensus as to which environmental variables should be theoretically linked to entrepreneurial activity.

Research needs in this area are many and multifaceted. Constructs must be developed and validated on the basis of multiple traits and multiple means of approach. Research should examine how entrepreneurs assess an environment before starting a new venture, the relative weight they give the different environmental aspects, and the information sources used in evaluation.

The costs of compliance with state and federal regulations have increased start-up costs. Research on these additional costs and their impact on the rate of innovation and start-ups could have significant implications for government policy-makers.

Incubator firms are believed to be important breeding grounds for prospective entrepreneurs, yet little is known about them. Research in this area could provide valuable insights into the incubator process.

The availability of venture capital has been established as a positive factor in the environment for entrepreneurship. It is, of course, not always available. Research into this unavailability could be of importance to governmental agencies contemplating possible interventions on behalf of viable but unfunded venture proposals.

Finally, research results will apply differently to different industries. The impact of certain factors on entrepreneurship will vary from setting to setting and must be assessed accordingly.

Research in the area of entrepreneurship and academia

The number of entrepreneurship courses in academia has increased nearly tenfold over the last decade. More recently, the trend at the collegiate level is toward entire programs in the area. There have been few entrepreneurship programs at the high school and elementary levels. A number of schools now combine entrepreneurial courses with innovation programs, business outreach activities, and private enterprise education programs.

As these new programs develop, educators themselves may need to adopt entrepreneurial approaches and to make substantial departures from traditional school patterns. Virtually nothing is known at present about what types of instruction stimulate potential entrepreneurs or assist practicing ones. Questions about alternate educational delivery systems are seldom raised. The objectives of entrepreneurial programs will need continual review. Each new course or program must be assessed for its impact on the aspiring entrepreneur.

Feedback from alumni could give clues as to which course formats and teaching techniques are more effective. This information and the incorporation of necessary changes could significantly improve entrepreneurial education.

As an academic discipline, entrepreneurship is still in its infancy. It is a complex phenomenon that includes a number of intertwined and difficult to measure variables. Entrepreneurship is developing as an outgrowth of management, finance, and economics as the pragmatic difficulties confronting innovative activity have become sufficiently distinct to demand separate analytical treatment. Studies are currently based on a broad spectrum of analytical devices, ranging from formal theoretical models to the anecdotal evidence of experienced practitioners. No definitive set of precepts and no universally accepted methodology exist at present.

If entrepreneurial research is to advance, the myriad of theories and assumptions must be organized into a unifying framework for investigation. Given the current state of research, however, a synthesis should not be expected in the immediate future. A forced synthesis would be counterproductive. However, current research should be as carefully and systematically designed as possible, given the topic choice and practical circumstances. Such action will enhance the validity of research findings.

In closing

The major purpose of this book is to develop directions for future research in the field of entrepreneurship. The approach was to divide the field into a number of topical areas and to review both earlier research and current research in an effort to define the "gaps" and problem areas. The purpose of the editors and authors has been well served. For those interested in the growing field of entrepreneurship, the opportunities are many and the challenges great. It is the hope of the contributors to this book that it will soon become obsolete as new and more advanced research further establishes the field of entrepreneurship as a significant area of inquiry and as an academic discipline.

Bibliography

AITKEN, H. A. J., ed., *The State and Economic Growth.* New York: Social Science Research Council, 1959.

ALBERT, KENNETH J., *How to Pick the Right Small Business Opportunity.* New York: McGraw-Hill, 1977.

ALDRICH, HOWARD E., *Organizations and Environment.* Englewood Cliffs, N.J.: Prentice-Hall, 1979.

ALEXANDER, ALEC P., "Industrial Entrepreneurship in Turkey: Origins and Growth," *Economic Development and Cultural Change* VIII, No. 4 (July 1960).

ALLISON, DAVID, "The University and Regional Prosperity," *International Science and Technology,* April 1965.

APLIN, J. C., and LEVETO, G. A., "Factors That Influence the Business Success of Minority Entrepreneurs," *American Journal of Small Business* 1, No. 2 (October 1976).

ARGYRIS, CHRIS, *Intervention Theory and Method.* Reading, Mass.: Addison-Wesley, 1970.

ARRINGTON, LEONARD, *Great Basin Kingdom: An Economic History of the Latter Day Saints.* Cambridge: Harvard University, 1958.

ARROW, KENNETH J., CHENERY, H. B., MINHAUS, B. S., and SOLOW, R. M., "Capital-Labor Substitution and Economic Efficiency," *Review of Economics and Statistics* XLIII (1961).

ATKINSON, JOHN W., "Motivational Determinants of Risk-Taking Behavior," *Psychological Review* 63 (1956).

ATKINSON, JOHN W., "Motivational Determinants of Risk Taking Behavior," *Psychological Review* 64 (1957).

ATKINSON, JOHN W., and FEATHER, NORMAN T., eds., *A Theory of Achievement Motivation.* New York: John Wiley, 1966.

AUBREY, H. G., "Industrial Investment Revisions: A Comparative Analysis," *Journal of Economic History*, December 1955.

BALAN, J., BROWNING, H. L., and JELIN, E., *Men in a Developing Society.* Austin: University of Texas, 1973.

BALDWIN, W. L., and CHILDS, G. L., "The Fast Second and Rivalry in Research and Development," *Southern Economic Journal* 36 (July 1969).

BALL, RAY, and BROWN, PHILIP, "An Empirical Evaluation of Accounting Income Numbers," *Journal of Accounting Research* 6 (Autumn 1968).

BALSAUBRAMANYAM, V. N., *International Transfer of Technology to India.* New York: Holt, Rinehart & Winston, 1973.

BANFIELD, EDWARD C., *Political Influence.* New York: Free Press, 1964.

BANGS, DAVID H., and OSGOOD, WILLIAM R., *Business Planning Guide.* Portsmouth, N.H.: Upstart Publishing Company, 1979.

BARANSON, JACK, *Industrial Technologies for Developing Economies.* New York: Holt, Rinehart & Winston, 1969.

BARNET, RICHARD, and MULLER, RONALD, *Global Reach: The Power of the Multinationals.* New York: Simon & Schuster, 1971.

BATY, GORDON B., *Entrepreneurship: Playing to Win.* Reston, Va.: Reston Publishing Co., 1974.

BATY, GORDON B., "Financing the New, Research-Based Enterprises in New England," (Master's Thesis, Sloan School, MIT, 1963).

BAUMBACK, CLIFFORD M., and LAWYER, KENNETH, *How to Organize and Operate a Small Business* (6th ed.). Englewood Cliffs, N.J.: Prentice-Hall, 1979.

BAUMBACK, CLIFFORD M., and MANCUSO, JOSEPH, *Entrepreneurship and Venture Management.* Englewood Cliffs, N.J.: Prentice-Hall, 1975.

BAUMBACK, CLIFFORD M., and SCHOEN, J. E., "Assessing Entrepreneurial Potential," *Proceedings* (24th Annual Conference, International Council for Small Business). Quebec City: Laval University, 1979.

BAUMOL, WILLIAM J., "Entrepreneurship in Economic Theory," *The American Economic Review* 58, No. 2 (May 1968).

BEALS, ALLEN, *Village Life in South India.* Chicago: Aldine, 1974.

BECKER, GARY S., "Investment in Human Capital: A Theoretical Analysis," *Journal of Political Economy* LXX (October 1962).

BEHARI, BEPIN, *Economic Growth and Technological Change in India.* New Delhi: Vikas Publishing House, 1974.

BELLUSH, JEWEL, and HAUSKNECHT, MURRAY, "Entrepreneurs and Urban Renewal: The New Men of Power," *Journal of the American Institute of Planners* XXXII, No. 2 (September 1962).

BENOIT, J. L., "Venture Capital Investment Behavior: The Risk-Capital Investor in New Company Formation in France" (Doctoral dissertation, University of Texas, 1974).

BERLEW, DAVID, *The First Annual Karl A. Bostrum Seminar in the Study of Enterprise.* Milwaukee: Center for Venture Management, 1969.

BERLEW, D. E., and LECLERE, W. E., "Social Intervention in Chicago: A Case Study," *Journal of Applied Behavioral Sciences* 10, No. 1 (1974).

BERLINGEN, J. S., *The Innovation Decision in Soviet Industry.* Cambridge: MIT, 1976.

BERNA, JAMES J., *Industrial Entrepreneurship in Madras State.* Bombay: Asia Publishing House, 1960.

BHATTASALI, B. N., *Transfer of Technology among the Developing Countries.* Tokyo: Asian Productivity Organization, 1972.

BHATTASALI, B. N., *U.N. Industrial Development Organization, Guidelines for the Acquisition of Foreign Technology in Developing Countries.* New York: United Nations, 1973.

BIRCH, D. L., *The Job Generation Process.* Washington, D.C.: U.S. Department of Commerce, 1979.

BLITZER, CHARLES R., CLARK, PETER B., and TAYLOR, LANCE, eds., *Economy-Wide Models and Development Planning.* London: Oxford University, 1975.

BOLTON, J. E., *Small Firms: Report of the Committee of Inquiry on Small Firms* (The Bolton Report). London: HMSO, 1971.

BONACICH, EDNA, "A Theory of Middleman Minorities," *American Sociological Review* 38 (1973).

BONIFAY, P. H., EON, J. F., LABRE, H., and MELER, J., *La Création D'Enterprise.* Marseille: Chambre de Commerce et D'Industrie de Marseille, 1977.

BOOMS, BERNARD H., and WARD, JAMES E., JR., "The Cons of Black Capitalism," *Business Horizons* 12, No. 5 (October 1969).

BORLAND, CANDACE, *Locus of Control, Need for Achievement and Entrepreneurship* (Doctoral dissertation, University of Texas, 1974).

BOSWELL, JONATHAN, *The Rise and Decline of Small Firms.* London: George Allen & Unwin, 1972.

BOUCHARD, T., "Field Research Methods: Interviewing, Questionnaires, Participant Observations, Systematic Observations, Unobtrusive Measure," in *Handbook of Industrial and Organizational Psychology*, ed. Marvin D. Dunnette. Chicago: Rand McNally, 1976.

BRADEN, PATRICIA, *Technical Entrepreneurship.* Ann Arbor: University of Michigan, 1977.

BRIGHT, J. R., "Some Lessons from Technological Innovations Research," *Les Nouvelles* 4, No. 5 (November 1969).

BROCKHAUS, ROBERT H., "The Effect of Job Dissatisfaction on the Decision to Start a Business," *Journal of Small Business Management* 18 (January 1980).

BROCKHAUS, ROBERT H., "I-E Locus of Control Scores as Predictors of Entrepreneurial Intentions," *Academy of Management Proceedings*, 1975.

BROCKHAUS, ROBERT H., "Psychological and Environmental Factors Which Distinguish the Successful from the Unsuccessful Entrepreneur: A Longitudinal Study," *Academy of Management Proceedings*, 1980.

BROCKHAUS, ROBERT H., "Risk Taking Propensity of Entrepreneurs," *Academy of Management Journal*, September 1980.

BROCKHAUS, ROBERT H., and NOLD, WALTER R., "An Exploration of Factors Affecting the Entrepreneurial Decision: Personal Characteristics vs. Environmental Calculations," *Academy of Management Proceedings*, 1979.

BROEHL, WAYNE G., JR., "A Less Developed Entrepreneur," *Columbia Journal of World Business* 5, No. 2 (March-April 1970).

BROEHL, WAYNE G., JR., *The Molly Maguires.* Cambridge: Harvard University, 1964.

BROEHL, WAYNE G., JR., *The Village Entrepreneur.* Cambridge: Harvard University, 1978.

BROOM, H. N., and LONGENECKER, JUSTIN G., *Small Business Management* (5th ed.). Cincinnati: South-Western Publishing Co., 1979.

BRUYAT, C., and CARNET, G., *Les Créateurs D'Enterprises Industrie.* Paris: Centre D'Etudes et de Formation des Assistants en Gestion Industrielle (CEFAGI), 1976.

BUCHELE, ROBERT, *Business Policy in Growing Firms.* San Francisco: Harper & Row, Pub., 1967.

BUNNS, VERNE A., and TERFLINGER, CURTIS D., *Buying and Selling a Small Business.* Wichita, Kans.: Wichita State University, 1963.

BURNS, TOM, and STALKER, G. M., *The Management of Innovation.* London: Tavistock Publications, 1961.

Business History Review. Boston: Harvard Business School, 1929-1933.

Business History Review. Boston: Harvard Business School, 1959-1964.

Business Manuals. Santa Monica, Ca.: International Entrepreneurs and Associations, 1979.

CAMPBELL, D., and FISKE, D., "Convergent and Discriminant Validation by the Multi-Trait Multi-Method Matrix," *Psychological Bulletin*, March 1954.

CAMPBELL, DONALD, and STANLEY, JULIAN, *Experimental and Quasi-Experimental Design for Research.* New York: Rand McNally, 1973.

"Capital Formation Survey of High Technology Companies" (unpublished paper by the American Electronic Association, 1977).

CARLTON, DENNIS W., "Models of New Business Location" (Working paper, University of Chicago, 1978).

CARLYLE, THOMAS, *Letters of Thomas Carlyle to John Stuart Mill*, ed. Alexander Carlyle. New York: Fredrick Stocker, 1923.

CARROLL, JOHN J., *The Filipino Manufacturing Entrepreneur: Agent and Product of Change.* New York: Cornell University, 1965.

CHAKRAVARTY, S., and LEFEBER, L., "An Optimizing Planning Model," *Economic Weekly* 17 (February 1965).

CHANDLER, ALFRED D., *Visible Hand.* Cambridge: Harvard University, 1979.

CHANDLER, ALFRED D., and REDLICH, FRITZ, "Comments," *Business History Review*, Autumn 1961.

CHANDLER, ALFRED D., and REDLICH, FRITZ, "Recent Developments in American Business Administration and Their Conceptualization," *Business History Review*, Spring 1961.

CHENERY, HOLLIS B., and SYRQUIN, MOISES, *Patterns of Development, 1950-1970.* London: Oxford University, 1975.

CHILD, JOHN, ed., *Management and Organization.* New York: Halstead Press, 1974.

CHRISTENSEN, R. C., ANDREWS, K. R., and BOWER, J. L., *Business Policy* (4th ed.). Homewood, Ill.: Richard D. Irwin, 1978.

CHURCHILL, B., "Age and Life Expectancy of Business Firms," *Survey of Current Business*, December 1955.

CLARK, N. G., "Science, Technology and Regional Economic Development," *Research Policy* 1, No. 3 (1972).

CLARKE, THOMAS E., *R & D Management Bibliography.* Ottawa: Innovation Management Institute of Canada, 1975.

COCHRAN, THOMAS C., *Business in American Life: A History.* New York: McGraw-Hill, 1972.
COCHRAN, THOMAS C., "The Entrepreneur in Economic Change," *Behavioral Science* IX, No. 2 (April 1964).
COCHRAN, THOMAS C., and REINA, RUBEN E., *Capitalism in Argentine Culture.* Philadelphia: University of Pennsylvania, 1962.
COHEN, A. M., and SMITH, D. R., *The Critical Incident in Growth Groups.* La Jolla, Ca.: University Associates, 1976.
COLE, ARTHUR H., "An Approach to the Study of Entrepreneurship," in *Explorations in Enterprise*, ed. Hugh G. J. Aiken. Cambridge: Harvard University, 1965.
COLE, ARTHUR H., *Business Enterprise in Its Social Setting.* Cambridge: Harvard University, 1959.
COLE, ARTHUR H., "Entrepreneurship as an Area of Research," *The Task of Economic History* (Supplement to *Journal of Economic History*), December 1942.
"Colleges Are Replacing School of Hard Knocks for Some Businessmen," *Wall Street Journal* XCVII, No. 113 (December 9, 1977).
COLLINS, ORVIS F., and MOORE, DAVID G., *The Organization Makers: A Behavioral Study of Independent Entrepreneurs.* New York: Meredith, 1970.
COLLINS, ORVIS F., MOORE, DAVID G., and UNWALLA, DARAB B., *The Enterprising Man.* East Lansing: Michigan State University Business Studies, 1964.
COMANOR, W. W., "Research and Technological Change in the Pharmaceutical Industry," *Review of Economics and Statistics*, May 1965.
COMEGYS, CHARLES, "Cognitive Dissonance and Entrepreneurial Behavior," *Journal of Small Business Management*, January 1976.
COMEGYS, CHARLES, "Research Needs of Prospective Entrepreneurs," *Atlantic Economic Review* 28, No. 3 (1978).
CONAN DOYLE, SIR ARTHUR, "A Study in Scarlet," *The Complete Original Illustrated Sherlock Holmes.* Secaucus, N.J.: Castle, 1887.
CONVERSE, P. E., "The Nature of Belief Systems in Mass Publics," in *Ideology and Discontent*, ed. D. E. Apter. New York: Free Press, 1964.
COOPER, ARNOLD C., "The Entrepreneurial Environments," *Industrial Research* 12 (September 1970).
COOPER, ARNOLD C., *The Founding of Technologically-Based Firms.* Milwaukee: Center for Venture Management, 1971.
COOPER, ARNOLD C., "Incubator Organizations and Other Influences on Entrepreneurship," in *Entrepreneurship and Enterprise Development: A Worldwide Perspective* (Proceedings of Project ISEED). Milwaukee: Center for Venture Management, 1975.
COOPER, ARNOLD C., "Incubator Organizations and Technical Entrepreneurship," in *Technical Entrepreneurship: A Symposium*, eds. Arnold C. Cooper and John L. Komives. Milwaukee: Center for Venture Management, 1972.
COOPER, ARNOLD C., "The Palo Alto Experience," *Industrial Research*, May 1970.
COOPER, ARNOLD C., "R & D Is More Efficient in Small Companies," *Harvard Business Review*, June 1964.
COOPER, ARNOLD C., "Spin-Offs and Technical Entrepreneurship," *IEEE Transactions Of Engineering Management* EM-18, No. 1 (February 1971).
COOPER, ARNOLD C., "Strategic Management: New Ventures and Small Business" (Working paper, Krannert Graduate School of Management, Purdue University, 1978).

COOPER, ARNOLD C., "Technical Entrepreneurship: What Do We Know?" in *Entrepreneurship and Venture Management*, eds. C. Baumback and J. Mancuso. Englewood Cliffs, N.J.: Prentice-Hall, 1975.

COOPER, ARNOLD C., "Technical Entrepreneurship: What Do We Know?" *Research and Development Management* 3 (February 1973).

COOPER, ARNOLD C., and BRUNO, ALBERT, "Success among High-Technology Firms," *Business Horizons* 20, No. 2 (April 1977).

COOPER, ARNOLD C., and KOMIVES, JOHN L., eds., *Technical Entrepreneurship: A Symposium.* Milwaukee: Center for Venture Management, 1972.

COPULSKY, WILLIAM, and MCNULTY, HERBERT W., *Entrepreneurship and the Corporation.* Amacom, 1974.

Copyright Management. Arlington, Mass.: Institute for Invention and Innovation.

CRAY, ED, *Levi's.* Boston: Houghton Mifflin, 1978.

DAHMÉN, ERIK, *Entrepreneurial Activity and the Development of Swedish Industry, 1919–1939*, transl. Axel Leijonhufvud. Homewood, Ill.: Richard D. Irwin, 1970.

DALTON, GEORGE, ed., *Primitive Archaic and Modern Economies: Essays of Karl Polanyi.* Garden City, N.Y.: Anchor Books, 1968.

D'AMBOISE, G. R., *Personal Characteristics, Organizational Practices, and Managerial Effectiveness: A Comparative Study of French and English-Speaking Chief Executives in Quebec.* Los Angeles: University of California, 1974.

DANIELS, LORNA M., comp., *Studies in Enterprise: A Selected Bibliography of American and Canadian Company Histories and Biographies of Businessmen.* Boston: Harvard Business School, 1957.

DANILOV, VICTOR J., "Research Parks and Regional Development," in *Technical Entrepreneurship: A Symposium*, eds. Arnold C. Cooper and John L. Komives. Milwaukee: Center for Venture Management, 1972.

DAVIS, LANCE E., NORTH, DOUGLASS, and SMORODIN, CALLA, *Institutional Change and American Economic Growth.* Cambridge: Cambridge University, 1971.

DECARLO, JAMES F., and LYONS, PAUL R., "A Comparison of Selected Personal Characteristics of Minority and Non-Minority Female Entrepreneurs," *Journal of Small Business Management* 17, No. 4 (October 1979).

DEEKS, JOHN, *The Small Firm Owner-Manager: Entrepreneurial Behavior and Management Practice.* New York: Holt, Rinehart & Winston, 1976.

DENISON, EDWARD F., *Accounting for Slower Economic Growth: The United States in the 1970's.* Washington, D.C.: Brookings Institution, 1979.

DENISON, EDWARD F., *Accounting for United States Economic Growth 1929–1969.* Washington, D.C.: Brookings Institution, 1974.

DENISON, EDWARD F., *The Sources of Economic Growth in the U.S. and the Alternatives before Us.* New York: Committee for Economic Development, 1962.

DENISON, EDWARD F., and CHUNG, WILLIAM K., *How Japan's Economy Grew So Fast.* Washington, D.C.: Brookings Institution, 1976.

DENISON, EDWARD F., and POULLIER, J. P., *Why Growth Rates Differ: Postwar Experience in Nine Western Countries.* Washington, D.C.: Brookings Institution, 1967.

DEROSSI, FLAVIA, *The Mexican Entrepreneur.* Paris: OECD, 1971.

DETERMANN, ELIZABETH, "Seeding Science-Based Industry," *Business Review* (Federal Reserve Bank of Philadelphia), May 1966.

DIBLE, DONALD M., *Up Your Own Organization.* Santa Clara, Ca.: Entrepreneur Press, 1971.

DILL, W. R., "Environment as an Influence on Managerial Autonomy," *Administrative Science Quarterly* 2 (1958).

DILLARD, DUDLEY, *Economic Development of the North Atlantic Community.* Englewood Cliffs, N.J.: Prentice-Hall, 1967.

DOCTORS, SAMUEL I., "The Impact of State and Local Governments on Small Business," *Academy of Management Proceedings*, 1980.

DOCTORS, SAMUEL I., and JURIS, HERVEY A., "Management and Technical Assistance for Minority Enterprise" (Working paper, Northwestern University, 1971).

DOMAR, EVSEY D., "Capital Expansion, Rate of Growth, and Employment," *Econometrica* 14 (April 1946).

DOMAR, EVSEY D., "Investment Losses and Monopolies," *Income Employment and Public Policy: Essays in Honor of Alvin Hansen.* New York: McGraw-Hill, 1948.

DONALDSON, GORDON, "Financial Management in the New, Small Manufacturing Enterprise" (Doctoral dissertation, Harvard Business School, 1955).

DOUDS, CHARLES, and RUBENSTEIN, ALBERT, "Methodology for Behavioral Aspects of Innovation," in *Technological Innovation: A Critical Review of Current Knowledge*, Vol. II, eds. P. Kelly, M. Kranzberg, et al. Washington, D.C.: Government Printing Office, 1975.

DOUGLASS, MERRILL E., "Entrepreneurial Education Level Related to Business Performance," *Academy of Management Proceedings*, 1976.

DOUGLASS, MERRILL E., and ERICKSEN, ERIC W., "Limits to Growth: Entrepreneurial Characteristics of Small Business Owners," *Academy of Management Proceedings*, 1980.

DRAHEIM, KIRK P., "Factors Influencing the Rate of Formation of Technical Companies," in *Technical Entrepreneurship: A Symposium*, eds. Arnold C. Cooper and John L. Komives. Milwaukee: Center for Venture Management, 1972.

DRAHEIM, KIRK P., HOWELL, RICHARD P., and SHAPERO, ALBERT, *The Development of a Potential Defense R & D Complex: A Study of Minneapolis–St. Paul.* Menlo Park, Ca.: SRI, 1966.

DRISCOLL, ROBERT E., and WALLENDER, HARVEY W., *Technology Transfer and Development: An Historical and Geographic Perspective.* New York: Fund for Multinational Management Education, Council of the Americas, 1974.

DUNCAN, R. B., "Qualitative Research Methods in Strategic Management," in *Strategic Management: A New View of Business Policy and Planning*, eds. D. E. Schendel and C. W. Hofer. Boston: Little, Brown, 1979.

DURAND, D. E., "Effects of Achievement Motivation and Skill Training on the Entrepreneurial Behavior of Black Businessmen," *Organizational Behavior and Human Performance* 14 (1975).

DURAND, DOUGLAS, "Training and Development of Entrepreneurs," *Journal of Small Business Management* 12, No. 4 (October 1974).

ECKAUS, RICHARD, and PAREKH, KIRIT, *Planning for Growth.* Cambridge: MIT, 1967.

Emerging Innovative Companies: An Endangered Species. Washington, D.C.: National Venture Capital Association, 1976.

Enterprise Statistics—1972. Washington, D.C.: U.S. Government Printing Office, 1977.

Entrepreneurial Discovery and Development: Progress of Action Research. Honolulu: East-West Center Technology and Development Institute, 1977.

Entrepreneurial Manager's Newsletter. Worcester, Mass.: Center for Entrepreneurial Management.

ERICKSON, GERALD A., *Another Look at the New Venture Approach* (M.B.A. thesis, University of Washington, 1978).

EVAN, W. M., *Organizational Theory: Structures, Systems and Environments.* New York: John Wiley, 1976.

FAST, NORMAN D., "Key Managerial Factors in New Venture Departments," *Industrial Marketing Management* 8 (1979).

FEDER, ERNEST, "Six Plausible Theses about the Peasant's Perspectives in the Developing World," *Development and Change* 5 (1973-1974).

FEDER, ERNEST, "Vendetta against Indigenous Technology," *Economic and Political Weekly* (Bombay), April 1975.

FILLEY, ALAN, and ALDAG, RAMON, "Policy Implications for Small Business Growth and Survival," in *The Regional Environment for Small Business and Entrepreneurship*, eds. A. Cooper and W. Dunkelbert. Milwaukee: Center for Venture Management, 1979.

Financing New Technological Enterprise. Washington, D.C.: U.S. Department of Commerce, 1970.

FINNEY, B. R., *Big Men and Business: Entrepreneurship and Economic Growth in the New Guinea Highlands.* Honolulu: University of Hawaii, 1973.

FLEMING, W. J., "The Cultural Determinants of Entrepreneurship and Economic Development: A Case Study of Mendoza Province, 1861-1914," *Journal of Economic History* XXXIX, No. 1 (March 1979).

FOSTER, GEORGE M., "Introduction: Peasant Characteristics and Personality," in *Peasant Society: A Reader*, ed. Jack M. Potter. Boston: Little, Brown, 1967.

FOSTER, GEORGE M., *Traditional Cultures: And the Impact of Technological Change.* New York: Harper & Row, 1962.

FROMM, ERICH, *Social Character in a Mexican Village: A Socio-Psychoanalytic Study.* Englewood Cliffs, N.J.: Prentice-Hall, 1970.

GALVIN, PAUL F., "Investigation and Start-up Costs: Tax Consequences and Considerations for New Business," *Taxes* 56 (July 1978).

GARZA, DANIEL, "Going It Alone," *Texas Parade*, November 1975.

GASSE, YVON, "Characteristics, Functions and Performance of Small Firm Owner-Managers in Two Industrial Environments," Evanston, Ill.: Northwestern University, 1978.

GASSE, YVON, *The Cognitive Functioning of Small Firm Owner-Managers.* Saskatchewan: University of Saskatchewan, 1979.

GASSE, YVON, *Entrepreneurial Characteristics and Practices: A Study of the Dynamics of Small Business Organizations and Their Effectiveness in Different Environments.* Sherbrooke, Quebec: Rene Prince, 1977.

GASSE, YVON, "The Processing of Information in Small Business and the Entrepreneur as Information Processor," *Academy of Management Proceedings*, 1980.

GERSCHENKRON, ALEXANDER, "A Schumpeterian Analysis of Economic Development," *Continuity in History and Other Essays.* Cambridge: Harvard University, 1968.

GERSCHENKRON, ALEXANDER, *Economic Backwardness in Historical Perspective.* Cambridge: Belknap Press, 1962.

GLUECK, WILLIAM F., and MESCON, TIMOTHY S., "Entrepreneurship: A Literature Analysis of Concepts," *Academy of Management Proceedings*, 1980.

GORDON, MYRON J., and HALPERN, PAUL J., "Cost of Capital for a Division of a Firm," *Journal of Finance* 29, No. 4 (September 1974).

GOUGH, J. W., *The Rise of the Entrepreneur*. New York: Schocken Books, 1969.

GRABOWSKI, HENRY G., "The Determinants of Industrial Research and Development," *Journal of Political Economy* 76 (1968).

GRABOWSKI, HENRY G., and BAXTER, N. D., "Rivalry in Industrial Research and Development," *Quarterly Journal of Economics* 84 (1973).

GRABOWSKI, HENRY G., VERNON, JOHN M., and THOMAS, LACY G., "The Effects of Regulatory Policy on the Incentives to Innovate: An International Comparative Analysis," in *Impact of Public Policy on Drug Innovation and Pricing*, eds. Samuel A. Mitchell and Emery Link. Washington, D.C.: American University, 1976.

GRAS, NORMAN S. B., *Business and Capitalism: An Introduction to Business History*. New York: F. S. Crofts, 1939.

GRASLEY, R. H., *The Availability of Risk Capital for Technological Innovation and Invention in Canada*. Ottawa: Ministry of State, Science and Technology, 1976.

GRIGGS, JACK, "The Commercial Banker and Industrial Entrepreneurship: The Lending Officer's Propensity to Make Loans to New and Different Companies" (Doctoral dissertation, University of Texas, 1972).

GRILICHES, ZVI, "Research Expenditures and Growth Accounting," in *Science and Technology in Economic Growth*, ed. B. R. Williams. New York: Halstad Press, 1973.

GUNDER FRANK, ANDRE, "Sociology of Development and Underdevelopment of Sociology," *Catalyst*, 1969.

GURIN, P., GURIN, G., LAS, R., and BEATTIE, M. M., "Internal-External Control in the Motivational Dynamics of Negro Youth," *Journal of Social Issues*, 1969.

GUSTAFSON, ROBERT, "An Entrepreneurial Spirit," *Mechanical Engineering News* 5, No. 4 (November 1968).

HAGE, JERALD, and AIKEN, MICHAEL, *Social Change in Complex Organizations*. New York: Random House, 1970.

HAGEN, EVERETT E., *The Economics of Development* (3rd ed.). Homewood, Ill.: Richard D. Irwin, 1980.

HAGEN, EVERETT E., "The Entrepreneur as Rebel against Traditional Society," *Human Organization*, Winter 1960–1961.

HAGEN, EVERETT E., *On the Theory of Social Change: How Economic Growth Begins*. Homewood, Ill.: Dorsey Press, 1962.

HAMBERG, D., *R & D: Essays in the Economics of Research and Development*. New York: Random House, 1966.

HAMMEED, K. A., *Enterprise: Industrial Entrepreneurship in Development*. London: Sage Publications, 1974.

HAMNER, W. C., and ORGAN, D. W., *Organizational Behavior*. Dallas: Business Publications, 1978.

HANAN, MACK, *Venture Management: A Game Plan for Corporate Growth and Diversification*. New York: McGraw-Hill, 1976.

HANNAN, MICHAEL T., and FREEMAN, JOHN H., "The Population Ecology of Organizations," *American Journal of Sociology* 82 (March 1977).

HANSEN, ALVIN H., *Business Cycles and National Income* (exp. ed.). New York: W. W. Norton & Co., Inc., 1964.

HANSEN, ALVIN H., *Economic Policy and Full Employment.* New York: McGraw-Hill, 1947.

HANSEN, ALVIN H., *Fiscal Policy and Business Cycles.* New York: McGraw-Hill, 1941.

HANSEN, ALVIN H., *Public Enterprise and Economic Development.* London: Routledge and Kegan Paul, 1959.

HARBISON, FREDERICK, "Entrepreneurial Organization as a Factor in Economic Development," *Quarterly Journal of Economics*, August 1956.

HARBISON, FREDERICK, and MYERS, CHARLES A., *Management in an Industrial World.* New York: McGraw-Hill, 1959.

HARRIS, JOHN R., "Entrepreneurship and Economic Development," in *Business Enterprise and Economic Change*, eds. L. P. Cain and P. J. Eselding. Kent, Ohio: Kent State University, 1973.

HARRIS, JOHN R., "Nigerian Entrepreneurship in Industry," in *Growth and Development of the Nigerian Economy*, eds. C. Eicher and C. Lieholm. East Lansing: Michigan State University, 1970.

HARROD, R. F., "An Essay in Dynamic Theory," *The Economic Journal* XLIX (March 1939), and errata, June 1939.

HART, GILLIAN P., *African Entrepreneurship* (Occasional paper, Institute of Social and Economic Research, Rhodes University, 1972).

HARTMAN, HEINZ, "The Enterprising Woman," *Columbia Journal of World Business* 5, No. 2 (March-April 1970).

HARTMAN, HEINZ, "Managers and Entrepreneurs: A Useful Distinction?" *Administrative Science Quarterly*, March 1959.

HARTWELL, R. M., and HIGG, ROBERT, "Good Old Economic History," *American Historical Review* 76, No. 2 (April 1971).

HAWLEY, AMOS, *Human Ecology.* New York: Ronald Press, 1950.

Hearings, Small Business Access to Equity and Venture Capital. Washington, D.C.: House Committee on Small Business, Subcommittee on Capital Investment and Business Opportunities, 1977.

Hearings, Small Business Investment Company Program. Washington, D.C.: House Committee on Small Business, Subcommittee on Capital Investment and Business Opportunities, 1978.

HEGEL, GEORG W. F., *The Philosophy of History.* New York: Dover, 1956 (Originally published in 1837).

HEILBRONER, ROBERT L., *An Inquiry into the Human Prospect* (rev. ed.). New York: W. W. Norton & Co., Inc., 1980.

HEKMAN, J. S., "What Attracts Industry to New England?" *New England Economic Indicators.* Federal Reserve Bank of Boston, December 1978.

HESS, NANCY R., "Retail Strategy—How to Avoid Failure by Success," *Business and Economic Dimensions* 10 (March-April 1974).

HEXTER, RICHARD M., "How to Sell Your Company," *Harvard Business Review*, September-October 1968.

HIGGINS, BENJAMIN, *Economic Development* (rev. ed.). New York: W. W. Norton & Co., Inc., 1968.

HILL, CHRISTOPHER, "Protestantism and the Rise of Capitalism," *Essays in the Economic and Social History of Tudor and Stuart England: In Honour of R. H. Tawney*, ed. F. J. Fisher. London: Cambridge University, 1961.

HIRSCH, P. M., "Organizational Effectiveness and the Institutional Environment," *Administrative Science Quarterly* 20 (1975).

HIRSCHMAN, ALBERT O., *Journeys Toward Progress: Studies of Economic Policy-making in Latin America.* New York: Twentieth Century Fund, 1963.

HIRSCHMAN, ALBERT O., *The Strategy of Economic Development.* New Haven: Yale University, 1958.

HLAVACEK, JAMES D., and THOMPSON, VICTOR A., "Bureaucracy and New Product Innovation," *Academy of Management Journal* 16 (September 1973).

HOAD, WILLIAM M., and ROSKO, PETER, "Management Factors Contributing to the Success and Failure of New Small Manufacturers." Bureau of Business Research: University of Michigan, 1969.

HOAD, WILLIAM M., and ROSKO, PETER, *Management Factors Contributing to the Success or Failure of New Small Manufacturers.* Ann Arbor: University of Michigan, 1964.

HODGINS, JOHN W., *Entrepreneurship in High Technology.* Hamilton, Ontario: Cromlech Press, 1972.

HOFFER, C. W., "Toward a Contingency Theory of Business Strategy," *Academy of Management Journal*, December 1975.

HOFFMAN, CARY A., "The Role of the Financial Community in the Formation, Growth, and Effectiveness of Technical Companies: The Attitude of Commercial Loan Officers," in *Technical Entrepreneurship: A Symposium*, eds. Arnold C. Cooper and John L. Komives. Milwaukee: Center for Venture Management, 1972.

HOFFMAN, CARY A., "The Venture Capital Investment Process" (Doctoral dissertation, University of Texas, 1972).

HOFFMAN, CARY A., and SHAPERO, A., *Providing the Industrial Ecology Required for the Survival and Growth of Small Technical Companies.* Austin: MDRI Press, 1971.

HOLLINGSWORTH, A. THOMAS, and HAND, HERBERT H., *A Guide to Small Business Management: Text and Cases.* Philadelphia: Saunders, 1979.

HORNADAY, JOHN A., "Reliability Person-to-Person Interest Measurement" (Paper presented at the American Psychological Association Convention, September 1979).

HORNADAY, JOHN A., and ABOUD, JOHN, "Characteristics of Successful Entrepreneurs," *Personnel Psychology* 24 (Summer 1971).

HORNADAY, JOHN A., and BUNKER, CHARLES S., "The Nature of the Entrepreneur," *Personnel Psychology* 23, No. 1 (Spring 1970).

HORNADAY, JOHN A., VESPER, KARL H., and MOORE, LYNN, "Effects of Entrepreneurial Courses on Careers" (Working paper, Babson College, 1980).

HOSMER, LARUE T., COOPER, ARNOLD C., and VESPER, KARL H., *The Entrepreneurial Function.* Englewood Cliffs, N.J.: Prentice-Hall, 1977.

"How the Classroom Turns out Entrepreneurs," *Business Week*, June 18, 1979.

HOWELL, R. P., "Comparative Profiles—Entrepreneurs Versus the Hired Executive: San Francisco Peninsula Semi-Conductor Industry," *Technical Entrepreneurship: A Symposium*, eds. Arnold C. Cooper and John L. Komives. Milwaukee: Center for Venture Management, 1972.

HUDSON, E. A., and JORGENSON, D. W., "Energy Prices and the U.S. Economy," *Data Resource Review*, September 1978.

HUGHES, JONATHAN R. T., "Entrepreneurship," in *Encyclopedia of American Economic History,* ed. Glenn Porter. New York: Scribner's, 1980.

HULL, D. L., BOSLEY, J. J., and UDELL, G. G., "Renewing the Hunt for the Heffalump: Identifying Potential Entrepreneurs by Personality Characteristics," *Journal of Small Business Management* 18, No. 1 (January 1980).

HYMER, STEVEN, and RESNICK, STEVEN, "Responsiveness of Agrarian Economies and the Importance of Z Goods" (Discussion paper Economic Growth Center, Yale University, 1967).

Invention Management. Arlington, Mass.: Institute for Invention and Innovation.

"Iranian Immigrants, Totaling Perhaps a Million, Bring Wealth and Diversity to the United States," *New York Times,* December 9, 1979.

JAMES, F., and STRUYK, R., *Intrametropolitan Industrial Location: The Pattern and Process of Change.* Lexington, Ky.: Lexington Books, 1975.

JAMESON, KEN, "Comment on the Theory and Measurement of Dynamic X-Efficiency," *Quarterly Journal of Economics* 86 (1972).

JANSYN, LEON E., KOHLHOF, C., SADOWDKI, C., and TOBY, J., "Ex-Offenders as Small Businessmen: Opportunities and Obstacles" (Final report under Office of Manpower Contract, Rutgers University, 1969).

JARDIM, ANNE, *The First Henry Ford: A Study in Personality and Business Leadership.* Cambridge: MIT, 1970.

JAVILLONAR, GLORIA V., and PETERS, GEORGE R., "Sociological and Social Psychological Aspects of Indian Entrepreneurship," *The British Journal of Sociology* 24, No. 3 (1973).

JESSUP, CLAUDIA, and CHIPPS, GENIE, *Super Girls.* New York: Harper & Row, Pub., 1972.

JEVANS, WILLIAM STANLEY, *The Theory of Political Economy* (4th ed.). London: Macmillan, 1911 (Originally published in 1871).

JEWKES, J., SAWERS, D., and STILLERMAN, R., *The Sources of Invention.* New York: St. Martin's Press, 1959.

JOHANSEN, LIEF, "Substitution vs. Fixed Production Coefficients in the Theory of Economic Growth: A Synthesis," *Econometrica* XXVII (April 1959).

JOHNSON, CURTIS S., *The Indomitable R. H. May.* New York: Vantage Press, 1964.

JOHNSON, P. S., and CATHCART, D. G., "The Founders of New Manufacturing Firms: A Note on the Size of Their Incubator Plants," *The Journal of Industrial Economics* 28, No. 2 (December 1979).

JONES, KENNETH A., and WILEMON, DAVID L., "Emerging Patterns in New Venture Management," *Research Management,* November 1972.

Journal of Economic and Business History. Boston: Harvard Business School, 1929–1933.

JUSENIUS, C. L., and LEDEBUR, L. C., *Where Have All the Firms Gone?* Washington, D.C.: Economic Development Administration, U.S. Department of Commerce, 1977.

JUSTIS, ROBERT T., and KREIGSMAN, BARBARA, "The Feasibility Study as a Tool for Venture Analysis," *Journal of Small Business Management* 17, No. 1 (January 1979).

KAIMEN, MORTON, and SCHWARTZ, NANCY L., "Market Structure and Innovation: A Survey," *Journal of Economic Literature* 13 (March 1975).

KAIMEN, MORTON I., and SCHWARTZ, NANCY L., "Timing of Innovations under Rivalry," *Econometrica* 40 (January 1972).

KALDOR, NICHOLAS A., *Essays on Value and Distribution: On Economic Stability and Growth: On Economic Policy*. London: Ducksworth, 1960.

KANTER, ROSABETH MOSS, *Men and Women of the Corporation*. New York: Basic Books, 1977.

KASER, M. C., "Russian Entrepreneurship," in *The Cambridge Economic History of Europe*, eds. P. Mathias and M. M. Postan, Vol. VII, Part 2. Cambridge: Cambridge University, 1978.

KAY, NEIL M., *The Innovating Firm*. New York: St. Martin's Press, 1979.

KERLINGER, N., *Foundations of Behavioral Research*. New York: Holt, Rinehart & Winston, 1964.

KETS DE VRIES, M. F. R., "The Entrepreneurial Personality: A Person at the Crossroads," *Journal of Management Studies* 14, No. 1 (1977).

KEYNES, J. M., *General Theory of Employment, Interest and Money*. New York: Harcourt Brace Jovanovich, Inc., 1936.

KIERULFF, HERBERT E., "Can Entrepreneurship Be Taught?" *MBA Magazine*, June-July, 1973.

KIERULFF, HERBERT E., "Education for Entrepreneurship," *A.A.C.S.B. Bulletin*, April 1974.

KIERULFF, HERBERT E., "Finding—and Keeping—Corporate Entrepreneurs," *Business Horizons*, February 1979.

KILBY, PETER, ed., *Entrepreneurship and Economic Development*. New York: Free Press, 1971.

KINDLEBERGER, CHARLES P., *Economic Development* (2nd ed.). New York: McGraw-Hill, 1965.

KINNARD, W., JR., and MALINOWSKI, Z., *The Turnover and Mortality of Manufacturing Firms in the Hartford Connecticut Economic Area, 1953–1958*. Hartford: University of Connecticut, 1960.

KIRZNER, ISRAEL M., *Competition and Entrepreneurship*. Chicago: University of Chicago, 1973.

KLEIN, RICHARD H., "Financial Results of the Small Business Administration Minority Business Loan Portfolio," *University of Michigan Business Review* 30, No. 1 (January 1978).

KNIGHT, FRANK, *Risk, Uncertainty and Profit*. Boston: Houghton Mifflin, 1921.

KOGAN, N., and WALLACH, M. A., *Risk Taking*. New York: Holt, Rinehart & Winston, 1964.

KOMIVES, J. L., "A Preliminary Study of the Personal Values of High Technology Entrepreneurs," (Proceedings) *Technical Entrepreneurship: A Symposium*, eds. A. C. Cooper and J. L. Komives. Milwaukee: Center for Venture Management, 1972.

KOPPEL, B., and PETERSON, R. E., "Industrial Entrepreneurship in India: A Re-evaluation," *The Developing Economies*, September 1975.

KRAMER, HUGH E., "New Entrepreneurial Dimensions of Business Education," *Collegiate News and Views* XXV, No. 1 (Fall 1971).

KRISTENSEN, THORKIL, *Development in Rich and Poor Countries: A General Theory with Statistical Analysis*. New York: Holt, Rinehart & Winston, 1974.

KUDER, FREDERIC, *Activity Interests and Occupational Choice*. Chicago: SRA, 1977.

KUDER, FREDERIC, *Kuder Occupational Interest Survey.* Chicago: SRA, 1970.

KUDER, FREDERIC, "People Matching," *Educational and Psychological Measurement*, Spring-Summer 1980.

KUDER, FREDERIC, "Some Principles of Interest Measurement," *Educational and Psychological Measurement* 30 (Spring-Summer 1970).

KUHN, THOMAS, *The Structure of Scientific Revolutions.* Chicago: University of Chicago, 1970.

KUNKEL, JOHN H., "Values and Behavior in Economic Development," *Economic Development and Cultural Change*, April 1965.

KURILOFF, ARTHUR H., SCHMIDT, W., and MENKIN, D., "An Educational Venture in Entrepreneurship" (Working paper, UCLA Graduate School of Management, 1972).

KUZNETS, S. S., "Notes on the Take-Off," in *The Economics of Take-Off into Sustained Growth*, ed. W. W. Rostow. London: Macmillan, 1964.

KUZNETS, S. S., "Quantitative Aspects of the Economic Growth of Nations," *Economic Development and Cultural Change* X, No. 2 (January 1962).

LACHO, K. J., and NEWMAN, A. A., "The Use of New Venture Projects as a Teaching Device at the Undergraduate Level" (Presented to the Southwest Division, Academy of Management, March 1974).

LAMONT, LAWRENCE M., "The Role of Marketing in Technical Entrepreneurship," in *Technical Entrepreneurship: A Symposium*, eds. Arnold C. Cooper and John L. Komives. Milwaukee: Center for Venture Management, 1972.

LAMONT, LAWRENCE M., *Technology Transfer, Innovation and Marketing in Science Oriented Spin-Off Firms* (Doctoral dissertation, University of Michigan, 1969).

LAMONT, LAWRENCE M., "What Entrepreneurs Learn from Experience," *Journal of Small Business Management*, July 1972.

LANDU, RALPH, "Entrepreneurship in the Chemical Industry and in the United States," *Innovators and Entrepreneurs: An Endangered Species.* Washington, D.C.: National Academy of Engineering, 1978.

LAO, R. C., "Internal-External Control and Competent and Innovative Behavior among Negro College Students," *Journal of Personality and Social Psychology* 14 (1970).

LAWRENCE, P., and LORSCH, J., *Organization and Environment: Managing Differentiation and Integration.* Boston: Harvard Business School, 1967..

LEHR, LEWIS W., "Top Management Attitude and Its Role in Innovation" (Mimeographed 3M Release, May 22, 1979).

LEIBENSTEIN, HARVEY, "Allocative Efficiency Versus 'X-Efficiency,'" *American Economic Review* 56 (1966).

LEIBENSTEIN, HARVEY, *Beyond Economic Man: A New Foundation for Microeconomics.* Cambridge: Harvard University, 1976.

LEIBENSTEIN, HARVEY, "Comment on the Nature of X-Efficiency," *Quarterly Journal of Economics* 86 (May 1972).

LEIBENSTEIN, HARVEY, "Competition and X-Efficiency: Reply," *Journal of Political Economy* 81 (May-June 1973).

LEIBENSTEIN, HARVEY, "Economic Backwardness and Economic Growth," in *Studies in the Theory of Economic Development.* New York: John Wiley, 1957.

LEIBENSTEIN, HARVEY, "Entrepreneurship and Development," *The American Economic Review* 58, No. 2 (May 1968).

LEIBENSTEIN, HARVEY, "Notes on X-Efficiency and Technical Progress," in *Micro*

Aspects of Development, ed. Eliezer B. Ayal. New York: Holt, Rinehart & Winston, 1973.

LEIBENSTEIN, HARVEY, "Organizational or Frictional Equilibria, X-Efficiency, and the Rate of Innovation," *Quarterly Journal of Economics* 83 (November 1969).

LEIBENSTEIN, HARVEY, *The Theory of Economic-Demographic Development.* Princeton: Princeton University, 1954.

LEONTIADES, MILTON, *Strategies for Diversification and Change.* Boston: Little, Brown, 1980.

LEVITT, THEODORE, "Innovative Imitation," *Harvard Business Review* 44 (September-October 1966).

LEVITT, THEODORE, "Production-line Approach to Service," *Harvard Business Review*, September-October 1972.

LEWIS, OSCAR, *The Children of Sanchez.* New York: Random House, 1963.

LEWIS, OSCAR, *Pedro Martinez.* New York: Random House, 1966.

LEWIS, OSCAR, *Typologies of Poverty: Life in a Mexican Village: Tepoztlan Restudied.* Urbana: University Of Illinois, 1951.

LEWIS, OSCAR, *Village Life in Northern India.* Urbana: University of Illinois, 1958.

LIGHT, I. H., *Ethnic Enterprise in America.* Berkeley: University of California, 1972.

LILES, P. R., *New Business Ventures and the Entrepreneur.* Homewood, Ill.: Richard D. Irwin, 1974.

LIPMAN, AARON, *The Colombian Entrepreneur in Bogota.* Coral Gables, Fla.: University of Miami, 1969.

LIPMAN, AARON, "Social Background of the Bogota Entrepreneur," *Journal of Inter-American Studies* VII, No. 2 (April 1965).

LITTLE, ROYAL, *How to Lose $100,000,000 and Other Valuable Advice.* Boston: Little, Brown, 1979.

LITVAK, I. A., and MAULE, C. J., *Canadian Entrepreneurship: A Study of Small Newly Established Firms.* Ottawa: Department of Industry, Trade and Commerce, 1971.

LITZINGER, WILLIAM D., "The Motel Entrepreneur and The Motel Manager," *Academy of Management Journal* 8, No. 4 (December 1965).

LIVESAY, HAROLD C., *American Made: Men Who Shaped the American Economy.* Boston: Little, Brown, 1979.

LJUNGMARK, LARS, *Swedish Exodus.* Carbondale: Southern Illinois University, 1979.

LORSCH, JAY W., *Product Innovation and Organization.* New York: Macmillan, 1965.

LOUCKS, KENNETH E., "An Experiment in Combining Financial and Management Assistance for New and Small Business, *Fourth International Symposium on Small Business* (Seoul, Korea) 1977.

LOUCKS, KENNETH E., "Survey of Small Business Management and Entrepreneurship Educational Activities in Canada," *Small Business Secretariat* (Ottawa, Canada), 1979.

LYNN, RICHARD, *The Entrepreneur: Eight Case Studies.* London: George Allen & Unwin, 1973.

MCCLELLAND, DAVID C., "Achievement Motivation Can Be Developed," *Harvard Business Review*, November-December 1965.

MCCLELLAND, DAVID C., *The Achieving Society.* Princeton: D. Van Nostrand, 1961.

McCLELLAND, DAVID C., "Entrepreneurship and Achievement Motivation," in *Approaches to the Science of Socio-Economic Development*, ed. P. Lengyel. Paris: UNESCO, 1971.

McCLELLAND, DAVID C., "Need Achievement and Entrepreneurship: A Longitudinal Study," *Journal of Personality and Social Psychology* 1 (1965).

McCLELLAND, DAVID C., ATKINSON, J. W., CLARK, R. A., and LOWELL, E. L., *The Achievement Motive*. New York: Appleton-Century-Crofts, 1953.

McCLELLAND, DAVID C., and WINTER, DAVID G., *Motivating Economic Achievement*. New York: Free Press, 1969. Rpt. 1971.

McGHEE, P. E., and CRANDALL, V. C., "Beliefs in Internal-External Control of Reinforcement and Academic Performance," *Child Development*, 1968.

McGRATH, J. E., "Toward a Theory of Method for Research in Organizations," in *New Perspectives in Organizational Research*, eds. W. W. Cooper, H. J. Leavitt, and M. W. Shelly. New York: John Wiley, 1964.

McMURTRY, B. J., "Institutional Venture Associates" (Unpublished working paper prepared for Conference on Innovation, Entrepreneurship and the University, University of California at Santa Cruz, 1978).

MacAVOY, PAUL W., *The Regulated Industries and the Economy*. New York: W. W. Norton & Co., Inc., 1979.

MacCOBY, MICHAEL, *The Gamesman*. New York: Simon & Schuster, 1976.

MAHAR, JAMES F., and CODDINGTON, DEAN C., "The Scientific Complex—Proceed with Caution," *Harvard Business Review*, January-February 1965.

MALINOWSKI, BRONISLAW, *Argonauts of the Western Pacific*. London: Routledge & Kegan Paul, 1922.

MALTHUS, THOMAS ROBERT, *Essay on the Principle of Population*, ed. Antony Flew. New York: Penguin, 1970.

MANCUSO, JOSEPH R., "The Entrepreneurs' Quiz," in Clifford M. Baumback and Joseph R. Mancuso, *Entrepreneurship and Venture Management*. Englewood Cliffs, N.J.: Prentice-Hall, 1975.

MANCUSO, JOSEPH R., *Fun 'n' Guts, The Entrepreneur's Philosophy*. Reading, Mass.: Addison-Wesley, 1977.

MANCUSO, JOSEPH R., *How to Start, Finance, and Manage Your Own Small Business*. Englewood Cliffs, N.J.: Prentice-Hall, 1978.

MANSFIELD, EDWIN, *The Economics of Technological Change*. New York: W. W. Norton & Co., Inc., 1968.

MANSFIELD, EDWIN, "Industrial Research and Development Expenditures: Determinants, Prospects, and Relation to Size of Firm and Inventive Output," *Journal of Political Economy*, August 1964.

MANSFIELD, EDWIN, "Size of Firm, Market Structure and Innovation," *The Journal of Political Economy* 71, No. 6 (December 1963).

MANSFIELD, EDWIN, "The Speed of Response of Firms to New Techniques," *Quarterly Journal of Economics* 77 (May 1963).

MANSFIELD, EDWIN, et al., *The Production and Application of New Industrial Technology*. New York: W. W. Norton & Co., Inc., 1977.

MAPES, GLYNN, "Profs and Profits: More Professors Put Campus Lab Theories to Work in Own Firms," *Wall Street Journal*, March 13, 1967.

MARRIS, P., and SOMERSET, A., *African Businessmen: A Study of Entrepreneurship and Development in Kenya*. London: Routledge & Kegan Paul, 1971.

MARSHALL, ALFRED, *Principles of Economics* (8th ed.). London: Macmillan, 1946.

MARTIN, ALBRO, *Enterprise Denied: Origins of the Decline of American Railroads, 1897-1917.* New York: Columbia University, 1971.

MARX, KARL, *Capital: A Critique of Political Economy*, ed. Friedrich Engels. Chicago: Henry Regency, 1936.

MAYER, K. B., and GOLDSTEIN, S., *The First Two Years: Problems of Small Firm Growth and Survival.* Washington, D.C.: Small Business Administration, 1961.

MEADE, J. E., *A Neo-Classical Theory of Economic Growth.* London: Allen & Unwin, 1961.

MEADOWS, D. H., et al., *The Limits to Growth: A Report on the Club of Rome's Project on the Predicament of Mankind.* New York: Universe Books, 1972.

MEYER, HERBERT, "If Men Fear to Fail, Can Organizations Succeed?" *Innovation*, December 1969.

MEYER, JOHN W., "Strategies for Further Research: Varieties of Environmental Variation," in *Environments and Organizations*, ed. Marshall W. Meyer. San Francisco: Jossey-Bass, 1978.

Midyear Review of the Economy: The Outlook for 1979. Washington, D.C.: U.S. Congress, Joint Economic Committee, 1979.

MILL, JOHN STUART, *Principles of Political Economy with Some of Their Applications to Social Philosophy.* London: John W. Parker, 1848.

MILLER, HARRY, *The Way of Enterprise.* London: Deutsch, 1963.

MILLER, WILLIAM, *Men in Business: Essays on the Historical Role of the Entrepreneur.* New York: Harper & Row, Pub., 1952.

MILLIKAN, M. F., *National Economic Planning.* New York: Columbia University, 1967.

MIRON, DAVID, and MCCLELLAND, DAVID C., "The Impact of Achievement Motivation Training on Small Businesses," *California Management Review* XXI, No. 4 (Summer 1979).

MISHAN, E. J., "Growth and Antigrowth: What Are the Issues?" *Challenge*, May-June 1973.

MORSE, R. S., and FLENDER, J. O., *The Role of New Technical Enterprises in the U.S. Economy.* Washington, D.C.: U.S. Department Of Commerce, 1976.

NATHUSIUS, KLAUS, *Venture Management.* Berlin: Duncker & Humbolt, 1979.

National Patterns of R & D Resources. Washington, D.C.: National Science Foundation, 1978.

NAUMES, WILLIAM, *The Entrepreneurial Manager in the Small Business.* Reading, Mass.: Addison-Wesley, 1978.

NECK, P., "Report on Achievement Motivation Training Program Conducted in Uganda, June, 1969 to December, 1970." Mimeo. International Labor Organization, 1971.

NEKVASIL, CHARLES A., "Plight of the Businessman," *Industry Week* 173, No. 11 (June 1972).

NELSON, R. R., "Economics of Invention," *Journal of Business*, April 1959.

NELSON, R. R., *The Rate and Direction of Inventive Activity: Economic and Social Factors.* Princeton: Princeton University, 1962.

NEVINS, ALAN, et al., *Ford* (3 vols.). New York: Scribner's, 1954-1963.

New England Business: Profile and Analysis. Boston: Price Waterhouse, 1976.

New England Business: Verification of Capital Gaps in New England. Boston: T. A. Associates, 1976.

News Releases, April and October 1979. Washington, D.C.: National Science Foundation, 1979.

NORTH, DOUGLASS C., *The Economic Growth of the United States 1790–1860.* Englewood Cliffs, N.J.: Prentice-Hall, 1961.

NORTH, DOUGLASS C., and THOMAS, ROBERT P., *The Rise of the Western World: A New Economic History.* London: Cambridge University, 1973.

OLSHAKER, MARK, *The Instant Image: Edwin Land and the Polaroid Experience.* Briarcliff Manor, N.Y.: Stein & Day, 1978.

O'NEIL, J. W., JR., "The New England Entrepreneurial Experience" (Unpublished paper, Whittemore School of Business and Economics, University of New Hampshire, 1971).

ORGAN, D. W., and GREENE, C. N., "Role Ambiguity, Locus of Control, and Work Satisfaction," *Journal of Applied Psychology* 59 (1974).

OSGOOD, C., SUCI, G., and TANNENBAUM, P., *Measurement of Meaning.* Chicago: University of Illinois, 1957.

OSGOOD, WILLIAM R., and WETZEL, WILLIAM E., "Systems Approach to Venture Initiation" (Paper presented to the Academy of Management Annual Meeting, 1967).

PALMER, MICHAEL, "The Application of Psychological Testing to Entrepreneurial Potential," *California Management Review* 13, No. 3 (1970–1971).

PANDEY, JANAK, and TEWARY, N. B., "Locus of Control and Achievement of Entrepreneurs," *Journal of Occupational Psychology* 52, No. 2 (June 1979).

PAPANEK, GUSTAV F., "The Development of Entrepreneurship," *American Economic Review* 52 (May 1962).

PARETO, VILFREDO, *The Mind and Society.* New York: Harcourt Brace Jovanovich, Inc., 1935.

PARETO, VILFREDO, *Sociological Writings*, ed. S. E. Finer. New York: Holt, Rinehart & Winston, 1966.

PARK, WILLIAM R., *How to Succeed in Your Own Small Business.* New York: John Wiley, 1978.

PARKS, GEORGE, "How to Climb a Growth Curve," *Journal of Small Business Management* 15, No. 1 (January 1977) and No. 2 (April 1977).

PATEL, V. G., "Venture Assistance Experiments in India," *Proceedings: International Symposium on Entrepreneurship and New Enterprise Development*, Summer 1975.

Patterns for Success in Managing a Business. New York: Dun & Bradstreet, 1967.

PAULIN, WILLIAM L., "Consulting of Small Business by Students: Experience at Three Universities" (Doctoral dissertation, University of Washington, 1980).

PAULIN, WILLIAM L., "Improving Small Business Student Consulting: An Empirical Study," *Academy of Management Proceedings*, 1980.

PEARCE, JOHN A., II, "Underwriting Small Business Community Growth through Tourism Development," *Academy of Management Proceedings*, 1980.

PELTZMAN, SAM, *Regulation of Pharmaceutical Innovation.* Washington, D.C.: American Enterprise Institute for Public Policy Research, 1974.

PENNINGS, JOHANNES M., "An Ecological Perspective on the Creation of Organizations," in *The Organization Life Cycle*, eds. John R. Kimberly and Robert H. Miles. San Francisco: Jossey-Bass, 1980.

PENNINGS, JOHANNES M., *Organizational Birth Frequencies: An Empirical Investigation* (Working paper, Columbia University Graduate School of Business, 1980).

PESSEMIER, EDGAR A., *Product Management.* New York: John Wiley, 1977.

PETERSON, REIN, *Small Business: Building a Balanced Economy.* Erin, Ontario: Porcepic, 1977.

PETERSON, RUSSELL W., "New Venture Management in a Large Company," *Harvard Business Review,* May-June 1967.

PETERSON, W., "Chinese Americans and Japanese Americans," in *American Ethnic Groups,* ed. Thomas Sowell. Washington, D.C.: The Urban Institute, 1978.

PFEFFER, JEFFREY, and SALANCIK, GERALD R., *The External Control of Organizations: A Resource Dependence Perspective.* New York: Harper & Row, Pub., 1978.

PHARES, E. J., *Locus of Control: A Personality Determinant of Behavior.* Morristown, N.J.: General Learning Press, 1973.

PICKLE, HAL B., and ABRAHAMSON, ROYCE L., *Small Business Management.* New York: John Wiley, 1976.

POLANYI, KARL, *The Great Transformation.* New York: Holt, Rinehart & Winston, 1944.

POLANYI, KARL, ARENSBERG, CONRAD W., and PEARSON, H. W., *Trade and Market in the Early Empires.* New York: Free Press, 1957.

POTTER, JACK M., ed., "Introduction: Peasant Character and Personality," *Peasant Society: A Reader.* Boston: Little, Brown, 1967.

PRAGER, D. J., and OMENN, D. S., "Research, Innovation, and University-Industry Linkages," *Science* 207 (January 1980).

QUIRT, J., "Why the Future No Longer Looks So Golden in California," *Fortune,* March 1978.

REDLICH, FRITZ, "A New Concept of Entrepreneurship," *Explorations in Entrepreneurial History* 5 (October 1952).

REDLICH, FRITZ, "Towards a Better Theory of Risk," *Explorations in Entrepreneurial History* 10, No. 1 (October 1957).

"Regional Reports" (Letter to all regional reports editors, January 28, 1980). Washington, D.C.: U.S. Small Business Administration, 1980.

Report of the SBA Task Force of Venture and Equity Capital. Washington, D.C.: U.S. Small Business Administration, 1977.

Report of the Task Force of Capital and Labor Markets. Boston: New England Regional Commission, 1975.

REUSS, GERHART E., "Entrepreneurship in the Area of Management," in *Peter Drucker,* eds. T. H. Bonaparte and J. E. Glaherty. New York: NYU, 1970.

RICARDO, DAVID, *Principles of Political Economy and Taxation.* London: Macmillan, 1921.

ROBERTS, EDWARD B., "Entrepreneurship and Technology," in *Factors in the Transfer of Technology,* ed. W. H. Gruber and D. G. Marquis. Cambridge: MIT, 1969.

ROBERTS, EDWARD B., "Entrepreneurship and Technology," *Research Management,* July 1968.

ROBERTS, EDWARD B., "Influences upon Performance of new Technical Enterprises," in *Technical Entrepreneurship: A Symposium,* eds. Arnold C. Cooper and John L. Komives. Milwaukee: Center for Venture Management, 1972.

ROBERTS, EDWARD B., "Insights into Innovation," *Proceedings of the 27th National Conference on the Administration of Research.* Denver: University of Denver, Denver Research Institute, 1974.

ROBERTS, EDWARD B., and WAINER, H. A., "Some Characteristics of Technical Entrepreneurs," IEEE Transactions on Engineering Management, EM-18, No. 3, 1971.

ROBINSON, JOAN, *Accumulation of Capital.* London: Macmillan, 1956.

ROBINSON, RICHARD B., JR., and GLUECK, WILLIAM F., "The Role of 'Outsiders' in Small Firm Strategic Planning: An Empirical Study," *Academy of Management Proceedings,* 1980.

ROBINSON, ROLAND, *Financing the Dynamic Small Firm.* Belmont, Ca.: Wadsworth, 1968.

ROCKWELL, WILLIARD F., "How to Acquire a Company," *Harvard Business Review,* September-October 1968.

ROGERS, EVERETT M., *Diffusion of Innovation.* New York: Free Press, 1962.

ROGERS, EVERETT M., and AGARWALA-ROGERS, REKHA, *Communication in Organizations.* New York: Free Press, 1976.

ROKEACH, M., *The Open and Closed Mind.* New York: Basic Books, 1960.

The Role of High Technology Industries in Economic Growth. Cambridge, Mass.: Data Resources, 1977.

"The Role of New Technical Enterprises in the U.S. Economy: A Report of the Commerce Technical Advisory Board to the Secretary of Commerce." Washington, D.C.: Department of Commerce, 1976.

ROSCOE, JAMES, "Can Entrepreneurship Be Taught?" *MBA Magazine,* June-July 1973.

ROSENBERG, NATHAN, "Capital Formation in Underdeveloped Countries," *American Economic Review* 50, Part 2, No. 4 (September 1960).

ROSS, D. F., "The Tribal Entrepreneur in the Emerging Liberian Economy," *Liberian Studies Journal* III, No. 2 (1970–1971).

ROSTOW, WALT W. *The Economics of Take-Off into Sustained Growth.* London: Macmillan, 1963.

ROSTOW, WALT W., *The Stages of Economic Growth.* Cambridge: Cambridge University, 1960.

ROSTOW, WALT W., "The Take-Off into Sustained Growth," *Economic Journal* LXVI (March 1956).

ROTTENBERG, SIMON, "Trade and Market in the Early Empires," *The American Economic Review* 48 (1958).

ROTTER, J. B., "Generalized Expectancies for Internal versus External Control of Reinforcement," *Psychological Monographs: General and Applied,* whole #609 80, No. 1 (1966).

ROUBIDOUX, J., "Profil Électif D'Entrepreneurs des Enterprises á Success au Québec" (Unpublished paper, University of Laval, 1975).

ROUBIDOUX, J., and GARNIER, G., *Facteurs de succès et faiblesses des petites et moyennes entreprises manufacturières au Québec, spécialement des entreprises utilisant des techniques de production avancées.* Sherbrooke, Quebec: Faculté d'Administration, 1973.

RUBENSTEIN, ALBERT, *Problems of Financing and Managing New Research-Based Enterprises in New England.* Boston: Federal Reserve Bank, 1958.

RUMELT, RICHARD, *Strategy, Structure, and Economic Performance.* Boston: Harvard Business School, 1974.

RUNKEL, P. J., and MCGRATH, J. E., *Research on Human Behavior.* New York: Holt, Rinehart & Winston, 1972.

SAMPSON, ANTHONY, *The Sovereign State of ITT.* Briarcliff Manor, N.Y.: Stein & Day, 1973.

SAWYER, JOHN E., "Entrepreneurial Studies: Perspectives and Directions 1948–1958," *Business History Review*, Winter 1958.

SAYIGH, YUSIF A., *Entrepreneurs in Lebanon.* Cambridge: Harvard University, 1962.

SCHARY, PHILIP B., "Transportation Problems of Small Business in the Pacific Northwest" (Working paper, Oregon State University, 1979).

SCHEIBER, HARRY, and FRIEDMAN, LAWRENCE, eds., *American Law and the Constitutional Order: A Historical Perspective.* Cambridge: Harvard University, 1978.

SCHEIRER, W. K., "Small Firms and R & D." Washington, D.C.: Department of Commerce, 1977.

SCHENDEL, D. E., and HOFER, C. W., *Strategic Management.* Englewood Cliffs, N.J.: Prentice-Hall, 1979.

SCHERER, FREDERICK M., "Firm Size, Market Structure, Opportunity and the Output of Patented Inventions," *American Economic Review* 55 (1965).

SCHERER, FREDERICK M., *Industrial Market Structure and Economic Performance.* Chicago: Rand McNally, 1970.

SCHERER, FREDERICK M., "Market Structure and Technological Innovation," in *Industrial Market Structure and Economic Performance.* Chicago: Rand McNally, 1970.

SCHLOSS, HENRY H., *Contribution of Private Investors to Development in a Mixed Economy.* Los Angeles: University of Southern California, 1971.

SCHMOOKLER, JACOB, *Invention and Economic Growth.* Cambridge: Harvard University, 1966.

SCHMOOKLER, JACOB, "Inventions Past and Present," *Review of Economics and Statistics* 39 (1957).

SCHOCH, SUSAN, "How Business Schools Handle Entrepreneurs," *Venture Magazine* 1, No. 8 (September 1979).

SCHOLLHAMMER, HANS, and KURILOFF, ARTHUR H., *Entrepreneurship and Small Business Management.* New York: John Wiley, 1979.

SCHON, DONALD A., "Champions for Radical New Inventions," *Harvard Business Review*, March-April 1963.

SCHON, DONALD A., *Technology and Change: The Impact of Invention and Innovation on American Social and Economic Development.* New York: Delta Publishing, 1967.

SCHRAGE, H., "The R & D Entrepreneur: Profile of Success," *Harvard Business Review*, November-December 1965.

SCHREIER, JAMES W., ed., "Training and Education for Entrepreneurship," in *Proceedings of Project ISEED.* Milwaukee: Center for Venture Management, 1975.

SCHREIER, JAMES W., and KOMIVES, JOHN L., *The Entrepreneur and New Enter-*

prise Formation: A Resource Guide. Milwaukee: Center for Venture Management, 1973.

SCHREIER, JAMES W., and KOMIVES, JOHN L., "Provisional Annotated Bibliography on Entrepreneurship and Small Enterprise Development" and Supplement No. 1. Honolulu: Technology and Development Institute, East-West Center, 1975.

SCHULMAN, JEFFREY, and HORNADAY, JOHN, "Experimental Learning in an Entrepreneurial Course" (Paper presented at the Annual Meeting of the Academy of Management, 1975).

SCHUMPETER, JOSEPH A., *Business Cycles: A Theoretical, Historical, and Statistical Analysis of the Capitalist Process.* New York: McGraw-Hill, 1939.

SCHUMPETER, JOSEPH A., *Capitalism, Socialism, and Democracy.* London: George Allen & Unwin, 1947. Rpt. Harper & Row, 1950; Simon & Schuster, 1958.

SCHUMPETER, JOSEPH A., "Economic Theory and Entrepreneurial History," in *Explorations in Enterprise,* ed. Hugh G. J. Aiken. Cambridge: Harvard University, 1965.

SCHUMPETER, JOSEPH A., *History of Economic Analysis.* New York: Oxford University, 1954.

SCHUMPETER, JOSEPH A., "The March into Socialism," *American Economic Review: Papers and Proceedings* XL (May 1950).

SCHUMPETER, JOSEPH A., *Theory of Economic Development.* Cambridge: Harvard University, 1936. Rpt. Oxford, 1961.

SCHWARTZMAN, DAVID, *Innovation in the Pharmaceutical Industry.* Baltimore: Johns Hopkins University, 1976.

"Science Indicators 1976." Washington, D.C.: National Science Foundation, 1977.

SEEMAN, M., and EVANS, J. W., "Alienation and Learning in a Hospital Setting," *American Sociological Review* 27 (1962).

SEXTON, DONALD L., "Characteristics and Role Demands of Successful Entrepreneurs," *Academy of Management Proceedings,* 1980.

SHAGORY, GEORGE, and SHUMANN, JEFFREY, "Entrepreneurship by Experience," *Journal of General Management* 3, No. 3 (Spring 1976).

SHAPERO, ALBERT, *An Action Program of Entrepreneurship.* Austin: Multi-Disciplinary Research, 1971.

SHAPERO, ALBERT, "The Displaced, Uncomfortable Entrepreneur," *Psychology Today,* November 1975.

SHAPERO, ALBERT, "Entrepreneurship and Economic Development" in *Entrepreneurship and Enterprise Development: A Worldwide Perspective,* eds. John Komives and James Schreier. Milwaukee: Center for Venture Management, 1975.

SHAPERO, ALBERT, "Have You Got What It Takes to Start Your Own Business?" *Savvy,* April 1980.

SHAPERO, ALBERT, "The Process of Technical Company Formation in a Local Area," in *Technical Entrepreneurship: A Symposium,* eds. Arnold C. Cooper and John L. Komives. Milwaukee: Center for Venture Management, 1972.

SHAPERO, ALBERT, "The Role of Entrepreneurship in Economic Development at the Less-Than-National Level" (Working paper, College of Administration Science, Ohio State University, 1979).

SHAPERO, ALBERT, BARCIA-BOUZA, JORGE, and FERRARI, ACHILLE, *Technical Entrepreneurship in Northern Italy.* Milano: IIMT, 1974.

SHAPERO, ALBERT, HOFFMAN, C., DRAHEIM, K. P., and HOWELL, R. P., *The Role of the Financial Community in the Formation, Growth and Effectiveness of Technical Companies.* Austin: Multi-Disciplinary Research, 1969.

SHETH, J. N., "A Model of Industrial Buying Behavior," *Journal of Marketing,* October 1973.

SHETTY, M. C., "Entrepreneurship in Small Industry," *International Development Review* I, No. 2 (June 1964).

SHILS, EDWARD B., and ZUCKER, WILLIAM, "Developing a Model for Internal Corporate Entrepreneurship," *Social Science* 54, No. 4 (Autumn 1979).

SIROPOLIS, NICHOLAS C., *Small Business Management: A Guide to Entrepreneurship.* Boston: Houghton Mifflin, 1977.

SLEVIN, DENNIS P., "The Innovation Boundary: A Specific Model and Empirical Results," *Administrative Science Quarterly* 16 (1971).

SLOAN, ALFRED P., *My Years with General Motors.* New York: Doubleday, 1963.

SLOCUM, DONALD H., *New Venture Methodology.* New York: American Management Association, 1972.

Small Business Administration Size Standards for the SBIC Program. Washington, D.C.: National Association of Small Business Investment Companies, 1977.

Small Business and Innovation. Washington, D.C.: House Committee on Small Business, 1979.

Small Business and Innovation. Washington, D.C.: U.S. Senate Select Committee on Small Business, 1978.

Small Business Bibliographies. Washington, D.C.: Small Business Administration, 1979.

The Small Business Company Program: Who Does It Benefit? Washington, D.C.: Comptroller General of the U.S., 1978.

Small Business Financing: The Current Environment and Suggestions for Improvement. Washington, D.C.: Joint Industry/Government Committee on Small Business Financing, National Association of Securities Dealers, 1979.

Small Business Reporter. San Francisco: Bank of America, 1979.

Small Firms and Federal Research and Development. Washington, D.C.: Office of Management and Budget, 1977.

SMITH, ADAM, *The Wealth of Nations,* ed. Edwin Cannon. New York: Modern Library, 1937.

SMITH, C. B., "Measurement Fundamentals in Entrepreneurship," in *Entrepreneurship and Enterprise Development: A Worldwide Perspective,* eds. J. W. Schreer, J. C. Susbauer, R. J. Baker, W. J. McCrea, A. Shapero, and J. L. Komives. Milwaukee: Center for Venture Management, 1975.

SMITH, NORMAN R., "The Entrepreneur and His Firm: The Relationship between Type of Man and Type of Company" (Unpublished paper, Graduate School of Business, Michigan State University, 1967).

SMITH, P. C., KENDALL, L. M., HULIN, C. L., *The Measurement of Satisfaction in Work and Retirement.* Chicago: Rand McNally, 1969.

SNIZCK, WILLIAM E., "The Use of Research Entrepreneurship as a Potential Role Conflict Reduction Mechanism," *Pacific Sociological Review* 19, No. 3 (1976).

SOLOMON, GEORGE T., "National Woman's Prebusiness Workshop Evaluation." *Academy of Management Proceedings,* 1980.

SOLOW, ROBERT M., "A Contribution to the Theory of Economic Growth," *The Quarterly Journal of Economics* LXX (February 1956).

SOLOW, ROBERT M., "Substitution and Fixed Proportions in the Theory of Capital," *Review of Economic Studies* 29 (June 1962).

SOLOW, ROBERT M., "Technical Change and the Aggregate Production Function," *Review of Economics and Statistics* XXXIX (1957).

SOLTOW, JAMES H., "The Entrepreneur in Economic History," *The American Economic Review* 58, No. 2 (May 1968).

SOMBART, WERNER, *The Jews and Modern Capitalism.* London: T. Fisher Unwin, 1913.

SOWELL, T., "Three Black Histories," in *American Ethnic Groups,* ed. T. Sowell. The Urban Institute, 1978.

SPENCER, DANIEL L., and WORONIAK, ALEXANDER, *The Transfer of Technology to Developing Countries.* New York: Holt, Rinehart & Winston, 1967.

SPIEGELMAN, ROBERT G., "A Method for Determining the Location Characteristics of Footloose Industries: A Case Study of the Precision Instruments Industry," *Land Economics* XL, No. 1 (February 1964).

STANFORD, MELVIN J., *New Enterprise Management.* Provo, Utah: Brigham Young University, 1975.

STARBUCK, W. H., "Organizations and Their Environments," in *Handbook of Industrial and Organization Psychology,* ed. M. D. Dunnette. Chicago: Rand McNally, 1976.

"Statement of William R. Hambrecht before the Senate Select Committee on Small Business." Washington, D.C.: U.S. Senate Select Committee on Small Business, 1979.

STEINER, GEORGE A., "Approaches to Long-Range Planning for Small Business," *California Management Review,* Fall 1967.

STEINHOFF, DAN, *Small Business Management Fundamentals* (2nd ed.). New York: McGraw-Hill, 1978.

STEPANEK, JOSEPH E., *Managers for Small Industry.* New York: Free Press, 1960.

STIGLER, GEORGE J., "Imperfections in the Capital Market," *Journal of Political Economy* 75 (June 1967).

STIGLITZ, JOSEPH E., and UZAWA, HIROFUMI, *Readings in Modern Theory of Economic Growth.* Cambridge: MIT, 1969.

STRAUSS, JAMES H., "The Entrepreneur: The Firm," *Journal of Political Economy* 52 (1944).

STRONG, EDWARD K., JR., *Strong Vocational Interest Blanks.* Palo Alto, Ca.: Consulting Psychologists Press, 1959.

STRONG, EDWARD K., JR., *Vocational Interests Eighteen Years after College.* Minneapolis: University of Minnesota, 1955.

A Study of Small Business in the Electronics Industry. Washington, D.C.: Small Business Administration, 1962.

SULLIVAN, JACK, "Entrepreneurship and Small Business Management: What Is Known and What Needs to Be Known" (Unpublished paper, Pennsylvania State University, 1979).

SUSBAUER, JEFFREY C., *Intracorporate Entrepreneurship: Programs in American Industry.* Cleveland: Cleveland State University, 1973.

SUSBAUER, JEFFREY C., "The Technical Company Formation Process: A Particular Aspect of Entrepreneurship" (Doctoral dissertation, University of Texas, 1969).

SUSBAUER, JEFFREY C., "The Technical Entrepreneurship Process in Austin, Texas," in *Technical Entrepreneurship: A Symposium*, eds. Arnold C. Cooper and John L. Komives. Milwaukee: Center for Venture Management, 1972.

SUSBAUER, JEFFREY C., "U.S. Industrial Intracorporate Entrepreneurship Practices," *R & D Management* 3, No. 3 (June 1973).

SUTHERLAND, ALLISTER, "The Diffusion of Innovation in Cotton Spinning," *Journal of Industrial Economics* 7, No. 2 (March 1959).

SUTTON, F. X., "Achievement Norms and the Motivation of Entrepreneurs," in *Entrepreneurship and Economic Growth.* Cambridge: Social Science Research Council and Harvard University Research Center in Entrepreneurial History, 1954.

SWAIN, CHARLES B., and TUCKER, WILLIAM R., *The Effective Entrepreneur.* Morristown, N.J.: General Learning Press, 1973.

TATE, CURTIS E., MEGGINSON, LEON C., SCOTT, CHARLES B., and TRUEBLOOD, LYLE R., *Successful Small Business Management* (Rev. ed.). Dallas: Business Publications, 1978.

TAWNEY, R. H., *Religion and the Rise of Capitalism.* London: Harcourt Brace Jovanovich, Inc., 1926. Rpt. Penguin, 1947; NAL, 1954.

TAYLOR, NORMAN W., "L'Industrial Canadien-Francais," *Recherches Sociographiques*, No. 11 (1960).

Technological Innovation: Its Environment and Management (The Charpie Report). Washington, D.C.: Technical Advisory Board, U.S. Department of Commerce, 1967.

THOMPSON, JAMES D., *Organizations in Action.* New York: McGraw-Hill, 1967.

THOMPSON, WILBUR, *A Preface to Urban Economics.* Baltimore: Johns Hopkins University, 1966.

THUROW, LESTER C., "The Implications of Zero Economic Growth," *Challenge*, March-April 1971.

TIMMONS, JEFFRY A., "Black Is Beautiful—Is It Bountiful?" *Harvard Business Review*, November-December, 1971.

TIMMONS, JEFFRY A., "A Business Plan Is More Than a Financing Device," *Harvard Business Review*, March-April 1980.

TIMMONS, JEFFRY A., "Careful Self-Analysis and Team Assessment Can Aid Entrepreneurs," *Harvard Business Review*, November-December 1979.

TIMMONS, JEFFRY A., "Motivating Economic Achievement: A Five Year Appraisal," *Proceedings of the Fifth Annual Meeting, American Institute for Decision Sciences*, 1973.

TIMMONS, JEFFRY A., BROEHL, WAYNE G., and FRYE, JOSEPH M., "Developing Appalachian Entrepreneurs," *Academy of Management Proceedings*, September 1980.

TIMMONS, JEFFRY A., SMOLLEN, LEONARD E., and DINGEE, ALEXANDER, *New Venture Creation* (rev. ed.). Homewood, Ill.: Richard D. Irwin, 1981.

"A Tiny, Remote Island Spawns Dynasties of Greek Shipowners," *New York Times*, May 6, 1979.

TOBIN, JAMES, "A Dynamic Aggregative Model," *The Journal of Political Economy* LXIII, No. 2 (April 1955).

TOWNSEND, HARRY, and EDWARDS, ROLAND S., *Business Enterprise: Its Growth and Organization.* London: Macmillan, 1961.

UDELL, GERALD G., and O'NEILL, MICHAEL F., *The New Product Decision Making Process: A Selected Annotated Bibliography of the Current Literature.* Washington, D.C.: National Science Foundation, 1975.

The U.S. Economy in the 1980's. Washington, D.C.: U.S. Congress, Joint Economic Committee, 1979.

VALECHA, G. K., "Construct Validation of Internal-External Locus of Reinforcement Related to Work-Related Variables," *Proceedings of the 80th Annual Convention of the American Psychological Association* 7 (1972).

VESPER, KARL H., "Commentary," in *Strategic Management: A New View of Business Policy and Planning,* eds. D. Schendel and C. Hofer. New York: Little, Brown, 1979.

VESPER, KARL H., *Entrepreneur Education: A Bicentennial Compendium.* Milwaukee: Center for Venture Management, 1976.

VESPER, KARL H., *Entrepreneurship Education.* Milwaukee: Center for Venture Management, 1979.

VESPER, KARL H., "New Venture Ideas: Do Not Over Look the Experience Factor," *Harvard Business Review* 57, No. 4 (1979).

VESPER, KARL H., *New Venture Strategies.* Englewood Cliffs, N.J.: Prentice-Hall, 1980.

VESPER, KARL H., "Research on Education and Entrepreneurship" (Paper presented at the Conference on Research and Education in Entrepreneurship, Baylor University, 1980).

VESPER, KARL H., "Sub-Fields of Entrepreneurial Research," *Proceedings of Project ISEED,* 1976.

VESPER, KARL H., "Two Approaches to University Stimulation of Entrepreneurship" in *Technical Entrepreneurship: A Symposium,* eds. Arnold C. Cooper and John L. Komives. Milwaukee: Center for Venture Management, 1972.

VESPER, KARL H., "Venture Initiation Courses in U.S. Business Schools," *Academy of Management Journal,* December 1971.

VESPER, KARL H., and ALBAUM, GERALD, "The Role of Small Business in Research, Development, Technological Change and Innovation in Region 10" (Working paper, University of Washington, 1979).

VESPER, KARL H., and HOLMDAHL, THOMAS G., "How Venture Management Fares in Innovative Companies," *Research Management* 16 (May 1973).

VESPER, KARL H., and SCHLENDORF, H., "Views on U.S. College Courses in Entrepreneurship," *Academy of Management Journal,* September 1973.

VESPER, KARL H., and VORHIES, KENNETH A., "Entrepreneurship in Foreign Trade," *Journal of Small Business Management* 17, No. 2 (April 1979).

VICARS, WILLIAM M., JAUCH, L. R., and WILSON, H. K., "A Scale to Measure General Entrepreneurial Tendency (GET)," *Academy of Management Proceedings,* 1980.

VOZIKIS, GEORGE, and GLUECK, WILLIAM F., "Small Business Problems and Stages," *Academy of Management Proceedings,* 1980.

WAGNER, G. R., and BRIGHT, J. R., "Technical Entrepreneurship for Engineering Seniors" (Working paper, University of Texas, 1973).

WAINER, HERBERT A., and RUBIN, IRWIN M., "Motivation of Research and Development Entrepreneurs: Determinants of Company Success," *Journal of Applied Psychology* 53, No. 3 (1969).

WALTON, SCOTT D., *Business in American History.* Columbus: Grid, Inc., 1971.

WATSON, D., and BAUMOL, E., "Effects of Locus of Control and Expectation of Future Control upon Present Performance," *Journal of Personality and Social Psychology* 6 (1967).

WATSON, JOHN G., and SIMPSON, LEO R., "A Comparative Study of Owner-Manager Personal Values in Black and White Small Businesses," *Academy of Management Journal* 21, No. 2 (1978).

WEAVER, PETER, *You, Inc.* Garden City, N.Y.: Doubleday, 1973.

WEBER, MAX, *General Economic History.* New York: Free Press, 1950.

WEBER, MAX, *The Protestant Ethic and the Spirit of Capitalism.* New York: Scribner's, 1930.

WEBER, MAX, *The Theory of Social and Economic Organization*, ed. and trans. A. M. Henderson and Talcott Parsons. New York: Scribner's, 1917.

WEBSTER, F. A., "A Model for New Venture Initiation: A Discourse on Rapacity and the Independent Entrepreneur," *The Academy of Management Review* 1, No. 1 (January 1976).

WEIDENBAUM, MURRAY L., *Business, Government and the Public.* Englewood Cliffs, N.J.: Prentice-Hall, 1977.

"Where Do You Get The Money?" *American Machinist*, August 10, 1970.

WHITE, RICHARD M., JR., *The Entrepreneur's Manual.* Radnor, Pa.: Chilton Books, 1977.

WILEMON, DAVID L., and GEMMILL, GARY R., "The Venture Manager as a Corporate Innovator," *California Management Review* 16 (Fall 1973).

WOLK, S., and DUCETTE, J., "International Performance and Incidental Learning as a Function of Personality and Task Dimensions," *Journal of Personality and Social Psychology* 29 (1974).

WOODWORTH, ROBERT, et al., "The Entrepreneurial Process and the Role of Accountants, Bankers, and Lawyers" (Unpublished paper, University of Washington, 1969).

YAMAMURA, KOZO, "Entrepreneurship, Ownership and Management in Japan," in *The Cambridge Economic History of Europe*, eds. P. Mathias and M. M. Postan, Vol. III, Part 2. Cambridge: Cambridge University, 1978.

YOUNG, ROBERT, "No Room for the Searcher," *Managing Advancing Technology*, Vol. II. New York: American Management Association, 1972.

ZALDUENDO, E. A., "El Empresario Industrial en America Latina," Argentina; CEPAL, 1963.

ZALEZNIK, ABRAHAM, "Managers and Leaders: Are They Different?" *Harvard Business Review*, May-June 1977.

ZALEZNIK, ABRAHAM, and KETS DE VRIES, MANFRED, *Power and the Corporate Mind.* Boston: Houghton Mifflin, 1975.

ZALTMAN, GERALD, DUNCAN, ROBERT, and HOLBEK, JONNY, *Innovations and Organizations.* New York: John Wiley, 1973.

ZERBE, RICHARD O., "Research and Development by Smaller Firms," *Journal of Contemporary Business*, Spring 1976.

ZYTOWSKI, DONALD G., *Contemporary Approaches to Interest Measurement.* Minneapolis: University of Minnesota, 1973.

Index